Making Community Law

'Civis Europeus sum'
AG Jacobs in Case C-168/91 *Konstantinidis*, Luxembourg,
9 December 1992

Making Community Law

The Legacy of Advocate General Jacobs at the European Court of Justice

Edited by

Philip Moser

Barrister, Monckton Chambers, London, UK

and

Katrine Sawyer

Barrister, Hailsham Chambers, London, UK and Référendaire, European Court of Justice, Luxembourg

Foreword by Sir Christopher Bellamy, President, UKAEL

Preface by The Right Honourable The Lord Slynn of Hadley

Edward Elgar

Cheltenham, UK • Northampton, MA, USA

Published by
Edward Elgar Publishing Limited
Glensanda House
Montpellier Parade
Cheltenham
Glos GL50 1UA
UK

Edward Elgar Publishing, Inc.
William Pratt House
9 Dewey Court
Northampton
Massachusetts 01060
USA

A catalogue record for this book
is available from the British Library

Library of Congress Control Number: 2008926577

ISBN 978 1 84720 137 9

Typeset by Cambrian Typesetters, Camberley, Surrey
Printed and bound in Great Britain by MPG Books Ltd, Bodmin, Cornwall

Contents

Contributors

Anthony Arnull, Birmingham University
Catherine Barnard, Trinity College, Cambridge
Paul Craig QC, St John's College, Oxford
Christopher Morcom QC, Hogarth Chambers
Philip Moser, Monckton Chambers
The Rt Hon. Lord Justice Mummery
Richard Plender QC LLD, 20 Essex Street
Sara Poli, University of Rome
Katrine Sawyer, European Court of Justice
Advocate General Eleanor Sharpston QC
Takis Tridimas, Queen Mary, University of London
David Vaughan CBE QC, Brick Court Chambers
Stephen Weatherill, Somerville College, Oxford
Richard Whish, King's College London

Editors' note

The inspirational ideas of The Rt Hon. Professor Sir Francis Jacobs are collected here for the first time in one volume, in a book that has emerged out of a UKAEL conference held at the Middle Temple on 30 June 2006 in celebration of Sir Francis's eighteen years as Advocate General at the European Court of Justice.

We are pleased that it has been possible to collect the thoughts of fourteen leading practitioners and academics in the field of EU law, and in particular that the book includes contributions by both Sir Francis's predecessor and successor at the Court. Each chapter deals with a discrete topic, ranging from human rights to the temporal limitation of Court judgments and from competition to citizenship. The development and current state of EU law is discussed and described by specialist authors, with specific reference to the opinions of Francis Jacobs. Each author also expresses his or her own views as to the future development of the law in their area. The majority of the contributions are based on the authors' lectures at the June 2006 conference, whilst Chapters 8 and 9 have been written specially for this book.

In our Introduction we aim to give a flavour of the chapters that follow it and to distil the essence of what makes a Francis Jacobs opinion. In the Annex to this book the reader will find a list of Sir Francis's opinions from 1988 to 2005.

We would like to thank all those who have contributed to this book and all those at UKAEL and Edward Elgar Publishing who have made this publication possible. The editors intend to blame each other for any errors or inaccuracies in the text.

Philip Moser
Monckton Chambers
Gray's Inn, London

Katrine Sawyer
Hailsham Chambers, London and
European Court of Justice, Luxembourg

June 2007

Foreword

Sir Christopher Bellamy QC[1]

This book arises out of the successful and well-attended conference which the United Kingdom Association of European Law, UKAEL, organized in the summer of 2006 to celebrate the 18 years of service given by one of our most distinguished members, and Vice President of this Association, Sir Francis Jacobs KCMG, as Advocate General at the European Court of Justice.

The UKAEL exists to foster the sound development of European Community law by organizing lectures, conferences and other occasions at which important issues can be discussed in depth between academics, judges, practitioners, administrators, students and all those interested in the subject matter. Our strong links with the Court of Justice and other European institutions, with our sister associations in the Member States through Fédération Internationale de Droit Européen (FIDE), and with the universities, enable this Association to bring together distinguished participants from many different backgrounds, as shown by the contents of this book.

The following chapters will highlight Francis's many achievements and discuss his brilliant and wide-ranging, and often courageous, contributions to many diverse fields of Community law. I of course associate myself with all those tributes and will, if I may, add just one remark. What is not perhaps generally known is Francis's work behind the scenes at the European Court to improve the functioning and effectiveness of that institution. Francis was there when the Court of First Instance was set up in 1989 and helped smooth some of the initial difficulties; Francis helped the evolution of the Court through no fewer than three treaties, Maastricht, Amsterdam and Nice. I would mention in particular his work on the ECJ/CFI *comité mixte* which worked up the Court's proposals for the Treaty of Nice; and more recently his work, at the invitation of President Skouris, as rapporteur and moving force behind some of the more recent procedural changes that the Court has introduced. Francis's contribution to the way in which the Court has evolved to meet the challenge of its expanding caseload is in my humble view one of his major achievements.

---

1 President, UKAEL; former judge of the Court of First Instance and former President of the Competition Appeals Tribunal.

I trust that the reader will enjoy and profit from the discussion in this book of some of the themes that emerge from the opinions given by an outstanding Advocate General between 1988 and 2006.

Preface

The Rt Hon. The Lord Slynn of Hadley*

The papers published in this book reflect and expand on speeches at a conference held in the Middle Temple on 30 June 2006. It was a warm, friendly, at times jolly, occasion when former colleagues and students of Francis Jacobs met to pay tribute to his work and to celebrate the Knighthood conferred on him on retirement as an Advocate General of the European Court of Justice.

Only a few people's career in the law in this country have been so devoted to matters European. He began his academic work of course on a broader (or should it be narrower?) basis – jurisprudence at Glasgow and 'law' at the London School of Economics. But the attraction of 'Europe' for him was evident from the beginning and it is in retrospect not surprising that he felt the urge to work at a European institution. When he was ready for that, however, the European Communities Act 1972 was not in force and so the right place to go, perhaps the only appropriate place for him to go in 1969, was to the Commission of Human Rights of the Council of Europe at Strasbourg. It was there that I first met him during the early cases in which the United Kingdom was a party or an intervener and he was a very valuable contact to ask about the procedures which the English team had to follow and which obviously were very new to us. It was not only appropriate that he went to Strasbourg but also in the long run beneficial for his future work both in the United Kingdom and in Luxembourg. His book jointly with Robin White on the European Convention of Human Rights in 1975, an early contribution on this subject by British lawyers, was widely used and appreciated.[1] As the European Court of Justice developed notions of human rights law, his knowledge of the jurisprudence on the Convention, his experience in Strasbourg and his enthusiasm for the subject affected both his teaching and writing and his opinions for the Court of Justice in Luxembourg. That experience, coupled with two years as

---

* The Rt Hon. Lord Slynn of Hadley, Lord of Appeal in Ordinary; former Advocate General (and Sir Francis Jacobs's predecessor) and Judge at the Court of Justice of the European Communities.

1 Now C. Ovey & R. White, *Jacobs and White, The European Convention on Human Rights*, 3rd ed (Oxford: OUP, 2002).

one of J.P. Warner's Legal Secretaries, between 1972 and 1974, laid the foundations for his future career in the law-making process.

However, human rights law and European law had begun to permeate the law faculties and King's College, University of London, was one of the leaders in the field. It wisely appointed him Professor of European Law as early as 1974 and as Director of The Centre of European Law in 1981.

Fourteen years of academic work, principally in European law, not only gave him a pre-eminent knowledge and status in the United Kingdom as a European law specialist, but it also meant that he was well known amongst Judges and Advocates General of the Court, many of whom had held academic posts. He was nominated by the United Kingdom and in 1988 appointed as an Advocate General of the Court. He thus arrived at the Court of Justice with a considerable knowledge of the legal structure of the Community and particularly the jurisprudence of the Court and the Court of Human Rights, whereas in the nature of things, Jack Mackenzie Stuart, J.P. Warner and I had largely to pick it up as we went along.

In the following seventeen years he wrote very many opinions, as the chapters in this book demonstrate. But he did more. He was a prodigious participant at conferences in Community law throughout the Community – indeed if conference organizers wanted an Advocate General to contribute, they usually, if not invariably, began by inviting Francis Jacobs. He did it so well that he himself found it difficult to say no. His contribution to law journals and the literature of Community law has been no less voluminous and important. His participation in the production of the Yearbook of European Law, even before his appointment, and in other journals such as the Common Market Law Review, the European Law Review, and the Cahiers de Droit Européen made considerable demands on his time when already he held an appointment itself very demanding. He continued throughout as a member of the Board and Vice-President of the United Kingdom Association for European Law and as a member of the Council of the King's College Centre.

However, in the end it is to his opinions at the Court that one must turn to see his contribution and the chapters in this book rightly pay warm tribute to that, both as to content and style and originality. I asked when invited to write this Preface whether I should comment on his 'top ten cases' and I was told firmly, and rightly, that I should not be concerned about that. The essays spoke for themselves and the editors were in any event going to write a thorough first introductory chapter on the law and King's was going to do a *festschrift*. So in effect I should write a short preface to the man rather than to the book. It is impossible, however, not to say two things. In the first phase of seventeen years in post there are few areas of Community law with which Francis Jacobs did not deal in these opinions and not many fewer where his opinions did not have a significant impact on the law directly or indirectly. That was so whether or not the Court wholly followed him. Many of his opinions provided fruitful material for the academic lectures of others – *Hag II*[2] is a good example – though my own view on first reading his opinion in that case was that his academic opinion in *Hag I*[3] produced a better result. That, however, was a minority view. *Konstantinidis*,[4] which Henry Schermers enjoyed lecturing about in a mirthful way; *UPA*[5] which advocated a loosening of the *Plaumann*[6] test, a result I had quietly lobbied for since 1981 (thereby shocking the President of the Court who did not approve of the Court reversing its earlier decisions) to no effect except in the case of the *Chilean Apples*.[7]

In the second place I pay tribute to the quality of the opinions apart of their jurisprudential correctness. His analysis and exposition of the points in issue is admirable and never pedestrian, as sometimes in the process of the domestic law courts one is almost inevitably driven to be. This I think explains why, when I asked him when I was leaving the Court 'do you want to be considered as a judge?' he firmly said no. I am sure that temperamentally that was a right decision for him. Moreover, it had the great advantage that he could write in depth, without being unnecessarily diffuse, and at the same time concentrate on the quality of expression (if you like the poetry as well as the clarity). The influence of such writing, exploratory and creative, may have a longer-term effect on the development of the law than the short-term importance of the immediate disposal of the case. In his case the confidence which came from his experience enabled him to be exploratory and creative. For myself I have not yet decided whether it is more agreeable to be 'in at the kill' (the judicial process) or to be able to write language and conclusions which afterwards are important in the long term. Francis Jacobs clearly decided this question for himself. Whichever is individually the more agreeable, in Francis's case being highly respected by his colleagues, he has made an important contribution which is there for the future.

His opinions on the free movement of goods and intellectual property; on free movement of people linked to the principles of human rights law; on taxation and, so important, the concept of the legal system as part of the Constitution of the Community are well known. These and many other cases are analysed by distinguished professors of European law in this book and it is not the function of the Preface writer to repeat them. On any view now that

[2] Case C-10/89 *CNL-Sucal v HAG GF* [1990] ECR I-3711.
[3] Case 192/73 *Van Zuylen v HAG* [1974] ECR 731.
[4] Case C-168/91 *Konstantinidis* [1993] ECR I-1191.
[5] Case C-50/00 P *Unión de Pequeños Agricultores v Council* [2002] ECR I-6677.
[6] Case 25/62 *Plaumann v Commission* [1963] ECR 95.
[7] Case C-152/88 *Sofrimport v Commission* [1990] ECR I-2477.

he is back here there will be a great deal more for him to write about, if not *ex cathedra*. I anticipate, I hope, I am sure that he will continue to write and to lecture for everyone's benefit.

Table of cases

European Court of Justice

Court of First Instance (CFI)

Opinions

Commission Decisions

Directorate of the European Commission (Competition) – DG COMP

European Court of Human Rights (ECtHR)

NATIONAL COURTS

Belgium

Canada

Germany

Ireland

United Kingdom

Competition Appeal Tribunal

Introduction: Making Community Law

The legacy of Advocate General Jacobs at the European Court of Justice

Philip Moser[1] and Katrine Sawyer[2]

Sir Francis Jacobs was the United Kingdom's Advocate General (AG) at the European Court of Justice (ECJ) from 7 October 1988 until 10 January 2006. He attended his first hearing on 9 November 1988 and delivered his first opinion on the thirtieth day of that same month.[3] Sir Francis's last case hearing was on 17 November 2005,[4] with a three-pack of final opinions delivered on 15 December 2005, in Cases C-167/04-P *JCB*,[5] C-423/04 *Richards*[6] and C-416/04-P *Sunrider*,[7] followed by a final attendance in the Chamber at the *audience solennelle* on 10 January 2006 which marked his retirement.

During Sir Francis's tenure at the ECJ both the European Communities and the wider world experienced fundamental changes. When Sir Francis arrived at the ECJ, there were twelve Member States. At the time of his departure, there were twenty-five Member States, with two more (Romania and Bulgaria) about to accede. In October 1988 the iron curtain was in place, Germany was divided into two states and the Soviet Union was just beginning its process of reform. In 2006 the Soviet Union was history and three former Soviet Socialist Republics (Estonia, Latvia and Lithuania) were actually within what was now

1 Of the Inner Temple, Barrister, Monckton Chambers, London.

2 Of the Middle Temple, Barrister, Hailsham Chambers, London; Référendaire, European Court of Justice, Luxembourg.

3 Both in Case 182/87 *Trouw & Co. BV v Hoofdproduktschap voor Akkerbouwprodukten* [1989] ECR 469 (a case about the calculation of aid for skimmed milk powder).

4 In Case C-416/04-P *Sunrider*, judgment 11 May 2006.

5 Judgment, 21 September 2006 (competition appeal from Court of First Instance; following the AG's opinion, the ECJ fined JCB €30,864,000.00).

6 Judgment, 27 April 2006 (pension entitlement of a post-operative male-to-female transsexual; following the AG's opinion the ECJ held that the applicant was entitled to a pension at age 60).

7 Judgment, 11 May 2006 (trade mark appeal from the CFI on similarity of a trade mark; following the AG's opinion, the ECJ dismissed the appeal).

the European Union. In all, no fewer than ten countries that were formerly part of the Eastern bloc were now part of the EU project, with more tied in by way of Association Agreements.

In 1988 the ECJ was an entirely single-tier institution. The years of Francis Jacobs's tenure saw the establishment of the Court of First Instance (CFI);[8] the introduction of judicial panels[9] and the creation of the Civil Service Tribunal.[10] Thus, the Court of Justice of the European Communities went from being a single-tier institution in every case to being a two-tier Court in many cases and a three-tier Court in some.[11] Sir Francis' s time in office spanned all these developments.

The role of the Advocate General itself underwent considerable change in the same period. Since 2000, Article 104(3) of the Court's rules of procedure has enabled it to respond to a preliminary reference by means of a reasoned order and without the opinion of an AG where the answer to such a question may be clearly deduced from existing case law or where the answer to the question admits of no reasonable doubt. The Nice Treaty, signed in 2001, amended the Statute of the Court and introduced the possibility for the Court to rule without the submission of an Advocate General's opinion where the case raised no new point of law.[12]

The same period also saw a reduction in the number of Advocates General in relation to the number of judges at the ECJ. The accession of ten new member states in May 2004 (and two more were to follow in January 2007) increased the number of judges but not the number of Advocates General at the ECJ. This resulted in a ratio of eight Advocates General to twenty-five (now twenty-seven) judges. This is in sharp contrast with the position at the Court's inception when there were seven judges and two Advocates General and with the position when Francis Jacobs arrived at the Court (and until

---

8 1 September 1989.

9 1 February 2003.

10 6 October 2005.

11 With the establishment of the Office of Harmonization for the Internal Market (OHIM) in 1999 it is arguable that in such trade mark appeals the ECJ is in fact the fourth tier, e.g.: Francis Jacobs's last case *Sunrider* (op cit) was an appeal against a judgment of the Court of First Instance upholding a decision of the First Board of Appeal of OHIM (Trade Marks and Designs) dismissing an appeal from a decision of the Opposition Division of OHIM.

12 After hearing the AG, see Article 20 of the Statute of the Court. In another innovation since the Nice Treaty, the First Advocate General can now also propose when the ECJ should review a CFI decision in a panel appeal, see Article 62 of the Statute (the position of First Advocate General rotates amongst the AGs on an annual basis – the primary function of the First AG is to decide on the distribution of cases amongst the Advocates General).

October 2000) when there were fifteen judges to nine Advocates General. Even with the procedural changes allowing the Court to decide some cases without the submission of an opinion by the AG, the current arrangement means that there is increased pressure on the Advocates General to produce their opinions within shorter time frames in order to keep up with the rate at which the Court is able to decide its judgments.

The Court may soon find itself at a turning point at which it must decide either to increase the number of Advocates General or else to reduce yet further the cases in which the Advocates General give an opinion. It is therefore timely to reflect on the very important contribution that an AG can make in the development of the Court's jurisprudence.

It is in this context that Advocate General Jacobs's eighteen years at the Court must be appreciated. Through the contribution made by Sir Francis in over five hundred and fifty opinions[13] in three decades, his views and arguments have helped shape EU law as it stands today. His opinions span the whole range of EU law: from milk quotas to VAT; social security to competition; free movement to fisheries; state aid to equal pay – the range of topics covered is simply too wide to list them all here, even by way of key words. The conference held by the United Kingdom Association for European Law (UKAEL) on 30 June 2006, which inspired this book, was held not only to honour Francis Jacobs the man and mark his achievements as Advocate General. It also provided an account of the state of EU law as we enter a 'post-Jacobs era'; a body of law that has been influenced by his opinions and which owes its current form to a significant degree to Francis Jacobs's thoughts and arguments. That it is possible to see a body of law through the prism of the opinions of one member of the Court is testament not merely to his professional longevity but also to the strength of his influence.

If one were to put together a complete account of EU law through the medium of Sir Francis's opinions, such an account would probably run to several volumes. Instead, this book has reduced the commentary on Sir Francis's *oeuvre* to just ten chapters, with a Preface by his predecessor as UK Advocate General, Lord Slynn of Hadley, and a Postscript by his former Référendaire, Professor Anthony Arnull. Between those most distinguished of bookends, there are contributions by a judge of the Court of Appeal, four professors of law, a Cambridge fellow and three distinguished QCs, as well as one from Sir Francis's successor as UK Advocate General, Eleanor Sharpston. In Chapter 1 Professor Stephen Weatherill has addressed Francis Jacobs's particular contribution to EU law, providing a useful and entertaining

[13] A list of opinions delivered by Sir Francis Jacobs 1988–2005 is to be found in the Annex to this book.

overview for the reader. In the subsequent chapters each author has taken one subject, highlighting the particular contribution made by Sir Francis in that field as well as commenting on the present state of the law and possible future developments. We hope therefore that this work is more than a mere personal celebration or *festschrift* and will serve as a useful reference text for academics and practitioners alike.

THE ROLE OF THE ADVOCATE GENERAL

In contrast to the role of a judge, that of Advocate General is not one that has its equivalent in the legal systems of England and Wales, or Scotland, nor is it a position found in many of the courts of the continental Member States. The result can be confusion amongst those who are not Community law specialists as to what an Advocate General is or does. The task of the Advocate General, in the case to which he or she is assigned, is to provide an independent and impartial opinion, after the parties have completed their submissions and before the judges begin their deliberations. The opinion examines the relevant law and facts, analyses the issues and concludes with a recommendation as to how the case should be decided. In the context of the ECJ, set up as a single instance court from which there is no appeal, there is great value in having each case judicially considered twice in this way, first by the Advocate General and then by the sitting judges. Even after the changes to the judicial architecture of the Court, addressed above, the ECJ will still often sit as a single-tier institution, especially in Article 234 EC references for preliminary rulings from national courts. The AG's opinion thus serves not only as a guide to the ECJ but will often provide crucial assistance to the national court in interpreting the eventual judgment of the Court.

As Francis Jacobs himself has commented extrajudicially, he was neither an advocate nor a general. The BBC website, reporting on one of Sir Francis's last opinions, delivered on 1 December 2005 in Case C-5/05 *Joustra*, described him as an 'adviser to the European Court of Justice'. Indeed, with typical understatement Sir Francis had once used that term himself in describing the role of Advocate General in the context of references to the ECJ: 'The purpose of the Advocate-General's Opinion is to advise the Court on the answers to be given to the questions referred. While the Court is at liberty to depart from it, the Advocate-General's Opinion often gives a useful pointer to the content of the eventual ruling.'[14] Whilst not inaccurate, the term 'adviser'

---

14 Francis G. Jacobs and David Anderson, 'References to the European Court' in G. Barling and M. Brealey (eds), *Practitioners' Handbook of EC Law* (London:Trenton Publishing, Bar European Group, Bar Council, 1998) p. 131.

considerably underplays the importance of the role of someone who is a member of the Court, equal to a judge and carrying out a judicial function.

That the Advocate General is a member of the Court, equal in rank to the other judicial members, was clarified by the ECJ itself in Case C-17/98 *Emesa Sugar v Aruba.*[15] In that case Emesa had argued that the lack of an opportunity for litigants to reply to the AG's opinion constituted a violation of the right to adversarial proceedings guaranteed by Article 6(1) of the European Convention on Human Rights (ECHR). This gave the ECJ the opportunity to consider the role of its own AG.[16] The ECJ held that:

> It is … appropriate to recall the status and role of the Advocate General within the judicial system established by the EC Treaty and by the EC Statute of the Court of Justice, as set out in detail in the Court's Rules of Procedure.
>
> In accordance with Articles 221 and 222 of the EC Treaty, the Court of Justice consists of Judges and is assisted by Advocates General. Article 223 lays down identical conditions and the same procedure for appointing both judges and Advocates General. In addition, it is clear from Title I of the EC Statute of the Court of Justice, which, in law, is equal in rank to the Treaty itself, that the Advocates General have the same status as the Judges, particularly so far as concerns immunity and the grounds on which they may be deprived of their office, which guarantees their full impartiality and total independence.
>
> Moreover, the Advocates General, none of whom is subordinate to any other, are not public prosecutors nor are they subject to any authority, in contrast to the manner in which the administration of justice is organised in certain Member States. They are not entrusted with the defence of any particular interest in the exercise of their duties.
>
> The role of the Advocate General must be viewed in that context. In accordance with Article 222 of the EC Treaty, his duty is to make, in open court, acting with complete impartiality and independence, reasoned submissions on cases brought before the Court of Justice, in order to assist the Court in the performance of the task assigned to it, which is to ensure that in the interpretation and application of the Treaty, the law is observed.
>
> Under Article 18 of the EC Statute of the Court of Justice and Article 59 of the Rules of Procedure of the Court, the Opinion of the Advocate General brings the oral procedure to an end. It does not form part of the proceedings between the parties, but rather opens the stage of deliberation by the Court. It is not therefore an opinion addressed to the judges or to the parties which stems from an authority outside the Court or which 'derives its authority from that of the Procureur Général's department [in the French version, "ministère public"]' (judgment in *Vermeulen v Belgium*[17] [. . .]). Rather, it constitutes the individual reasoned opinion, expressed in open court, of a Member of the Court of Justice itself.

---

15 [2000] ECR I-665.

16 In the instant case contrasting it with, e.g., the role of the Procureur Général in the Belgian Cour de Cassation, which was the subject matter of the ECtHR case of *Vermeulen v Belgium* [1996] I, Reports of Judgments and Decisions 224, on which Emesa had relied.

17 See footnote immediately above.

> The Advocate General thus takes part, publicly and individually, in the process by which the Court reaches its judgment, and therefore in carrying out the judicial function entrusted to it. Furthermore, the Opinion is published together with the Court's judgment.[18]

Thus the Advocate General acts with 'complete impartiality and total independence', is 'not subordinate to any other' and gives his 'reasoned submissions' without having regard to 'any particular interest'. It is for this reason that the position of Advocate General, whether by accident or design,[19] is arguably the most influential in the whole structure of EU law. Alone amongst the members of any part of the Court, the AG produces a single-authored ruling, without having to have regard (indeed, obliged not to have regard) to the views of any of the other members. By contrast, when the Court comes to give its judgment, it will be a compromise document, produced by up to twenty-seven authors with no dissenting opinions allowed. Inevitably, a judgment produced in this way may sometimes end up as the lowest common denominator; the minimum to which all the members of the collegium could agree. Being independent and free from individual (or national) interests, the AG can also attempt to move the law forward. In particular, the Advocate General may take the opportunity to reflect on the development of the ECJ's case law, suggesting a new direction that it could (perhaps should) take and even pointing out where previous case law has taken a wrong turn, something that the Court itself might find difficult to do. This dialogue between the Advocate General and the Court can lead to progressive developments of the law. As will be seen, Sir Francis has not infrequently used just this opportunity to influence the development of the ECJ's case law.

If one compares the opinions of the Advocates General to the judgments of the Court, they will immediately seem more familiar to the common lawyer: a more rigorous analysis of the facts and the law, with an opportunity to present arguments in a more discursive style before reaching a conclusion. These opinions read more like an English court's judgment than the ECJ judgments themselves. It may well be that the more 'English' style of opinions is due in no small part to the contributions of Francis Jacobs and his two UK predecessors, Gordon Slynn and Jean-Pierre Warner. It is however also the whole nature and purpose of an AG's opinion to provide a thorough analysis of this kind. The draughtsmen of the EC Treaty deliberately intended the AG not to be a final arbiter and his opinions are never binding, and there is perhaps a certain safety in knowing that the opinion is not the final judgment. On occasion it can be an opportunity to launch an idea, which may not find its way into

---

18 Case C-17/98 *Emesa*, op cit, Order at paras 10–15.

19 One suspects it is more accident.

the judgment in the instant case but which may develop and grow and come to fruition when the time is right. All these facets can be identified in the opinions delivered by Francis Jacobs between 1988 and 2006, and they provide the material which has allowed the contributors to produce this book.

In the first chapter of this book, Stephen Weatherill reflects on what it is that makes a good Advocate General. He identifies five characteristics or qualities demonstrated by those Advocates General who exploit the full potential of their role in shaping the law. These are: first, clarity of expression. Second, clarity of vision, namely a vision of the direction in which the Community legal order is or should be heading. Third, contextual richness, by which is meant that the Advocate General should explore the wider implications and broader context of the facts and issues in hand than the ruling itself could do. Fourth, leadership, in which an Advocate General may suggest the future direction of the law and challenge received wisdom where necessary. Finally, the fifth characteristic that Weatherill identifies as important is the capacity to inspire. In this first chapter, Weatherill examines whether, or rather how, Sir Francis demonstrates all of these characteristics in his opinions.

Weatherill's assessment of Sir Francis's work as Advocate General is that of an outsider, or a 'consumer', as Stephen Weatherill describes himself. He has not worked for Sir Francis or for the Court. His perceptions are derived purely from the opinions themselves. By contrast, a more informal and anecdotal look at Sir Francis's characteristics as Advocate General is given in the final chapter of this book, in the Postscript authored by Anthony Arnull, who worked as a référendaire to Francis Jacobs from 1989 until 1992. Arnull gives an insider's view of the approach that Sir Francis took to his cases, which in many ways reflects the perceptions that our outsider has noted in Chapter 1, in particular Francis's attention to the context of the issues in hand, both as concerns the facts of a given case and the relevant jurisprudence, and also his willingness to challenge existing jurisprudence and to show leadership in his arguments as to the proposed future direction of the Court's case law. According to Arnull, Francis Jacobs also found a place in his opinions for jokes. It seems to us, however, that Arnull sums up the particular quality of Sir Francis's contribution as Advocate General when he reflects on the two aspects of Francis's experience prior to becoming Advocate General which doubtless influenced his approach to that role. Arnull writes: '[Francis's] capacity to combine an academic's sensitivity to the deep rhythms of Community law with a practitioner's ability to identify the really crucial issues [I believe] played a big part in his success.'

Given the range of subject matter that Sir Francis has covered in his opinions and the long duration of his tenure as Advocate General, there is barely an area of Community law which he has not touched on. The authors of this volume deal with those aspects that seemed to us to be amongst the most important topics of EU law and those where Francis Jacobs made some of his most notable contributions to the jurisprudence of the Court. No doubt there will be some aspects of Sir Francis's work that are not covered and that will appear like glaring omissions to certain readers. To some engaged in the implementation of directives it might perhaps be what Sir Francis had to say about the interpretation of national law according to *Marleasing* principles in criminal and non-criminal cases in Case C-456/98 *Centrosteel N/H*;[20] for those dealing with discrimination issues it might perhaps be Sir Francis's careful explanation of the workings of direct discrimination, indirect discrimination and objective reasons in the context of equal treatment of men and women in Case C-79/99 *Schnorbus*,[21] or for certain charitable bodies offering childcare services and their VAT advisers it may even be the case of *Kinderopvang Enschede*.[22] There will be dozens (and probably more) of similar examples. However, we have not set out to provide an encyclopaedic guide to the opinions of AG Francis Jacobs. Rather, we hope that from these twelve studies it is possible to identify some of the ways in which Sir Francis's influence as Advocate General has been felt in the development of Community law.

HUMAN RIGHTS AND THE ECJ

In Chapter 2 Paul Craig examines the ways in which Sir Francis has contributed to the development of the fundamental rights jurisprudence of the ECJ. He also looks at the relationship as it now stands between the ECJ in Luxembourg and the European Court of Human Rights (ECtHR) in Strasbourg and how far the latter Court appears to accept that the ECJ does, generally, satisfactorily protect the human rights and fundamental freedoms guaranteed by the European Convention. Craig takes his cue from the case of *Konstantinidis*,[23] which exemplifies Francis Jacobs's approach to fundamental rights, in that case the right to one's name, as being an EU law entitlement independent of other Treaty concepts (such as – for example – discrimination), summed up in the following declaration of the rights of an EU citizen: '. . . he is entitled to say 'civis europeus sum' and to invoke that status in order to oppose any violation of his fundamental rights'.[24] Several authors return to this theme in subsequent chapters. In Chapter 6 Catherine Barnard sees it as

20 [2000] ECR I-6007, opinion paras 31–35.
21 [2000] ECR I-10997.
22 C-415/04, judgment 9 February 2006.
23 Case C-168/91, *Konstantinidis v Stadt Altensteig, Standesamt, and Landratsamt Calw, Ordnungsamt* [1993] ECR I-1191.
24 Opinion, para. 46.

an important recognition of the changing attitude towards migrants. In Chapter 7 Advocate General Sharpston points out the biblical source for that particular concept of citizenship, namely the martyrdom of St Paul.[25]

Konstantinidis was an example of the ECJ not going as far (or not yet going as far) as its AG. Craig traces the developments of case law through the leading case of *Bosphorus*,[26] concluding with a thoughtful discussion of the implications if the EU were to accede to the ECHR.

Bosphorus concerned the impounding of a Turkish aircraft, and the opinion of AG Jacobs contains a rigorous analysis of the right to property as protected by Article 1 of the First Protocol to the ECHR, and thus part of fundamental EU rights. Impounding aircraft was a severe restriction on Bosphorus Airways' property rights, but there was a powerful public interest justification: stopping a civil war. Sir Francis found that in this case the actions of the authorities could not be regarded as unreasonable, particularly in the light of the aims of the UN sanctions regulation. The ECJ concurred, and in due course – and this is the particular feature of *Bosphorus* – the ECtHR approved. The *Bosphorus* case again cuts across the topics covered in this book, and Richard Plender returns to the issue in Chapter 8 on international relations, where he takes it as his cue to discuss an aspect not directly addressed in *Bosphorus*: whether UN Security Council resolutions are binding on the EU.

ACCESS TO THE COURT AND *LOCUS STANDI*

Craig also discusses the case of *UPA*,[27] which addressed the vexed question of standing to bring a direct action before the ECJ. This is an issue of such

---

25 AG Jacobs may also have had in mind the stirring speech by Cicero, in 70 BC, during the trial of Gaius Verres, the corrupt governor of Sicily. The particular accusation concerned the whipping of a prisoner, despite his calling out that he was a Roman citizen and therefore entitled to due process and the protection of Roman law: see Cicero, *In Verrem* II.V, 162: 'Caedebatur virgis in medio foro Messanae civis Romanus, iudices, cum interea nullus gemitus, nulla vox alia illius miseri inter dolorem crepitumque plagarum audiebatur nisi haec, "Civis Romanus sum." Hac se commemoratione civitatis omnia verbera depulsurum cruciatumque a corpore deiecturum arbitrabatur; is non modo hoc non perfecit, ut virgarum vim deprecaretur, sed cum imploraret saepius usurparetque nomen civitatis, crux, – crux, inquam,– infelici et aerumnoso, qui numquam istam pestem viderat, comparabatur.'

26 In the ECJ: Case C-84/95 *Bosphorus Hava Yollari Turizm Ve Ticaret AS v Minister for Transport, Energy and Communications and others* [1996] ECR I-3953; in the ECtHR: *Bosphorus Hava Yollari Turizm Ve Ticaret Anonim Sirketi v Ireland* ECHR (2005) No. 45036/98.

27 Case C-50/00 P, *Union de Pequenos Agricultores v Council* [2002] ECR I-6677.

importance in the case law of the ECJ in general, and in any discussion of Francis Jacobs's contribution in particular, that it is the subject of the whole of Chapter 3 by Takis Tridimas and Sara Poli. Tridimas and Poli trace the development of what they term the 'trialogue' between AG, ECJ and CFI in *UPA* and the parallel direct access case, *Jégo-Quéré*.[28] Tridimas and Poli explain how AG Jacobs criticized the restrictive interpretation of Article 230(4) EC and proposed an alternative definition of 'individual concern'. *UPA* is the most celebrated example of AG Jacobs's progressive views being thwarted by a more restrictive Court. For the time being at least, the ECJ's approach to effective judicial protection and access to justice continues to prevail, an approach that dictates, in essence, that fundamental concepts of access to justice nevertheless cannot effect an express disapplication of the wording of Article 230 of the Treaty.[29]

This is an area addressed by Francis Jacobs himself at the UKAEL conference which inspired this book. As Sir Francis pointed out (and as Tridimas and Poli remark in Chapter 3), at the time of its *UPA* judgment, on 25 July 2002, the ECJ was aware of the then ongoing review of the EC Treaty, including Article 230, in the course of the Constitutional Convention (which reported on 18 July 2003). The outcome of that review was not known in 2002, but its publication and the ratification of the resulting Treaty seemed imminent. This may go some way towards explaining the ECJ's reluctance to reinterpret the Treaty article concerned. Viewing it from the position as it was in June 2006, Sir Francis suggested that (with no relevant amendment in prospect and in view of the failure to ratify the draft Treaty establishing a Constitution for Europe) the ECJ might revisit its definition of 'individual concern' accordingly.[30]

In an intriguing footnote to the *UPA* case, Francis Jacobs (the AG in *UPA*) and Judge Gulmann (the reporting judge in *UPA*) both retired from the Court on the same day, 10 January 2006. In the public session of the Court, the *audience solennelle*, each of them made reference to the *UPA* case and their differing views on Article 230 and 'individual concern'. Using the image of the front door (Article 230 direct action) and the back door (Article 234 refer-

[28] Case T-177/01 *Jégo-Quéré v Commission* [2002] ECR II-2365.

[29] For a restatement of the European Courts' current approach to the principle of access to the Courts and effective judicial protection, see e.g. paragraphs 55 and 56 respectively of Case T-2/04 *Korkmaz & Ors v Commission* (unrep.), order 30 March 2006; but cf. the ECJ's recent permissive use of *UPA* in its reliance upon effective judicial protection of rights derived from the Community legal order and Articles 6 and 13 of the ECHR in Case C-229/05 P *PKK and KNK v Council*, judgment 18 January 2007, paras 109 following.

[30] Speaking at the UKAEL conference, held at Middle Temple, London, 30 June 2006.

ence), Sir Francis, returning to the theme of his opinion, remarked that 'the front doors of the Court are too narrow, while the back door is not always open'.[31]

As Tridimas and Poli point out, this is a chapter in the development of the jurisprudence of the Court that may not be closed, albeit that the narrow interpretation of 'individual concern' in *UPA* and *Jégo-Quéré* continues to apply.

LINKS WITH THE NATIONAL COURTS

In addressing Article 234 references, Sir Francis was referring to one of the safeguards for the uniform application of EU law that the ECJ relied on in *UPA* and *Jégo-Quéré*: it is intended to be part of the working of the Community legal order that it should always be possible for individual litigants to approach the ECJ via the mechanism of a reference from a national court.[32]

As Sir Francis pointed out (restating the settled ECJ case law in his opinion in Case C-306/99 *BIAO*[33]): 'the procedure provided for in Article 177 [now 234] of the Treaty is a means of cooperation between the Court of Justice and national courts'.[34] The nature of that cooperation is addressed, from a personal perspective, by a serving member of the Court of Appeal of England and Wales, Lord Justice Mummery, in Chapter 4. Mummery sees the Article 234 procedure as a 'dialogue', which works well precisely because the national courts and the ECJ are not in competition with one another, each being supreme in its own sphere.

Within the Community legal order, the national courts are of course themselves Community courts, bound to ensure the uniform application of EU law. Sir Francis himself recognized this in his joined opinion in *Leur-Bloem* and *Giloy*:[35]

---

31 (Unreported), speaking in the European Court of Justice, Luxembourg, 10 January 2006.

32 If the Community law issue is critical and the national court cannot with complete confidence resolve the issue itself, see e.g. *ex parte Else* [1993] QB 534.

33 [2003] ECR I-1 at para. 44 of the opinion.

34 Francis Jacobs's opinion in *BIAO* provides a striking example of the AG exhorting the Court to address an area of law, where Francis had delivered two earlier opinions, in Case C-28/95 *Leur-Bloem* [1997] ECR I-4161 and Case C-130/95 *Giloy* [1997] ECR I-4291, and where in his view a failure by the Court unequivocally to resolve the issue now would continue to generate uncertainty in future cases. That question is whether the Court is competent to interpret provisions of national legislation which in effect apply Community legislation to situations to which that Community legislation is not required to be applied as a matter of Community law. The ECJ ducked the issue in *BIAO*, and the issue continues to generate uncertainty about the Article 234 jurisdiction.

35 Op cit; at para. 49.

> the Court's concern about . . . remote threats to the uniform application of Community law is difficult to reconcile with the fact that Article 177 [now 234] envisages that Community law will be interpreted and applied primarily by national courts. Community law is applied every day by national courts; only in the relatively small number of cases heard by final appeal courts is there an obligation to refer.

Mummery also provides a critique of the nature and workings of the ECJ and highlights what he sees as 'avoidable uncertainty and unpredictability'. The result, according to Mummery, is instability. Some of these criticisms have been addressed by Francis Jacobs in his Foreword to *Kerly's Law of Trade Marks and Trade Names*,[36] and in Chapter 4 Mummery sets out the cases for the prosecution and the defence.

Francis Jacobs has taken a close interest in the preliminary reference procedure under Article 234 EC, which (as Mummery points out) is unique to the ECJ and which, as we have seen, can be characterized as essentially one of dialogue between the national courts and the ECJ. Sir Francis's concern has always been to facilitate this dialogue so far as possible, encouraging national courts and tribunals of all levels to make use of the procedure where appropriate. However, he has also voiced concerns against inappropriate use, or over-use, of the reference procedure. Sir Francis's most general discussion of the power to refer came in Case C-338/95 *Wiener* [1997] ECR I-6495, a case on the customs classification of women's nightdresses. *Wiener* is sometimes relied upon by litigants to urge restraint in the making of references (and possibly contrary to the way in which Francis Jacobs intended it to be read), but is in fact a thoughtful analysis of the purpose and proper use of references, and the interplay between national courts and the ECJ. The problem identified in *Wiener* was references 'which, through the creativity of lawyers and judges, are couched in terms of interpretation, even though the reference might in a particular case be better characterized as concerning the application of the law rather than its interpretation'. Sir Francis's solution was twofold: (1) 'self-restraint' on the part of both national courts and the ECJ[37] and (2) an 'evolutionary approach', with national courts extrapolating from the principles already developed in the ECJ's case law.[38] Sir Francis said this on references from courts not of last instance:

---

[36] D. Kitchin, D. Llewelyn, J. Mellor, R. Meade, T. Moody-Stuart and D. Keeling, *Kerly's Law of Trade Marks and Trade Names* (London: Sweet & Maxwell, 14th edn, 2005).

[37] In the case of the ECJ this would mean a 'declaration of self-restraint' that would not lead to a decision of inadmissibility but would be couched in terms of a non-specific reply to the referring court's questions, merely recalling the principles and rules of interpretation developed by the previous case-law, and leaving it to the national court to decide the particular issue with which it is confronted (opinion, para. 21).

[38] Opinion, paras 59 and 60.

> A reference will be most appropriate where the question is one of general importance and where the ruling is likely to promote the uniform application of the law throughout the European Union. A reference will be least appropriate where there is an established body of case-law which could readily be transposed to the facts of the instant case; or where the question turns on a narrow point considered in the light of a very specific set of facts and the ruling is unlikely to have any application beyond the instant case. Between those two extremes there is of course a wide spectrum of possibilities; nevertheless national courts themselves could properly assess whether it is appropriate to make a reference, and the Court of Justice, even if it continued to maintain that the decision to refer was exclusively within the discretion of the national courts, could perhaps give some informal guidance and so encourage self-restraint by the national courts in appropriate cases.

And on references from courts of last instance, subject to the *CILFIT* test,[39] Sir Francis said this:[40]

> The Court thus imposed strict conditions which had to be satisfied before a final court could be absolved of its obligation to refer. But the very fact that the Court imposed such strict conditions might suggest that the Court again had in mind questions of law of general interest and the need to avoid the development of 'a body of national case-law' inconsistent with Community law. In *CILFIT* the Court did not consider, and had no need to consider, whether all questions of Community law, however detailed and specific, should be subject to the conditions laid down in that judgment; the substantive issue in that case was a question of general importance, namely whether a health inspection levy was payable on imported wool. If the *CILFIT* judgment were applied strictly, then every question of Community law, including all questions of tariff classification, would have to be referred by all courts of last instance.
>
> . . . it is necessary to interpret Article 177, like all other general provisions of Community law and in particular the provisions of the Treaty, in an evolutionary way. . . .
>
> If an evolutionary approach is adopted to the interpretation of Article 177, then it seems to me impossible to ignore a number of developments at least some of which should condition the interpretation of Article 177 today. Community legislation has recently extended to many new fields; and the volume of legislation has greatly increased. Excessive resort to preliminary rulings seems therefore increasingly likely to prejudice the quality, the coherence, and even the accessibility, of the case-law, and may therefore be counter-productive to the ultimate aim of ensuring the uniform application of the law throughout the European Union.
>
> . . . Experience has shown that case-law now provides sufficient guidance to enable national courts and tribunals – and in particular specialized courts and tribunals – to decide many cases for themselves without the need for a reference. . . .
>
> Moreover if the obligation to refer of courts of last instance is interpreted too strictly, then as Community law develops the incidence of that obligation will increasingly fall unevenly across the Member States, if only because their court

---

39 Case 283/81 [1982] ECR 3415.

40 *Ibid*, paras 58 to 61.

> systems are very different. In some Member States the courts of last instance may decide tens of thousands of cases a year; in another Member State – the United Kingdom – the court which is for most purposes the sole court of last instance – the House of Lords – may decide fewer than one hundred cases a year. A vastly greater number of references will therefore come from some Member States than from others. If however only cases raising a point of some general importance are referred to the Court, then a more balanced case-law – and a more balanced development of the case-law – is likely to result.[41]

In recent years, Sir Francis has been concerned that the enlargement of the European Union will ultimately lead to a greatly increased number of references, with the possibility that the time taken for the Court's judgments to be handed down would be increased further, thus reducing the willingness of national courts to make references.

Building on the 'self-restraint' and 'evolutionary' approaches in *Wiener*, one solution that Sir Francis has supported extrajudicially is that national courts should be encouraged, or perhaps even required, to supply their own proposed responses to questions that they refer which could enable the Court to expedite proceedings where the national court has arrived at the correct solution. This proposal has become known as the 'green light system'.[42] Whilst this proposed system has not yet been expressly implemented, the basic tools for at least one variation of it to be developed are in place. First, the Information Note on references from national courts for a preliminary ruling[43]

---

[41] NB that national courts, including courts of final appeal, are increasingly accepting of the responsibility to resolve certain issues themselves, particularly where such issues can be characterized as being within the application of EU law and within the discretion of the Member State, see e.g. the recent decision of the House of Lords in *Lonsdale v Howard & Hallam* [2007] UKHL 32 in the context of the Community law concept of 'compensation' under the Commercial Agents Directive (*per* Lord Hoffmann, at para. 40): 'the differences in opinion between the Scottish and the English courts and between various English judges show that the law is uncertain. That is true, but what is uncertain is not the meaning of the directive. It is clear that the agent is entitled to compensation for "the damage he suffers as a result of the termination of his relations with the principal" and that the method by which that damage should be calculated is a discretionary matter for the domestic laws of the Member States. It is the way in which our domestic law should implement that discretion which has been uncertain and the resolution of that uncertainty is the task of this House and not the European Court of Justice.'

[42] Francis Jacobs (2004) 'Possibilities for further reforming the preliminary ruling procedure', *Papers from the Colloquium on the Judicial Architecture of the European Union, 15th November 2004* (CCBE), pp. 62–9; this could at some stage even become a 'red light' system, whereby the national court would issue a judgment nisi at the same time as it made its reference. The judgment would then become absolute after a certain time limit if the Court of Justice failed to respond to the reference (*ibid*, p. 67).

[43] OJ [2005] C-143/01.

was amended in 2005 and introduced, at point 23, an invitation to the referring court that it 'may, if it considers itself to be in a position to do so, briefly state its view on the answer to be given to the questions referred for a preliminary ruling'. Encouraging referring courts to set out what is, in their view, the answer to their own question is a first step in the direction of establishing the green light procedure and the amendment of the Information Note may be seen as one result of Sir Francis's contribution to the debate. Secondly, there already exists the possibility for the Court to deliver the answer to a preliminary reference in the form of a reasoned order.[44] If a referring court were to indicate what it considered the answer to its own question to be and the ECJ agreed, the ECJ might more readily turn to the option of disposing of the case by reasoned order. These two aspects could gradually lead to the *de facto* adoption of a green light procedure and could speed up the responses to preliminary references whilst still protecting the useful dialogue that the procedure has engendered between national courts and the ECJ. Francis Jacobs has noted in particular that one of the attractive features of a green light procedure is that the national courts would be enabled to contribute fully to the making of Community law:

> the green light system would enable national courts to contribute more directly and substantially in the development of Community law by encouraging them not merely to identify and pass on the relevant questions of Community law which arise before them, but also to contribute their own analysis of those questions which might then be endorsed by the Court of Justice. That would be a particular advantage in the case of the highest national courts, which might be able to contribute substantially to the development of Community law but which may currently see themselves having the role of a judicial post-box.[45]

It remains to be seen whether this change in the reference procedures and in the links between the national and European Courts will prove to be another aspect of Francis Jacobs's legacy.

COMPETITION LAW

One area where, until relatively recently, the European Courts enjoyed an unrivalled jurisdiction is competition law. In Chapter 5 Richard Whish analyses Francis Jacobs's influence on this field, citing examples of opinions that have had a lasting effect on EU law. Whish begins with a discussion of two competition

---

44 Article 104(3) of the Court's rules of procedure.
45 Jacobs, op cit, p. 68.

cases, *Tournier* and *JCB*, that are over sixteen years apart;[46] yet another example of the longevity and consistency of Francis Jacobs's output.

Whish then highlights for particular attention Jacobs's opinions in the cases of *Bronner*[47] and *Syfait*.[48] In both these cases, Whish considers that the impact of Jacobs's opinions has been more extensive than the impact of the judgments themselves. In *Bronner* Francis Jacobs reviewed and analysed the law of refusal to supply and the so-called 'essential facilities doctrine' under Article 82 EC. He reached the conclusion that Article 82 could lead to mandatory access to the essential facility of a competitor only in cases where there was a genuine stranglehold on a related market and that it was impossible or extremely difficult to duplicate that facility. Whish sets out the cogent and compelling nature of Sir Francis's discussion of the law and observes that although the ECJ judgment reached the same conclusion, it did so without the clarity and authority of the Advocate General. The result is a tendency to cite the opinion 'as if it were the judgment of the Court'. In *Syfait* the issue was once again refusal to supply, in that case the refusal by GlaxoSmithKline to supply certain drugs to pharmaceutical wholesalers in Greece in order to limit parallel trade from that country to other Member States where the drugs commanded higher prices. Francis Jacobs reached the view that the refusal to supply should not be regarded as abusive *per se*. On the question of objective justification, he reached the conclusion that, in the specific circumstances of the European pharmaceutical sector, there was such a justification. In its subsequent judgment, however, the ECJ did not answer these substantive questions given that the Court reached the conclusion that the Greek Competition Commission was not a court or tribunal within the meaning of Article 234 EC and that therefore the preliminary reference was inadmissible. The result, as Whish observes, was that there is no authoritative judgment by the Court and yet we have the view of a highly experienced Advocate General as to where the law stood, a view which is likely to be highly influential.

Whish also emphasizes two aspects of competition law which are not often addressed: the social dimension of competition law and the difficult concept of 'undertakings' in Community competition law. Francis Jacobs had to wrestle with both these concepts and his opinions are prime amongst the authoritative sources on the matter; opinions which must now be read with Professor Whish's commentary in Chapter 5 of this book.

---

[46] Case 395/87 [1989] ECR I-2521 and Case C-167/04, judgment of 21 September 2006.

[47] Case C-7/97 *Oscar Bronner GmbH & Co. KG v Mediaprint* [1998] ECR I-7791.

[48] Case C-53/03 *Syfait* [2005] ECR I-4609.

THE FOUR FREEDOMS

In Chapter 6 Catherine Barnard discusses Francis Jacobs's contribution in the context of freedom of movement for goods, services and persons, which, along with capital, constitute the four fundamental freedoms at the very heart of the European Community project. Barnard observes how, in the wake of the decision in *Keck*[49] in which the ECJ limited the *Dassonville*[50] case law, Francis's opinions must have helped to steer the Court away from any temptation of applying the *Keck* ruling in a formalistic way. In *Keck* the Court held that certain selling arrangements fell outside the scope of Article 28.[51] An overly formalistic application of that principle could have risked taking outside the scope of Article 28 measures that, albeit capable of being described as such 'selling arrangements', in fact had the effect of restricting trade between Member States. Jacobs's opinions advocated a more functional approach, in order to achieve the fundamental aim of the Treaty, which in these cases was the realization of the internal market. Barnard compares this approach with the opinion in *Leclerc-Siplec*.[52] That case concerned a prohibition in France of television advertising of petrol and other fuel. AG Jacobs, having observed that the role of advertising could be crucial in facilitating access to the market of another Member for a foreign manufacturer, proposed that the Court should not simply rule out a breach of Article 28 where a measure was non-discriminatory but should apply a test that asked whether the measure was liable 'substantially to restrict access to the market'.[53] The Court did not follow its AG's opinion on this occasion. Rather than apply a 'substantial restriction' test, the ECJ ruled that the measure was a selling arrangement that applied to and affected the marketing of products from domestic and other Member States in the same manner and so Article 28 was not engaged. However, in an exercise of legal detective work, Barnard follows the subsequent case law relating to restrictions on advertising and concludes that Sir Francis's opinions must have 'seeped into the pores of the Court's jurisprudence'. She observes that in *De Agostini*,[54] the Court, following AG Jacobs's opinion in that case, accepted that an outright ban on a form of promotion for a product might have a greater impact on products from other Member States. The Court concluded

---

49 Joined Cases C-267 & 268/91 *Keck and Mithouard* [1993] ECR I-6097.

50 Case 8/74 *Dassonville* [1974] ECR 837.

51 I.e. that quantitative restrictions on imports and all measures having equivalent effect shall be prohibited between Member States.

52 Case C-412/93 *Leclerc-Siplec* [1995] ECR I-179.

53 Para. 49.

54 Joined Cases C-34-36/95 *De Agostini* [1997] ECR I-3843.

that if an unequal burden in law or fact was found, then the national restriction would be caught by Article 28.

In *Alpine Investments*,[55] which concerned the free movement of services rather than goods, Jacobs proposed a similar test to that which he had proposed in *Leclerc-Siplec*, namely 'whether [the restriction] substantially impedes the ability of persons established in its territory to provide intra-Community services'. In that case, the Court followed Sir Francis's approach, finding that the measure in question, albeit general and non-discriminatory, directly affected access to the market in services in other Member States and was thus capable of hindering intra-Community trade in services contrary to Article 49. So we see the Court steering away from a formalistic approach towards the functional approach advocated by Jacobs; the approach which is most consistent with achieving the fundamental aims of the Treaty. Also on services and the free movement of persons, Barnard emphasizes the importance of the case of *Säger*[56] and the development, inspired by Francis Jacobs, that services should be treated by analogy with goods, and that 'non-discriminatory restrictions on the provision of services' (and, in this context, also persons) should be approached in the same way as non-discriminatory restrictions on the free movement of goods.

It should be added that in a different field of application of the free movement of goods, Francis Jacobs was thwarted one last time in his instinctive inclination towards greater liberalization: in Case C-5/05 *Staatssecretaris van Financiën v Joustra*,[57] (in which judgment was delivered after Sir Francis's retirement from the Court) Mr Joustra and friends had formed a 'cercle des amis du vin' in The Netherlands and each year he ordered a quantity of wine from France for private consumption. He also arranged for its transportation to his home by a Dutch transport company. He argued that there should be no payment of excise duty on this wine in The Netherlands, such duty having already been paid in France and this being a purchase by a private individual for non-commercial use within the single market. Mr Joustra relied on the provisions of Directive 92/12/EEC on excise duty. The ECJ held that the correct interpretation of the Directive was that the wine will be free of duty if transported across the border personally by the purchaser, but not if ordered by telephone or online and then transported by a third party. The ECJ recognized that its ruling could be a retrograde step, in that personal effects transported in the course of a removal to another Member State or small consignments of a non-commercial nature sent from one private individual to another could also be caught. The ECJ reached its conclusion by a restrictive interpretation of the

55 Case C-384/93 *Alpine Investments* [1995] ECR I-1141.
56 Case C-76/90 [1991] ECR I-4221.
57 Judgment, 23 November 2006.

phrase 'products acquired by private individuals for their own use and transported by them' in Article 8 of the Directive. According to the Court's ruling in *Joustra*, 'transported by them' means literally transported by the individuals, rather than by a transport company hired for that purpose. Sir Francis in his opinion had managed to give the phrase 'transported by them' a wider definition, albeit that he called for a revised version of Directive 92/12 (which is now being drafted): 'Whilst I have sought to derive a workable interpretation from the present wording, it seems to me that revised legislation is an urgent necessity in order to deal clearly with those problems.'[58]

It is perhaps predictable that Sir Francis should have sought such a workable interpretation, at the same time giving a purposive interpretation to the provision; the purpose in this case being the free movement of goods in a single market. It is also pointed out, with respect, that (by its own admission) the solution reached by the ECJ led to a flawed result, whilst the AG's solution would have provided greater consistency.

Barnard concludes Chapter 6 with a comprehensive analysis of derogations and justifications that may apply once a breach has been established, with reference to fundamental rights and social provisions. She explores the outer limits of the Treaty provisions, using Francis Jacobs's opinions as her guide.

The sheer volume of case law dealt with by Barnard in Chapter 6 demonstrates the importance of at least three of the four freedoms, goods, persons and services, to the Community *acquis*. There is rather less to say about the fourth freedom, capital, always the somewhat neglected sibling to the other three. However, for the sake of completeness it should be added that when Francis Jacobs had the opportunity to comment on the free movement of capital in Case C-329/03 *Trapeza tis Ellados AE v Banque Artesia*,[59] he once again unsurprisingly followed his *communautaire* instincts in favour of the promotion of greater freedom. In the context of a case on the First Capital Movements Directive,[60] he said:

> It will be recalled that the single recital in the preamble to the directive states that the attainment of the objectives of the Treaty 'requires the greatest possible freedom of movement of capital between Member States and therefore the widest and most speedy liberalisation of capital movements'. In the light of that overriding objective, I consider that any ambiguity in the directive should be construed so as to promote such liberalisation.[61]

---

58 Para. 92.

59 Judgment of 27 October 2005.

60 First Directive for the implementation of Article 67 of the Treaty (OJ, English Special Edition 1959–62, p. 49); repealed with effect from 1 July 1990 by Council Directive 88/361/EEC of 24 June 1988 for the implementation of Article 67 of the Treaty (OJ 1988 L 178, p. 5).

61 Opinion, 14 April 2005, para. 58.

FROM FREE MOVEMENT OF PERSONS TO CITIZENSHIP

Francis Jacobs's efforts (along with other AGs, notably Advocate General Geelhoed) to develop the Treaty provisions, particularly those introduced by the Treaty of Amsterdam,[62] by taking freedom of movement for persons to a new level have led to a new appreciation of the concept of European citizenship. It is fitting that in Chapter 7 it falls to Sir Francis's successor, Advocate General Sharpston, to analyse the law on citizenship.

AG Sharpston takes three specific examples where citizenship rights have come into play: the right to one's own language in criminal proceedings (*Bickel and Franz*[63]), the right to have one's income taken into account before being deprived of property (*Pusa*[64]) and the right to one's own name (*García Avello*, *Niebüll*[65]). Sharpston cites the striking passage in *Bickel and Franz* where Sir Francis describes the encapsulation of Community law rights within the concept of EU citizenship, simply and in one sentence, thus: 'The notion of citizenship of the Union implies a commonality of rights and obligations uniting Union citizens by a common bond transcending Member State nationality.' Building on these cases, Sharpston concludes that in an EU in which nationals of Member States are also citizens of the Union, then in order for that citizenship to have real meaning, administrative rules should not automatically be applied in a rigidly national way and that 'cultural diversity allied to the consequences of free movement may sometimes require greater flexibility of thought and spirit'.

Reading Chapter 7 of this book, it may be surmised that Francis Jacobs's flexibility of thought and spirit will continue to be applied at the ECJ;[66] in itself a legacy of Sir Francis's seventeen years at the Court.

THE EU AND THE WORLD: EXTERNAL RELATIONS

In Chapter 8 Richard Plender reminds us that Francis Jacobs began his professional career as a public international lawyer. The external competence of the

---

62 Signed 2 October 1997.

63 Case C-274/96 [1998] ECR I-7637.

64 Case C-224/03, judgment 29 April 2004.

65 Case C-148/02, judgment 2 October 2003 and Case C-96/04, judgment 27 April 2006.

66 On the subject of continuity it may be worth noting that in her first opinion, delivered on 7 March 2006 in Case C-166/05 *Heger* [2006] ECR I-7749 (a case about VAT on fishing permits), AG Sharpston relied on two of the opinions of her predecessor AG Jacobs: Case C-108/00 *Syndicat des producteurs independents* [2001] ECR I-2361 and Case C-315/00 *Maierhofer* [2003] ECR I-563.

EU (and more particularly the European Community[67]) has been enhanced by the ECJ, which has developed the concept of implied external powers for the Community in case law stretching back to 1971.[68] Sometimes this competence is shared with the Member States and where the Community and the Member States are parties to the same international agreement, it is called a 'mixed agreement'. Plender uses the example of Case C-89/99 *V.O.F. Schieving-Nijstad*[69] to illustrate the political sensitivity of cases where the rights of individuals may be decided by the ECJ ruling on the meaning of provisions in a mixed international agreement, even if that agreement does not itself produce direct effects. Plender goes on to trace the consequences of the *Schieving-Nijstad* ruling in the light of the cases that followed it.

Taking his cue from Francis Jacobs's opinion in *Bosphorus*,[70] Dr Plender then goes on to make the case for UN Security Council resolutions being binding upon the Community (a consequence which the ECJ did not have to, and therefore did not, consider in *Bosphorus*). Time will tell whether this will be accepted by the Court and the Member States.

Commenting on the *Regione Friuli-Venezia Giulia* case[71] (like so many important ECJ cases, a case concerning alcohol), Plender provides a critique of the arguments in that case, centring around Article 1 of the First Protocol of the ECHR proprietary right to use the name of the region in which a wine is produced. Further, commenting on Case C-171/01 *Wählergruppe Gemeinsam Zajedno*,[72] which dealt with the delicate subject of the direct effect of the EU–Turkey Association Agreement, Plender shows how the tests of direct applicability may apply equally to agreements with international scope as they do to inner-EU instruments.

It is a sign of the development of EU law and of the jurisprudence of the ECJ that it can now be said, as Plender concludes, that 'the judgments of the European Courts constitute an indispensable source of international law'.

INTELLECTUAL PROPERTY

The case of *Cnl-Sucal NV SA v Hag GF AG*,[73] known as '*HAG II*', stands out

---

67 Which has long enjoyed legal (and thus international legal) personality: Article 281 EC.
68 See Case 22/70 *Commission v Council* (ERTA) [1971] ECR 263.
69 [2001] ECR I-5851.
70 Op cit.
71 [2005] ECR I-3785.
72 [2003] ECR I-4301.
73 Case C-10/89 [1990] ECR I-3711.

amongst the opinions of Francis Jacobs, not just as a model of legal reasoning but because it resulted in the ECJ expressly overruling a previous decision, namely *Van Zuylen Freres SA v HAG AG*[74] (now known as '*HAG I*'). In Chapter 9 Christopher Morcom sees Advocate General Jacobs as having come to the rescue of trade mark law in *HAG II*, exposing 'the fallacy, indeed the heresy, of the *HAG I* common origin doctrine'. It is instructive to read paragraphs 22 to 25 of the opinion in *HAG II* and note the way in which, in just a few paragraphs, sixteen years of errant case law are disposed of, leading to one inevitable result (at para. 26): 'The unpalatable but inescapable conclusion that emerges from the above analysis is that the doctrine of common origin is not a legitimate creature of Community law. There is no clear basis for it in the Treaty and no explanation of its necessity was put forward in *HAG I*.' So the old common origin doctrine was eliminated from the menagerie of creatures of Community law as being an illegitimate member of that species. What took its place was the notion that the trade mark owner may rely on his right against the owner of a parallel right in another Member State.

How Sir Francis dealt with the (then wholly novel) issue of the ECJ overruling its previous decision is also typical of the clarity of thought and purpose found in his opinions:[75] 'It would, I think, be healthier to recognize that *HAG I* was wrongly decided, rather than to compound that error by inventing a spurious distinction between the two cases' and 'the Court should in my view make it clear, in the interests of legal certainty, that it is abandoning the doctrine of common origin laid down in *HAG I*. . . . That the Court should in an appropriate case expressly overrule an earlier decision is I think an inescapable duty, even if the Court has never before expressly done so.' Again, viewed at the time of Sir Francis's departure in 2006, that seems unarguably correct. When Mr Francis Jacobs arrived in 1988, it had not been thought of.

In the remainder of Chapter 9, Morcom guides the reader through the full panoply of Community trade mark law (the author's specialist subject): the exhaustion of rights (Community exhaustion and international exhaustion); the registrability of trade marks; infringement of registered trade marks and the opposition to registration of trade marks. Morcom confidently asserts that the protection of trade mark rights in the EU has been greatly enhanced as a result of the work of Sir Francis Jacobs, and Morcom's explanation of the law in Chapter 9 will demonstrate the same to any reader.

---

74 Case 192/73 [1974] ECR 731.

75 At paras 66 and 67.

TEMPORAL LIMITATIONS

Advocate General Jacobs was always interested in the procedural aspects of the work of the ECJ. In Chapter 10 David Vaughan tackles the origins and future of temporal limitation in EU law, from its beginnings in Case 43/75 *Defrenne No. 2*[76] to Francis Jacobs's opinion in Case C-475/03 *Cremona.*[77] As Vaughan points out, the introduction of temporal limits, limiting the effect of judgments of the ECJ, has always been an innovative business. This was recognized by Sir Francis in *Cremona* and it is interesting to note Sir Francis, after years of innovative opinions of his own, giving a roll-call of similar cases dating from the time prior to his arrival at the Court:[78]

> For this Court to take such a step[79] would be a considerable innovation. Such innovations have however been made in the past. It was an innovation for example in 1976 when in *Defrenne*[80] the Court limited the retroactive effect of its interpretation of a Treaty article. There were further innovations in 1980, when in *Providence Agricole de la Champagne*[81] the Court applied the second paragraph of what is now Article 231 EC by analogy in a preliminary ruling, limiting the retroactive effect of a finding that certain Commission regulations were invalid, and again in 1988, when in *van Landschoot*[82] it went a stage further, maintaining the effects of an invalid Community provision until such time as it was replaced by a valid provision.

Since a departure from the Court's customary approach (in favour of a novel finding of incompatibility that would only come into effect at a future date to be set by the Court) had not been debated during the proceedings, the AG suggested the reopening of the oral procedure in *Cremona*, which was duly done. As Vaughan points out, after the rehearing the ECJ eventually decided *Cremona* on other grounds, so that the question of a temporal limitation did not have to be considered. So we are left with a situation similar to that identified by Whish in Chapter 5 in relation to *Syfait* in the field of competition law (see above): the innovative and authoritative opinion of an experienced Advocate General, but no ruling from the Court. It seems more than

---

76 [1976] ECR 455.

77 Opinion of 17 March 2005.

78 Para. 87 of the opinion.

79 The finding in question being a finding of incompatibility subject to a future date before which individuals may not rely on the incompatibility in any claims against the state, the date in question being chosen in order to allow sufficient time for new legislation to be enacted: see para. 86 of the opinion.

80 Case 43/75 [1976] ECR 455, at paras 69 to 75.

81 Case 4/79 [1980] ECR 2823, at paras 42 to 46.

82 Case 300/86 [1988] ECR 3443, at paras 22 to 24.

likely that the solution suggested by Francis Jacobs in *Cremona* will fall to be reconsidered in a suitable future case.

FROM *WACHAUF* TO *RICHARDS*: MAKING COMMUNITY LAW AND THE LEGACY OF AG JACOBS

It may be concluded from the cases discussed above that Sir Francis Jacobs's legacy at the Court is not merely the body of work that he leaves behind; nor is it limited to the contents of his individual opinions, valuable though these are as a rich treasury of ideas for future cases. Sir Francis combines clarity of reasoning with a straightforward application of the law, instinctively striving for outcomes that are both workable and accord with the fundamental principles of EU law. This can be observed in the opinions that deal with free movement as much as in opinions dealing with the regulation of competition or the purpose of trade marks. In each case the relevant interest is kept clearly in view, be it the freedom to establish oneself in another Member State, the achievement of a single market or the protection of the consumer. Sir Francis's true legacy is this clarity of approach, combined with a willingness to depart from the accepted way of doing things if the justice of the case demands it.

Francis Jacobs's influence has also been felt particularly keenly in the development of the Court's jurisprudence on the general principles of Community law; that is to say those principles that fall outside the formal sources of Community law such as the Treaties and the Community legislation. In particular, Sir Francis's contribution has been notable as regards the development of the Court's jurisprudence on the protection of fundamental rights. It is fitting therefore to conclude this Introduction by looking at one of Advocate General Jacobs's first cases and one of his last: Case 5/88 *Wachauf*[83] (opinion delivered 27 April 1989) and Case 423/04 *Richards*[84] (opinion delivered 15 December 2005).

Wachauf was one of the earliest opinions that Sir Francis delivered. It concerned the dry and technical subject of milk quotas. However, it also raised an important underlying issue of fundamental rights. In an attempt to reduce milk production the Community legislature provided for a system of milk quotas and also enabled Member States to grant compensation to producers who discontinued milk production entirely. Germany took advantage of the latter option, but as a condition of entitlement to compensation in the case of tenant farmers, the authorization of the landlord was required. The result was

---

83 Case 5/88 *Wachauf* [1989] ECR 2609.
84 Judgment, 27 April 2006.

that the Community rules, if they were to be implemented in this way, could mean that a tenant farmer, who had acquired the milk quota as a result of his labours, could be deprived without compensation of the fruits of his labour by a landlord who might never have engaged in milk production. AG Jacobs argued that although it was up to the national legislature to implement the regulations in a way that balanced appropriately the interests of tenant farmers and landlords, Community law also played a role in determining how that balance should be struck. He argued that when implementing Community law it was incumbent upon Member States to have regard to the principle of respect for the right to property which was guaranteed in the Community legal order in accordance with the ideas common to the constitutions of the Member States and which was also reflected in Article 1 of the First Protocol to the European Convention on Human Rights. The Court agreed. It held that the requirements of the protection of fundamental rights in the Community legal order were also binding on the Member States when they implement Community rules. This was the first case in which the ECJ expressly established that fundamental rights are binding on Member States when implementing Community law. *Wachauf* was an early example of what would come to be typical in the opinions of Francis Jacobs: a simple statement of the fundamental right, followed by the self-evident conclusion that the responsible authority (in this case the Member State) must be bound by it. As was so often the case, the application of the appropriate right led to the resolution of the question referred to the ECJ.

Richards was one of the three last opinions delivered by Sir Francis on the same day in December 2005. That case dealt with the question of whether it is contrary to Directive 79/7[85] for a Member State to refuse to grant a retirement pension before the age of sixty-five to a male-to-female transsexual[86] where that person would have been entitled to a pension at the age of sixty had she been regarded as a woman as a matter of national law. Sir Francis cited two previous rulings of the ECJ on gender reassignment, *P v S* and *KB*,[87] identifying the fundamental right concerned, namely the right not to be discriminated against on grounds of sex, which is one of the fundamental human rights whose observance the Court has a duty to ensure, and the correct comparator

85 Council Directive 79/7/EEC of 19 December 1978 on the progressive implementation of the principle of equal treatment for men and women in matters of social security (OJ 1979 L 6, p. 24).

86 Quoting the House of Lords in *Bellinger v Bellinger* [2003] 2 AC 467, AG Jacobs defined transsexuals as people who were 'born with the anatomy of a person of one sex but with an unshakeable belief or feeling that they are persons of the opposite sex' (opinion, para.1).

87 Case C-13/94 [1996] ECR I-2143 and Case C-117/01 [2004] ECR I-541.

for someone in the situation of a female-to-male transsexual; that is, a male person whose identity was not the result of gender reassignment surgery. The AG then applied the relevant fundamental right to the situation in hand in a way that a scholar of Francis Jacobs's opinions over the preceding seventeen years would find wholly unsurprising (at paras 54 to 56):

> It is clear from its terms that the prohibition on discrimination in Article 4(1) of Directive 79/7, which states 'that there shall be no discrimination whatsoever on grounds of sex either directly, or indirectly by reference in particular to marital or family status', is intended to be all-encompassing. The Court has ruled that the provision 'precludes, generally and unequivocally, all discrimination on grounds of sex'. . . .
>
> In contrast, the Court has ruled that, in view of the fundamental importance of the principle of equal treatment, the exception to the prohibition of discrimination on grounds of sex provided for in Article 7(1)(a) must be interpreted strictly. As explained above, that provision permits the maintenance of a specific instance of different treatment of men and women, namely in the determination of pensionable age for the purposes of granting old-age and retirement pensions and the possible consequences thereof for other benefits. That type of sex discrimination is not in issue in the present case.
>
> In the present case the conduct complained of falls within the general prohibition in Article 4(1) of the Equal Treatment Directive and outside the derogation therefrom in Article 7(1)(a).[88]

The AG concluded that it was contrary to Article 4(1) of Directive 79/7 for a Member State to refuse to grant a retirement pension before the age of sixty-five to a post-operative male-to-female transsexual where that person would have been entitled to a pension at the age of sixty had she been regarded as a woman as a matter of national law. The ECJ concurred.

In both *Wachauf* and *Richards* one finds a staunch defence of fundamental rights. In neither case however is the point made in a grandstanding or dramatic fashion; rather, the strength of the arguments is enhanced by the matter-of-fact delivery of Francis Jacobs. In both cases the innovation is framed in terms of continuity and conformity with previous case law. Another aspect of these cases is that they directly affect the rights, and thus the everyday lives, of the individual applicants: for both Hubert Wachauf and Sarah Margaret Richards these were not matters of abstract principle but issues of considerable personal and financial importance. Francis Jacobs's recourse to fundamental rights was not an arid exercise in building the Community *acquis*. In each case the end in view was justice for the individual.

---

88 The question of the stage at which a transsexual person becomes entitled to equal treatment within the meaning of Directive 79/7 with persons of his or her acquired gender was discussed but it was not necessary for the AG or the Court to consider this, and so they did not do so.

As a modest man, Sir Francis Jacobs may well be appalled at the sheer volume of praise contained in this book (and in this introductory chapter). However, the authors of this work have not set out to flatter. Francis Jacobs has made a unique contribution to EU law and it is hoped that this book can go some way towards explaining and perpetuating that contribution.

1. A consumer's appreciation of the contribution of Advocate General Francis Jacobs to the shaping of the EC's legal order

Stephen Weatherill[1]

INTRODUCTORY REMARKS[2]

In a recent paper Kamiel Mortelmans made the following perceptive observation about the store of literature which examines the contribution of the Advocates General to the shaping of the EC legal order: 'The role of the Advocates General in the development of Community law is discussed most frequently by the Advocates General themselves and their legal secretaries in articles and farewell addresses … One advantage of this obviously is that insiders know what they are talking about.'[3]

I am not an insider. It does not necessarily follow that I do not know what I am talking about. However, it does follow that if Mortelmans is correct in his view of the most fecund source of writing about Advocates General – and I think he is – then I will be writing with a handicap. For since I have never worked at the Court and since, in fact, my direct experience of its Luxembourg home is limited to a very few visits, there is much upon which I cannot comment. I am sure, for example, that an important quality of a successful Advocate General is his or her ability to work efficiently and to meet dead-

[1] Jacques Delors Professor of European Community Law, Somerville College, Oxford.

[2] This is a lightly edited and re-arranged version of a paper delivered at Middle Temple in June 2006. I have largely retained the flavour of an oral presentation in preference to converting my remarks into more conventional academic tone. Moreover, much of the chapter offers a rather general survey of developments across a range of areas of EC law and practice, in line with its intent in June 2006 as an introduction to a day's discussion which subsequently pursued more detailed sector-specific analysis in other contributions.

[3] K. Mortelmans, 'The Court under the influence of its Advocates General' (2005) 24 YEL 127, 130–31.

lines. I would know nothing about that. Probably Advocates General are prized or feared in Luxembourg for their compassion or its absence shown to those on their team. I expect that advocates appearing before the Court have their own favourites among the Advocates General. In practice the pattern of distribution of cases between the Advocates General also doubtless matters. But I am not an insider. I have nothing to say about these enormously important practical aspects of the job.[4] I am a consumer. I judge Advocates General by what they offer me in their Opinions. When I read an Opinion, I want to be better informed as a result and perhaps wiser too. For eighteen years I have felt that Francis Jacobs offers me, as a consumer, very good value for money indeed.

In the next section of this chapter I summarize what are the five most important characteristics of a good Advocate General to me as a consumer. Then, in the section that follows, I skip across a number of areas of EC law to explore the extent to which Francis Jacobs has displayed those characteristics in eighteen years at the Court. Next, I select one area in particular for closer analysis. This is the phenomenon of so-called 'incidental' direct effect of directives in the context of the rules governing notification of technical standards, which in my view deserves attention as an example of carefully phrased, closely argued analysis by Francis Jacobs in an environment of woeful inattention to its learned Advocate General by the Court. Finally, I conclude my remarks; but briefly, I am a satisfied consumer.

THE FUNCTION OF THE ADVOCATE GENERAL

What makes a good Advocate General? And what makes a bad one, or at least one who would fail to exploit to the full the potential of the Advocate General in shaping the law?

The Treaty offers little help. Article 222 EC provides simply that:

> The Court of Justice shall be assisted by eight Advocates-General. Should the Court of Justice so request, the Council, acting unanimously, may increase the number of Advocates-General.
>
> It shall be the duty of the Advocate-General, acting with complete impartiality and independence, to make, in open court, reasoned submissions on cases which, in accordance with the Statute of the Court of Justice, require his involvement.

---

4 On this – and a great deal more! – see e.g. T. Tridimas, 'The role of the Advocate General in the development of community law' (1997) 34 CMLRev 1349; L. Neville Brown and T. Kennedy, *Brown and Jacobs: The Court of Justice of the European Communities* (London: Sweet and Maxwell, 5th edn, 2000), Ch. 4.

Roughly, of course, we recognize that the Advocate General should address relevant issues, offer a solution or solutions and generally offer the Court a pathway to resolution of the dispute before it. Normally the Court agrees more or less with its Advocate General but not always and in any event frequently without being explicit. It is not possible to make a systematic qualitative assessment of the influence of the Advocates General.[5] More broadly we expect the Advocate General to provide a fuller discussion of the law and the factual background than is to be found in the judgment of the Court. There is nothing precisely like the Advocate General in any national legal order but after fifty years of the EC legal order we have a rough idea of what to expect.

I offer five characteristics which seem to me as a consumer typical of the most successful Advocates General.

First: clarity of expression. This is self-evident. One needs to understand the arguments advanced in an Opinion. Most Advocates General are blessed by skills of clarity of expression.

Second: clarity of vision. This is also self-evident but deserves a little elaboration. First of all, I believe that sometimes, though certainly not always, vision is not too grand a word to describe what one should expect from an Advocate General. Some cases are admittedly minute in their impact but others raise issues of profound impact. A vision of which complex issues are involved is needed. There is also a call for a vision of the direction in which the EC legal order is headed. This vision is more readily shaped by an Advocate General than by a Court, which takes as its overwhelming priority the resolution of the particular dispute at stake. But there is a second element. The Court is limited by the need to produce a single collegiate judgment. I understand the importance of speaking with one voice as a means to confer legitimacy on the Court in its early years as it sought (successfully) to harness national courts to its mission to ensure the deep penetration of EC law into national legal orders. My own view is that times have changed and that the Court would show strength, not weakness, were it to allow dissenting judgments. Institutional adhesiveness would ensure they would be rare, I think, but if permitted they would help us to understand the Court's shaping of the law rather better than the current situation in which we are on occasion forced to put up with troublingly opaque rulings which are plainly merely the minimum that can be agreed in common by a divided chamber. But that is a debate for another day: my main point is that the Advocate General has a considerable advantage over the Court in showing clarity of vision. The Court in truth sometimes does not speak with one voice despite the comforting deception of

5 The track record is explored by both Mortelmans and Tridimas, op. cit. See also A. Arnull, *The European Union and its Court of Justice* (Oxford: OUP, 1999), pp.7–10.

its single collegiate judgment whereas the Advocate General always does. An Opinion is not undermined by the committee-like deliberations that are unavoidable in the Court itself. It is a purer source.

Third: contextual richness. This has some connection with the point I made above about the Advocate General's ability to go further than the Court in offering more than a resolution of the dispute. One would commonly expect to see a fuller exploration of the wider implications of the decision at hand in an Opinion than in the ruling itself. But my claim here is more ornate. I expect to see an Advocate General prepared to embark on comparative analysis. I expect to see an Advocate General prepared to draw on academic writing. Not always and certainly not where it would add nothing. But there is a close interconnection between the universities of Europe and the Court; many professors have become judges or Advocates General and many members of the Court have returned to academic life. Where appropriate, reference to academic writing can help us to understand the trajectory of legal development. This is much more the preserve of the Opinions of the Advocates General than judgments of the Court. So, generally, I expect to see the Advocate General helping to shed light on the broad intellectual context within which a particular piece of litigation is situated. Broader still, where an Opinion shows contextual richness the Advocate General can demonstrate and help shape the EC legal order's systemic qualities more overtly than the Court.

Fourth: leadership. A factor explaining my call for contextual richness is a belief that an Advocate General can be responsible for helping to piece together the legal order as a (more or less) coherent structure, not simply a set of accidents of litigation. That is a form of leadership. Leadership is a quality generally associated with the more prominent Advocates General. Boldness is a necessary ingredient in a successful Advocate General. He or she should not be afraid to challenge received wisdom. It is not always helpful simply to invite the Court to take the line of least resistance in deciding a case. Sometimes the law needs to be adjusted. This is not to say that the Advocate General will always be able to persuade the Court but if he or she can contribute to a debate about whether to renovate the law then he or she is doing a good, constructive job. Simply to identify looming problems is a service. An Advocate General can sow the seeds of change. In this sense measuring influence is necessarily a matter for the long term.

Fifth: capacity to inspire. This quality may simply constitute the sum of the four above-mentioned qualities, but I think it can be something extra. The Advocate General can present a more sweeping understanding of the shape and direction of the law than can the Court, especially in circumstances where the Court has to squeeze dissent into a single collegiate judgment. The Advocate General can easily choose to go beyond understandable judicial reticence to test new ideas, especially where they are unnecessary to dispose of the case at hand. Without being incautious or over-elaborate the Advocate General can adopt a more vivid tone than the Court.

I think that Francis Jacobs scores very well on all five counts. I will seek to demonstrate this in the sections that follow.

THE QUALITIES OF A SUCCESSFUL ADVOCATE GENERAL: BRIEF EXAMPLES FROM ACROSS A RANGE OF AREAS OF THE LAW

The Law of Free Movement of Goods: What Is a Trade Barrier?

These issues will be examined in more depth by Catherine Barnard.[6] My concern here is therefore not to offer a systematic account. Rather, I use this area to illustrate some of my points about the role of an Advocate General in general and Francis Jacobs in particular.

My understanding of the current state of the law governing the free movement of goods separates out three types of national measure. First, there are measures that discriminate on the basis of nationality or origin. These measures clearly fall within the scope of the law of free movement as trade barriers and therefore require justification but are unlikely to be justified. Second, there are measures that do not make explicit reference to nationality or origin but which exert a protectionist effect in favour of the home market. This will typically arise where compliance with the rules of the Member State of production is insufficient to secure access to the market of the target Member State because the rules there are different. Imports therefore face an extra regulatory burden when compared with similar products made and marketed in the target state. The target state must justify that extra regulatory burden and, if it cannot, it must not impose it on imports. This is the fact pattern familiar from the Court's landmark ruling in *Cassis de Dijon*.[7] The third type of national measure is that which constitutes a restriction on commercial freedom but which applies to all operators equally in law and in fact. The rule is origin-neutral and its interference with market freedom has no cross-border dimension. It affects the market but it does not affect the making of the EU internal market. In short, this is the type of rule which the Court in *Keck and Mithouard*[8] intended to place beyond the reach of Article 28 EC.

---

6 Chapter 6.

7 Case 120/78 *Rewe-Zentrale AG v Bundesmonopolverwaltung für Branntwein* [1979] ECR 649.

8 Cases C-267 and C-268/91 [1993] ECR I-6097.

Such national rules are not inter-state trade barriers and therefore the state does not need to justify them according to standards recognized by EC law.

The literature in this area is plentiful and there remains much that is unsettled.[9] However, for the purposes of this chapter I do not choose to dig more deeply into the mountain of case law and scholarly investigation. I want only to observe that I think this threefold classification of national measures makes good sense when placed in the context of the internal market project. The first and second categories of measure damage the interpenetration of markets in the EU and must be subject to review under EC trade law. The third category of measure poses no threat to the internal market project. Diversity between national laws is not in itself a sufficient reason for the invocation of the law of free movement.[10] That is, in my judgement, the core of the message delivered in *Keck and Mithouard*. The challenged French rules were different from those used elsewhere but they did not amount to obstacles to trade between Member States. They applied equally in law and in fact to all traders operating on French territory. They were treated as a permissible exercise of local regulatory competence.

So I believe the Court was right in *Keck and Mithouard* to adjust its case law and to insist that a genuine connection exist between the challenged measure and the process of product market integration as a pre-condition to the potential application of Article 28 EC. I had, and have, my reservations about the precise formula it used to achieve that re-direction. Most of all, I feared that a formal approach to the presence of inequality between local and imported goods and traders might lead to an under-use of Article 28: that even barriers to inter-state trade might escape scrutiny.[11] To put it another way, I had anxieties that national measures that should be treated as falling into my second category would instead be placed in the third category as a result of an inappropriately rigid application of the '*Keck* formula' and a consequent

---

[9] It is a matter of persisting controversy whether the law covering all the freedoms will be aligned and, equally, it is controversial whether it should be aligned. For discussion see e.g. M. Andenas and W.-H. Roth (eds), *Services and Free Movement in EU Law* (Oxford: OUP, 2002); E. Spaventa, 'From Gebhard to Carpenter: towards a (non-)economic European constitution' (2004) 41 CMLRev 743; J. Snell, *Goods and Services in EC Law* (Oxford: OUP, 2002); C. Barnard, *The Substantive Law of the EU: The Four Freedoms* (Oxford: OUP, 2004); P. Oliver and W.-H. Roth, 'The internal market and the four freedoms' (2004) 41 CMLRev 407.

[10] Cf. S. Weatherill, 'Diversity between national laws in the internal market', Ch. 10, pp.131–50, in U. Drobnig, H.J. Snijders and E.-J. Zippro (eds), *Divergences of Property Law, an Obstacle to the Internal Market?* (Munich: Sellier European Law Publishers, 2006).

[11] S. Weatherill, 'After *Keck*: some thoughts on how to clarify the clarification' (1996) 33 CMLRev 885.

undue deference to national regulatory autonomy. The Court moved quickly to address this concern by finding that national rules governing product packaging obstructed inter-state trade, refusing to accept analogies with *Keck* which concerned the way in which products were sold rather than their physical characteristics.[12] However, it was cases dealing with advertising techniques which presented the sternest challenges to the viability of the '*Keck* formula' in providing a reliable basis for the future direction of the law governing the free movement of goods. It is in large measure thanks to Francis Jacobs that the challenges were met and the case law placed on an intellectually stable footing.

The awkward aspect of advertising techniques is that commonly they are not physically attached to the product. Indeed, they may be found remote from it: on billboards, on televisions, on cinema screens. Imagine a state which bans a particular type of advertising campaign and imagine that it does so for all relevant products and traders with no hint of reference to origin or nationality. The regulator argues that the physical composition of products remains unaffected: all that is affected is a means of inducing consumers to favour a product; all operators are subject to this inhibition. Is this, after *Keck*, a matter of even-handed local regulation which escapes the supervision of EC trade law?

The flaw in this approach is that it rests on a static view of the market. In reality markets are dynamic and advertising is a key motor for change. Suppressing advertising tends to prevent markets from altering and therefore tends to confer an advantage on existing incumbents. So, in *Keck* terms, the effect of the national measure is not equal in fact, even if it may be equal in law.

In *Konsumentombudsmannen v Gourmet International Products* Francis Jacobs drew attention to this phenomenon with the vivid depiction of the 'primordial' importance of advertising in penetrating new markets.[13] This phrase has galvanized the Court, which has followed the vitally important lead set by Francis Jacobs in understanding that a restriction on advertising may have a damaging effect on inter-state trade even where on the face of it all operators are confronted by the same restriction on their opportunities to publicize their wares.

So, in the judgment of the Court:

> Even without its being necessary to carry out a precise analysis of the facts characteristic of the Swedish situation, which it is for the national court to do, the Court is

---

[12] e.g. Case C-470/93 *Verein gegen Unwesen in Handel und Gewerbe Köln eV v Mars GmbH* [1995] ECR I-1923.

[13] Case C-405/98 *Konsumentombudsmannen v Gourmet International Products* [2001] ECR I-1795.

> able to conclude that, in the case of products like alcoholic beverages, the consumption of which is linked to traditional social practices and to local habits and customs, a prohibition of all advertising directed at consumers in the form of advertisements in the press, on the radio and on television, the direct mailing of unsolicited material or the placing of posters on the public highway is liable to impede access to the market by products from other Member States more than it impedes access by domestic products, with which consumers are instantly more familiar. (Paragraph 21)

Precisely so!

In *Douwe Egberts* the Court confirmed that 'an absolute prohibition of advertising the characteristics of a product is liable to impede access to the market by products from other Member States more than it impedes access by domestic products, with which consumers are more familiar',[14] citing the above-mentioned ruling in *Gourmet International Products*.

The point is not that any rule affecting advertising or other methods of boosting sales is now within the scope of Article 28. That conclusion would go too far and would undo much of the good done by *Keck*'s readjustment of Article 28. Rather, the point is that one must carefully examine the impact of a particular challenged national measure on the market which it affects.[15] The margin between what I choose to describe as category two measures and category three measures is not dictated by the form of the national measure. That is the trap set by the slightly careless wording of the *Keck* ruling itself. It is tempting but wholly misconceived to inflate the notion of rules affecting 'selling arrangements' into some definable category divorced from what really counts, which is to examine the economic impact of the measures in question. The point is that only if the national measure imperils the quest to create an integrated market for Europe does it fall for consideration in the light of Article 28.

Francis Jacobs deserves great credit for helping us to understand this in the particularly awkward area of national rules affecting advertising. This demonstrates his clarity of expression and clarity of vision; his concern to found the law of free movement on the basis of its true economic purpose demonstrates contextual richness; and there is clear evidence of leadership here as the Court has accepted the steer away from a rigidly formalist interpretation of *Keck*.

---

14 Case C-239/02 *Douwe Egberts* [2004] ECR I-7007, para. 53.

15 Cf. Case C-20/03 *Burmanjer et al.* judgment of 26 May 2005; Case C-71/02 *Herbert Karner GmbH v Troostwijk GmbH* [2004] ECR I-3025. For recent academic discussion, see S. Enchelmaier, 'The awkward selling of a good idea, or a traditionalist interpretation of Keck' (Oxford: OUP, 2003) 22 YEL 249.

The Law of Free Movement: The Significance of Discrimination

My first category of trade barrier was rules that discriminate on the basis of nationality or origin. My second was those that do not make explicit reference to nationality or origin but which exert a protectionist effect in favour of the home market. Why distinguish between the two? After all, both are inter-state barriers to trade. The orthodox answer is that the two categories must be distinguished because available justifications vary according to the type of measure, discriminatory or not, that is at stake. Here too Francis Jacobs has been active.

The orthodox view holds that discriminatory measures are capable of justification only pursuant to Article 30 EC, whereas indistinctly applicable measures benefit from more generous treatment in the shape of the 'mandatory requirements' developed (under that inelegant and misleading name[16]) in *Cassis de Dijon* and elaborated since as a broader notion of public interest justification. So the nature of the trade barrier affects the scope of available justification.

This, at least, is what the Court says is the law. But in some instances, in particular in connection with challenges to national measures of environmental protection, the Court confronts the awkwardness of a test that is reliant on discrimination and on some accounts it sacrifices purity of reasoning in order to achieve a result that is consistent with good environmental practice, recognized inter alios loci elsewhere in the EC Treaty. In the *Walloon Waste* case[17] Wallonia (a region of Belgium) prohibited the storage, tipping or dumping of waste from other Member States or from elsewhere in Belgium. The measure was aimed at protecting Wallonia from becoming the target for waste from areas with tighter regulatory regimes. This was a restriction on the importation of goods of commercial value, but the Court found it justified as a measure of environmental protection. The Court observed that '[t]he accumulation of waste . . . constitutes a threat to the environment because of the limited capacity of each region or locality for receiving it'. It drew on the principle expressed in Article 130r(2) of the EC Treaty (now, after amendment, Article 174(2) EC) that 'environmental damage should as a priority be rectified at source', which dictates a need to minimize transport of waste.

The result is receptive to national measures designed to counter 'waste tourism' and it may be applauded as consistent with good environmental prac-

---

16 On mistranslation, see S. Weatherill and P. Beaumont, *EU Law* (London: Penguin Books, 3rd edn, 1999) p. 575, n. 35.

17 Case C-2/90 *Commission v Belgium* [1992] ECR I-4431, [1993] 1 CMLR 365.

tice.[18] But in law there is a problem. Waste originating from one source was unambiguously treated differently from waste from another. Therefore, one might suppose, this was a discriminatory measure capable of justification only by reference to Article 30 EC, which does not include any mention of environmental protection. Only those measures which do not discriminate on the basis of origin benefit from access to the longer list of justifications encompassed by the mandatory requirements and including environmental protection.

For some commentators, in *Walloon Waste* the Court therefore took a discriminatory measure and allowed it to be justified on grounds extending beyond Article 30 EC and the case is in this vein used to support an argument that in fact the Court has tacitly accepted that all trade barriers, discriminatory or not, are subject to the same test of justification.[19] However, this is not what the Court said. It may not even be what it did. It is not self-evident that this was truly a discriminatory measure. The Court commented that 'having regard to the differences between waste produced in one place and that in another and its connection with the place where it is produced, the contested measures cannot be considered to be discriminatory'. It has a point: if, as Article 174(2) EC suggests, waste is in part defined by its origin then waste created in one locality is not the same thing as waste created elsewhere and it is not discriminatory to treat the two types of waste in a different manner. On that analysis, the case law remains consistent with the principle that environmental protection and other mandatory requirements outside Article 30 EC are justifications available only for non-discriminatory measures.

Wherever one stands in this debate, it is an awkward one. In his Opinion, Francis Jacobs himself treated the measure as discriminatory. So one can be sceptical whether the law is sufficiently clear and stable. The problem lies in the heavy load carried by the notion of discrimination in structuring the law on the scope of available justifications. Use of discrimination as a relevant legal test presupposes a need to decide what constitute legitimate subjects for comparison. Is transported waste the same as locally produced waste? What really is the proper basis of comparison?[20] Is a pregnant woman sacked by a ruthless employer the same as an ill man similarly dismissed? Many areas of the law reveal that identifying discrimination is itself a deeply contested process.

---

[18] There is of course a body of Community secondary legislation dealing with these issues, some of which is visible in the ruling itself.

[19] Peter Oliver takes this view in *Free Movement of Goods in the European Community* (London: Sweet and Maxwell, 4th edn, 2003): a 'manifestly discriminatory' measure (p. 219).

[20] See e.g. the contributions of G. De Burca and of J. Scott to C. Barnard and J. Scott (eds), *The Law of the Single European Market* (Oxford: Hart Publishing, 2001).

The law invites renovation. The Court has not explicitly abandoned the separation of discriminatory and non-discriminatory measures for the purposes of assessing justification. On the contrary, it has affirmed it. However, should the Court abandon that separation? This concession has been pressed on the Court by Francis Jacobs, who has pointed out the deficiencies in the current structure of the law with characteristic clarity and vigour. More than that, he has constructively set out a better approach. In *Preussen Elektra*[21] Francis Jacobs called on the Court to improve legal certainty by adopting a unified test that would apply the full spectrum of justifications to all barriers to trade, and relegate the presence of discrimination to the assessment of whether the national rules should be accepted as proportionate. He advanced this argument once again in *Danner*, a subsequent case dealing with the free movement of services.[22]

The Court did not address the point in either decision and without attempting to clarify the law it maintained its orthodox approach.[23] I think this is unfortunate.

The proposal is that in principle all barriers to trade, whatever their character, should be susceptible to justification according to the same criteria and that discrimination should become simply an element in the factual assessment. This eliminates the importance of discrimination in the analysis of which justifications are in principle available. It moves it and its conundrums to the concrete assessment of whether a particular justification is made good in the case: presumably direct discrimination on the basis of origin will not be readily justified. Peter Oliver has also championed this approach, and though I do not hold to his view that the Court has in effect already adopted this line, I would be inclined to accept the normative view that this is the right road for the future.[24] The principal orthodox counter-argument has been that any extension in the scope of justification for discriminatory measures opens the door to devious protectionism. My view is that appreciation of the now well-established tough standard of review applied to national measures that act as barriers to inter-state trade is enough to allay that concern. In the cause of superior legal coherence I hope that ultimately the Court will embrace the improvement suggested by Francis Jacobs. It is likely to be prodded again in future.

---

21 Case C-379/98 *Preussen Elektra* [2001] ECR I-2099.

22 Case C-136/00 *Danner* [2002] ECR I-8147.

23 The same is true of its decision in Case C-320/03 *Commission v Austria* judgment of November 2005, although, as para. 39 makes clear, the Court had again been pressed to address the matter.

24 In *Free Movement of Goods in the European Community* (op. cit.), esp. Chapter VIII which weaves together Article 30 cases with Cassis 'mandatory requirements' cases.

This issue has been the subject of comment by at least two other Advocates General recently. Advocate General Geelhoed commented in *Commission v Austria* that 'The case-law remains unclear and fragmented in this regard'[25] and Advocate General Poiares Maduro advised in *Marks and Spencer* that 'it would be useful for the Court to put an end to these uncertainties'.[26] In both instances the pioneering trail cut by Francis Jacobs was noted with approval.

Here again I believe that Francis Jacobs has demonstrated clarity of expression and clarity of vision; he has shown leadership here too. That the Court has not yet followed that lead is unfortunate. Nevertheless, Francis has invigorated a debate and sown the seeds for future improvement in the shape of the law.

Other Examples of Trendsetting

I will skip more briefly over a group of other areas where I think one can identify Francis Jacobs to have made a major contribution to the shaping of the EC legal order and, more specifically, to have displayed the sterling qualities which I expect to find in a successful Advocate General.

In *Germany v Commission*[27] Francis made the following observation:

> EC law in its present state does not confer on the Commission, the [Court of First Instance] or the [European Court of Justice] the function of a criminal tribunal. It should, however, be noted that that would not in itself preclude the EC from harmonising the criminal laws of the Member States if that were necessary to attain one of the objectives of the Community.

This, it seems to me, was a classic case of an Advocate General being able to raise awareness of an issue without the need to address it in its full complexity. How far might the EC bite into the criminal sphere in its quest to attain its widely drawn objectives? Francis gave that Opinion in 1992. Over a decade later the Court addressed the matter squarely in its remarkable judgment in September 2005 in *Commission v Council*.[28] It stated that

> As a general rule, neither criminal law nor the rules of criminal procedure fall within the Community's competence . . . [that] does not prevent the Community legislature, when the application of effective, proportionate and dissuasive criminal penalties by the competent national authorities is an essential measure for combating serious environmental offences, from taking measures which relate to the criminal law of the Member States which it considers necessary in order to ensure that the rules which it lays down on environmental protection are fully effective.

---

25 Para. 104 of his Opinion in Case C-320/03 *Commission v Austria*.

26 Para. 33 of his Opinion in Case C-446/03 *Marks and Spencer*.

27 Case C-240/90 *Germany v Commission* [1992] ECR I-5383.

28 Case C-176/03 *Commission v Council* judgment of 13 September 2005.

This immediately invites attention to the point raised by Francis Jacobs because there is no obvious logical basis for confining this statement to criminal law adopted in support of effective environmental protection. Intriguing questions arise about the extent to which the Court has given a green light to EC competence to adopt criminal measures across a wide range of areas, including in the context of harmonization designed to create an internal market.[29] I have some anxieties about whether the Court's slippery test is capable of serving as a reliable basis for deciding when the threshold has been crossed for the purposes of authorizing EC legislative action affecting criminal law.[30] That is to say, judging what is 'effective' is not easily measured,[31] and I fear this judgment is conducive to legislative 'competence creep', which has a corrosive effect on the EC's legitimacy.[32] I also wonder more generally whether the EC is really an appropriate place to develop criminal law, the shaping of which needs a great deal more subtlety than simply prescribing penalties. For present purposes, however, I limit myself to observing that this is another good example of Francis Jacobs sowing the seeds for future debate, which I consider to be an important attribute of a successful Advocate General.

Oscar Bronner GmbH v Mediaprint[33] provides a powerful example of Francis acting to stabilize a line of case law that had the potential to list dangerously. Richard Whish will tackle competition law more intensively,[34] but the background to the ruling in *Oscar Bronner* is provided by the strikingly interventionist use of Article 82 EC by the Commission, approved by the Community judicature, to require a reluctant dominant firm to respond to consumer demand in the so-called *'Television Guides'* cases.[35] The television companies were forced to surrender exclusive rights over programme listings, allowing third parties to pay a reasonable fee in order to acquire the right to use the information and to produce a single guide, for the benefit of consumers previously denied such an attractive product. Consumer choice prevailed over

---

29 Cf. Case C-440/05 *Commission v Council* (action brought on 8 December 2005).

30 Cf. in this vein C. Tobler, 'Annotation', (2006) 43 CMLRev 835; E. Herlin-Karnell, '*Commission v Council*: some reflections on criminal law in the first pillar' (2007) 13 European Public Law 47.

31 Cf. M. Ross, 'Effectiveness in the European legal order(s): beyond supremacy to constitutional proportionality?' (2006) 31 ELRev 476.

32 S. Weatherill, 'Competence creep and competence control' (2004) 23 *Yearbook of European Law* 1.

33 Case C-7/97 [1998] ECR I-7791.

34 Chapter 5.

35 Decision 89/205 OJ 1989 L78/43, [1989] 4 CMLR 757, Cases T-69, T-70, T-76/89 [1991] ECR II-485, 535, 575, Joined Cases C-241/91P and C-242/91P *RTE and ITP v Commission* [1995] ECR I-743.

commercial freedom not to contract and, in my view, rightly so in the special circumstances of the case.[36] However, the risk is that this interventionism becomes over-inflated, with the result that firms lose incentives to invest in innovation for fear that their profits will be curtailed by assertive application of Article 82. That could be severely damaging in the long term. Article 82 must not be used routinely to strip exclusivity out of the hands of right-holders.[37] *Oscar Bronner GmbH v Mediaprint* provided that necessary corrective and it was Francis Jacobs who showed the way forward.[38] His Opinion, delivered on 28 May 1998, contains assessment of US law and practice, with particular reference to the so-called 'essential facilities' doctrine as a basis for intruding on the commercial autonomy of dominant firms. The US analogy is not used as an example to be followed slavishly or uncritically. Nor is it mere window-dressing. Instead it is used to inform and illuminate and to ensure that the full legal and economic context is appreciated. This approach is fully in line with my argument that a good Advocate General should provide necessary contextual richness within which to guide a Court that will typically not take such a discursive tack.

In *Oscar Bronner* Francis Jacobs took the view that

> intervention whether understood as an application of the essential facilities doctrine or, more traditionally, as a response to a refusal to supply goods or services, can be justified in terms of competition policy only in cases in which the dominant undertaking has a genuine stranglehold on the related market. That might be the case for example where duplication of the facility is impossible or extremely difficult owing to physical, geographical or legal constraints or is highly undesirable for reasons of public policy. It is not sufficient that the undertaking's control over a facility should give it a competitive advantage.

This is highly significant in alerting us to the real peril involved if one accedes to the short-term appeal of allowing third parties to share in the economically valuable distribution facilities built up by a dominant firm. This was not a case where intervention was appropriate. Francis Jacobs offered a broader reminder of why one should be circumspect in asserting a right to undermine commercial autonomy pursuant to Article 82:

---

36 As explained in G. Howells and S. Weatherill, *Consumer Protection Law* (Aldershot: Ashgate Publishing Company, 2nd edn, 2005), Chapter 12.3.4.

37 Cf. in the wake of the 'Television Guides' cases, anxiety in this vein expressed by P. Crowther, 'Compulsory licensing of intellectual property rights' (1995) 20 ELRev 521. See more generally C. Twigg-Flesner, 'Innovation and EU consumer law' (2005) 28 JCP 409.

38 Case C-7/97 [1998] ECR I-7791.

> To accept Bronner's contention would be to lead the Community and national authorities and courts into detailed regulation of the Community markets, entailing the fixing of prices and conditions for supply in large sectors of the economy. Intervention on that scale would not only be unworkable but would also be anti-competitive in the longer term and indeed would scarcely be compatible with a free market economy.

In its judgment in *Oscar Bronner* the Court showed it had paid attention. In that ruling and the subsequent ruling in *IMS Health*,[39] in which Advocate General Tizzano was able to rely on the commentary on the 'essential facilities' doctrine already prepared by Francis Jacobs, a conspicuously cautious judicial approach is evident. A refusal to license an exclusive right is not *per se* abusive within the meaning of Article 82. The Court sets out three cumulative criteria that must be satisfied before Article 82 may be used to intervene in such circumstances of refusal to deal. The refusal must be preventing the emergence of a new product for which there is a potential consumer demand, it must be unjustified (or, to put it another way, it must not be justified by objective considerations) and it must be such as to exclude any competition on a secondary market. This does not mean that a ruling such as that in the *'Television Guides'* cases, provoking the release of a new product onto the market, could not in future be extracted from Article 82 EC. The three criteria were satisfied in that case. However, the recent judicial practice underlines that this is not the norm. It is Francis Jacobs who has played a major part in stabilizing the case law.

Leadership, as I have already suggested, is not necessarily judged only by whether others follow. I will not dwell at length on the vigorously debated matter of the standing rules governing access to the Court under Article 230(4).[40] I will only comment that Francis Jacobs has been active in exposing the weaknesses of the established approach and in putting forward constructive alternatives. Whether his lead will ultimately be picked up by the Court or whether we must await revision of the Treaty, I do not know. But I think his view will ultimately win the day. Ami Barav sums up a view I share:

> In *Union de Pequenos Agricultores* Advocate General Jacobs has bravely invited the Court to depart from its previous case-law . . . Advocate General Jacobs put

---

39 Case C-418/01 [2004] ECR I-5039. For discussion see E. Derclaye, 'The IMS Health decision and the reconciliation of copyright and competition law' (2004) 29 ELRev 687.

40 For extended analysis and copious cross-referencing see S. Enchelmaier, 'No-one slips through the net? Latest developments, and non-developments, in the European Court of Justice's jurisprudence on art. 230(4) EC' (2005) 24 YEL 173.

> forward several forceful reasons for inviting the Court to reconsider the case-law . . . He correctly stated that the wording of the fourth paragraph of Article 230 did not preclude reconsideration by the Court of its case-law on individual concern.[41]

The strength of purpose to which Barav refers is typical of the contribution of Francis Jacobs to the shaping of the EC legal order.

I will not reflect at length on the complex case law which seeks to weave together the status of citizenship of the Union introduced by the Maastricht Treaty with effect from 1993 and the pre-existing provisions dealing with the rights of individuals, in particular those concerning the free movement of persons. How far Union citizenship reaches as a legal concept is a matter of persisting obscurity. What is not in doubt is that Francis Jacobs is responsible for one of the most vivid statements to be found in this area. In *Christos Konstantinidis* he stated that:

> In my opinion, a Community national who goes to another Member State as a worker or self-employed person under Articles 48, 52 or 59 of the Treaty is entitled not just to pursue his trade or profession and to enjoy the same living and working conditions as nationals of the host State; he is in addition entitled to assume that, wherever he goes to earn his living in the European Community, he will be treated in accordance with a common code of fundamental values, in particular those laid down in the European Convention on Human Rights. In other words, he is entitled to say 'civis europeus sum' and to invoke that status in order to oppose any violation of his fundamental rights.[42]

Perhaps the Court will one day adopt this approach, perhaps it will not. Perhaps it should, perhaps it should not. The literature is abundant.[43] What is plain for present purposes is that Francis Jacobs has here chosen to cut through the confusion and offer a shining vision of where he thinks the law should be taken – in a direction which takes very seriously the centrality of fundamental rights protection. Clarity of expression and vision, contextual richness, leadership and . . . civis europeus sum – this is also truly inspirational.

---

41 Ami Barav, 'The European Court and the use of judicial discretion', in Ola Wiklund (ed), *Judicial Discretion in European Perspective* (Stockholm: Kluwer Law International, 2003), pp. 136–7.

42 Case C-168/91 *Christos Konstantinidis* [1993] ECR I-1191 para. 46.

43 For synthesis see C. Barnard, *The Substantive Law of the EU* (Oxford, OUP, 2004), ch. 15.

MARKET MANAGEMENT: THE ROLE OF NATIONAL COURTS

I offer this as the one case study that I will pursue in depth for the purposes of this chapter. In part, I am attracted to it because I find it unusually intriguing; in part, I examine it in depth because it will not be covered by other contributors. Most of all I think this case study reveals the great value of an alert and thoughtful Advocate General.

It is well known that EC trade law has exerted a powerful deregulatory impact on the economy. A host of peculiar and often anachronistic national rules have been set aside where their damaging effect on inter-state trade has been judged to outweigh any beneficial regulatory purpose that they may serve. However, the deregulatory impulse is not absolute. The Court has insisted that 'the fact that one Member State imposes less strict rules than another Member State does not mean that the latter's rules are disproportionate and hence incompatible with Community law'.[44] As the Treaty makes plain in Articles 30 EC, 46 EC and 55 EC, EC trade law does not generate automatic deregulation of national markets. Justification of trade-restrictive rules remains possible. This acknowledges regulatory diversity amongst the Member States (pending possible legislative intervention by the EC). In other words, the mutual recognition principle widely understood to capture the Court's approach in and since *Cassis de Dijon*[45] is not an unconditional one.

A key question is to ask: is this a reliable and workable basis for building and maintaining the internal market? How do traders devising their pan-European commercial strategy know when obstructive national rules can safely be ignored as incompatible with Article 28 EC? They can be confident that the regulator bears the burden of showing an adequate justification,[46] but they cannot be certain whether the burden will prove too heavy. So EC trade law's deregulatory effect on national practice (its role as a form of 'negative' harmonization) is less apt to set a clear basis for an integrated commercial strategy than would common rules adopted under EC legislation ('positive' harmonization). That does not necessarily mean that one should therefore eagerly support initiatives for more EC harmonization – although business interests often do press for the security of more EC rules, often whilst also

---

[44] E.g. in connection with the free movement of goods, Case C-294/00 *Deutsche Paracelsus Schulen* [2002] ECR I-6515, and in connection with the free movement of services, Case C-3/95 *Reisebüro Broede v Gerd Sanker* [1996] ECR I-6511.

[45] Case 120/78, note 4 above.

[46] E.g. Case 227/82 *Van Bennekom* [1983] ECR 3883, Case C-14/02 *ATRAL SA* [2003] ECR I-4431.

claiming to be averse to more regulation – but it does mean that one should appreciate that the free movement rules are more effective in delivering an integrated market on paper than they are in practice. Conditional mutual recognition is part of a strategy for making and maintaining an internal market but more is needed.

The Commission has made the point neatly in its Communication of May 2003 on Internal Market Strategy: Priorities 2003–2006.[47] It points out that:

> Mutual recognition is a corner stone of the Internal Market. It enables products to circulate freely on the basis of conformity with the national laws in the Member State where the product is first marketed. The principle is that there are no specific procedural rules and no extra paperwork. This is its strength, but at the same time its weakness. When problems occur, there is little or no transparency, there is no commonly agreed approach to evaluating whether levels of protection are equivalent and there is no clear procedure for a company to challenge a negative decision. As a result, many companies decide to abandon certain markets or are forced to modify their products to comply with local requirements.

What is at stake is the building of a European market, not a European state. However, can we really make and maintain a European market in the absence of a state-like institutional and constitutional infrastructure at European level? This is the challenge of market management.

An example of a specific instrument of market management, designed to provide practical support for the Treaty rules on (conditional) mutual recognition, is provided by the 'early warning system' for technical regulations. Council Directive 83/189 provided for Member States to give advance notice to the Commission and to other Member States of plans to introduce new product specifications (including from 1989 food products). The amendments were consolidated in Directive 98/34, which was itself amended by Directive 98/48.[48] Member States must comply with a 'standstill obligation' for a defined period after notification of draft measures before bringing them into force. The Commission's job is to inspect the planned measures. If the Commission considers the measures to be contrary to the Treaty provisions on free movement, it will advise the Member State not to introduce them. So the purpose of the regime is to forestall the introduction of new trade-restrictive measures (and also to supply the Commission with a possible basis for developing its harmonization programme in so far as it considers national regulatory initiatives to be worthwhile). It is an 'early warning system' and, in principle, one would suppose that ex ante control of potential trade barriers is

---

47 COM(2003) 238 final.
48 OJ 1998 L204/37, OJ 1998 L217/18 respectively.

a good deal superior to ex post control through expensive and lengthy litigation to remove barriers that have already caused economic damage.[49]

Member States notify draft rules to the Commission with a varying degree of conscientiousness.[50] They are not infallible. For reasons of inadvertence or, likely, sometimes for the purposes of achieving protection of domestic traders, some measures are not notified, or, if they are notified, they are put into effect before the mandatory standstill period has expired. This is a breach of EC law and could be the subject of Commission infringement proceedings. That is cold comfort: the whole point of the notification system is to prevent resort to laborious litigation. Would it not help a lot if national courts could play a role in penalizing delinquent public authorities where they seek to rely on technical regulations which have not been fed through the early warning notification procedure in the correct manner?

The Commission certainly thought so. Its view was that non-notification of a draft technical regulation, as defined by the Directive, should rob it of enforceability in proceedings involving third parties before national courts of the defaulting Member State.[51] It had no explicit textual support for this view. The Directive does not address the matter at all but the Court was not deterred. It decided to rule on the matter in the way favoured by the Commission. In *CIA Security International SA v Signalson SA and Securitel Sprl*[52] it held that breach of the procedural obligation to notify robs the measure of enforceability in proceedings before national courts involving third parties. Accordingly a trader was unable to rely on Belgian law to secure a court order against another trader dealing in products (burglar alarms) that were not in conformity with a Belgian technical regulation that had not been notified to the Commission in accordance with Directive 83/189. The Belgian courts were required to disapply the Belgian technical specification without any question

---

49 See S. Weatherill, 'Compulsory notification of draft technical regulations: the contribution of Directive 83/189 to the management of the internal market' (1996) 16 YEL 129; J. Jans, 'National legislative autonomy? The procedural constraints of European Law' LIEI [1998/1] 25; S. Weatherill, 'A case study in judicial activism in the 1990s: the status before national courts of measures wrongfully un-notified to the Commission', Ch. 31 in D. O'Keeffe (ed.), *Judicial Review in European Union Law: Liber Amicorum Gordon Slynn* (The Hague: Kluwer, 2000); R. Munoz, 'The development of the ex-ante control mechanism regarding implementation of the internal market', Ch. 7 in T. Tridimas and P. Nebbia (eds), *European Union Law for the 21st Century – Rethinking the New Legal Order* (Oxford: Hart, 2005).

50 For statistics relating to notification of technical regulations in 2003, see OJ 2004 C216/2, in 2004, see OJ 2005 C158/20, in 2005, see OJ 2006 C166/2.

51 Commission Communication OJ 1986 C245/4; this interpretation of the law was regularly added by the Commission as a footnote to published lists of notified drafts, e.g. OJ 1993 C237/3, OJ 1994 C3/2, C8/2, C129/5.

52 Case C-194/94 [1996] ECR I-2201.

of its compatibility with Article 28 EC being at stake: the procedural default in the shape of non-compliance with the early warning system by the Belgian public authorities was sufficient.

The Court was, of course, thereby granting the Commission significant support in its quest to achieve effective market management under the notification Directive. This penalty of unenforceability before national courts induces Member States to stick to the promise made in the Directive to cooperate with the Commission, and thereby to allow the Commission the chance to make the ex ante review system for technical regulations work effectively.[53] The Commission was pleased: it now routinely cites this judgment in notifications of technical rules published in the Official Journal.[54]

However, ingenious case law generates ingenious litigation. The Court's ruling in *CIA Security* offered a new route for enhancing commercial freedom. A technical rule obstructing trade in non-conforming products could be set aside without the need to show incompatibility with Article 28 EC if it could be shown to be a measure that fell within the notification regime established by Directive 83/189 and if it could be shown that the state had not conscientiously complied. So the definitional issue of whether a national measure fell within the scope of Directive 83/189, or now Directive 98/34, became very significant;[55] as, more broadly, did the question of whether the reasoning employed in *CIA Security* might be applied to regimes of compulsory notification operating elsewhere in the Community system.[56]

The most startling attempt to exploit the ruling in *CIA Security* arrived in *Johannes Martinus Lemmens*.[57] The Court ruled that a conviction for driving whilst drunk could not be challenged on the basis that the equipment for recording the level of intoxication was designed according to standards that had not been notified under Directive 83/189. A general argument based on the 'effet utile' of the notification Directive which had found favour with the

---

53 There is a clear parallel with the law governing consequences of non-notification of state aids to the Commission: for a vigorous examination of the law, and explicit discussion of the incentives of Member States, see the Opinion of Francis Jacobs in Case C-368/04 *Transalpine Ölleitung* delivered on 29 November 2005.

54 See e.g. OJ 2001 C152/4, OJ 2004 C230/3, OJ 2005 C259/4.

55 E.g. Case C-13/96 *Bic Benelux v Belgian State* [1997] ECRI-1753; Case C-278/99 *Georgius van der Burg* [2001] ECR I-2015; Case C-267/03 *Lindberg* 21 April 2005.

56 Cf. Case C-235/95 *AGS Assedic Pas-de-Calais v Francois Dumon* [1998] ECR I-4531; Case C-201/02 *Wells* [2004] ECR I-723. Inclusion of a notification procedure in the proposed 'Services Directive' would raise similar questions about the applicability of the *CIA Security* case law: see Article 15(7) of the Council Common Position reached in July 2006.

57 Case C-226/97 [1998] ECRI-3711.

Court in *CIA Security* might have encouraged the Court to uphold the offender's submission. After all, a state would certainly be impelled to take seriously its obligations of notification under Directive 83/189 if it were to discover that failure to do so sliced deep into its ability to apply orthodox rules of criminal law. One may assume that the Court was of the view that improving effective market management could not safely be regarded as a trump card such as to override other important interests in society, such as the effective suppression of drunken driving. The Court, provoked by the ingenious submissions presented to it in *Lemmens* to realize that caution was called for, took the opportunity to fix a limit to the scope afforded to private parties to escape obstructive national technical rules. In *Lemmens* it adopted a legal formula that is noticeably more precise than that found in *CIA Security*. The Court observed that failure to notify rendered regulations inapplicable only inasmuch as they hindered the use or marketing of non-conforming products. This pins down the key distinction between *CIA Security*, where the private individual was able to evade the obstructive but non-notified rules, and *Lemmens*, where he was not.

So far, so good. But in my view the Court took a wrong turning in the next key case in this sequence, *Unilever Italia SpA v Central Food SpA*.[58] *Unilever* applies the reasoning pioneered by *CIA Security* and finessed in *Lemmens* in proceedings involving a contract between private parties.

Unilever had supplied Central Food with a quantity of virgin olive oil. Central Food rejected the goods on the basis that they were not labelled in accordance with a relevant Italian law. This law had been notified to the Commission but Italy had not observed the Directive's standstill obligation.[59] Unilever submitted that the law should not be applied and sued Central Food for the price of the goods. The Court pointed out that were the Italian rules applied they would have the effect of hindering trade in a product not complying with those rules. The Court acknowledged that its own case law denies that a directive can of itself impose obligations on an individual but flatly stated that that case law does not apply where violation of the obligations arising under Directive 83/189 renders a national measure inapplicable. The Court asserted that the Directive 'does not in any way define the substantive scope of the legal rule on the basis of which the national court must decide the case before it. It creates neither rights nor obligations for individuals.'[60] So, it seems, Central Food would have to accept the goods.

[58] Case C-443/98 [2000] ECR I-7535.

[59] So the default in *Unilever* was not precisely the same as that at stake in *CIA Security*. The significance of this was another point of disagreement between the Court and Advocate General Jacobs but I do not explore that here.

[60] Para. 51.

The European Court is correct in *Unilever* to point out that were the Italian rules to be applied they would have the effect of hindering trade in a product not complying with them. This repeats the core of the Court's reasoning in *Lemmens* which was evidently directed at identifying precisely when the Directive bites in national proceedings. The striking element of the ruling in *Unilever* is the Court's readiness to adopt this reasoning even in a case where the impact of the unenforceability of the state measure was felt directly in a contractual dispute between private parties. The Court makes light of this novelty. It observes that in *CIA Security* it has already held that state default under the Directive is capable of impinging on a dispute between private parties. It is submitted that this underplays the differences between the cases. There was no contract in *CIA Security*. In fact the Belgian law at stake was a form of quasi-regulatory power, placing in private hands the possibility of taking court action to secure the withdrawal from the market of a product not in conformity with the Belgian law (which had not been notified). In many states this type of power would be exercised by a public body. In Belgium it so happened that a private party performed this function. The Court's brisk assumption that the factual background of *CIA Security* was materially similar to that which arose in *Unilever* because both cases involved a pair of private litigants is not persuasive and it seems that the Court has embraced the application of the notification Directive in a contractual dispute between private parties without fully considering the size of the leap beyond existing case law which it is thereby making.[61]

Admittedly one could re-fashion the arguments to provide support for the Court's view that the cases are materially similar. If one adopts the view that EC law rejects the possibility that an unimplemented directive may itself be relied on to impose an obligation on a private party, but that it accepts the possibility that an unimplemented directive may have the effect of setting aside a rule of national law on which a private party wished to rely, then one has thereby found a rational basis for classifying the case law. This would arguably mean that *Unilever* should indeed be decided in the same way as *CIA Security*, for what is at stake is not using an EC directive as a source of obligations imposed on an individual but rather using an EC directive to set aside a provision under national law which provides an individual with some form of legal protection. These are different phenomena. EC law rejects the former but accepts the latter.[62] After all, the notification Directive did not impose an

---

61 And I criticize it in this vein in S. Weatherill, 'Breach of Directives and breach of contract' (2001) 26 ELRev 177.

62 For discussion see Figuero Reguiero, Jean Monnet Working Paper 7/02 via http://www.jeanmonnetprogram.org/papers/papers02.html; T. Tridimas, 'Black, white and shades of grey: horizontality of Directives revisited' (2002) 21 YEL 327; D.

obligation on Central Food. The contract imposed the obligation. At this level the Court is therefore perfectly justified in treating *Unilever* as distinct from the case law in which it refuses to attribute horizontal direct effect to directives.[63]

I understand this argument and I do not wish to quarrel with its intellectual appeal. There are, however, good reasons for drawing the line in a different place and for embracing *CIA Security* as a correct decision but taking the view that *Unilever* should have been treated as a case where an EC directive did not have an impact on the private litigation involved. That is, I submit that the fact pattern in *Unilever*, whilst not one of 'horizontal direct effect', raises the same type of concerns and should generate the same outcome, namely the exclusion of the Directive from the national legal proceedings. The powerful arguments which persuade me are connected with the preservation of legal and commercial certainty and they are set out with vigour and clarity in the Opinion of Francis Jacobs in *Unilever*. It is regrettable that the Court chose not to accept his view; it is even more regrettable that it chose not even to address his concerns.

Francis Jacobs took the view that the Court in *CIA Security* cannot have intended that the sanction of unenforceability should apply in all types of proceedings between individuals. He fixed on two important arguments of principle:

> That is, first, because such effects would be difficult to justify in the light of the principle of legal certainty. For the day-to-day conduct of trade, technical regulations which apply to the sale of goods must be clearly and readily identifiable as enforceable or as unenforceable. Although the present dispute concerns a relatively small quantity of bottled olive oil of a value which may not affect the finances of either Unilever or Central Food to any drastic extent, it is easy to imagine an exactly comparable case involving highly perishable goods and sums of money which represent the difference between prosperity and ruin for one or other of the parties concerned. In order to avoid difficulties in his contractual relations, an individual trader would have to be aware of the existence of Directive 83/189, to know the judgment in *CIA Security*, to identify a technical regulation as such, and to establish with certainty whether or not the Member State in question had complied with all the procedural requirements of the directive. The last element in particular might prove to be extremely difficult because of the lack of publicity of the procedure under the directive. There is no obligation on the Commission to publish the fact that a Member State has notified or failed to notify a given draft technical regulation. In respect of the standstill periods under Article 9 of the directive, there is no

Voinot, 'Le droit communautaire et l'inopposabilité aux particuliers des regles techniques nationales' (2003) 39 RTDE 91. See also S. Prechal, *Directives in EC Law* (Oxford: OUP, 2nd edn, 2006), Chapter 9.5.

[63] Case C-91/92 *Faccini Dori* [1994] ECR I-3325; Case C-192/94 *Blazquez Rivero* [1996] ECR I-1281.

> way for individuals to know that other Member States have triggered the six-month standstill period by delivering detailed opinions to the Commission. Similarly, the Commission is also not required to publish the fact that it has informed a Member State of intended or pending Community legislation.
>
> The second problem is possible injustice. If failure to notify were to render a technical regulation unenforceable in private proceedings an individual would lose a case in which such a regulation was in issue, not because of his own failure to comply with an obligation deriving from Community law, but because of a Member State's behaviour. The economic survival of a firm might be threatened merely for the sake of the effectiveness of a mechanism designed to control Member States' regulatory activities. That would be so independently of whether the technical regulation in question constituted an obstacle to trade, a measure with neutral effects on trade, or even a rule furthering trade . . . The only redress for a trader in such a situation would be to bring ex post a hazardous and costly action for damages against a Member State. Nor is there any reason for the other party to the proceedings to profit, entirely fortuitously, from a Member State's failure to comply with the directive.[64]

Therefore, he urged, the technical regulation's compatibility with Article 28 EC should be of relevance to the litigation, but not its mishandling by the Italian public authorities under the notification Directive.

Quite so! *Unilever* is perilous to certainty in commercial planning. One may accept as dogmatically pure the analysis that the Directive did not impose an obligation directly on Central Food and that this was therefore not to be assimilated to a case of horizontal direct effect,[65] but nevertheless the injection into the proceedings of the consequences of Italy's failure to suspend its law as required by the Directive entirely changed the circumstances in which the pattern of rights and obligations arising under the contract fell to be judged. Goods which could have been refused under domestic law now had to be accepted. This is not horizontal direct effect according to its classic meaning but it is so very close to it in its destabilizing effect on the legal position of private parties before national courts that it seems to me to be seriously wrong to treat it in such a completely different manner under EC law. Francis has shown a better way in a powerful, contextually rich opinion demonstrating the commercial implications of the constitutional choices involved in determining the effect of directives in national legal proceedings.

The Court has had the opportunity to reconsider the matter. It did so, but in a rather infelicitous way. In *Sapod Audic* some similar issues arose.[66] In the

---

64 Paras 100–101 of the Opinion.

65 See, making exactly this case (which is convincing on its own terms), V. Skouris, '*Effet utile* versus legal certainty: the case law of the Court of Justice on the Direct Effect of Directives' (2006) 17/2 Euro. Bus. L. Rev. 241, 248.

66 Case C-159/00 [2002] ECR I-5031, noted by M. Dougan (2003) 40 CMLRev 193.

Opinion of Francis Jacobs the matter was apt to be disposed of on definitional grounds. He considered that the (French) provisions in question did not fall within the scope of the notification Directive. So, as he pointed out, it was not necessary to consider what would have been the consequences, in the context of national legal proceedings, of a failure to comply with the duty of notification. But he made a couple of cautionary observations:

> It may, however, be noted that the present case illustrates the difficulties which may arise as a result of the Court's ruling in *Unilever.* It appears from documents in the file that a ruling in the present case to the effect that the French State violated its obligations under the Directive might affect the validity and enforceability in national courts of several thousand contracts which have been concluded, in reliance upon the rules laid down in the Decree, between Eco-Emballages and producers of household goods since the Decree entered into force nearly 10 years ago.

A forceful point, made gently. The Court, by contrast, did not rule out the possibility that the national court could conclude that the relevant provision constituted a technical regulation within the meaning of the notification Directive. This, therefore, raised precisely the concern about contractual enforceability in national proceedings to which Francis Jacobs had drawn attention. The Court found that:

> It should, however, be observed that the question of the conclusions to be drawn in the main proceedings from the inapplicability of the second paragraph of Article 4 of Decree No 92-377 as regards the severity of the sanction under the applicable national law, such as nullity or unenforceability of the contract between Sapod and Eco-Emballages, is a question governed by national law, in particular as regards the rules and principles of contract law which limit or adjust that sanction in order to render its severity proportionate to the particular defect found.[67]

So the tough line taken in *Unilever* is maintained. State default under the notification Directive has a potentially dramatic impact on private contracts. However, it seems, this may be softened under national law. Quite what 'the rules and principles of contract law which limit or adjust that sanction in order to render its severity proportionate to the particular defect found' may be, I could not say. Probably there are such rules in some national legal systems in the EU but not in all. The Court has opened the door to some peculiar and diverse results. It would have been much better to have reconsidered *Unilever*, to have digested Francis Jacobs's warnings and to have held that the notification Directive has no role to play in actions for breach of contract before national courts. After all, preservation of legal certainty is a general principle

---

[67] Para. 52 of the judgment.

of the Community legal order[68] and it should deter the Court from holding that state default under the notification Directive is directly relevant in private law proceedings. If, as seems now inescapable, the Court will not admit the horizontal direct effect of directives it should acknowledge that the incidental application of directives is permitted, if at all, only in cases involving the public authorities of the state or quasi-regulatory powers such as those at stake in *CIA Security* but not in contractual proceedings involving private parties. It has been shown how and why by the clear vision and leadership offered by Francis Jacobs.

CONCLUSION

I concluded the previous sub-section with the observation that the Court 'has been shown how and why by the clear vision and leadership offered by Francis Jacobs', and that will serve as my overall conclusion. Francis has provided this service so very frequently. I have suggested that a successful Advocate General is marked by five qualities: clarity of expression, clarity of vision, contextual richness, leadership and capacity to inspire. Francis Jacobs scores very highly when measured against these standards.

---

68 E.g. Case C-469/00 *Ravil* [2003] ECR I-5053; Case C-209/04 *Commission v Austria* judgment of 23 March 2006; Case C-212/04 *Adeneler* judgment of 4 July 2006. On the principle's multi-faceted nature, see T. Tridmas, *The General Principles of EC Law* (Oxford: OUP, 2nd edn, 2006), Chapter 6.

2. Fundamental rights

Paul Craig[1]

INTRODUCTION

This chapter examines fundamental rights in Community law and the contribution made by Advocate General Jacobs to this jurisprudence. The discussion begins with analysis of some of the important Opinions that Francis Jacobs has given on fundamental rights during his tenure as Advocate General. The focus then shifts to the more general relationship between fundamental rights within the Community legal order and the European Convention on Human Rights (ECHR). This is a topic of considerable importance. It is more especially relevant in the present context given that Francis Jacobs is an acknowledged expert on the case law of the European Court of Human Rights (ECtHR) as well as that of the European Court of Justice (ECJ).

ADVOCATE GENERAL JACOBS AND FUNDAMENTAL RIGHTS

In his long and distinguished career Advocate General Jacobs has given a number of Opinions concerning fundamental rights relating both to their reach and their application. Prominent examples of these will be considered in turn.

(A) The Reach of Fundamental Rights: *Konstantinidis*

Advocate General Jacobs's best-known and most oft-quoted contribution to fundamental rights jurisprudence came in *Konstantinidis*.[2] A self-employed Greek masseur who worked in Germany argued that the German authorities were infringing his Community rights in their official mistranslation of his name. The question addressed by the Advocate General was whether a

---

[1] Queen's Counsel, Professor of English Law, St John's College, Oxford.

[2] Case C-168/91, *Konstantinidis v Stadt Altensteig, Standesamt, and Landratsamt Calw, Ordnungsamt* [1993] ECR I-1191.

national of a Member State, who was established as a self-employed person in another Member State, was entitled by what were then Articles 7 and 52 EC to oppose the transliteration of his names, in a manner that grossly misrepresented the pronunciation of those names, for the purpose of entries into registers of civil status. Advocate General Jacobs found that the German rule was discriminatory. Nonetheless, he continued to consider whether it might be contrary to the applicant's right to personal identity. He surveyed various human rights instruments and national constitutions and concluded that it was possible to infer from them 'the existence of a principle according to which the State must respect not only the physical well-being of the individual but also his dignity, moral integrity and sense of personal identity'.[3] Advocate General Jacobs had no doubt that such rights were violated if a state required an individual to abandon or modify his name, unless there was good justification. His reasoning is captured in the following striking quotation:[4]

> A person's right to his name is fundamental in every sense of the word. After all, what are we without our name? It is our name that distinguishes each of us from the rest of humanity. It is our name that gives us a sense of identity, dignity and self-esteem. To strip a person of his rightful name is the ultimate degradation, as is evidenced by the common practice of repressive penal regimes which consists in substituting a number for the prisoner's name.

Having established the existence of the relevant right, he then considered whether it could be invoked by the applicant in the instant case. He referred to the existing case law, establishing that fundamental rights could be used against a Member State either when it was implementing EC law[5] or when it sought to rely on a derogation from principles of free movement.[6] Advocate General Jacobs was clear that if the German measure were discriminatory it could not therefore be justified on grounds of public policy because it infringed the applicant's fundamental rights.[7]

The novelty of his contribution in *Konstantinidis* is that he argued that the German measure could be contrary to what was Article 52 even if it was not

---

3 *Ibid.* at para. 39, Jacobs AG.

4 *Ibid.* at para. 40, Jacobs AG.

5 Case 5/88, *Wachauf v Germany* [1989] ECR 2609.

6 Case C-260/89, *Elliniki Radiophonia Tileorassi AE v Dimotiki Etairia Pliroforissis and Sotirios Kouvelas* [1991] ECR I-2925, at para. 43; Case C-368/95, *Vereinigte Familiapress Zeitungsverlags- und vertriebs GmbH v Heinrich Bauer Verlag* [1997] ECR I-368, at para. 24; Case C-60/00, *Carpenter v Secretary of State for the Home Department* [2002] ECR I-6279, at paras 40–41; Cases C-482 and 493/01, *Orfanopoulos v Land Baden-Württemberg* [2004] ECR I-5257, at paras 97–8.

7 Case C-168/91 *Konstantinidis*, n. 2, para. 44.

discriminatory, simply on the ground that it infringed fundamental rights. He gave the following graphic example to drive home his point:[8]

> Suppose that a Member State introduces a draconian penal code under which theft is punishable by amputation of the right hand. A national of another Member State goes to that country in exercise of the rights of free movement conferred on him by Article 48 et seq of the Treaty, steals a loaf of bread and is sentenced to have his right hand cut off. Such a penalty would undoubtedly constitute inhuman and degrading treatment punishment contrary to Article 3 of the European Convention of Human Rights. But would it also be a breach of the individual's rights under Community law, even though it were applied in a non-discriminatory manner? I believe that it would.

It was in the light of this hypothetical that Advocate General Jacobs penned the paragraph for which his Opinion is best known.[9]

> In my opinion, a Community national who goes to another Member State as a worker or self-employed person under Articles 48, 52 or 59 of the Treaty is entitled not just to pursue his trade or profession and to enjoy the same living and working conditions as nationals of the host State; he is in addition entitled to assume that, wherever he goes to earn his living in the European Community, he will be treated in accordance with a common code of fundamental values, in particular those laid down in the European Convention on Human Rights. In other words, he is entitled to say 'civis europeus sum' and to invoke that status in order to oppose any violation of his fundamental rights.

The force of this statement is readily apparent from the reasoning that preceded it. Fundamental rights derived from Community law should be respected whenever a Community national ventured to another Member State irrespective of whether the national measure infringing human rights was discriminatory or not and irrespective of whether there was any connection with his or her work.

The ECJ's ruling was far more cautious. It made no reference to fundamental rights and based its reasoning on settled EC law relating to the right of self-employed people to establish themselves in a Member State without being disadvantaged in their business on account of their nationality. Thus the German measure concerning transliteration of the applicant's name would be caught by Article 52 in so far as it might lead to confusion for the applicant's customers, who would not recognize the modified name.

Nor have the seeds sown by Advocate General Jacobs been developed thus far in later jurisprudence. The one overt reference to his reasoning was by

---

8 *Ibid.* at para. 45, Jacobs AG.
9 *Ibid.* at para. 46, Jacobs AG.

Advocate General Gulman, who felt that it was too radical.[10] Moreover, the ECJ has not taken the opportunity in later cases to apply Advocate General Jacobs's reasoning, even though the facts might well have lent themselves to this.[11]

Advocate General Jacobs has not therefore always secured acceptance of his views by the ECJ. His Opinion in *Konstantinidis* is nonetheless powerful and there is nothing to prevent the ECJ revisiting the issue on some future occasion and adopting his reasoning if it is so minded. It could indeed be argued that the iteration in more recent jurisprudence to the effect that 'Union citizenship is destined to be the fundamental status of nationals of the Member States, enabling those who find themselves in the same situation to enjoy the same treatment in law irrespective of their nationality, subject to such exceptions as are expressly provided for',[12] is fertile terrain for such a development. This is so notwithstanding the fact that this principle is cast in terms of non-discrimination and equality of treatment. It would not be difficult if the ECJ so wished to modify this reasoning in order to accommodate the substance of the position suggested by Francis Jacobs in *Konstantinidis*.

(B) The Application of Fundamental Rights: *Schmidberger*

Whilst the reasoning of Advocate General Jacobs was not adopted in *Konstantinidis*, it is, as those familiar with EC law will attest, far more common for the ECJ to follow or be strongly influenced by his line of argument. This is exemplified by the reasoning and result in *Schmidberger*.[13]

The Austrian government gave permission for a demonstration by an environmental group on the Brenner motorway, the effect of which was to close it for 30 hours. Schmidberger ran a transport firm and argued that the closure of the motorway was in breach of EU law on free movement of goods. The issue before the ECJ was the relation between Article 28 EC on free movement, and freedom of expression and assembly as protected by Articles 10 and 11 of the ECHR and the Austrian Constitution.

---

[10] Case C-2/92, *R. v Ministry of Fisheries, Agriculture and Food, ex parte Bostock* [1994] ECR I-955, at 971.

[11] Case C-291/96, *Criminal Proceedings Against Grado and Bashir* [1997] ECR I-5531; Case C-177/94, *Criminal Proceedings against Perfili* [1996] ECR I-161; Case C–299/95, *Kremzow v Austria* [1997] ECR I-2629.

[12] Case C-184/99, *Rudy Grzelczyk v Centre Public D'Aide Sociale d'Ottignes-Louvain-la-Neuve (CPAS)* [2001] ECR I-6193, at para. 31.

[13] Case C-112/00, *Schmidberger Internationale Transporte und Planzuge v Austria* [2003] ECR I-5659.

Advocate General Jacobs considered that the action of the Austrian government constituted a prima facie breach of Article 28 and that this was so notwithstanding the fact that the action constituting the limitation of free movement was by private individuals, namely the protestors. He followed in this respect the earlier decision of the ECJ in *Commission v France*,[14] where it held that France was responsible for impeding free movement by not taking adequate steps to control the actions of its farmers who were angry at imports from other Member States. Advocate General Jacobs acknowledged that there were important differences between that case and *Schmidberger*, but felt that these should be taken into account when considering justification.

When considering justification he recognized the novelty of the case before the Court: this was the first time that a Member State had invoked the need to protect fundamental rights as a reason for limiting one of the fundamental freedoms.[15] The Advocate General said that the case should be approached in two stages.

The first stage was to determine whether Austria, when relying on the particular fundamental right, was, as a matter of Community law, pursuing a legitimate objective in the public interest that was capable of justifying a restriction on a fundamental Treaty freedom. The Advocate General acknowledged that the answer to this inquiry might seem to be obvious in the instant case given that Austria was protecting the fundamental right to peaceful protest. Nonetheless, he hypothesized about instances where a Member State might seek to advance its domestic fundamental rights as a reason for resisting a Treaty freedom where the nature of the national right was very different from that in the instant case. The example he proffered was of a Member State that had a right to be protected against unfair trade competition or where the fundamental right to free economic activity was interpreted in the same manner. In such circumstances,[16]

> It cannot therefore be automatically ruled out that a Member State which invokes the necessity to protect a right recognised by national law as fundamental nevertheless pursues an objective which as a matter of Community law must be regarded as illegitimate.

No such problem existed in the instant case and Advocate General Jacobs therefore passed on to the second stage of the inquiry, which was whether the restriction was proportionate to the objective pursued. He prefaced this inquiry by making clear that proportionality should not be applied too strictly since the

---

14 Case C-265/95, *Commission v France* [1997] ECR I-6959.

15 Case C-112/00, *Schmidberger*, n. 13, at paras 89, 94, Jacobs AG.

16 *Ibid.* at para. 98, Jacobs AG.

'issue is not so much what the Austrian authorities did, but whether they failed to prevent action by others and what action they should have taken to do so'.[17] In such circumstances the Member State had a margin of discretion in determining when to take action and which measures were most appropriate to limit the interference with trade.[18] A number of factors led the Advocate General to conclude that the action by the Austrian government was proportionate: the disruption was of limited duration on an isolated occasion; measures were taken to limit the disruption caused; and excessive restrictions on the demonstration would not only have deprived the protestors of their right to protest peacefully, but might have led also to greater disruption to trade, since there might have been numerous unauthorized demonstrations.[19]

The ECJ closely followed the reasoning and result in Advocate General Jacobs's Opinion. Thus the ECJ reaffirmed that Article 28 EC required the state to refrain from imposing obstacles to free movement of goods itself, and also to take all necessary action to ensure that free movement was not impeded by the acts of private parties.[20] The failure by the Austrian government to ban the demonstration was therefore prima facie a breach of Article 28 EC unless it could be objectively justified.[21]

The ECJ, like the Advocate General, accepted the justification proffered by the Austrian government cast in terms of respect for the right to freedom of expression and assembly guaranteed by the ECHR and the Austrian Constitution. It held that Member States and the Community were required to respect fundamental rights and that therefore those rights could justify a restriction of other Community obligations including even a fundamental freedom such as free movement of goods.[22] The ECJ noted however that Articles 10 and 11 of the ECHR protecting freedom of expression and assembly were not absolute. They could be limited provided that the restrictions corresponded to objectives of general interest and did not constitute disproportionate and unacceptable interference that impaired the very substance of the right.[23] It was therefore necessary to decide whether the restrictions placed on Community trade were proportionate in the light of the relevant fundamental rights. The ECJ once again closely followed the reasoning of the Advocate General. It held that the restriction was proportionate because: the disruption

---

17 *Ibid.* at para. 106, Jacobs AG.
18 *Ibid.* at para. 106, Jacobs AG.
19 *Ibid.* at paras 107–11, Jacobs AG.
20 *Ibid.* at para. 59, reaffirming Case C-265/95, *Commission v France* [1997] ECR I-6959.
21 *Ibid.* at para. 64.
22 *Ibid.* at para. 74.
23 *Ibid.* at para. 80.

of Community trade was for a limited time on a limited route; it was in pursuit of a genuine environmental aim; it was not designed to keep foreign goods out of a particular state; efforts had been made to limit the disruption caused by the demonstration; and a ban on the demonstration would have been an unacceptable limit on the right to peaceful demonstration.[24]

(C) The Application of Fundamental Rights: *UPA*

In *Konstantinidis* the ECJ declined to follow the reasoning of Advocate General Jacobs; in *Schmidberger* by way of contrast the ECJ's judgment followed closely that of the Advocate General. The *UPA* case reveals a rather different interplay between the Advocate General and the ECJ in the sense that both acknowledged the importance of the fundamental right at stake in that case, namely the right to effective judicial protection, but the importance accorded to that right differed markedly. Takis Tridimas and Sara Poli have explored the case in depth in their chapter on standing.[25] The present brief discussion will focus on the differential weight given to the right to effective judicial protection in the Opinion of the Advocate General and the Court's judgment.

In the *UPA* case[26] an association of farmers, UPA, sought the annulment of Regulation 1638/98, which substantially amended the common organization of the olive oil market. The Court of First Instance dismissed the application because the members of the association were not individually concerned by the Regulation under Article 230(4) EC. UPA argued, *inter alia*, that it was denied effective judicial protection because it could not readily challenge the measure via Article 234.

Advocate General Jacobs made an extensive analysis of the law relating to standing. He began by considering the right to effective judicial protection which framed the entirety of his analysis. The ability of an individual to contest, whether indirectly or directly, the legality of a Community norm was tested against this background right. The Advocate General considered whether this basic right could be adequately protected by indirect challenge via Article 234. He concluded that there were serious difficulties in regarding the preliminary reference as providing full and effective judicial protection against general measures. This was so for a number of reasons.[27] The applicant had no right under the preliminary ruling procedure to decide whether a

---

24 *Ibid.* at paras 83–94.

25 See below, Chapter 3.

26 Case C-50/00 P, *Union de Pequenos Agricultores v Council* [2002] ECR I-6677.

27 *Ibid.* at para. 102(1), Jacobs AG.

reference was made, which measures were referred for review or what grounds of invalidity were raised, and thus had no right of access to the Court of Justice. The national court could not itself grant the desired remedy of declaring the measure invalid because of the rule preventing national courts annulling Community norms.[28] There could be cases where it was difficult or impossible for an applicant to challenge a general measure indirectly, for example where there were no challengeable implementing measures or where the applicant would have to break the law in order to be able to challenge ensuing sanctions.

Advocate General Jacobs considered whether the problem could be overcome by expanding direct actions only where the particular legal system made the indirect action especially difficult, but rejected this solution. He also discussed whether a solution could be found through an obligation for national legal orders to ensure that references on the validity of general Community measures were available in their legal systems. He rejected such an approach since it would 'leave unresolved most of the problems of the current situation such as the absence of remedy as a matter of right, unnecessary delays and costs for the applicant or the award of interim measures'.[29] It was for these reasons that Advocate General Jacobs concluded that the only way to secure the effective right of judicial protection was to have a test for direct challenge based on substantial adverse impact. This would accord applicants 'a true right of direct access to a court which can grant a remedy'.[30]

The Opinion is a classic example of the use of background rights as a mechanism for the re-assessment of existing doctrine. The reality is that although the right to effective judicial protection is part of Community jurisprudence this right had not featured significantly in the case law on *locus standi*. It had more commonly been part of the reasoning in cases concerned with the effectiveness of national remedial protection. The very fact that the right to effective judicial protection had not featured prominently in the case law on challenges to Community acts was one of the reasons why that case law had continued to develop in an illiberal fashion. It is clear that placing the right to effective judicial protection at the centre of the analysis exerted a powerful force in the demand for re-evaluation of the case law.

The role afforded to the right to effective judicial protection in the Advocate General's Opinion stands in sharp relief to the place of that right in the ECJ's reasoning. The major premise of the ECJ's reasoning was that the applicants had not fulfilled the standard requirements for *locus standi* under

---

28 Case 314/85, *Firma Foto-Frost v Hauptzollamt Lubeck-Ost* [1987] ECR 4199.

29 *Ibid.* at para. 102(3), Jacobs AG.

30 *Ibid.* at para. 102(4), Jacobs AG.

Article 230 EC. They had not shown they were affected by the regulation by reason of certain attributes peculiar to them or by reason of factual circumstances in which they were differentiated from all others, as required by the *Plaumann* test.[31] The ECJ emphasized this major premise by stating that if the *Plaumann* condition were not fulfilled then a natural or legal person would not have standing to seek the annulment of a regulation 'under any circumstances'.[32]

The right to effective judicial protection entered the ECJ's reasoning against the backdrop that the applicants had failed to meet the normal rules for *locus standi*. The ECJ held that it was necessary to see whether 'in those circumstances' the applicant could 'nonetheless' have standing on the ground that the absence of a remedy before the national courts meant that there must, in the light of the right to effective judicial protection, be a direct action.[33] The ECJ acknowledged that the right to effective judicial protection was a fundamental right, which was part of the Community legal order based on the rule of law. It read the existing *locus standi* rules against this fundamental right to see if those rules required amendment.[34]

The ECJ decided that no such amendment was warranted. It held that the Treaty established a complete system of legal remedies for challenging the legality of Community action.[35] The ECJ concluded its judgment by reaffirming its major premise and the secondary, limited role accorded to the right to effective judicial protection. The Court declined to follow the lead of the Advocate General. It concluded its judgment in the same vein that it had begun.[36] The applicants had failed to satisfy the legal requirements for standing in Article 230. Whilst the meaning of individual concern must be interpreted in the light of the right to effective judicial protection this could only be in the context of defining the circumstances that could distinguish an applicant individually. An interpretation of individual concern in the light of the right to effective judicial protection could not have the effect of setting aside that condition, which was expressly laid down in the Treaty. This would be to go beyond the jurisdiction of the Community Courts and would require an amendment of the Treaty.

The contrast between the ECJ's judgment and the Advocate General's Opinion is marked. The ECJ paid heed to the right to effective judicial protection but its role in the Court's judgment was minimal. The Court began and

31 *Ibid.* at paras 32, 34–6.
32 *Ibid.* at para. 37.
33 *Ibid.* at para. 33.
34 *Ibid.* at paras 33, 38–9.
35 *Ibid.* at para. 40.
36 *Ibid.* at paras 44–5.

ended its judgment with the *Plaumann* formula coupled with the fact that the applicants had been unable to meet this test. The right to effective judicial protection was accorded a secondary role of determining whether some extension of standing was required or warranted. This secondary role was moreover interpretative in a minimalist sense. The right to effective judicial protection might influence the meaning of individual concern only in the limited sense of helping to define the circumstances that could distinguish an applicant individually, as exemplified by *Codorniu*.[37] It could not have any greater impact since this would, in the view of the Court, entail the setting aside of a Treaty condition.

THE RELATIONSHIP BETWEEN THE EU AND THE ECHR: THE ECJ'S PERSPECTIVE

The discussion thus far has focused on some of the important contributions made by Advocate General Jacobs to the evolution of the ECJ's fundamental rights jurisprudence. It is however well known that Francis Jacobs is an authority on ECHR law as well as EU law, and it is therefore fitting to consider more generally the relationship between the EU and the ECHR. This is more especially so given that the nature of the inter-relationship between the two regimes has been the subject of recent jurisprudence by the Strasbourg Court. Before considering this case law, it is fitting to consider briefly the relationship between the EU and the ECHR as perceived by the ECJ.

The relationship between the EU and the ECHR as perceived by the ECJ is well known. Whilst the EU is not bound by the ECHR, the ECJ nonetheless regards the ECHR as a very important source of inspiration for its own decisions in the field of fundamental rights. It is therefore a standard feature of fundamental rights adjudication in the EU for the Community Courts to have detailed recourse to Convention jurisprudence on the relevant matter. The Community Courts will moreover strive for an interpretation in the instant case that is compatible with that reached in the Strasbourg jurisprudence, and the ECJ has been willing to revise some previous judgments in order to bring them into line with subsequent Strasbourg case law.[38]

The ECJ however ruled in Opinion 2/94 that the EU lacked competence to

---

37 Case C-309/89, *Codorniu v Council* [1994] ECR I-1853.

38 Case C-94/00, *Roquette Freres SA v Directeur General de la Concurrence, de la Consommation et de la Repression des Fraudes and Commission* [2002] ECR I-9011, at para. 29; Cases C-238, 244, 245, 247, 250–52 and 254/99 P, *Limburgse Vinyl Maatschappij (LVM) and Others v Commission* [2002] ECR I-8375, at paras 273–5.

accede to the ECHR in the absence of a Treaty amendment.[39] It began with established orthodoxy, to the effect that the Community could only act within the limits of the powers assigned to it, noting that this principle of conferred powers should be respected in relation to both internal and international action by the Community. The ECJ acknowledged that the Community could possess implied power as well as express power. It referred to its previous case law, holding that in the field of international relations the competence of the Community to enter into international commitments could flow not only from express provisions of the Treaty but could also be implied from those provisions. This was so whenever Community law created internal powers to attain a specific objective, the consequence being that the Community was empowered to enter into international commitments that were necessary for attainment of that objective even in the absence of an express provision to that effect. This jurisprudence did not however avail the Community in relation to accession to the ECHR since no 'Treaty provision confers on the Community institutions any general power to enact rules on human rights or to conclude international conventions in this field'.[40]

The ECJ then considered whether accession might be based on Article 308 EC which 'is designed to fill the gap where no specific provisions of the Treaty confer on the Community institutions express or implied powers to act, if such powers appear none the less to be necessary to enable the Community to carry out its functions with a view to attaining one of the objectives laid down by the Treaty'.[41] The ECJ prefaced its consideration of whether accession could be based on Article 308 with the following cautionary observation:[42]

> That provision, being an integral part of an institutional system based on the principle of conferred powers, cannot serve as a basis for widening the scope of Community powers beyond the general framework created by the provisions of the Treaty as a whole and, in particular, by those that define the activities and tasks of the community. On any view, Article 235 [308] cannot be used as a basis for the adoption of provisions whose effect would, in substance, be to amend the Treaty without following the procedure which it provides for that purpose.

The ECJ noted that respect for human rights had been emphasized in various declarations of the Member States and of the Community institutions and that reference to human rights could be found in the preamble to the Single European Act 1986 as well as in various Articles of the Treaty on European

---

39 Opinion 2/94, *On Accession by the Community to the ECHR* [1996] ECR I-1759.
40 *Ibid.* at para. 27.
41 *Ibid.* at para. 29.
42 *Ibid.* at para. 30.

Union (TEU), more especially what was then Article F TEU, which provides that the Union is to respect fundamental rights as guaranteed, in particular, by the Convention. The ECJ acknowledged also that fundamental rights formed an integral part of the general principles of law whose observance the Court ensured and that the ECHR had a special significance in that respect. Respect for human rights was therefore a condition of the lawfulness of Community acts. The ECJ nonetheless concluded that the Community lacked competence to accede to the ECHR in the absence of a Treaty amendment. This was because,[43]

> Accession to the Convention would . . . entail a substantial change in the present Community system for the protection of human rights in that it would entail the entry of the Community into a distinct international institutional system as well as the integration of all the provisions of the Convention into the Community legal order.
>
> Such a modification of the system for the protection of human rights in the Community, with equally fundamental institutional implications for the Community and for the Member States, would be of constitutional significance and would therefore be such as to go beyond the scope of Article 235 [308]. It could be brought about only by way of Treaty amendment.

This is not the place for detailed exegesis on the reasoning in Opinion 2/94.[44] Two brief points can however be made in this context. First, the language chosen by the ECJ when discussing the limits of recourse to Article 308 was surely not fortuitous. There had been concern in some quarters over what was seen to be excessively liberal usage of Article 308, both legislatively and judicially, as the foundation for Community action. This culminated in the 'warning' given by the German Federal Constitutional Court in the *Brunner* case.[45] The case was concerned with the issue of whether Germany could ratify the TEU. The Federal Constitutional Court held ultimately that it could do so but in the course of its judgment it sounded this warning note:[46]

> Inasmuch as the Treaties establishing the European Communities, on the one hand, confer sovereign rights applicable to limited factual circumstances and, on the other hand, provide for Treaty amendments . . . this distinction is also important for the future treatment of the individual powers. Whereas a dynamic extension of the existing Treaties has so far been supported on the basis of an open-handed treatment of Article 235 of the EEC Treaty as a 'competence to round off the Treaty' as a whole, and on the basis of considerations relating to the 'implied powers' of the

43 *Ibid.* at paras 34–5.

44 *The Human Rights Opinion of the ECJ and its Constitutional Implications* (Cambridge University CELS, Occasional Paper No. 1).

45 *Brunner v The European Union Treaty* [1994] 1 CMLR 57.

46 *Ibid.* at para. 99.

Communities, and of Treaty interpretation as allowing maximum exploitation of Community powers (*effet utile*), in future it will have to be noted as regards interpretation of enabling provisions by Community institutions and agencies that the Union Treaty as a matter of principle distinguishes between the exercise of a sovereign power conferred for limited purposes and the amending of the Treaty, so that its interpretation may not have effects that are equivalent to an extension of the Treaty. Such an interpretation of enabling rules would not produce any binding effects for Germany.

The language used by the ECJ when discussing the limits of Article 308 is strikingly similar to that used by the Federal Constitutional Court in the *Brunner* case. The ECJ's acknowledgment that Article 308 could not be used as the basis for the adoption of provisions that would be tantamount to Treaty amendment without following the requisite procedure signalled that the ECJ had heard the concerns voiced by the German Court and that it would be mindful of them when considering the remit of Article 308.

Secondly, the ECJ in all probability did not unduly regret the conclusion that it had reached on the limits of Community competence in this instance. Accession to the ECHR would entail entry into a 'distinct international institutional system',[47] one consequence of which would be that the ECJ would no longer be the ultimate judicial decision-maker on fundamental rights issues so far as they pertained to EC law. To put the same matter a different way, the ECJ would be in the same position *vis-à-vis* the European Court of Human Rights as any other top national court. If a litigant disliked the ruling given by the ECJ on the fundamental rights issue he or she could take the case before the Strasbourg Court in the hope of a better outcome. If this was forthcoming it would constitute the ultimate determination on the fundamental rights and the EU would be under a Treaty obligation to comply with the ruling. The ECJ's ruling in Opinion 2/94 therefore left open the possibility of accession but only after due consideration through Treaty amendment in order that the full implications of membership could be understood.

THE RELATIONSHIP BETWEEN THE EU AND THE ECHR: THE PERSPECTIVE FROM THE EUROPEAN COURT OF HUMAN RIGHTS

The relationship between the EU and the ECHR is also dependent on how the ECtHR views the nature of that relationship.[48] Cases such as *Matthews* had

---

47 Opinion 2/94, n. 2, at para. 34.

48 I. Canor, '*Primus inter pares:* who is the ultimate guardian of fundamental

shown that a Member State of the EU could be held in violation of the Convention even where the cause of the breach was an act of the EU.[49] The leading decision on the relationship between fundamental rights protection afforded by the EU and the ECHR is now the *Bosphorus* case.[50]

(A) *Bosphorus* and the ECJ

The applicant had leased two planes from the Yugoslav Airlines, JAT, and one of these planes was impounded in Ireland pursuant to an EC regulation. This regulation had been enacted in furtherance of UN sanctions against the former Federal Republic of Yugoslavia. The applicant argued that the seizure infringed its property rights under the Convention. This issue was considered by the ECJ, which found against the applicant.[51]

Article 8 of Regulation 990/93 concerning trade between the EC and Yugoslavia provided that all aircraft in which a majority or controlling interest was held by a person or undertaking in or operating from Yugoslavia should be impounded by the competent authorities of the Member States. The ECJ held that this applied to an aircraft that was owned by an undertaking based in or operating from Yugoslavia even though the owner had leased it for four years to another undertaking and even though that other undertaking was not based in or operating from Yugoslavia.

In response to the applicant's plea that this infringed its property rights, the ECJ held that such rights were not absolute and could be restricted pursuant to objectives of general interest pursued by the Community. Moreover, the restrictions could be substantial where the aims pursued by the Community measure were themselves of substantial importance. That was so here since the objectives of the challenged Regulation were to contribute at Community level to the implementation of the sanctions regime against Yugoslavia with the objective of bringing to an end the war in the region and the human rights violations that had occurred. The impounding of the aircraft pursuant to

---

rights in Europe?' (2000) 25 ELRev 3; C. Costello, 'The *Bosphorus* ruling of the European Court of Human Rights: fundamental rights and blurred boundaries in Europe' (2006) HRLRev 1.

49 *Matthews v United Kingdom*, ECHR (1999) No. 24833/94.

50 *Bosphorus Hava Yollari Turizm Ve Ticaret Anonim Sirketi v Ireland*, ECHR (2005) No. 45036/98.

51 Case C-84/95, *Bosphorus Hava Yollari Turizm Ve Ticaret AS v Minister for Transport, Energy and Communications and Others* [1996] ECR I-3953; I. Canor, '"Can two walk together, except they be agreed?" The relationship between international law and European law: the incorporation of United Nations sanctions against Yugoslavia into European Community law through the perspective of the European Court of Justice' (1998) 35 CMLRev 137; N. Burrows, 'Caught in the cross-fire' (1997) 22 ELRev 170.

Regulation 990/93, even where it had been leased to another undertaking that did not operate in Yugoslavia, was therefore found not to be disproportionate in the light of the objectives that the Regulation sought to achieve.

(B) *Bosphorus* and the ECtHR: The General Approach

The applicant then brought an action against Ireland before the European Court of Human Rights arguing that the impounding of the plane violated Article 1 of Protocol No. 1 ECHR, which protects property rights.

The Strasbourg Court considered the relationship between the EU and the ECHR since Ireland had taken the aircraft pursuant to a Community Regulation.[52] The Court accepted that it was legitimate for contracting parties to the ECHR to transfer power to an international organization such as the EU even if the organization was not itself a contracting party under the ECHR. The state contracting party however remained responsible for all acts and omissions of its organs irrespective of whether they were the result of domestic law or the need to comply with an international obligation flowing from membership of an international organization. If this were not so then the state's obligations under the ECHR could be evaded when power was transferred to an international organization.

State action taken in compliance with such international obligations could nonetheless be justified as long as the relevant international organization was considered to protect fundamental rights 'as regards both the substantive guarantees offered and the mechanisms controlling their observance, in a manner which can be considered at least equivalent to that for which the Convention provides'.[53] The Strasbourg Court made it clear that 'equivalent' meant comparable, not identical, and that the finding of equivalence might alter if there was a relevant change in fundamental rights' protection by the international organization.[54] Where equivalent protection was provided by the international organization there was a presumption that a state had not departed from the ECHR when it did no more than implement legal obligations flowing from its membership of that international organization. This presumption could be rebutted if it could be shown in the circumstances of a particular case that the protection of Convention rights was manifestly deficient.[55]

The Strasbourg Court found that the protection afforded to fundamental rights by the EU was equivalent in the preceding sense, thereby raising the presumption that Ireland had not departed from the ECHR by complying with

---

[52] *Bosphorus Hava Yollari*, n. 50, at paras 152–8.
[53] *Ibid.* at para. 155.
[54] *Ibid.* at para. 155.
[55] *Ibid.* at para. 156.

the EC Regulation. It also found that the protection afforded in this instance was not manifestly deficient and hence that the presumption was not rebutted.[56]

The reasoning and result reached by the Strasbourg Court render it unlikely that a ruling of the ECJ would be held to violate the ECHR given that the EU was held to have met the test for equivalence, thereby raising the presumption of compliance with Convention standards which could only be rebutted by showing that the result in a particular case was manifestly deficient. This may well be so but this conclusion needs to be qualified in two ways.

(C) *Bosphorus* and the ECtHR: The General Approach Qualified

Lawyers, academics and practitioners alike are properly mindful of exceptions or qualifications to general rules. The need for caution in this respect is exemplified by the *Bosphorus* judgment. The Strasbourg Court, having set out its general approach based on equivalence leading to a presumption of compliance with the Convention that could only be rebutted by showing manifest deficiency in the instant case, immediately qualified this. It emphasized that a 'State would be fully responsible under the Convention for all acts falling outside its strict international legal obligations',[57] that numerous Convention cases had confirmed this and that such cases concerned review by the Strasbourg Court 'of the exercise of State discretion for which EC law provided'.[58]

It is clear from the majority's judgment that it did not regard the *Bosphorus* case on its facts as raising such an issue since the impugned act only concerned compliance by Ireland with an EC obligation flowing from a directly applicable Regulation that left no discretion to the Irish authorities.[59]

It is however less clear what the Strasbourg Court meant when it said that the state would remain fully responsible under the Convention for all acts falling outside its strict international legal obligations and that this enabled the Strasbourg Court to review the exercise of state discretion for which EC law provided. The case law cited by the Court provides some guidance in this respect.

There are some cases where the review of 'State discretion for which EC law provided' is uncontroversial in terms of principle and entails no real conflict or tension between the EU and the ECtHR. This includes cases such as *Van de Hurk* where the Strasbourg Court considered whether the state had

56 *Ibid.* at paras 165–6.
57 *Ibid.* at para. 157.
58 *Ibid.* at para. 157.
59 *Ibid.* at paras 148, 158.

complied with Article 6 of the Convention when applying EC agricultural regulations.[60] Similarly uncontroversial is a case such as *Dangeville*, which raised the issue of whether a state that failed to implement a directive within the assigned time, with the consequence that it levied taxes that it should not have done if the directive had been properly implemented, was thereby in breach of Article 1 of Protocol No. 1.[61]

There are however other cases that raise more problematic issues concerning the relationship between the EU and the ECtHR. It is significant that the case singled out for special mention[62] as being one in which the Strasbourg Court would review the exercise of discretion for which EC law provided was *Cantoni*, a judgment of the Grand Chamber.[63] The applicant was prosecuted for unlawfully selling pharmaceutical products in supermarkets contrary to French law. The applicant argued by way of defence that the products in question were not medicinal products within the meaning of the French law and that the definition of such products was not sufficiently clear to satisfy the requirements of Article 7(1) of the Convention.

The French approach allowed a product to be defined as 'medicinal' by virtue of its function, presentation or composition. It followed in this respect the meaning given by the ECJ to 'medicinal product' in Directive 65/65. This Directive was primarily concerned with the authorization for placing medicinal products on the market and the application of the test for medicinal product was often left to national authorities, subject to review by the ECJ. The ECJ held moreover that in principle a Member State could reserve to pharmacists the sale of medicinal products, since this would safeguard public health, subject to a proportionality test designed to check whether such a monopoly was really required for products the use of which would not involve any serious danger to public health.[64]

The Strasbourg Court concluded that the French definition of medicinal product was not in breach of Article 7 of the ECHR. The Strasbourg Court will nonetheless exercise its normal review in cases such as *Cantoni* and this review is clearly more extensive than review bounded by the ideas of equivalence and manifest deficiency. There are at least two kinds of situation in which *Cantoni* as interpreted in *Bosphorus* can apply, both of which can give rise to problems, especially the latter.

---

60 *Van de Hurk v Netherlands*, ECHR (1994) Series A, No. 288.

61 *Dangeville v France*, ECHR (2002) No. 36677/97.

62 *Bosphorus Hava Yollari*, n. 50, at para. 157.

63 *Cantoni v France*, ECHR (1996) No. 45/95.

64 Case C-60/89, *Criminal Proceedings against Jean Monteil and Daniel Sammani* [1991] ECR I-1547.

The first type of situation is where the Strasbourg Court reviews the way in which a state implemented a directive and the way in which it applied the directive to particular cases. The assumption underlying the *Cantoni* judgment is that the Strasbourg Court can and will review such matters and this reading is reinforced by the *Bosphorus* judgment, which held that *Cantoni* exemplified 'review by this Court of the exercise of state discretion for which EC law provided'.[65] There is however potential for tension between Strasbourg and Luxembourg because the ECJ already exercises review over such matters. The ECJ clearly has authority to decide whether the way in which a directive was implemented by the Member State sufficed to ensure that the ends stipulated by the directive were properly attained. It is clear also that the ECJ can review the manner in which the directive was implemented in order to check whether the implementation complied with Community conceptions of fundamental rights. This is exemplified by *Caballero*.[66] The ECJ held in essence that where a directive left the definition of 'pay' to a Member State the meaning accorded to that term had to comply with the requirements of Community law, which included fundamental rights. The Member States were therefore bound by Community fundamental rights when they implemented Community law, in this instance through a directive, the ECJ reasoning by analogy from the *ERT* case.[67] There could therefore be instances where the ECJ and the ECtHR reach different conclusions as to whether the manner of implementation complied with fundamental rights, more especially so given that the ECtHR will exercise full review in such circumstances.

The second type of case is more problematic. It is important to recognize that in *Cantoni* the Strasbourg Court was indirectly assessing whether the definition given to a term in Community legislation, which was then applied by a Member State, was compatible with the ECHR. This was the actual legal issue posed by *Cantoni*. It was the definition of medicinal product adopted by the ECJ and then applied in French law that was said by the applicant to be contrary to Article 7. Thus the Strasbourg Court held that the fact that the French law was based almost word for word on the ambit of the Community Directive did not remove it from the ambit of Article 7 of the Convention.[68] The difficulty with this is apparent once it is recognized that in *Cantoni* France did not have, nor was it exercising, discretion for which EC law provided. The

---

65 *Ibid.* at para. 157.

66 Case C-442/00, *Caballero v Fondo de Garantia Salarial (Fogasa)* [2002] ECR I-11915, at paras 29–32. See also Cases C-465/00, 138 and 139/01, *Rechnungshof v Österreichischer Rundfunk and Others* [2003] ECR I-4989.

67 Case C-260/89, *Elliniki Radiophonia Tileorassi AE v Dimotiki Etairia Pliroforissis and Sotirios Kouvelas* [1991] ECR I-2925.

68 *Cantoni*, n. 63, at para. 30.

case was not concerned with the way in which a state chose to implement a Community directive. The issue was not whether the manner or method of implementation was defective. The essence of the applicant's claim was not simply that the French authorities had misapplied the definition, but that the very definition itself was contrary to Article 7 since it did not give those potentially affected by it adequate opportunity to know whether they would come within its remit. That was how the case was pleaded, reasoned and decided. The salient issue was therefore whether the meaning accorded to a certain term in a Community directive by the ECJ, which was then applied in French law, was compatible with Convention rights. On this issue the French authorities had no discretion provided by EC law. They could not have adopted a definition of medicinal product that differed in substance from that laid down by the Community Courts.

The judgment throws into sharp relief the relationship between the general principle propounded by the majority in *Bosphorus* with their endorsement of the principle flowing from *Cantoni*. The position appears to be that where the state is simply applying a legal obligation pursuant to a Community regulation, as in *Bosphorus*, then the Strasbourg Court will consider whether the EU provides equivalent protection for fundamental rights and, if it does so, the ECtHR will then only intervene if it feels that this was manifestly deficient in the instant case. The *Cantoni* decision and its endorsement in *Bosphorus* means however that the Strasbourg Court will continue to hold the state 'fully responsible' for acts done 'outside its strict international legal obligations' and that this includes review by the Strasbourg Court of the 'exercise of state discretion for which EC law provided'.[69]

The precise dividing line between the limited review provided for by *Bosphorus* and the fuller scrutiny exemplified by *Cantoni* remains unclear. The reasoning in the latter would appear to allow the Strasbourg Court indirect review over the definition of terms in a Community directive through the claimant's ability to argue that its application by a state was contrary to the Convention, even where the state had no discretion as to whether to apply that definition. If this is so then the '*Cantoni* exception' could well overshadow the '*Bosphorus* rule'. It is moreover difficult in terms of logic to see why the *Cantoni* reasoning should not apply to regulations as well as directives. If Strasbourg is willing indirectly to engage in fuller review as to whether the meaning of a term in a Community directive is compatible with the Convention, why should it not do so when the disputed meaning relates to a term in a regulation? The state against whom the action is brought has no discretion in the relevant sense in either such instance.

---

69 *Bosphorus Hava Yollari*, n. 50, at para. 157.

(D) *Bosphorus* and the ECtHR: The Concurring Opinion by Judge Ress

Lawyers interpreting judicial opinions will not only be mindful of exceptions to the general rule laid down by the majority, but also of concurring opinions that imbue terms used by the majority with a different meaning.

This is exemplified by Judge Ress's concurring Opinion, which was more nuanced both about equivalence and about the meaning of manifest deficiency. Thus whilst Judge Ress was willing to accept the majority's findings that the EU met the test of equivalence judged generally in terms of substantive guarantees of rights, he was a good deal more equivocal as to whether the EU's method of protection for those rights, with its limited standing rules, was really in accord with Article 6 of the ECHR, and he was also less willing to conclude that the presumption of Convention compliance could be said to exist in relation to all Convention rights.[70]

Judge Ress also in effect transformed the concept of manifest deficiency into a far more potent tool of review. He was willing to find such a deficiency where there was no adequate review because the ECJ lacked competence; where the ECJ had been too restrictive in its interpretation of individual access; where there had been an obvious misinterpretation or misapplication by the ECJ of a Convention right; where the ECJ departed from well-established Strasbourg case law, or where the result of the ECJ's judgment was that the level of protection was not the same as that which would be afforded under the ECHR.[71] This was, it should not be forgotten, an individual concurring Opinion. It shows nonetheless that there are diverse strands of opinion within the Strasbourg Court as to the proper relationship between it and the ECJ. The reality is that under the guise of manifest deficiency Judge Ress would in effect assure the Strasbourg Court's dominance over the ECJ.

Judge Ress's willingness to find a manifest deficiency where the ECJ had been too restrictive in its interpretation of individual access is especially interesting. Rights demand remedies. This is an obvious proposition, but important nonetheless. It is axiomatic, as van Gerven states, that 'fundamental rights are only truly respected when the legal order concerned makes them enforceable against those who have breached them'.[72] The problems with standing for individuals in direct actions before the ECJ are well known, and this has forced many litigants to seek access to the ECJ indirectly via Article 234 EC. It remains to be seen what impact if any the Community Charter of

[70] *Ibid.*, n. 50, Judge Ress concurring Opinion at para. 2.

[71] *Ibid.* at para. 3.

[72] W. van Gerven, 'Remedies for infringements of fundamental rights' (2004) 10 EPL 261.

Fundamental Rights[73] might have, more especially if it is accorded binding legal status. Article 41 enshrines a right to good administration, which is said to inhere in every person. Article 41(2) sets out certain more specific rights that are included in this right. Article 47 provides that everyone whose rights and freedoms guaranteed by EU law are violated has the right to an effective remedy before a tribunal in compliance with the conditions laid down in this Article. Standing rules are not explicitly mentioned in either Article. It would be open to the Community Courts, if they wished to do so, to regard these provisions as the basis for expanding the existing standing rules. They are however unlikely to do so given their approach to standing hitherto. This is especially so given that the explanatory memorandum stated in relation to Article 47 that there was no intent for this provision to make any change to the rules on standing other than those embodied in Article III-365(4) of the Constitutional Treaty.[74]

It should nonetheless be recognized that there is an uneasy tension between the Charter rights and the standing rules for direct actions. The Charter accords *individual rights*, yet the application of the standing rules means that a person who claims that his rights have been infringed by Community law would normally not be able to meet the requirements of *individual concern*. There is something decidedly odd about the infringement of an individual right not counting as a matter of individual concern. The ECJ touched on this in *Bactria*:[75] the ECJ held that the fact that a Regulation dealing with biocidal products provided that a list of existing substances was to be drawn up with the help of information from producers did not mean that the Commission was required to hear producers such as the applicant when adopting the Regulation. The applicant argued that it should be regarded as individually concerned by the Regulation because it affected its property and data-protection rights. The ECJ briefly concluded that the alleged infringement of the applicant's property right was insufficient to distinguish it individually for the purposes of standing. This conclusion is sustainable in formalistic terms, since the Regulation could equally affect the property rights of other operators in the area. This merely serves to demonstrate the limits of the formalistic reasoning. The fact that a regulation might affect equally a number of traders does not alter the fact that the affect in the instant case is on the individual right that each possesses. In this sense *Bactria* fails to resolve or recognize the tension between individual rights and individual concern.

---

73 OJ 2000 C364/01.

74 Charte 4473/00, Convent 49, 11 October 2000, at 41; CONV 828/03, Updated Explanations Relating to the Text of the Charter of Fundamental Rights, 9 July 2003, at 41.

75 Case C-258/02 P, *Bactria Industriehygiene-Service Verwaltungs GmbH v Commission* [2003] ECR I-15105, at para. 43.

THE RELATIONSHIP BETWEEN THE EU AND THE ECHR IF THE EU ACCEDES

We should now consider the relationship between the EU and the ECHR if the EU accedes to the Convention. This was always open to the EU if the necessary Treaty amendment was made.[76] Many commentators advocated the step, as did Working Group II of the Convention on the Future of Europe.[77] This issue was addressed by the Constitutional Treaty, Article I-9(2) of which provided that the EU should accede to the ECHR, although no precise time line for this was stipulated. The fate of the Constitutional Treaty means that this obligation to accede is unlikely to become a legal reality. This does not of course preclude the EU from deciding on some other occasion to accede to the ECHR, although it is very likely that this would still require a Treaty amendment.

The effect of any future accession is however more complex than is often imagined. Decisions would have to be made as to whether, for example, to build in a preliminary reference relationship between the Luxembourg and Strasbourg Courts.[78] Accession would not moreover, as is sometimes claimed, obviate the need for the EU to have its own Charter. This is so for both substantive and jurisdictional reasons.

In substantive terms, a political entity with the power of the EU should, as a matter of principle, be subject to rights-based constraints on the exercise of that power. The absence of such constraints was the source of the initial revolt by the German and Italian courts, which served as the catalyst for the introduction of the ECJ's fundamental rights jurisprudence. The Charter has enhanced the political legitimacy of the EU by furnishing its citizens with a comprehensive, transparent document that includes a broad range of rights. The Charter was premised on the political choice made by the heads of state in the European Council that it should cover social and economic, as well as more traditional civil and political rights. The ECHR covers only some of the rights included in the Charter, and for that reason accession would not obviate the need for the EU's own document enshrining the rights that it believes are worthy of protection.

In jurisdictional terms accession to the ECHR would not render moot the choices open to citizens as to how they protect their human rights. This point would hold true even if the EU's human rights document had been an exact copy of the ECHR. This is because of the differing impact of the EU and

---

[76] Opinion 2/94, n. 39.

[77] CONV 354/02, Final Report of Working Group II, 22 October 2002, at 11.

[78] A. Arnull, 'From Charter to Constitution and beyond: fundamental rights in the new European Union' [2003] PL 774, 788–9.

ECHR Treaties in at least some states, as exemplified by the UK. The supremacy doctrine is a central principle of EU law. The UK courts have held that even primary legislation that is inconsistent with EU law can be declared inapplicable to the instant case. Such legislation will be 'disapplied' by the national court.[79] The status of the ECHR is different. Under the Human Rights Act 1998, where primary legislation is incompatible with Convention rights, the UK courts can issue a declaration of incompatibility.[80] This declaration does not however affect the validity of the legislation. It serves to send the legislation back to the political forum, with the expectation that Parliament will remove the offending provision. There is therefore an incentive for those minded to challenge primary legislation to do so through EU rights where that is possible.

CONCLUSION

Other contributors to this volume will doubtless have gleaned the following statistic from a search on EUR-Lex: Francis Jacobs produced 544 Opinions during his tenure as Advocate General. He has made a major contribution, judged both by the quantity of his Opinions and more especially their quality over this period. His ability to shift between topics as diverse as fundamental rights and customs regulations, principles of free movement and VAT, and agriculture and trade marks is a testimony to his legal skills and his depth of understanding of Community law. These skills are exemplified by the contributions that he made to the Community's fundamental rights jurisprudence, and his broader appreciation of human rights grounded in his knowledge of the ECHR jurisprudence.

---

79 *R. v Secretary of State for Transport, ex p. Factortame Ltd (No. 2)* [1991] 1 AC 603; *R. v Secretary of State for Employment, ex p. Equal Opportunities Commission* [1995] 1 AC 1.

80 Human Rights Act 1998, ss. 2–4.

3. *Locus standi* of individuals under Article 230(4): the return of Euridice?

Takis Tridimas and Sara Poli[1]

INTRODUCTION

Sir Francis Jacobs has been one of the most influential Advocates General (AsG) in the history of the European Court of Justice (ECJ). He became a member of the Court in October 1988 and served until January 2006, thus being the second longest-serving Advocate General and one of the longest-serving members of the Court.[2] The function of the AG, which in the eyes of a common lawyer remains a somewhat esoteric and quaint office, is 'to make, in open court, reasoned submissions' on cases 'acting with complete impartiality and independence'.[3] The Opinion of the Advocate General fulfils essentially three functions.[4] It assists the Court to find a solution to the case and thus in preparing the judgment. It sheds light on the factual and legal background to the dispute. It thus complements and assists in explaining the judgment, which is collegiate and much more compact. It also offers an opportunity to analyse and, on occasion, re-evaluate the case law, taking a step back from the facts of the case and assessing the impact of possible solutions to the dispute on the wider matrix of the law. It is no secret that Sir Francis excelled in performing all these functions. In his years at the Court, he became renowned for his intellectual vigour, his persuasive arguments and his efficiency. He was

1 Takis Tridimas is Sir John Lubbock Professor of Banking Law at Queen Mary, University of London; Professor at the Dickinson School of Law, Pennsylvania State University and barrister, Matrix Chambers. Sara Poli is lecturer in Law at the University of Rome. Sara Poli has been primarily responsible for writing sections 2–5 of this chapter and Takis Tridimas for the remaining. The authors undertake collective responsibility for the views expressed.

2 Karl Roemer AG served from 1953 until 1973. The longest-serving judges have been Andreas Donner (1958–79) and Pierre Pescatore (1967–85), who served for 21 and 18 years respectively.

3 Article 222(2) EC.

4 For more details, see T. Tridimas, 'The influence of the Advocate General in the development of Community law: some reflections' (1997) 34 CMLRev, 1349.

a pioneer, procuring by his Opinion in *HAG II* the first ever express overruling of 'precedent' by the Court.[5] His Opinions touched almost every aspect of European Community law. He was particularly present in some areas, such as free movement of goods and services, external relations, social security and taxation. In the field of human rights especially he often represented the Court's 'embodied conscience',[6] as his Opinions in *Konstantinidis* and *Schmidberger* testify.[7]

This chapter focuses on Francis Jacobs's contribution on *locus standi* of individuals under Article 230(4) EC, a particularly troubled area of Community law. Article 230(4) EC is one of the few provisions of the Treaty where, save with few exceptions, the case law has remained virtually unevolved. The ECJ has shown an uncharacteristic reluctance to broaden the *locus standi* of individuals, elevating the *Plaumann* formula[8] to an effective litigation filter. In determining *locus standi*, the ECJ is not pre-occupied with injury-based considerations but follows an 'alternative forum' approach. This approach views national courts as the appropriate forum for challenges by individuals against the validity of Community acts of general application, irrespective of whether they are truly legislative or regulatory, and promotes a decentralized system of justice.

The 'closed category' test adopted in *Plaumann*[9] appears to be counter-intuitive and has been criticized as not corresponding to economic reality. A firm is denied locus where it is a member of a potentially open category, which effectively limits standing to cases where some kind of a retroactive element is present.[10] It does not seem persuasive to deny *locus standi* to a person who is adversely affected by a measure on the ground that other persons may also be affected in the future.[11]

The contribution of AG Jacobs in this area of law can be traced primarily

---

5 Case C-10/89 *CNL-Sucal v HAG GF* [1990] ECR I-3711.

6 This term was coined by C. Hamson, *Executive Discretion and Judicial Control*, (London: Stevens & Sons, 1954) p. 80.

7 Case C-168/91 *Konstantinidis* [1993] ECR I1191; Case C-112/00 *Schmidberger* [2003] ECR I-5659.

8 Case 25/62 *Plaumann* [1963] ECR 95.

9 In *Plaumann*, the ECJ held that persons other than those to whom a decision is addressed may only claim to be individually concerned if that decision affects them by reason of certain attributes peculiar to them or by reason of circumstances in which they are differentiated from all other persons and by virtue of these factors distinguishes them individually just as in the case of the person addressed.

10 See Craig and De Burca, *EU Law, Text, Cases, and Materials* (Oxford: OUP, 3rd edn, 2003), pp. 462–3.

11 Id.

by reference to his Opinions in *Extramet*,[12] *UPA*[13] and, more recently, *ARE*.[14] This chapter focuses on his Opinion in *UPA* and the resulting trialogue amongst AG Jacobs, the Court of First Instance (CFI) and the ECJ as it unravelled in *UPA* and subsequent case law. There is no intention to be exhaustive and the examination of the case law is highly selective.

THE PRE-*UPA* CASE LAW: SOME KEY JUDGMENTS

Before embarking on an examination of *UPA*, it may be interesting to recall briefly some key judgments delivered in earlier years. At an early stage, a consistent line of cases established that, as a general rule, an individual may only contest the validity of an act which is in substance a decision. Regulations are normative acts and as such were perceived to be, in principle, beyond the reach of individuals. The rationale of this approach was explained in *Koninklijke Scholten Honig*.[15] The Court stated that the objective of Article 173(2) (now Article 230(4)) is to prevent the Community institutions from being in a position, merely by choosing the form of a regulation, to exclude an application by individuals against a decision which concerns them directly and individually. It became important therefore to distinguish between normative acts and decisions. The distinction is by no means easy to draw and resulted in some complex case law.[16]

Although some allowances were made in the field of state aid, competition law and anti-dumping in view of the special features of these sectors, the interpretation of 'individual concern' remained narrow and, save in the field of anti-dumping, the applicant had to establish – in addition to direct and individual concern – that the contested measure was, in substance, a decision.

The first case where the Court showed a willingness to depart from its traditional, strict approach was *Extramet*.[17] The Council had imposed anti-dumping duties on imports of calcium metal originating from China and the Soviet Union. The applicant was an independent Community importer whose prices had not been taken into account for the determination of the export price and

12 Case C-358/89 *Extramet Industrie v Council* [1991] ECR I-2501.

13 Case C-50/00 P *Unión de Pequeños Agricultores v Council* [2002] ECR I-6677.

14 Case C-78/03 P *Commission v Germany (ARE case)*, judgment of 13 December 2005.

15 Case 101/76 *Koninklijke Scholten Honig* [1979] ECR 797, para. 6.

16 See e.g. Joined Cases 789 and 790/79 *Calpak v Commission* [1980] ECR 1949; Case 138/79 *Roquette Frères v Council* [1980] ECR 3333; Joined Cases 41-44/70 *Fruit Company v Commission* [1971] ECR 411; Case 26/86 *Deutz and Geldermann* [1987] ECR 941.

17 See n. 12.

therefore, according to the case law as it stood, did not have *locus standi* to challenge the imposition of anti-dumping duty. The Court, however, led by Francis Jacobs, held that in the circumstances of the case, the applicant was able to establish individual concern. It was the largest Community importer. Its business activities depended on imports from China and the Soviet Union and were seriously affected by the contested regulation. There were effectively no alternative sources of supply as there was a limited number of manufacturers of the product concerned and the sole Community producer was a competitor of the applicant.[18] Although the result reached by the Court in *Extramet* was correct, its reasoning was limited to the facts. It focused on the prejudice which the regulation caused to the applicant in the circumstances and did not make any general pronouncements regarding *locus standi* in anti-dumping cases, despite being invited to do so by the Advocate General.

The Court went one step further in *Codorniu v Council*.[19] In 1989 the Council adopted a regulation by which it reserved the term 'crémant' to certain quality sparkling wines produced in France and Luxembourg. The applicant was a Spanish company which had registered in Spain the graphic trade mark 'Gran Cremant de Codorniu' in 1924. It alleged that the regulation was discriminatory and deprived it of the right to use the terms it traditionally used for the description of its products. The Court accepted that the regulation was, by virtue of its abstract and general application, of a legislative nature. That however did not prevent it from being of individual concern to some traders. The applicant was able to establish individual concern because the contested regulation, by reserving the term 'crémant' to French and Luxembourg producers, prevented it from using its graphic trade mark.[20]

Codorniu was the first case outside the limited field of anti-dumping where the Court expressly acknowledged that an individual may challenge directly a true legislative measure. It may be taken as evidence that, where an applicant has a very strong case on the merits, the Court may be prepared to grant him *locus standi* to challenge a legislative measure despite the restrictive requirements of Article 230(4).[21] It may thus be viewed as a triumph of substance over form but, nonetheless, has remained very much the exception. It did not detract from the application of the *Plaumann* formula and the narrow interpretation of individual concern.

---

18 Op. cit., para. 17.

19 Case C-309/89 [1994] ECR I-1853.

20 Op. cit., paras 19–21.

21 After declaring the application admissible the Court proceeded to annul the regulation for breach of the principle of equal treatment. The regulation can be seen as a blatant disregard of acquired rights, indeed, as verging on expropriation; See T. Tridimas, *The General Principles of EC Law* (Oxford: OUP, 1999), p. 58.

In *Campo Ebro*[22] the Council adopted a regulation reducing sugar prices in Spain so as to align them with those in the rest of the Community. The applicants, who were producers of isoglucose, argued that the regulation discriminated against them because it did not grant them temporary aid to mitigate the reduction in prices, whereas it granted such aid to sugar producers. The CFI held that, even if the applicants were the only producers of isoglucose in Spain, they were only affected in their objective capacity as isoglucose producers in the same way as any other trader in the sugar sector.[23] They were not therefore members of a closed class.

Similarly, in *Buralux*,[24] the appellants were undertakings carrying out the collection, shipment and dumping of household waste from Germany to France. They sought annulment of Article 4(3)(i)(a) in Council Regulation No. 253/93 which authorized Member States to restrict the shipment of waste. The Court held that that provision concerned the appellants only in their capacity as economic operators in the business of waste transfer between Member States in the same manner as any other operator in that business. The fact that they were practically the only operators who transported waste from France to Germany was not sufficient to differentiate them, nor was the fact that they had entered into long-term contracts with German public agencies for the shipment of waste before the Regulation was issued. In response to the argument that such a restrictive approach to *locus standi* denied effective protection, the Court pointed out that the appellants could challenge the refusal of national authorities to ship waste based on the Regulation before national courts; in support of such a challenge, the Court continued, they could claim that Article 4(3)(i)(a) was unlawful, thus obliging the national court to make a preliminary reference.

In *Campo Ebro* and *Buralux* the Community Courts applied the traditional approach according to which the possibility of determining more or less precisely the number or even the identity of the persons to whom a measure applies does not in any way imply that it must be regarded as being of individual concern to them, as long as it is established that such application takes effect by virtue of an objective legal or factual situation defined by the measure in question in relation to its purpose. For such persons to be capable of being regarded as individually concerned, their legal position must be affected because of a factual situation which differentiates them from all other persons and distinguishes them individually in the same way as a person to whom a measure is addressed.[25]

---

22 Case T-472/93 *Campo Ebro v Council* [1995] ECR II-421.

23 Op. cit., para. 33.

24 Case C-209/94 P *Buralux v Council* [1996] ECR I-615, paras 31–4.

25 See e.g. Case C-264/91 *Abertal and Others v Council* [1993] ECR I-3265,

This test is detached from economic reality. It may lead to the refusal of *locus standi* even in cases where the applicant is the only person of a potentially open class at the time the contested measure is adopted and there is economically no realistic prospect that other undertakings will become part of the same group.[26]

THE *UPA* OPINION

In his Opinion in *Unión de Pequeños Agricultores v Council* (*UPA case*),[27] AG Jacobs criticized the restrictive interpretation of Article 230(4) EC and proposed an alternative definition of 'individual concern'. The facts of the case, as such, are unremarkable. A Spanish trade association sought the annulment of a Council agricultural Regulation. At first instance, the CFI rejected the action as inadmissible, following the established case law.[28] On appeal, the applicant relied essentially on the right to judicial protection and AG Jacobs took the opportunity to revisit the case law. It is worth examining in some detail the arguments put forward in his Opinion.

The Advocate General criticized the view, enshrined in traditional case law, that the preliminary reference procedure provided an effective alternative means of judicial review.[29] Preliminary references suffer from the disadvantages of extra costs and delay. They are contingent, since they are for the national court to decide and access to the ECJ is not granted to an applicant as a matter of right. Furthermore, they make it impossible for individuals to challenge Community measures which do not require any implementing measures. Direct actions, by contrast, have procedural advantages since they entail a full exchange of pleadings and allow for the intervention of interested third parties. They also increase legal certainty since challenges must be brought within the short time limit of two months from the adoption of the contested measure.

The Advocate General then concentrated on how the annulment action could become more accessible to private applicants. One option might be to grant individuals standing to challenge a regulation where an examination of the particular case revealed that they would otherwise be denied effective judicial protection at national level. The applicant in *UPA* favoured this solution

---

para. 16; Case C-131/92 *Arnaud and Others v Council* [1993] ECR I-2573, para. 13; Case 26/86 *Deutz und Geldermann v Council* [1987] ECR 941, para. 9.

26 That was argued to be the case in *Campo Ebro*, op. cit.; see paras 10, 25 and 33 of the judgment.

27 See n. 13.

28 Case T-173/98 *Unión de Pequeños Agricultores v Council* [1999] ECR II-3357.

29 Op. cit., at 6693 *et seq.*

and some support for it could be drawn from previous case law, including the judgment in *Greenpeace*.[30] AG Jacobs however found this solution unsatisfactory for three reasons. First, Article 230 EC made no reference to the availability or absence in particular instances of alternative remedies in national courts. Secondly, Community Courts were not competent, and were ill-equipped, to rule on the interpretation of national law. Thirdly, national rules on standing diverged: there were therefore risks that Community citizens who were affected by a Community regulation in a similar way, might not enjoy the same possibilities to challenge it.

Another option, suggested by the Commission and the Council, was to shift the burden to Member States by requiring them not to apply rules of national law which rendered it difficult or impossible to challenge Community measures in the national courts. The Advocate General highlighted the weaknesses of this suggestion.[31] It would not resolve the problems linked to the preliminary procedure. It would make far-reaching intrusions into the national legal systems in the sensitive areas of remedies and procedure, which are viewed as falling within the national procedural autonomy. Finally, any required changes of national rules would be very difficult to monitor and enforce effectively.

According to the Advocate General, the time was ripe to give the notion of individual concern a wider reading. He proposed a new test according to which a person was to be regarded as individually concerned 'where, by reason of his particular circumstances, the measure had, or was liable to have, a substantial adverse effect on his interests'.[32] This test does away with the closed category approach of the *Plaumann* case law. The Advocate General celebrated this extension, pinpointing the fallacy of the traditional test: under *Plaumann*, the greater the number of persons affected by a measure, the less

---

30 See Case C-321/95 P *Greenpeace Council and Others v Commission* [1998] ECR I-1651, para. 33. There, in rejecting the action brought by Greenpeace, the ECJ stated that the appellants did not remain without any effective judicial protection since in the circumstances their rights were 'fully protected by national courts'. This gave the impression that the Court might have rendered the action admissible if Greenpeace had had no alternative possibility to pursue a claim in national courts. It is not however clear whether this was the Court's intention. The above dictum might have served to highlight that, in the specific circumstances of the case, the contested Commission decision which concerned the financing of a power station affected the applicants' interests only indirectly. See further Case C-300/00 *Federatión de Cofradías de Pescadores de Guipúzcoa* P-R [2000] ECR I-8797, para. 37, but see also the judgment in *Buralux*, op. cit., where reference to the preliminary reference procedure as an alternative remedy was made. For subsequent case law, see below.

31 *UPA*, op. cit., 6697–8.

32 *UPA*, op. cit, 6698 at para. 60 of the Opinion.

likely that an action under Article 230(4) would succeed. However, the fact that a measure adversely affected a large number of individuals, causing widespread rather than limited harm, provided 'a positive reason for accepting a direct challenge by one or more of those individuals'.[33]

The Advocate General then went on to explain the advantages of the proposed *locus standi* test and deal with possible objections to it. The new test would avoid a *déni de justice* and encourage the use of direct actions. This would have beneficial effects in terms of legal certainty and the uniform application of Community law. The new definition would bring clarity and simplicity to a compounded body of case law and remove a number of anomalies.[34] Finally, it would shift the emphasis of judicial review from questions of admissibility to questions of substance, as is the case with actions in damages.

The Advocate General dismissed the argument that the new test was contrary to the wording of Article 230(4). Rather, it was one of the interpretations which the notion of individual concern was capable of carrying. He also found exaggerated the concern that the new test would open the floodgates. An increase in the number of annulment actions was to be expected but it would be manageable. In many cases, applicants would challenge the same act. Moreover, procedural and jurisdictional reforms of the Community judicial architecture would enable the system to cope with the growth of litigation. He further argued that the restrictive *locus standi* of individuals under Article 230(4) was increasingly out of line with the administrative laws of the Member States.

Finally, AG Jacobs drew attention to the evolving case law on the effective protection of Community rights in national courts. That principle was enunciated in 1986, in the case of *Johnston*,[35] and reaffirmed in subsequent judgments such as *Factortame*[36] and *Verholen*,[37] where it was held that the principle of effective judicial protection may require national courts to review all national legislative measures; to grant interim relief and to grant individu-

---

33 Op. cit., 6698 at para. 59 of the Opinion.

34 The Opinion highlighted the following anomalies. First, the restrictive interpretation of the notion of individual concern contrasts with the generous and dynamic interpretation of other aspects of Article 230 EC adopted by the Court in cases such as Case 22/70 *Commission v Council (ERTA Case)* [1971] ECR 263; Case 294/83 *Partie Ecologiste 'Les Verts' v European Parliament* [1986] ECR 1339; and Case C-70/88 *Parliament v Council (Chernobyl case)* [1990] ECR I-2041. Second, there are no restrictions on the standing of individuals to bring actions for damages under Articles 235 EC and 288 EC.

35 Case C-222/84 *Johnston v Chief Constable of the Royal Ulster Constabulary* [1986] ECR 1651.

36 Case C-213/89 [1990] ECR I-2433.

37 Joined Cases C-87/90, C-88/90 and C-89/90 [1991] ECR I-3757.

als standing to bring proceedings, even where they would be unable to do so under national law. The Advocate General viewed the restrictive *Plaumann* formula as untenable in the light of the case law on judicial protection.

In its judgment, the ECJ did not heed the recommendations of the Advocate General and reiterated the traditional case law. The next act in this drama was to unravel not in the *UPA* litigation but in *Jégo-Quéré*, which highlighted much more sharply the injustices of the *Plaumann* formula, and to which we now turn.

THE CFI'S TEST IN *JÉGO-QUÉRÉ*

In *Jégo-Quéré v Commission*[38] a French fishing company sought to challenge a Commission Regulation which imposed minimum mesh sizes for fishing nets. The objective of the Regulation was to protect the stock of hake. Jégo-Quéré claimed that, whilst it caught only a negligible quantity of hake, the enlargement of the mesh size prescribed by the Regulation seriously reduced its catch of whiting, which represented the bulk of its activity. It argued that the Regulation penalized its business in violation of the principles of proportionality and equality.

The CFI had no difficulty in finding that the Regulation was of direct concern to the applicant. It left no discretion to the Member States and no additional measures, either at Community or national level, were needed for its implementation. The crucial obstacle however was the condition of individual concern. The CFI found that Jégo-Quéré was not individually concerned within the meaning of the *Plaumann* test. The fact that it was the only operator fishing for whiting in the waters south of Ireland with vessels with a specific length was not sufficient to differentiate it from all operators specialized in fishing for whiting. The CFI then distinguished the case from *Piraiki-Patraiki*.[39] It held that the fact that a person was 'involved in some way or other in the procedure leading to the adoption of a Community measure was capable of distinguishing that person individually in relation to the measure in question only if the applicable Community legislation granted him certain procedural guarantees'.[40] Neither the EC Treaty, however, nor any Community measure, required the Commission to hear Jégo-Quéré before adopting the Regulation. In addition, the Court held that Jégo-Quéré was not in a special position comparable to that of the applicants in *Codorniu* or *Extramet*.

38 Case T-177/01 *Jégo-Quéré v Commission* [2002] ECR II-2365.
39 Case 11/82 *Piraiki-Patraiki v Commission* [1985] ECR 207.
40 *Jégo-Quéré*, op. cit., para. 40.

This would have been the end of the inquiry, had it not been for another argument raised by Jégo-Quéré. It argued that, if the CFI held the action to be inadmissible, it would face a denial of justice since there were no alternative ways of challenging the Regulation. This argument had been raised before[41] but the CFI had never upheld it on the ground that 'such circumstances, even if they [were] established, [could not] warrant modifying by way of judicial interpretation the system of legal remedies and procedures laid down in the Treaty'.[42] But in *Jégo-Quéré*, given the particular circumstances of the case, it underwent a change of heart, reasoning as follows:

The CFI acknowledged that access to the Courts was one of the essential elements of a Community based on the rule of law and that the Treaty established a 'complete system of legal remedies'.[43] It then proceeded to examine whether the right to an effective remedy, based on Articles 6 and 13 of the European Convention on Human Rights (ECHR) and reaffirmed by Article 47 of the EU Charter of Fundamental Rights, could justify a relaxation of the *locus standi* conditions. The CFI first searched for alternative remedies and pointed out that neither the preliminary reference procedure nor an action in damages provided workable solutions. The applicant could not introduce an action under Article 234 since the contested Regulation did not need any implementation measures in national law. The only chance for individuals to challenge it before a national court would be to violate its provisions and then contest its validity by way of defence in possible proceedings initiated against them. However, as AG Jacobs had already pointed out in *UPA*, requiring indi-

---

41 This argument had been invoked for example in the following cases before the CFI: Joined Cases T-198/95, T-171/96, T-230/97, T-174/98 and T-225/99 *Comafrica SpA and Dole Fresh Fruit Europe Ltd & Co. v Commission* [2001] II-1975 para. 111; Case T-172/98 *Salamander and Others v Parliament/Council* case ECR [2000] II-2487, paras 72–3; Case C-321/95 P *Stichting Greenpeace* [1998] ECR I-1651, para. 32; Case T-138/98 *Armement Coopératif Artisanal Vendéen* (ACAV) [2000] II-341, para. 68; Case T-100/94 *Kapniki A. Michailidis AE* [1998] ECR II-3115, para. 72; Case T-14/97 and T-15/97 *Sofivo v Council* [1998] ECR II-4191, para. 40; Case T-122/96 *Federazione Nazionale del Commercio Oleario (Federolio)* [1997] ECR II-1559, para. 79. For examples of cases where parties had raised this argument in appeals before the ECJ, see Joined Cases C-300/99 P and C-388/99 P *Area Cova and Others v Council* [2001] I-983, para. 26; Case 87/95 P *Cassa Nazionale di Previdenza ed Assistenza a favore degli avvocati e dei Procuratori v Council* [1996] ECR I-2003, para. 22.

42 See *Armement Coopératif Artisanal Vendéen* (ACAV), op. cit., para. 68. Similar wording was used in Case T-212/00 *Nuove Industrie Molisane v Commission* [2002] ECR I-347, para. 48; Case T-339/00 *Bactria Industriehygiene-Service Verwaltungs GmbH*, judgment of 29 April 2002, para. 54; Case T-172/98 *Salamander*, op. cit., para. 74; Case T-69/96 *Hamburger Hafen- und Lagerhaus Aktiengesellschaft* [2001] ECR II-1037, para. 51.

43 *Jégo-Quéré*, op. cit., para. 41.

viduals to breach the law in order to gain access to justice fell short of the requirements of effective judicial protection. An action in damages did not offer a better alternative. The rationale of an action under Article 235 EC was to compensate for damages arising from the application of a Community measure and not to remove an illegal act from the Community legal order. Furthermore, the annulment action and the action for damages were based on different criteria of admissibility and substance. The review undertaken by the Court in an action for damages was not as comprehensive as in an annulment action, since in the former the Court's scrutiny was limited to identifying a sufficiently serious breach and did not cover all the factors which might affect the legality of the measure in question. The CFI concluded that, in the light of Articles 6 and 13 of the ECHR and of Article 47 of the Charter of Fundamental Rights, Articles 234, 235 and 288(2) EC could not be regarded as guaranteeing individuals the right to an effective legal remedy.[44]

The CFI then proceeded to redefine the notion of individual concern to ensure private parties' effective judicial protection. Drawing inspiration from the wording of Article 47 of the Charter of Human Rights, it proposed the following new test of admissibility:

> a natural or legal person will be regarded as individually concerned by a Community measure of general application that concerns him directly if the measure in question affects his legal position, in a manner which is both *definite* and *immediate*, by restricting his rights or by imposing obligations on him. The number and position of other persons who are likewise affected by the measure, or who may be so, are of no relevance in that regard.[45]

Applying the new test to the case in issue, the CFI concluded that Jégo-Quéré was individually concerned by the contested Regulation since it imposed specific obligations on it concerning the mesh size of nets.

A COMPARISON OF THE TWO TESTS IN *UPA* AND *JÉGO-QUÉRÉ*

There are obvious similarities between the test proposed by AG Jacobs in *UPA* and the test of the CFI in *Jégo-Quéré*. Both viewed the *Plaumann* formula as running counter to the fundamental right to judicial protection. They both considered the narrow interpretation of individual concern not as being dictated by the letter of the Treaty but as a judicial choice of construction. The

44 Op. cit., para. 47.
45 Op. cit., para. 51, emphasis added.

broadening of *locus standi* endorses a hierarchy of remedies absent in the ECJ case law. Both the CFI and the Advocate General took the view that a direct annulment action should take precedence over a preliminary reference or an action for damages. This marks a stark contrast with past case law, where individuals wishing to contest the effects of a Community measure were systematically redirected towards other remedies, mainly an indirect challenge in the national courts via the preliminary ruling[46] or, occasionally, the action in damages.[47] The Community judicature had pointed out the avenue of the preliminary ruling procedure to applicants not vested with legal standing, without considering whether that possibility was real or hypothetical.[48]

There are also other similarities between the two tests. The number of parties which are affected by a given Community measure is irrelevant to pass the test of individual concern. Further, applicants are no longer required to show that the contested act is in substance a decision in order to challenge it. Although the importance of this requirement had declined since *Codorniu*,[49] the CFI had not been consistent in skipping the legal nature test. As a result, there was still some confusion as to whether or not the proof of the legal nature of an act was a preliminary requirement to claim individual concern.[50]

The two tests however are by no means identical. The *Jégo-Quéré* test is not as far reaching as the test proposed by AG Jacobs in *UPA*. Semantically, the CFI test is drawn in narrower terms. It requires a 'definite and immediate effect' on the 'legal position' of the applicant, whilst Jacobs's test only demands a 'substantial' effect on his legal 'interests' and a potential effect

---

46 See e.g. Case T-244/00 *Coillte Teoranta* [2001] ECR II-1275, para. 63; Case T-330/94 *Salt Union Ltd v Commission* [1996] ECR II-1475, para. 39. There have been instances where the parties took up the suggestion of the Community Courts and, after having unsuccessfully challenged a Community act through Article 230(4) EC, they sought a preliminary ruling on the validity of the contested measure but their action was dismissed. See, for example, the reference in Case C-328/00 *Weber* [2002] ECR I-1461 where a party unsuccessfully attempted to challenge the validity of a regulation via the preliminary ruling procedure after being denied individual concern by the CFI in Case T-482/93 *Weber v Commission* [1996] ECR II-609.

47 See Case T-172/98 *Salamander*, op. cit., para. 77.

48 This is effectively what the ECJ did in *Jégo-Quéré* on appeal. See below. For a case where it was argued that it would be impossible to challenge a Community decision before national courts, see Case T-398/94 *Kahn Scheppvaart BV v Commission* [1996] ECR II-447, para. 35.

49 See A. Ward, *Judicial Review and the Right of Private Parties in EC Law*, (Oxford: OUP, 2000), p. 225.

50 The expression 'legal nature test' is borrowed from A. Albors-Llorens, *Private Parties in European Community Law* (Oxford: Clarendon Press, 1996). Note that in annulment actions against directives the Community judicature continued to analyse whether the contested directive was in substance a decision. See, for example, Case C-321/95 *UEAPME v Council* [1998] ECR II-2335, para. 63.

seems to suffice. Further, the reasoning of the CFI suggests that the new test applies only where the contested Community measure requires no implementing measures 'capable of forming the basis of an action before national courts'.[51]

The CFI test is clearly less ambitious: understandably, the Court was preoccupied with the facts of the case and less concerned about articulating a general theory of *locus standi*. It identified an injustice and sought to avoid a *déni de justice* by doing away with the *Plaumann* formula in specific circumstances. The new test seems to be superimposed upon, and does not change, the existing exceptions of *Codorniu* and *Extramet*. It preserves the possibility for private parties to attack a regulation where they have 'special rights' (as in *Codorniu*) or they establish the existence of a specific 'set of factors' (as in *Extramet*). Indeed, in considering whether Jégo-Quéré could rely on these cases to gain *locus standi*, the CFI stated that the applicant 'had not produced enough evidence' to that effect. By contrast, Jacobs's test, being broader, extinguishes the need to preserve *Codorniu*.

It would be interesting to speculate how certain cases that reached the ECJ might have been decided under each test. The test of AG Jacobs in *UPA* appears broad enough to provide *locus standi* to applicants in circumstances similar to those in *Plaumann*, *Buralux* and *Greenpeace*. Would the same be true for the *Jégo-Quéré* test? In our view, it is doubtful whether the applicant in *Plaumann* would have met the conditions for *locus standi* as defined in *Jégo-Quéré*. In that case, the direct annulment action did not appear to be, strictly speaking, the only available remedy to attack the validity of the Commission decision, which appeared to require implementing measures by the German authorities. The applicant could therefore have challenged the national measure giving effect to the Commission decision before a national court. It is also uncertain whether the application of the *Jégo-Quéré* test would have been favourable to the applicants in *Buralux* and *Greenpeace* since the possibility of utilizing the preliminary reference procedure by challenging national measures appeared to exist. Also, it might be argued that the contested Community measures in those cases did not affect the legal position of the applicants in a manner which was both *definite* and *immediate*.

---

[51] *Jégo-Quéré*, op. cit., para. 45. The CFI stated that the *Jégo-Quéré* test applies to measures of general application. It did not consider whether the test is also applicable to individual acts such as decisions. It is submitted, however, that the test applies *a fortiori* to such measures since decisions, just like regulations, are directly applicable and do not require any implementing acts.

THE ECJ JUDGMENT IN *JÉGO-QUÉRÉ*

On appeal by the Commission, the ECJ reversed the judgment of the CFI in *Jégo-Quéré* and reiterated the strict definition of individual concern. The following points may be made in relation to the judgment: The Court correctly confirmed that an action for annulment under Article 230(4) should not become available if it could be shown that national law did not allow the applicant to bring proceedings to contest the validity of the Community measure at issue. Such an interpretation would require the CFI or the ECJ to examine and interpret national procedural law in each individual case, and exceed their jurisdiction to review the legality of Community measures.[52] The Court felt unable to endorse the liberal interpretation of the CFI on the ground that, if it disregarded the requirement of individual concern, it would set aside a condition which is expressly laid down in the Treaty, thus exceeding its jurisdiction. This is however a circular argument. As AG Jacobs observed in *UPA*,[53] and indeed the CFI in its judgment under appeal, there is nothing in the Treaty which dictates that the concept of individual concern should be interpreted so restrictively; that is, that the individual must be differentiated from all other persons: what the Court views as an inescapable constraint imposed by the letter of the Treaty is in fact no more than a constraint imposed by its own preferred interpretation of the provision.

The Court then proceeded to shift the burden of providing an effective remedy to the national legal systems, following its judgment in *UPA*. It stated that the fact that the Commission's contested Regulation applied directly, without intervention by the national authorities, did not mean that a party who was directly concerned by it could only contest its validity if he had first contravened it. It is possible for domestic law to permit an individual directly concerned by a general legislative measure of national law which cannot be directly contested before the courts to seek from the national authorities under that legislation a measure which may itself be contested before the national courts, so that the individual may challenge the legislation indirectly. It is likewise possible that under national law an operator directly concerned by the Commission regulation may seek from the national authorities a measure under that regulation which may be contested before the national court, enabling the operator to challenge the regulation indirectly.[54]

In effect, the Court identifies a gap in the system of judicial protection and requires the national legal systems to fill it, thus preserving the presumed

---

52 See *UPA*, op. cit., paras 37 and 43.
53 See para. 59 of the Opinion.
54 Para. 35.

integrity of the letter of the Treaty. It is however highly doubtful whether the alternative remedy proposed by the ECJ provides a workable solution. In many legal systems, a firm in the position of Jégo-Quéré would find it in practice very difficult to obtain a national act amenable to challenge given that a regulation of the type in issue would not normally require implementation. The success of any such action would be costly, time consuming and highly uncertain.

The judgment of the ECJ is based on an assumption – that indirect challenge in national courts provides an effective alternative – which is simply not valid. The most striking aspect of the judgment is that it is so prescriptive as regards the remedies that should be available in national courts. The Court held that, in accordance with Article 10 EC, it is for the Member States to establish a system of legal remedies and procedures which ensure respect for the right to effective judicial protection and that, therefore, it is for the Member States to provide a remedy in a Jégo-Quéré situation. Ironically, this obligation finds much less of a basis in the letter of the Treaty than the more liberal interpretation of individual concern proposed by the CFI, or AG Jacobs in *UPA*.

Locus standi of individuals is an area where there has been consistent disagreement between the ECJ and the CFI and a higher than average success rate in appeals against decisions of the CFI.[55] The relationship between the two Courts in this area seems to be an uneasy one, with the CFI pressing unsuccessfully for a liberalization of the case law. It is notable that the EU Constitutional Treaty adopted the solution of the CFI in *Jégo-Quéré*.[56] Why then has the ECJ been so reluctant to accept the liberalization of *locus standi*? The following reasons may be given:[57]

1. The ECJ and the CFI are already overburdened by a heavy workload. If *locus standi* was liberalized, that would open the floodgates and the judicial system would be unable to cope. This is particularly so in view of the enlargement of the Union.

---

55 This can be illustrated by reference to the litigation in Case T-32/98 *Nederlandse Antillen v Commission* [2000] ECR II-201, reversed by Case C-142/00 [2003] ECR I-3483; *Jégo-Quéré*, op. cit.; Case T-54/99 *max.mobil Telekommunikation Service GmbH v Commission,* judgment of 30 January 2002, reversed by Case C-141/02 P *Commission v T-Mobile Austria GmbH*, judgment of 22 February 2005; *ARE* case, infra.

56 See Article III-365(4) of the Constitutional Treaty and, for a discussion, T. Tridimas, 'The European Court of Justice and the Draft Constitution: a Supreme Court for the Union?', in T. Tridimas and P. Nebbia (eds), *EU Law for the 21st Century: Rethinking the New Legal Order* (Oxford: Hart Publishing, 2004), pp. 113–41.

57 Op. cit., pp. 123–4.

2. A class of litigants which would benefit particularly from liberalization of standing would be large corporations or associations of undertakings. These would be likely to challenge Community legislative measures which affected their interests adversely even if they had little chance of success on the merits, simply in order to delay the coming into effect of a measure,[58] which would still benefit them financially because it would postpone for a period the regulatory costs of compliance. This further stresses the danger of the proliferation of cases.
3. Apart from those arguments which are costs-based, there is a majoritarian argument. Community legislative measures tend to have a long period of gestation and to be the product of painstaking negotiations conducted by political actors who are directly or indirectly accountable to their electorates. The jurisdiction of the Courts to annul such measures at the instigation of individuals should therefore be restricted.
4. The limited standing of individuals to challenge legislative acts is in conformity with the constitutional traditions of most Member States.
5. Every system of law has mechanisms which seek to restrict undesirable litigation. Common law systems tend to have more liberal rules of standing but this is counterbalanced by the fact that, traditionally, they exercise less rigorous review on the merits. In this light, a restrictive *locus standi* requirement can be seen as a *quid pro quo* for maintaining comparatively strict standards of substantive judicial review.
6. In any event, the system as it currently stands has its own internal economy and works satisfactorily. The right to judicial protection is safeguarded since individuals may challenge the validity of Community acts indirectly before national courts.

These arguments are potent but none of them is without a counter-argument. Suffice it to say here that arguments of costs appear particularly important and one assumes that they must have weighed especially in the policy of the ECJ not to liberalize standing for individuals.

POST-*UPA* DEVELOPMENTS

Although the ECJ had already rejected the invitation to revise its approach to Article 230(4) in *UPA*, applicants continued to invoke the right to an effective

---

[58] For an example of a challenge before a national court, see Case C491/01 *The Queen v Secretary of State for Health ex parte British American Tobacco Ltd* [2002] ECR I-11453.

remedy as an argument in favour of a more liberal interpretation. Such arguments were presented in direct actions against decisions,[59] regulations[60] and even directives.[61] In an attempt to circumvent the *Plaumann* straitjacket, the CFI was also asked to examine the substance before ruling on admissibility.[62] The CFI however reverted to the classic case law and rejected arguments based on the right to an effective remedy on the basis of the reasoning deployed by the ECJ in *UPA*.[63] By way of exception, in two sets of cases, *Pfizer* and *Alpharama*,[64] and *Sony*[65] the application was held to be admissible; but only in *Sony* did the party succeed on the merits.

In *Pfizer* and *Alpharama* the CFI ruled in favour of the applicants on the basis of *Codorniu*. It will be noted that the possibility to use *Codorniu* had cautiously been left open by the CFI in *Jégo-Quéré*.[66] Since both cases essentially shared the same legal and factual background, it suffices to refer to *Alpharama*. The applicant challenged a Council Regulation which withdrew authorization to market, amongst others, an antibiotic of which it was the only manufacturer and the largest supplier.[67] The CFI stated that the fact that, at the

---

59 See e.g. Case T-45/02 *DOW AgroSciences BV* [2003] ECR II-1973; Joint Cases C-346/03 and C-529/03 *Francesco Atzori, Giuseppe Atzeni, Giuseppe Ignazio Boi* [2003] ECR II-6037; Case T-142/03 *Fost Plus VZW*, order of 16 February 2005; Case T-141/03 *Sniace SA*, judgment of 14 April 2005; T-2/04 *Korkmaz v Commission*, order of 30 March 2006.

60 See Case T-231/02 *Gonnelli*, order of 2 April 2004; Case T-391/02 *Bundesverband der Nahrungsmittel*, order of 10 May 2004.

61 Case T-167/02 *Établissements Toulorge* [2003] ECR II-1111; Case T-154/02 *Villiger* [2003] ECR II-1921; Case T-321/02 *Paul Vannieuwenhuyze-Morin*, unpublished, order of 6 May 2003; Case T-213/02 *SNF SA v Commission*, order of 6 September 2004; Case T-196/03 *European Federation for Cosmetic Ingredients*, order of 10 December 2004.

62 T-142/03, *Fost Plus VZW*, op. cit.

63 The ECJ has also reiterated the *UPA* test when it has had occasion to do so, and in doing so has emphasized individuals' entitlement to effective judicial protection of the rights they derive from the Community legal order and Articles 6 and 13 of the ECHR (*UPA*, paras 38 and 39), without however extending its definition of individual concern (see e.g. Case C-229/05P *PKK v Council*, judgment of 18 January 2007, at para. 109, in the unusual context of the ECJ overturning a finding of a lack of standing by the CFI on the question of the legal existence and capacity of the applicant).

64 Case T-13/99 *Pfizer Animal Health v Council* [2002] ECR II-3305; Case T-70/99 *Alpharama v Council* [2002] ECR II-3495.

65 Case T-243/01 *Sony Computer Entertainment LTD v Commission* [2003] ECR II-4189.

66 Op. cit.

67 Regulation 2821/98 amending, as regards withdrawal of the authorization of certain antibiotics, Directive 70/524/EEC concerning additives in feedingstuffs (OJ [1998] L 351/4).

time when the contested Regulation was adopted, the applicant was the only manufacturer and by far the largest supplier in the EU was not in itself capable of distinguishing it from all other traders concerned. According to established case law, the fact that it is possible to determine the number or even the identity of the persons to whom a measure applies does not mean that they must be considered to be individually concerned as long as the measure applies by virtue of an objective legal or factual situation defined by it. However, it found the applicant to be individually concerned because, as the firm first responsible for putting the product into circulation, under the Community rules applicable, it was the only person in a legal position enabling it to obtain authorization to market it. It therefore enjoyed legal safeguards which granted a specific right comparable to the applicant in *Codorniu*. Furthermore, the effect of the contested Regulation was to suspend a procedure which had already been initiated by the applicant for the purpose of obtaining authorization for the antibiotic in question and in the course of which it enjoyed procedural rights. It thus affected the applicant by reason of a legal and factual situation which differentiated it from all other persons.[68]

Alpharama and *Pfizer* do not provide much of an extension to the *Codorniu* exception and reiterate, rather than question, the narrow reading of individual concern. Their distinct feature which enabled the applicants to be successful was that, under the applicable regime, the authorization of a product was linked to the person responsible for putting it into circulation. By contrast, the CFI rejected the action as inadmissible in *Bactria v Commission*[69] as it found no specific link between the product subject to regulation and the applicant. The legal background to that dispute was defined by Directive 98/8, the purpose of which was to establish Community rules for the authorization and placing on the market of biocidal products. The Directive provided that Member States may authorize a biocidal product only if its active substance is listed in the annexes to the Directive and introduced a procedure for inclusion of an active substance into them. The Directive also envisaged a ten year programme for the systematic examination of all active substances already on the market on 14 May 2000. As a result, the Commission adopted a Regulation which required producers to provide the Commission with information on existing active substances and introduced a notification procedure enabling producers and other interested parties to inform the Commission of their wish to request the inclusion of an existing active substance in the annexes to the Directive.

---

[68] *Alpharama*, op. cit., paras 87–90 and 96; and see *Pfizer*, op. cit., paras 93–8 and 104.

[69] Case T-339/00 [2002] ECR II-2287.

The applicant produced and marketed the active substance peracetic acid and biological products containing it. It sought the annulment of the Regulation on the ground that it provided insufficient protection to commercially sensitive information. The CFI rejected the argument that the Regulation applied only to a closed group of operators, namely companies which had placed a biocidal product containing existing active substances on the Community market before 14 May 2000. The Regulation was addressed to all those who have an interest in the identification and notification of existing active substances and biological products and not only operators who placed such a product on the market before 14 May 2000. Given that the very argument of the applicant was that the Regulation caused it harm precisely because it enabled companies not participating in the review process to profit without cost from the notifications made by diligent competitors, the narrow reading of individual concern appeared to lead to lack of judicial protection.

In *Sony Computer Entertainment Europe Ltd.*[70] the applicant sought to challenge a customs tariff classification Regulation which applied to PlayStation®2, a product of which Sony was the sole importer into the Community. Under the established case law, individuals may not normally challenge tariff classification regulations because, despite their apparent specificity, they concern all products of the type described regardless of their individual characteristics and origin, and take effect in relation to all customs authorities in the Community and all importers.[71] The CFI however found that there were special circumstances which made Sony individually concerned. As a result of the contested Regulation, the UK customs authorities had revoked a Binding Tariff Information (BTI) which had been issued before its adoption and which was favourable to Sony. Also, the administrative procedure which led to the adoption of the contested Regulation concerned specifically the tariff classification of the PlayStation®2. No other similar product had been discussed before the Nomenclature Committee as part of that procedure. The applicant was therefore the only undertaking whose legal position was affected by the adoption of the Regulation. Furthermore, a number of considerations showed that, although the contested Regulation was worded in a general and abstract manner, it focused specifically on the classification of the PlayStation®2: it described in detail all of the features of that product and there were no other products with identical features, at least not at the time the contested Regulation entered into force. The description in fact corresponded exactly to the technical specifications of the PlayStation®2 and it was so specific that it could not have applied to any other products.

---

70 See n. 65.

71 See e.g. Case 40/84 *Casteels v Commission* [1985] ECR 667, para. 11.

Sony is the first case where an undertaking has succeeded in annulling a customs classification regulation in a direct action. It is true that the position of the applicant was exceptional and 'hinged on quite particular circumstances'.[72] Still, the case evinces the willingness of the CFI to depart from established case law and might open up the possibility of Article 230(4) being applied more leniently in the area of customs law, as is the case in the areas of anti-dumping, competition law and state aids. An interesting aspect of the case is that the applicant could have challenged the Regulation through a plea of illegality: Sony could have attacked the revocation of the BTI by UK customs on the ground that it was based on an invalid Community act. It opted instead for a direct challenge on the grounds that it was quicker to do so and because 'success in these proceedings would put it in a better financial position'.[73]

STATE AID PROCEEDINGS

A final case that deserves consideration in this context is *Commission v Germany (ARE case)*.[74] The case is important because it provides a further illustration that the CFI is more liberal than the ECJ in granting standing to individuals and also because AG Jacobs proposed a re-assessment of standing in state aid proceedings.

The origins of the case lie in the scheme for the privatization of agricultural land situated in the former East Germany introduced following re-unification. Under the German Compensation Act, certain agricultural land held by the state could be acquired by eligible persons for less than half its market value. The Act gave priority to certain categories of persons, such as those who held a farming lease and the successors to the former cooperatives, provided that they fulfilled two conditions, namely that they were resident in the former German Democratic Republic on 3 October 1990 and had, on 1 October 1996, a long-term lease in respect of certain land owned by the state. By Decision 1999/268, the Commission found the land acquisition scheme to be unlawful state aid insofar as it was tied to the condition of residence and also insofar as the purchase price exceeded the so-called maximum intensity rate; that is, it was available at a discount greater than 35 per cent below the actual value which was applicable under Community law.[75] Following the adoption of the

---

[72] See Case T-243/01 DEP, *Sony Computer Entertainment LTD v Commission*, of 18 March 2005, para. 25.

[73] Case T-243/01 *Sony Computer*, op. cit., para. 55.

[74] See n. 14.

[75] See Council Regulation No. 950/97 on improving the efficiency of agricultural structures, OJ 1997 L 142/1.

Commission's decision, Germany produced an amended law which abolished the condition of residence and fixed the intensity rate at 35 per cent. The draft law was notified to the Commission which, without initiating the review procedure provided for in Article 88(2), authorized the amended aid. ARE, a representative association, sought to challenge the Commission's new decision. The CFI found that ARE was individually concerned in two respects:

First, it held that ARE was entitled to bring the action on behalf of those of its members whose competitive position was affected by the aid. Such members were parties concerned within the meaning of Article 88(2) EC and could therefore have challenged the Commission's decision individually. Secondly, the CFI held that ARE had *locus standi* because its negotiating position was affected by the Commission's decision.

AG Jacobs disagreed with the CFI and the ECJ followed its Advocate General. Recalling its case law, the ECJ drew a distinction between the procedure of Article 88(2) and that of Article 88(3). Where the Commission initiates the formal review procedure of Article 88(2), a competitor may challenge the Commission's decision finding aid compatible with the common market where its market position is substantially affected by the aid.[76]

Where the Commission finds aid to be compatible with the common market at the end of a preliminary examination under Article 88(3), without initiating the formal procedure provided for in Article 88(2), a further distinction is drawn. A person who has the status of a 'party concerned' under Article 88(2) may challenge the Commission's decision in order to enforce the procedural rights available to him under Article 88(2). This includes persons, undertakings or associations whose interests might be affected by the grant of the aid, in particular competing undertakings and trade associations. There is however no need to show that the market position of the applicant has been affected in a substantial manner.[77]

Where, by contrast, the applicant does not merely seek to enforce the procedural rights of Article 88(2) but calls into question the merits of the decision appraising the aid, the mere fact that it may be regarded as concerned within the meaning of Article 88(2) cannot suffice to render the action admissible. It must then demonstrate that it has a particular status within the meaning of the *Plaumann* case law. That applies in particular where the applicant's market

---

[76] See Case 169/84 *Cofaz and Others v Commission* [1986] ECR 391; Case C-406/96 P *Sveriges Betodlares* [*Centralförening*] *and Henrikson v Commission* [1997] ECR I-7531.

[77] Case C-198/91 *Cook v Commission* [1993] ECR I-2487; Case C-225/91 *Matra v Commission* [1993] ECR I-3203; Case C-367/95 P *Commission v Sytraval and Brink's France* [1998] ECR I-1719.

position is substantially affected by the aid to which the decision at issue relates.[78]

In the case in issue, the ECJ held that ARE was seeking to challenge the Commission's decision on substantive grounds but lacked individual concern since it had not been proved that the competitive position of its members was substantially affected by the aid scheme. The CFI had wrongly taken the view that the application of ARE should be construed as criticizing the Commission for failing to initiate the formal review procedure rather than the merits of the decision. The ECJ also rejected the view that ARE was individually concerned because it had participated actively in the formal review procedure leading to the adoption and implementation of the initial Commission decision. Its role was much less significant than that of the applicants in *Van der Kooy* and *CIRFS* where the ECJ had accorded standing to the applicant associations.[79]

In his Opinion, AG Jacobs criticized the case law on *locus standi* in state aid cases as being complex, unsatisfactory and inconsistent.[80] In contrast to his Opinion on *UPA*, AG Jacobs called here for narrowing rather than extending standing. His main points of criticism were as follows. The *Cook* and *Matra* line of case law[81] provided liberal standing to competitors in cases where the Commission decided not to initiate the Article 88(2) procedure to compensate for the fact that the applicant may not have sufficient information to establish individual concern. This however conferred standing to a very wide category of persons, since many could claim that they would have been parties concerned if the Article 88(2) procedure had been initiated. This led in turn to subsequent refinements that made the case law confusing and incoherent. Furthermore, AG Jacobs was not convinced that the more lenient interpretation of *locus standi* in the context of Article 88(3) was justified. He accepted that, because a decision under Article 88(3) is taken at an early stage, a person potentially affected by the proposed aid might have little information about its likely effect and therefore might find it difficult to establish individual concern. He considered however that in the course of the proceedings before the CFI sufficient information would be produced by the Commission and, possibly, by the Member States concerned to enable the Court to decide on the existence of individual concern. In the view of the Advocate General, the best solution would be to apply in all cases where an applicant challenges a decision under Article 88(3) the test of direct and individual concern irrespective

---

78 See *ARE*, op. cit., para. 37 and also *Cofaz and Others v Commission*, op. cit., paras 22–25; *Sveriges*, op. cit., para. 45.

79 Joined Cases 67/85, 68/85 and 70/85 *Van der Kooy and Others v Commission* [1988] ECR 219; Case C-313/90 *CIRFS and Others v Commission* [1993] ECR I-1125.

80 See paras 138–42 of the Opinion.

81 Op. cit.

of the grounds on which the action is brought. The test of individual concern however should not be interpreted as narrowly as it was in *Plaumann* but in accordance with the broader approach taken in relation to competition and anti-dumping proceedings.[82]

CONCLUSION

The Opinion of AG Jacobs in *UPA* and the judgment of the CFI in *Jégo-Quéré* generated the hope that the ECJ would re-consider the much criticized narrow construction of individual concern. But the ECJ reiterated *Plaumann*, signalling the 'return of Euridice'. Both the CFI and Advocate General Jacobs offered progressive interpretations of individual concern, facilitating access to justice for private applicants. Post-*UPA* case law has developed within the constraints of *Codorniu* but this remains an area where the CFI and the ECJ frequently disagree, with the former favouring a less strict adherence to *Plaumann*. Although there are powerful arguments, mainly based on cost considerations, which would favour limiting the standing of individuals to challenge truly legislative acts, the current over-restrictive interpretation of Article 230(4) poses an obstacle to the right to judicial protection and is liable to cause injustice. The Constitutional Treaty extended *locus standi* somewhat, and it is a pity that in its judgment in *Jégo-Quéré* the ECJ declined the opportunity to anticipate this development. The Court shows no appetite for a quantum leap so it seems that, at least in this area, and unlike the wider field of fundamental rights, the legacy of Advocate General Jacobs will remain that of a dissident.

---

82 This line of reasoning however is not thoroughly persuasive. It is submitted that the protection of the rights of the applicant should not be left to the information that the Commission, being the opposite party in the litigation, might be required to produce in the proceedings. In any event, the ensuing argumentation as to whether the applicant is able to prove *locus standi* will be time consuming and may lead to further nuances and inconsistencies in the case law. Whilst acknowledging the need for simplicity, the present authors take the view that standing in state aid cases should be liberal rather than strict.

4. Links with national courts

Sir John Mummery[1]

THEME

'Links' normally conjure up the image of a golf course on sandy dunes close to the estuaries and the incoming tides, which, for Lord Denning, were metaphors of the relationship of English law with the European Community law.[2] The *Oxford English Dictionary* offers other examples of English usage and what better than 'links' to describe 'the divisions in a string of sausages or black puddings'?

The links of the European Community with national courts are *not* of the sausage or black pudding sort. In essence the links are informal and formal channels of communication serving the common purpose of constructive and structured judicial conversation and co-operation between national courts and the European Court of Justice. The shared goal is making sense of this uniquely ambitious legal order and, above all, making it work.

National courts decide cases. When it is necessary to do so, they ask the Court of Justice to supply them with authoritative rulings on the interpretation of Community law for them to use in deciding cases in their own legal systems.[3] The realistic aim is not perfection, which is impossible, but an acceptable level of uniformity in the interpretation of Community law and its local application and enforcement by the national courts in Member States.

INFORMAL LINKS

My experience of informal and formal links with the European Court of Justice spans the last 25 years, first as a barrister, then as a first instance judge and for the last 10 years as an appellate judge.

---

1 The Rt Hon. Lord Justice Mummery has been a Lord Justice of Appeal in the Court of Appeal for England and Wales since 1996.

2 *H.P. Bulmer Ltd v J. Bollinger SA* [1974] Ch. 401 at 418.

3 Article 234 EC.

The informal links are less well known than the formal links described in the legal texts, but they should be better known and understood. It is at gatherings like the conference for Sir Francis Jacobs on 30 June 2006 that their real and enduring value can be appreciated. The value and place of informal links between participants in different legal systems are liable to be underestimated by those responsible for creating and operating institutions and by critical observers of them. In our national courts Sir Francis Jacobs, whose contribution to European Community law over the last 18 years is celebrated in this collection of conference papers, and his gifted colleagues in Luxembourg have been the strongest links of all with the Court of Justice. For the judiciary, the legal profession and the academic community, who make a particularly important contribution to the understanding and development of this area of the law, they are the human face of the European Community legal order. What links can be stronger than those with people you know and trust? They are the friendly faces of otherwise faceless institutions, impersonal laws and hostile heaps of paper.

Francis Jacobs and I first met in litigation. We were both junior counsel for the Crown, led by Sam Stamler QC, in the state aids case of *R. v HM Attorney General ex parte ICI*[4] in the mid-1980s. I had forgotten, until Francis reminded me at the conference, that in my first case in the Court of Justice he was on the other side. Twenty-five years ago, in May 1981, the Court of Justice heard arguments on a reference in a tax case involving an accountant MEP, Lord Bruce of Donington,[5] who objected to the Inland Revenue's tax treatment of his travelling expenses to and from Strasbourg. Francis Jacobs was counsel for the taxpayer. I was counsel for the United Kingdom. Needless to say he won the case.

Links with Community law as counsel ended in 1989 on a high note. I was junior counsel in *Factortame*[6] from the start and for long enough, with Sir Nicholas Lyell QC (then Attorney General), John Laws (then the common law Treasury Devil) and Christopher Vajda, to be awarded a commemorative Factortame tie. On the other side were David Vaughan QC and Gerald Barling. Needless to say, they won in the end, many years later, by which time I was in the Court of Appeal and disqualified from hearing the appeals in *Factortame*.[7]

In our system links with national courts include the Bar, not just office holders in the national judiciary. The independence of the Bar, its high professional

4 *R. v Attorney General ex p. ICI* [1987] 1 CMLR 72.

5 Case 208/80 *Lord Bruce of Donington* [1981] ECR 2205.

6 *R. v Secretary of State for Transport ex parte Factortame (Factortame I)*, CA [1989] 2 CMLR 353.

7 *R v Secretary of State for Transport ex parte Factortame (Factortame IV)*, CA [1998] EuLR 457.

standards and its specialization in the skills of advocacy, as well as in substantive subjects such as competition law, intellectual property, tax and employment law, are vital to the ability of the courts to grapple with changing and challenging areas of the law like Community law.

As a judge since 1989, I have had more than my fair share of Community law in the form of cases and references, particularly on employment law – mainly equal treatment, equal pay, discrimination and TUPE and labour relations generally – VAT, social security law, intellectual property, parallel imports and competition law. I have refused to make references and decided points of Community law. I have made references and then acted on the rulings received. It is for others to decide whether judges like me have over-referred or under-referred.

I am vulnerable to the criticism that I have not always applied the correct legal criteria for making references. One of my criteria, not found in the authorities, is that, if I cannot understand the case, then I cannot have the requisite degree of confidence to decide it myself, and off to Luxembourg it goes.

Over the years I have also enjoyed and valued the informal judicial visits to Luxembourg on three or four occasions, brilliantly and generously hosted by Sir David Edward, Francis, Sir Christopher Bellamy and Nicholas Forwood QC and their colleagues in Luxembourg. I have also participated in the activities of professional associations, such as the United Kingdom Association for European Law (UKAEL) and the Bar European Group, who, in addition to their activities here, meet annually with local judges and lawyers in a different part of the expanding Community, Slovenia in 2006 and Rome for the 50 year celebrations in 2007.

Like the rest of you I have greatly benefited for almost the whole of my life in the law from the wisdom and unique European experience of Lord Slynn of Hadley, who is the Honorary Life President of UKAEL, and who chaired the opening session at the Conference on 'Eighteen Years of Community Law' in honour of Sir Francis Jacobs on 30 June 2006.

To sum up on informal links: all sorts of connections are necessary to make a system of the scale and complexity of the Community legal order work. The value of the personal element and the human factor should not be underestimated. Links do not just consist of formal procedures, Article 234 references, Advocate Generals' opinions and judgments of the Court of Justice. Forging informal links is essential to promote co-operation, to increase practical understanding of the way it all works and to give a proper sense of direction to the whole Community project.

I would add that the United Kingdom has been fortunate in the high judicial abilities and personal qualities of those appointed to the Community Courts. From the very beginning the contribution of the UK judges in Luxembourg has enhanced the standing of the UK in the Community and in the Court of Justice, surely one of the most effective Community institutions. It has established strong links and good relations with the UK courts, both on an institutional and on a personal basis.

What is required of the occupants of judicial office in a legal order like the European Community is not the remoteness and aloofness often associated with judicial office, but the skills and aptitude of good teachers and educators and the charm, tact and persuasiveness of skilled diplomats. Good teachers dispel the ignorance and stupidity in which suspicion flourishes and they replace it with knowledge, understanding and wisdom. Education can take place formally through the judgments and informally through writings, talks, lectures and meetings. Then add a generous helping of diplomacy for good measure and the wheels run more smoothly.

FORMAL LINKS

Next the formal links with national courts. I will deal very briefly with three areas: the reception of Community law, the division of functions between the Court of Justice and national courts, and the procedure for references by national courts to the Court of Justice.

Reception

The courts have received the basic doctrines of Community law into English law and litigation. They have adapted well to the new constitutional arrangements and to their role in them. They have been remarkably resilient and free of dogmatism in accommodating the changes. The basic elements of Community law – its supremacy, its doctrines of direct effect and proportionality and its principles of purposive interpretation – are all well understood and frequently applied by the courts via the European Communities Act 1972 that links domestic law with European Community law. The breakthroughs were made in a series of leading cases in the House of Lords: in particular, *Litster*,[8] *EOC*,[9] and *Factortame*.[10]

---

8 *Litster v Forth Dry Dock and Engineering Co. Ltd* [1990] 1 AC 546.

9 *R. v Secretary of State for Employment ex parte Equal Opportunities Commission* [1994] 1 AC 1.

10 *R. v Secretary of State for Transport ex parte Factortame (Factortame I)*, HL(1) [1990] 2 AC 85; *R. v Secretary of State for Transport ex parte Factortame (Factortame I)*, HL(2) [1991] 1 AC 603; *R. v Secretary of State for Transport ex parte Factortame (Factortame IV)*, HL [2000] EuLR 40. (The numbering of the different *Factortame* cases and decisions used here is taken from D. Vaughan, 'The *Factortame* saga', *The European Advocate* (Winter edition, 2005–2006).)

This has been achieved with relatively less fuss than was anticipated in the heated debates about the impact on national and parliamentary sovereignty, entrenched legislation, the status of treaties, dualist theories, implied repeal, and so on.

Modesty is a judicial virtue compatible with independence and impartiality. Enthusiasm is not. The right tone has been struck by the courts in finding pragmatic solutions for legal problems as and when they arise in the cases. The courts have proved quite adept at methods of interpretation appropriate to a different legislative style which survives the transposition of directives into national law. On the whole, conflict and incompatibility have been avoided.

There are even some signs of more subtle influences at work: working cautious cross-fertilization in the grounds for judicial review; in the canons of statutory construction; in styles of judgment; in the development in some courts of the single judgment; in the more generous use of legal materials; in greater use of written procedures and in court control over the form and length of oral hearings. It is truly remarkable what has been achieved in less than a generation, in the time that Francis Jacobs has spent as Advocate General in Luxembourg.

Division of Functions

The allocation of functions between the national courts and the Court of Justice is clear enough to be workable by well-disposed and sensible people, but not so inflexible as to obstruct development of the relationship. It has not led to any judicial clash or political crisis. It should not do so, as the national courts and the Court of Justice are not in competition with one another. Each is master in its own sphere and each complements the other. The Court of Justice rules on the interpretation and validity of Community law, but not on questions of national law. It respects the sphere of the national courts and has not sought to dominate the national courts.

The national courts apply Community and national law to the facts found by them, decide questions of the compatibility of national law and Community law, and are responsible for enforcing the law within their own countries.

Article 234 EC References

The system by which the Court of Justice receives specific requests, not cases, from national courts and by which the national courts receive rulings for them to apply, not final judgments on the merits of the case, from the Court of Justice, works reasonably well. It is a profitable dialogue. UK courts and tribunals now have enough confidence to decide some points for themselves in the light of the growing body of jurisprudence, but they are not so presumptuous as to reject the assistance of the Court of Justice as and when they need it.

There are problems: delay, aggravated by differences in language and legal traditions and by enlargement; sometimes there is difficulty in telling the difference between the interpretation of the law and the application of it to deciding the case. The system works least well when the Court of Justice gives decisions which are too concrete, factual and interventionist, appearing to control the outcome of the particular case in the national courts.

However, the reference system is infinitely preferable to the alternative of a system of appeals. It is quite a good sandwich, with the national court supplying the slices of bread at the beginning and the end of the case and the Court of Justice making some input into the filling. A centralized system of appeals from national courts would be too ambitious to be practicable. It would be perceived as extending too much control over the courts of Member States. In any case, the potential increase in the workload makes it an impracticable proposition. It would be even more crushing and unmanageable than under the Article 234 reference regime.

Indeed, within the reference system a good case can be made for the Court to receive fewer references from national courts and to move to a more supervisory or oversight role. It could concentrate more on the more general decisions to be made on legal policy and not be obliged to take every reference. The Court of Justice could and should decline jurisdiction, without giving offence to the referring court, where the answer has already been given, or where the point is simply not significant enough to require a decision of the Court of Justice, or the point raised is irrelevant to the resolution of the case.

A CASE STUDY: EC TRADE MARK LAW

Now for some concrete detail, without which a judge begins to feel uncomfortable. This is not the place for a detailed review of formal links. I am not the right person even to attempt it. Instead, I will take just one example from a very specialized area of law in order to illustrate a few problematic aspects of the links between national courts, the Court of Justice and the development of European Community law.

Last year saw the publication of the most recent and the most European edition of one of the oldest, most respected and widely used English legal textbooks on intellectual property – the 14th edition of *Kerly's Law of Trade Marks and Trade Names* (2005).[11] The Preface, the Foreword and the first few chapters tell the reader quite a lot about links with national courts.

---

11 D. Kitchin, D. Llewelyn, J. Mellor, R. Meade, T. Moody-Stuart and D. Keeling, *Kerly's Law of Trade Marks and Trade Names* (London: Sweet & Maxwell, 14th edn, 2005).

The first edition was by D.M. Kerly in 1894. For 100 years the book dealt only with English law on this topic. No other trade mark law really mattered. All that changed with the advent of the Trade Marks Directive,[12] the Trade Marks Act 1994 implementing the Directive and the Community Trade Marks Regulation[13] for a new type of trade mark, a Community trade mark.

The Editor in Chief of the current edition is Mr Justice Kitchin, the newest Intellectual Property judge on the High Court Bench. The Consulting Editor, Lord Justice Jacob, wrote the Preface for the new edition. It contains some cogent criticisms of the impact of Community law on UK trade mark law. Wedged between the title page and the Preface is the Foreword contributed by Advocate General Jacobs.

The informal links between national courts and the Court of Justice which I have described could hardly be closer or more evident. A large part of the Foreword answers the criticisms of Community law in the Preface. There, within the opening pages of an English legal text book, is incontrovertible proof of the vitality and proximity of the links with national courts. Both first instance and appellate judges in the national courts and an Advocate General of the Court of Justice attempt to come to grips with the impact of Community law and the interpretive decisions of the Court of Justice and the Court of First Instance on trade mark law applied and enforced in national courts.

Perspective of National Courts

The signal from the specialist national judges in the Preface and in the text (principally Chapters 1 and 2) is that not much happened in the law of trade marks until the advent of the EU Directive and Regulation 40/94; now a lot has happened very quickly, not all of it for the better. Five substantial criticisms are made of the new Community trade mark law in the Directive and the Regulation and of the decisions of the Community courts, both the Court of Justice and the Court of First Instance, on their interpretation. They illustrate the kind of constructive dialogue which epitomizes the links between the Community Courts and the national courts.

The points made about trade mark law and the Community are broadly similar to points made on other areas of Community law interpreted and administered by English courts and which are the subject of references under Article 234 of the Treaty. They indicate weaknesses and suggest improvements.

---

12 Directive 89/104/EEC (OJ 1989 L40/1).

13 Council Regulation (EC) No. 40/94 of 20 December 1993 (OJ 1994 No. L 11/1).

Broadly speaking the national courts would prefer trade mark solutions which would produce less complexity, more certainty and less litigation, while making more use of national experience and specialist expertise:

1. Complexity

The law on almost every topic affected by the European Community has become more complicated. Complexity is prejudicial to the effectiveness of the national legal systems and to the links between them and the Community. The efforts of all concerned should be to make laws simpler as far as possible.

Some complexity is inevitable, because the problems addressed by the law are increasingly complex, but there is avoidable complexity. For example, trade mark law has been made more complicated for the courts and for the users by the way in which the UK legislation (the Trade Marks Act 1994) has implemented the Trade Marks Directive of 1988, re-numbering it and partly re-writing it. Why? Is it for a legal reason or for a political reason or what? It would be better to go straight to the Directive, which is what Jacob LJ does in the national courts, just as if he were Jacobs AG in the Court of Justice.[14]

2. Uncertainty

Trade mark law has become more uncertain and less precise in fundamental respects, such as in what a trade mark is, what it is for and what is meant by such fundamental characteristics as 'distinctiveness'. There are sometimes real difficulties in extracting meaning and sense from the Trade Marks Directive and the Trade Mark Regulation and from the general interpretations of them by the Court of Justice when seeking to apply them to the facts of particular cases.

In a different area I predict that considerable problems will arise from the Employment Equality (Age) Regulations 2006[15] implementing the Framework Directive[16] on age discrimination with its vague requirements that the treatment of those affected must be a proportionate means of achieving a legitimate aim. This style of legislation tends to undermine the authority of the law and the rule of law, because it is too vague to predict what is prohibited by law and what is permitted by it. How can a law or the Law be respected and obeyed if it is difficult to know what it is? The citizen is entitled to have 'fair warning' of the law which may be enforced against him. A law which increasingly needs judges as

---

14 Confusing methodology is not an isolated instance. The same problem arose with the transposition of the Acquired Rights Directive (77/187/EEC) into the Transfer of Undertakings (Protection of Employment) Regulations 1981.

15 S.I. 2006/2408.

16 Council Directive 2000/78/EC of 27 November 2000 establishing a general framework for equal treatment in employment (OJ 2000 L 303/16).

'law detectors' is of decreasing practical value to the everyday users, whose activities it is intended to regulate.

Recent long-running cases on the registrability of shape marks and of word marks, such as advertising slogans, illustrate the increase in the uncertainty of the fundamentals of trade mark law.

I have encountered similar criticisms of the impact of Community law on the protection of employees during a merger or takeover and in numerous cases of contracting-out and outsourcing and in the field of the free movement of services.

The recent ruling in the case of *Yvonne Watts v Bedford Primary Care Trust*[17] on the free movement of health services is an example. On a reference from the English courts, the Court of Justice ruled that the NHS was liable to refund patients the cost (£3,900) of foreign medical treatment (hip replacement surgery in France) where there is 'undue delay' in the provision of treatment under the NHS. This is a new law of public liability to fund cross-border treatment, bypassing the national waiting list. The ruling has been described as a 'vaguely worded interference' in the complex area of medical treatment and priorities in patient care in a Member State.[18]

I am inclined to agree. The interpretation and application of the concept of 'undue delay' and of 'what is acceptable in the light of an objective medical assessment of the patient's clinical needs' (the degree of pain, the nature of the patient's disability, and so on) by national courts in individual cases promises much work for them, as well as for medical and legal practitioners. Vaguely worded criteria invite protracted legal wrangling that has little to do with the development of national healthcare policy and the improvement of delivery of healthcare to patients. Doctors and NHS administrators will be second guessing lawyers and vice-versa. Is there really a European health market? Is this ruling in the long-term interests of the sick? Will patients generally come first? Has judicial intervention in medicine really improved the position or helped to solve the underlying problems?

I know that there are jurists and others who think that the belief in legal certainty is an infantile delusion and that certainty is not the paramount goal or consideration in a legal system. I agree up to a point. I also appreciate the difficulties of struggling with the ambivalences of judicial power. Judicial decisions, especially those at a high degree of generality, are easy targets for those who fire from safe positions and do not have the burden of responsibilities of those who are entrusted with public power. Laws are inevitably general. The circumstances of cases are invariably particular. The world is

---

[17] Case C-372/04 *R. (Watts) v Bedford Primary Care Trust*, judgment 16 May 2006.

[18] *The Times*, 'Unhealthy law', 17 May 2006.

incurably uncertain. The application of the general to the particular in a changing world necessarily involves a degree of uncertainty.

What I am against, however, is avoidable uncertainty and unpredictability, the increase of it accompanied by the growing judicialization of more and more issues that are ill-suited to resolution by adversarial procedures and judicial processes. The result is instability, which undermines the authority of the law and the society it exists to serve. It even makes it difficult to change the law because of the lack of certainty as to what the law is. A basic core of certainty is necessary for a law and a legal system to function, even to exist. People must be able to know what the law is so that they can arrange their affairs on the basis that the legal consequences of one's actions are predictable.

3. Neglect of national experience

Part of this problem is not the fault of the Court of Justice. The complaint is that the content of the Trade Marks Directive shows a lack of attention to the lessons of national experience. It ignores a century of experience of the laws of Member States in dealing with trade mark problems, such as what is meant by 'distinctive' and by 'use'. National experiences may differ, but they can provide useful lessons that serve as foundations on which to build and develop the law. Of course, law must adapt to change, but the changes should be made in the light of experience and for valid reasons.

Our increasingly hurried society cuts itself off more and more from the past and sometimes displays arrogance and ignorance, and a lack of respect and humility in the face of the lessons of accumulated experience. It also tends to ignore the long-term perspective. Laws, like people, should be valued for what they have accomplished and for the experience gained, even if it is negative in some respects. There is a tendency, pushed forward by political and business agendas, to value experiment at the expense of experience, to be over-optimistic and short-term about the potential of untried laws and what might be achieved by them in the long term. This does not always have a healthy effect on the development of the law or on the wider social order. You can underestimate the importance not just of people, history and geography but of traditions and traditional concepts of law, justice and national and local cultural identity, which may lead to disillusionment with remote legislators and courts.

4. Litigation

These defects are bound to lead to an increase in complex multi-layered litigation, both on references from the national courts of Member States and on appeal from the OHIM[19] to the Court of First Instance and then the Court of

19 The Office of Harmonization for the Internal Market (OHIM) registers the Community Trade Mark in the European Union.

Justice. Even the decided cases have not made the law sufficiently certain for the needs of industry. There are inconsistencies in the decisions. Jacob LJ describes the guidance from the Court of Justice as 'less than perfect'. Knowing that perfection in human affairs is impossible, I would say 'less than helpful' in some cases.

5. Lack of specialist expertise

Jacob LJ attributes the proliferation of litigation in part to lack of expertise and relevant experience on the part of the Community judges in a subject full of pitfalls, ambiguities and complex concepts. In the UK the patent court is a specialist court supported by a specialist Bar and specialist firms of solicitors and patent agents. The same is true of other areas such as competition law, tax law and employment law. They all have their specialist tribunals and practitioners. Specialists have their weaknesses, but their strengths should not be neglected by those responsible for making and interpreting the law.

Problem of Change

One should add the problem of change. It takes too long to amend Community legislation. I will take the example of the TUPE Regulations 2006,[20] which have recently replaced the 1981 Regulations. It took nearly five years to implement the underlying Directive 2001/23/EC.

Response to Criticisms

Anticipating some of the said criticisms in the Preface to Kerly, Sir Francis Jacobs makes valid points in his Foreword about the general problems of linking the Community, its law and institutions with national legal systems and national courts and the Court of Justice. Identifying and understanding the problems is obviously the first step to finding solutions and improving the situation.

1. Different legislative styles

As the Trade Marks Directive and the Trade Mark Regulation are broadly framed, they will often call for interpretation by references from the national

---

[20] The Transfer of Undertakings (Protection of Employment) Regulations 2006 (SI 2006/246) revoked the Transfer of Undertakings (Protection of Employment) Regulations 1981 (SI 1981/1794) – commonly known as the TUPE Regulations – and implemented Council Directive 2001/23/EC on the approximation of the laws of the Member States relating to the safeguarding of employees' rights in the event of transfers of undertakings or businesses, which had in turn replaced Council Directive 77/187/EEC, as amended.

court or, in the case of Community marks, from the Board of Appeals to the Court of First Instance and the Court of Justice. Rulings are necessary to attain uniformity, but they add to the expense and delays of litigation and to the unpredictability of outcome, which is not good for business.

2. Different principles of interpretation

The principles of interpretation applied by the Court of First Instance and Court of Justice may differ from those traditionally applied in national courts, taking account of a wider range of non-legislative materials. This factor increases the references and the uncertainty.

3. Need for uniformity of interpretation

The Community Courts are best placed to resolve points of principle in the interpretation of the directive and the Regulations.

4. Awareness of criticisms

Despite criticisms of its decisions by some practitioners and national judges, there is a high level of appreciation for the main lines of the case law.

5. Need for national adjustment

It takes two to achieve co-operation. National courts and practitioners are adjusting to the Community dimension and recognize that past practice may have to be re-considered.

6. Increase in experience and response to criticism

For their part the Community Courts are still learning from experience and reaction in confronting new issues. Sir Francis recognizes that there are areas in which criticism is both justified and necessary. The overall message is that there has to be revision, rethinking, re-structuring and reflection about the direction of the law all round.

TENTATIVE CONCLUSIONS

The Preface and the Foreword in Kerly illustrate a lot of what is good about the links between the Courts of the European Community and the courts of the Member States: a continuing conversation in which the participants treat each other as equals or at least as worthy of equal respect in an open, courteous, self-critical way.

As I have mentioned, the informal links can be just as important as the formal links: in the exchange of views, the increase of understanding, and the promotion of trust between the institutions and the people in them.

As a modest contribution to the debate on links with national courts I would make two positive general points:

1. Sound Structure

The links between the Community Courts and the national courts are central to the structure of the entire Community project. The basic structure is strong and sound. It has withstood many pressures inherent in such a project and in its expansion.

Tribute should be paid to the architects of the Community, who hit on the brilliant notion of having laws and decisions made at a trans-national Community level, without there being a supra-national state, and then getting them implemented by agreement through the national courts and authorities in the Member States, to whose laws, courts and enforcement bodies its citizens owe loyalty and a duty of obedience. This structure has enabled the Court of Justice to emerge in an indirect and rather imprecise way, keeping a relatively low profile in the Member States into which its decisions are received.

Remarkably it has avoided divisive and damaging doctrinal disputes. It has not attracted any real effective political or popular opposition. The doctrines developed by the Court of the supremacy of Community law, direct effect and unifying principles of interpretation have contributed to what is a truly amazing achievement for the judges of a multinational court.

2. Wholesome Ambivalence

Realistically a degree of ambivalence on the part of national courts in their links with the Court of Justice must be recognized. National courts are naturally inclined to be ambivalent about enforcing laws made outside national boundaries, drafted in an unfamiliar style, interpreted under different rules, and intended to be uniform in many countries communicating in foreign languages and having a wide range of legal traditions. The ambivalence is wholesome. It is the right judicial attitude to adopt. Enthusiasm and scepticism are not on the judicial agenda, which has never been better expressed as no more and no less than the form of the judicial oath.

The European Union is a very ambitious legal enterprise which requires new approaches and demands changes in the way we think about law, with continuing and due respect for the value of national legal traditions, methods and experience, which should be observed.

A POSTSCRIPT ON FAILED LAWS WITH NO LINKS

The key point which I hope emerges from this chapter is that both informal human links and carefully structured formal links are absolutely crucial to the working of the Community legal order. Laws and legal institutions, national and supra-national, need human and institutional links to join them up and to make them work. Without links between the people who want the law to work and who know how to make it work – that is, people like Sir Francis Jacobs – the law will simply not work. You will have failed laws.

If this fact is not self-evident, the point can be made good from an obscure corner of medieval legal history. A recent monograph on sumptuary law in Italy from 1200 to 1500 written by Catherine Killerby,[21] covers a topic that, although recondite, has lessons for all lawmakers, judges and lawyers, even for politicians and economists, who entertain extravagant ideas about what law can achieve.

In a 300 year period over 300 sumptuary laws were passed in medieval Italy criminalizing extravagant expenditure. They legislated against luxury, aiming to prevent the dissipation of capital by the conversion into vanities and frippery. From our perspective they seem to be pointless, sexist laws directed at lavish spending on female 'bling'.

There were even 'Proclamations on Apparel' in Tudor England designed to regulate expenditure on clothing and food, partly (being England) to mark class distinctions, keeping people in their place, and partly to moderate extravagance. The laws soon became obsolete and were all repealed at the beginning of the 17th century.

Laws of this kind were as doomed to failure as the Prohibition laws in the United States of America 500 years later. The economic and commercial reality was that handsome profits could be made and capital could be accumulated from the production of luxuries for the shoppers of medieval Italy. Conspicuous consumption might have been seen by some as sinful on certain occasions, but industrious production of luxury and designer items came to be seen as blessed and approved by God. The result was that the sumptuary laws were mostly talk and not much action. They were ignored by contemporaries and ridiculed by posterity. They never worked. They never stood a chance of working in practice. They were never enforced. There was no will to enforce them. They were unenforceable. The result was centuries of conflict, compromise and ultimate inevitable failure.

The laws were impossible to execute, despite provisions for detailed guidelines on sanctions and penalties. Enforcement and effectiveness depended on

---

21 C. Killerby, *Sumptuary Law in Italy 1200–1500* (Oxford: OUP, 2002).

co-operation from several quarters. The co-operation and the links were non-existent. Noone was willing to take on responsibility for enforcing the laws and there was no realistic means of enforcing them. There were provisions for confiscation, but no machinery providing the means as to who could confiscate and how confiscation was to be made. There was no clear legislative policy and no economic incentive or political will to enforce them.

Law was simply not an appropriate way of controlling the consumption of luxury consumable items like fashion and jewellery. The law was too general in its terms and public and official attitudes towards it were ambivalent. To be enforced it needed to be more specific, but that was impracticable because the target, the infinite forms of excess and fashion, constantly changed, as fashion still does, and the law could not keep up with the 'spend, spend, spend' of the fashion victims of medieval Italy.

Yet, astonishing as it may seem, this futile set of laws went on being made century after century, more as a set of ideals and aspirations to ease social tension than as enforceable laws. Symbolic reasons – religious, social and political – seemed to serve some purpose. There is, of course, a serious point in this strange example of failed laws. The links necessary for the legal efficacy of the sumptuary laws were quite simply not there.

The links we have been considering in this chapter are crucial. The truth is that we need one another. These links are an expression of the need for one another in an effective legal order, whether national or supra-national. The national courts are essential for finding facts and for applying and enforcing the law. They are also responsible for seeing that references are made to the Court of Justice in appropriate cases. The Court of Justice is in its turn essential as the ultimate source of authoritative guidance on the interpretation of the laws to be enforced. This depends on the co-operation of national courts for case referrals.

If laws are to be more than just political talk, aspiration and gesture, there must be strong human and institutional links and resources for that purpose: education and diplomacy in a two-way process with a view to co-operation and action. Vital formal and informal links, like old friendships, need constantly to be kept in good repair to make law work. Without the links laws become increasingly remote from the reality of the people whose conduct is to be regulated by them. Laws imposed from on high by institutions with no local links to make them effective will lack credibility and, in the long run, will become failed laws, ignored by contemporaries and ridiculed by posterity.

5. Competition law

Richard Whish[1]

INTRODUCTION[2]

In his remarkable career as Advocate General at the European Court of Justice ('the ECJ'), Sir Francis Jacobs delivered Opinions on many aspects of Community law. Amongst those Opinions were many in the field of competition law – I believe the number to be 20 – beginning with *Ministère Public v Jean-Louis Tournier*[3] on 26 May 1989 and ending with *JCB Service v Commission*[4] on 15 December 2005. The Opinion in *JCB* was the final one that Sir Francis delivered to the ECJ. It is rather interesting to look at these two cases, separated by a period of more than 16 years, before examining in greater depth the contribution that Sir Francis has made to the development of the competition law of the Community during his time at the ECJ.

Ministère Public v Jean-Louis Tournier

In *Ministère Public v Jean-Louis Tournier*[5] complex issues in relation to the activities of copyright management societies fell to be considered, including the compatibility with Article 81 EC of reciprocal agreements between such societies for the management of each others' repertoires in their respective territories; the application of Article 82 EC to the 'global' licence which SACEM, the society in question, granted to discothèques, irrespective of the type or number of musical works actually used by them; and the difficult question of how to determine whether the fees charged by SACEM were excessive. On this last point, we often say in 2006 that there is little jurisprudence on what is meant by an excessive price under Article 82; there was much less known on this subject in 1989.

---

[1] Professor of Law, King's College, London.

[2] I would like to acknowledge the invaluable help of Dimitris Mourkas, my research assistant at the Centre of European Law, King's College, London.

[3] Case 395/87 [1989] ECR I-2521, [1991] 4 CMLR 248.

[4] Case C-167/04 [2006] ECR I-0000, judgment of 21 September 2006.

[5] See n. 3 above.

Two points in the Opinion in *Ministère Public* particularly struck me on re-reading it. First, the Advocate General noted that 'it should be stated at the outset that this is no ordinary dominant position'.

SACEM enjoyed 'a near-absolute freedom of action' and there was 'a clear inequality of bargaining power as between SACEM and the discothèques'. This sounds very like a reference to so-called 'super-dominance', long before that expression started to be used in discussions of competition law.[6] The Advocate General noted that SACEM's very strong position on the market did not in itself point to the existence of an abuse; nor did it require a higher standard of conduct from SACEM than from other dominant firms. However, SACEM's position did 'point to the need for a particularly stringent examination by the national courts of the justification for the practices alleged to be abusive'.

It can be imagined that DG COMP, the Directorate of the European Commission responsible for competition policy, as well as the national competition authorities of the Member States, would also take into account the extent of a firm's market power – in particular its proximity to absolute monopoly – when deciding, as a matter of prioritization, which cases to select for investigation and prosecution.

A second point about the Opinion in *Ministère Public* is that the Advocate General, when discussing the issue of the 'global' licence, referred to jurisprudence in the US on this subject, where it had been established that a 'rule of reason' rather than a *per se* approach should be taken to global licensing, so that a balance could be achieved between the effective management of copyright on the one hand and the oppressive conduct towards customers on the other. This willingness to invoke experience from other jurisdictions was a most welcome feature of Sir Francis's Opinions, and was particularly important in his Opinion on so-called 'essential facilities' in the *Bronner* case, discussed below. It would have been most regrettable if the ECJ had not had available to it the rich jurisprudence of the US courts in antitrust matters deriving from the provisions of the Sherman Act of 1890 when deciding novel cases under Community competition law.

It is interesting to note in passing that DG COMP adopted its first decision under Article 82 – in 1971 – in a case concerning a copyright management society, *GEMA I*,[7] and that it remains very active in the area, having adopted

---

6 See e.g. Case No. 1000/1/1/01 *Napp Pharmaceutical Holdings Ltd v Director General of Fair Trading* [2002] CAT 1, [2002] CompAR 13, para. 219, where the Competition Appeal Tribunal of the UK recognized, when applying the domestic equivalent of Article 82 EC, that certain firms may be 'super-dominant', with the result that the 'special responsibility' that they bear may be particularly onerous.

7 *GEMA I v Commission* OJ [1971] L 134/15, [1971] CMLR D35.

two commitment decisions under Article 9 of the Modernisation Regulation in the last year,[8] and having sent a statement of objections to the International Confederation of Societies of Authors and Composers (CISAC) on 7 February 2006.[9]

JCB Service v Commission

In *JCB Service v Commission*[10] JCB appealed against a judgment of the Court of First Instance (CFI)[11] substantially upholding a decision of the Commission imposing a fine on JCB for various infringements of Article 81 in its distribution arrangements, including restrictions on passive sales by authorized distributors and the fixing of discounts and resale prices. The Advocate General dismissed JCB's arguments in their entirety, noting that, to a large extent, JCB was asking the ECJ to review facts and assess evidence, which is beyond the scope of its jurisdiction in appeals on points of law from the CFI. The Advocate General agreed with the Commission's cross-appeal, which dealt with a technical point in relation to the now-defunct system of notification of agreements to the Commission for negative clearance and/or individual exemption. The issue concerned the extent to which the fact that JCB had notified its standard distribution agreement afforded it immunity from being fined under Article 15(5) of Regulation 17/62. The particular point was that a notified term of the agreement had been used to enforce an unlawful practice, and the Commission had regarded this as an aggravating factor; the CFI thought that, since the term had been notified, it was irrelevant to the quantification of the fine on JCB. In the Opinion of the Advocate General the CFI was wrong to have reduced the fine by €864,000, given that JCB had specifically stated that no sanctions would be used to enforce the term in question, which was contradicted by later events: he therefore advised the ECJ that this element of the fine should be reinstated. The ECJ's judgment in *JCB*, on 21 September 2006, followed the Opinion of its Advocate General; at paragraph 242 of its judgment the ECJ held that the CFI had erred in making the reduction, and the level of the fine was increased to €30,864,000.

It is interesting to note that there was a similar outcome in a later appeal by the Commission against a judgment of the CFI (though not one with which Sir

---

8 *BUMA/SABAM-Santiago Agreement* OJ [2005] C 200/11; *Cannes Extension Agreement*, Commission Press Release IP/06/1311, 4 October 2006.

9 *International Confederation of Societies of Authors and Composers*, Commission Press Release, 7 February 2006, MEMO/06/63.

10 See n. 4 above.

11 Case T-67/01 *JCB Service v Commission* [2004] ECR II-49, [2004] CMLR 24.

Francis was involved), *Commission v SGL Carbon*.[12] There the ECJ set aside a reduction of a fine allowed by the CFI: the reason on this occasion was that the Court considered that the CFI had wrongly applied the principles of the law against self-incrimination to a legitimate request by the Commission for documents (as opposed to a request for answers to questions) from a firm being investigated for participation in a suspected cartel.

OPINIONS DELIVERED IN MANY OF THE LEADING CASES OF THE ECJ ON COMPETITION LAW

It is noticeable that Advocate General Jacobs gave Opinions in many of the leading competition law cases of the ECJ, including, for example, *Spanish Banks*,[13] *Hilti v Commission*,[14] *Oscar Bronner GmbH & Co. KG v Mediaprint*,[15] *CIF Consorzio Industrie Fiammeriferi v Autorità Garante della Concurrenza e del Mercato*[16] and *Syfait*.[17] Two of these Opinions, for different reasons, are particularly well known and will regularly be cited in the future: indeed it is certainly the case that they will be more influential than the ECJ's judgments themselves.

Oscar Bronner

In *Oscar Bronner* a publisher of an Austrian daily newspaper was seeking access to Mediaprint's nationwide home-delivery service for daily newspapers against payment of reasonable remuneration. Having concluded (contrary to the arguments of both Mediaprint and the Commission) that the Article 234 reference from the Kartellgericht in Austria was admissible, the Advocate General reviewed the law of refusal to supply, and in particular the so-called 'essential facilities' doctrine, under Article 82. At paragraphs 46 to 47 of his Opinion the Advocate General explained the origins of this doctrine in US law, and the five conditions that must be met for its application there, before moving on, at paragraphs 56 to 58, to the adoption of the doctrine in the deci-

---

12 Case C-301/04 P *Commission v SGL Carbon AG* [2006] ECR I-000, judgment of 29 June 2006.

13 Case C-67/91 *Dirección General de Defensa de la Competencia v Asociación Española de Banca Privada and Others* [1992] ECR I-4785.

14 Case C-53/92 P [1994] ECR I-677, [1994] 4 CMLR 614.

15 Case C-7/97 [1998] ECR I-7791, [1999] 4 CMLR 112.

16 Case C-198/01 [2003] ECR I-8055, [2003] 5 CMLR 829.

17 Case C-53/03 *Synetairisimos Farmakopoion Aitolias & Akarnanias (Syfait) and Others* [2005] ECR I-4609, [2005] 5 CMLR 7.

sional practice of the European Commission. At paragraph 53 the Advocate General noted that, although the laws of the Member States generally regard freedom of contract as an essential element of free trade, nevertheless examples could be found – for example in Spain, Finland, France, Greece and Portugal – of situations in which an unjustified refusal to deal could amount to an infringement of local competition law; he also noted that in some countries there were specific laws on access to essential facilities. Sir Francis then gave his appraisal of the issues, and it is this passage of the Opinion that has been (and will be) the focus of so much attention. Paragraphs 56 to 58, in which he sets out a number of general points, merit citation in full:

> 56. First, it is apparent that the right to choose one's trading partners and freely to dispose of one's property are generally recognised principles in the laws of the Member States, in some cases with constitutional status. Incursions on those rights require careful justification.
>
> 57. Secondly, the justification in terms of competition policy for interfering with a dominant undertaking's freedom to contract often requires a careful balancing of conflicting considerations. In the long term it is generally pro-competitive and in the interest of consumers to allow a company to retain for its own use facilities which it has developed for the purpose of its business. For example, if access to a production, purchasing or distribution facility were allowed too easily there would be no incentive for a competitor to develop competing facilities. Thus while competition was increased in the short term it would be reduced in the long term. Moreover, the incentive for a dominant undertaking to invest in efficient facilities would be reduced if its competitors were, upon request, able to share the benefits. Thus the mere fact that by retaining a facility for its own use a dominant undertaking retains an advantage over a competitor cannot justify requiring access to it.
>
> 58. Thirdly, in assessing this issue it is important not to lose sight of the fact that the primary purpose of Article [82] is to prevent distortion of competition – and in particular to safeguard the interests of consumers – rather than to protect the position of particular competitors. It may therefore, for example, be unsatisfactory, in a case in which a competitor demands access to a raw material in order to be able to compete with the dominant undertaking on a downstream market in a final product, to focus solely on the latter's market power on the upstream market and conclude that its conduct in reserving to itself the downstream market is automatically an abuse. Such conduct will not have an adverse impact on consumers unless the dominant undertaking's final product is sufficiently insulated from competition to give it market power.

The Advocate General then discussed the well-known *Magill* case,[18] noting

---

[18] Cases C-241/91 P etc. *RTE and ITP v Commission* [1995] ECR I-743, [1995] 4 CMLR 718.

a number of 'special circumstances' that helped to explain the controversial obligation to license on that occasion; that the existing products (individual weekly guides to the television programmes of each of the BBC, ITV and RTE) were inadequate; that there was an obvious demand for a composite listings guide, as shown by the experience of other countries; the difficulty of justifying copyright protection for a mere list of television programmes that involved no creative endeavour; and the permanent nature of the barrier to entry represented by copyright protection for information that only had a useful life of a week or so. The Advocate General concluded, at paragraph 65, that the cases in which Article 82 could lead to mandatory access to the essential facility of another could be justified only in cases of 'a genuine stranglehold' on the related market, where duplication of the facility 'is impossible or extremely difficult owing to physical, geographical or legal constraints or is highly undesirable for reasons of public policy'. In his view Bronner's claim fell 'well short' of the situation in which access should be mandated under Article 82.

This is a most cogent and compelling discussion of Article 82 and the law of refusal to supply. The ECJ's judgment also came to the conclusion that the reference by the Kartellgericht was admissible and that it would not be unlawful for Mediaprint to deny Bronner access to its distribution system, but did so without the clarity and authority of the Advocate General. It is noticeable that there is a widespread tendency, in subsequent discussions of *Oscar Bronner*, to cite the Opinion of Sir Francis Jacobs as if it were the judgment of the Court. Of course the law is as laid down by the ECJ, but it is testament to the force of the Advocate General's argument that so much attention has been given to his Opinion.

Syfait

The *Syfait* case is a fascinating one. The Greek Competition Commission referred the case to the ECJ, seeking an opinion as to whether GlaxoSmithKline had abused a dominant position by refusing to supply certain drugs to pharmaceutical wholesalers in Greece in order to limit parallel trade from that country to higher-priced Member States. The issue is a familiar one, and has occupied the ECJ since the 1960s: all Member States intervene in the market to fix or limit the price of drugs within their territories, and this acts as an inducement to parallel traders, not least because of the low transport costs relative to the price of the products. However, pharmaceutical companies depend on revenues from their successful drugs to pay for their research and development costs in a highly risky business, and parallel trade could have a serious impact on these revenues. Community law has to decide how to balance the desirability of parallel trade, the 'holy cow' of much

Community jurisprudence, against the need not unduly to undermine the position of the pharmaceutical companies.

The first issue in *Syfait* was to determine whether the Competition Commission was competent to make the reference in the first place. Advocate General Jacobs concluded that it was a 'court or tribunal' for the purpose of Article 234, so that the case was admissible, although he acknowledged at paragraph 31 that the case was 'finely balanced', not least given the structure and composition of the Commission, only two of whose nine members were required to be lawyers, and that there were doubts about the separateness of the Commission from its secretariat. It is interesting to note that the ECJ had accepted a reference from the Spanish competition authority in 1992 in *Spanish Banks*, where Sir Francis had also been the Advocate General: as he noted in *Syfait*, the Spanish authority 'shared many of the same attributes as the Greek Competition Commission'. However, the ECJ declined to follow the Advocate General on this issue, concluding at paragraph 37 of its judgment that, as a result of a number of factors examined, the Commission was not a court or tribunal for the purpose of Article 234 EC: these factors included, for example, that the Commission was subject to the supervision of the Minister for Development; that there were insufficient safeguards to ensure that members of the Commission would not be subject to undue intervention or pressure, and that the European Commission could relieve the Greek Commission of the competence to act by using Article 11(6) of the Modernization Regulation.[19]

As a result of its finding on the question of admissibility the ECJ declined to answer the question of substance, namely whether GlaxoSmithKline had abused its dominant position by refusing to supply the Greek wholesalers. *Syfait* left this hugely important question unanswered at the level of the ECJ, but we do know the answer of the Court's Advocate General. The Opinion, from paragraph 53 onwards, contains a very careful examination of the jurisprudence on refusal to supply under Article 82. Many of the cases concern the refusal to supply existing customers (paragraphs 54 to 60), but others concern refusals to allow third parties access to intellectual property or physical infrastructures for the first time (paragraphs 61 to 65). At paragraph 68 the Advocate General notes that the factors that determine whether a refusal is abusive 'are highly dependent on the specific economic and regulatory context in which the case arises'. This leads him to the view, at paragraph 69, that the refusal to supply on the part of GlaxoSmithKline should not be regarded as abusive *per se*. The Opinion then moves on to the question of whether there could be an objective justification for the refusal and concludes that, in the

[19] OJ [2003] L 1/1, [2003] 4 CMLR 551.

very specific circumstances of the pharmaceutical industry, there was such a justification: in particular he noted the extent to which there was regulation of price and distribution in the European pharmaceutical sector, the economics of the innovative pharmaceutical sector and the consequences of parallel trade for consumers and purchasers in the Member State of import.

The *Syfait* case raised the obvious question for both pharmaceutical companies and parallel traders as to where the law now stood: the ECJ had declined to address the issue of substance, whereas a highly experienced Advocate General, with considerable knowledge of competition law in general and of the law of refusal to supply in particular, had given a cogent explanation as to why the behaviour in question might not be illegal. Where did this now leave (a) the Greek Competition Commission, (b) the European Commission, (c) other national competition authorities, (d) national courts and (e) professional advisers who might be called upon to deal with the issue? What, precisely, is the status of an Opinion of the Advocate General of the ECJ, in particular in circumstances where the ECJ has not adjudicated upon a matter considered in depth in the Opinion? And, as a particular point of UK law, what standing would the Opinion have in terms of section 60 of the Competition Act 1998, which requires that UK courts maintain consistency with the principles of the Community, but which says nothing about the particular position of the Opinions of the Advocates General?[20] The Court of First Instance subsequently handed down a very important judgment in *GlaxoSmithKline v Commission*[21] in which it found that an agreement that provided for the dual pricing of pharmaceuticals in Spain, designed to discourage parallel trade from Spain to the higher-priced UK market, did not have as its object the restriction of competition; the CFI went on to hold that the agreement did have a restrictive effect on competition, but that it might be justifiable under the criteria set out in Article 81(3) EC. As a result the Commission's decision condemning the agreement was set aside and the matter was remitted to the Commission for further consideration. It remains to be seen what the Commission will do in the light of this judgment but, if it were to decide in a future decision that the dual pricing scheme does indeed satisfy Article 81(3) because of the specificities of the pharmaceutical market, this would be consistent with the Opinion of Advocate General Jacobs in *Syfait* on the refusal to supply under Article 82.

---

[20] In *Napp Pharmaceutical Holdings Ltd v Director General of Fair Trading* [2002] EWCA Civ 796, [2002] 4 All ER 376 Buxton LJ considered that an Opinion of an Advocate General should be considered as 'important and authoritative'.

[21] Case T-168/01 [2006] ECR II-000, judgment of 27 September 2006.

OPINIONS DELIVERED IN MANY COMPETITION LAW CASES HAVING A SOCIAL DIMENSION

The discussion so far has already indicated the range of competition law cases with which Sir Francis Jacobs was involved in his time at the ECJ, and the strength of his contribution in this field. However, perhaps the most interesting series of cases in which he was concerned is that which examines the potential application of the competition rules to what might be termed 'non-obvious' situations, such as collective bargaining between employers' and employees' organizations and cases having a social dimension such as the provision of public ambulance services and of healthcare to citizens. It is interesting to note in recent years how often the ECJ has been asked to consider, first, which activities come within the scope of the competition rules and, secondly, what is to be done when it appears that the application of the competition rules might produce an outcome which is in conflict with some different Community policy. One way for the ECJ to resolve a particular case is simply to determine that an entity whose conduct is challenged under Article 81 or Article 82 is not acting as an undertaking, with the consequence that it is not within the 'personal scope' of those provisions. A different approach, necessitating careful consideration of the behaviour in question, is to decide that the entity is, indeed, acting as an undertaking, and then to examine whether its behaviour is restrictive of competition and, if so, whether it may nevertheless be justified in some way. The second of these analytical approaches is more likely to lead to outcomes consistent with the requirement of Article 3(1)(g) of the Treaty that one of the activities of the Community shall be the institution of an undistorted system of competition. Insofar as an entity is acting as an undertaking, and therefore falls within the personal scope of the competition rules, there are numerous ways in which it might nevertheless be able to argue that its behaviour is not unlawful under Articles 81 and/or 82:

- that an agreement to which it is party does not have as its object or effect the prevention, restriction or distortion of competition;
- that the agreement does not have an appreciable effect on competition;
- that the agreement does not affect trade between Member States (although it might still infringe the domestic law of a Member State);
- that the agreement satisfies the criteria of Article 81(3);
- that the agreement restricts competition but satisfies the 'public interest' test set out in *Wouters*;[22]

---

[22] Case C-309/99 *Wouters v Algemene Raad van de Nederlandse Orde van Advocaten* [2002] ECR I-1577, [2002] 4 CMLR 913.

- that conduct of which an undertaking is accused does not amount to an abuse of a dominant position;
- that apparently unlawful conduct satisfies one of the defences set out in paragraphs 77 to 92 of the Commission's *Discussion Paper on the application of Article 82 of the Treaty to exclusionary abuses*;[23]
- that an agreement or conduct benefits from the derogation set out in Article 86(2) EC.

It is obvious from the foregoing discussion that a definition is needed of the term 'undertaking' in order to determine when the competition rules are applicable. The subject is complex.[24] Sir Francis Jacobs was the Advocate General in several of the leading cases in which the meaning of the term 'undertaking' has been discussed by the ECJ:

Höfner and Elser

The usual starting point in any discussion of the term 'undertaking' is *Klaus Höfner and Elser v Macrotron*.[25] This is a most fascinating case, one of three landmark judgments in 1991 in which the ECJ explored the application of Article 82 in conjunction with Article 86(1) EC.[26] Höfner and Elser were personnel consultants in Germany, and they provided recruitment services for Macrotron. They sued for their fee, and Macrotron refused to pay. Macrotron's defence was that the Bundesanstalt für Arbeit in Germany had a legal monopoly over the provision of such services, and that the contract with Macrotron was therefore void as it violated the Bundesanstalt's monopoly. The Landgericht in Munich agreed with Macrotron and dismissed the claim. However, the Oberlandesgericht made an Article 234 reference. One of the questions for the ECJ was whether Article 82, in conjunction with Article 86(1), called into question the lawfulness of the Bundesanstalt's monopoly.

---

23 December 2005, available at http://ec.europa.eu/comm/competition/index_en.html.

24 For discussion of the term 'undertaking' see Bellamy and Child, *European Community Law of Competition* (London: Sweet & Maxwell, 5th edn, 2001, ed. P. Roth) paras 2-003 to 2-014; R. Whish, *Competition Law* (Oxford: Oxford University Press, 5th edn, 2003), pp 80–87; O. Odudu, 'The meaning of undertaking within Article 81 EC', Cambridge Yearbook of European Legal Studies, Volume 7 (2005), slightly revised in Chapter 3 of O. Odudu, *The Boundaries of EC Competition Law: The Scope of Article 81* (Oxford: Oxford University Press, 2006).

25 Case C-41/90 [1991] ECR I-1979, [1993] 4 CMLR 306.

26 See also Case C-260/89 *ERT v Dimotiki* [1991] ECR I-2925, [1994] 4 CMLR 540; Case C-179/90 *Merci Convenzionale Porto di Genova v Siderurgica Gabrielli* [1991] ECR I-5889, [1994] 4 CMLR 422.

Famously, the ECJ's conclusion was that it did do so, since Germany had created a situation in which the Bundesanstalt could not avoid infringing Article 82: it was manifestly incapable of satisfying demand on the market for recruitment services, and the pursuit of those activities by private recruitment services was rendered impossible by the maintenance in force of the statutory prohibition. It followed that Germany was in violation of Article 86(1) in conjunction with Article 82, and that the monopoly granted to the Bundesanstalt was invalid under Community law.

Advocate General Jacobs did not find it necessary to discuss the meaning of the term 'undertaking'. He simply said that:

> I have no difficulty in accepting that the Bundesanstalt . . . is a 'public undertaking', within the meaning of Article [86(1)], and an 'undertaking entrusted with the operation of services of general economic interest,' within the meaning of Article [86(2)]. As such, it is – contrary to the German Government's view – subject to the competition rules and to the other rules of the Treaty, unless it can be shown that the application of those rules would obstruct the performance of its tasks.

The ECJ however did discuss the term, stating at paragraph 21 of its judgment that:

> It must be observed, in the context of competition law, first that the concept of an undertaking encompasses every entity engaged in an economic activity, regardless of the legal status of the entity and the way in which it is financed and, secondly, that employment procurement is an economic activity.

Paragraph 21 of *Höfner and Elser* has become the starting point of any discussion of the term 'undertaking'. However, it requires only a moment's reflection to realize that 'engagement in economic activity' is by no means a simple concept, and there have been numerous subsequent cases, not always easily reconcilable, in which the concept has had to be explored further. Whilst it can be seen that some activities are inherently *not* economic because they involve the exercise of the power of the state – an obvious example would be air traffic control, the subject-matter of the *Eurocontrol* case[27] – this does not in itself help us to understand which activities *are* economic.

---

[27] Case C-364/92 *SAT Fluggesellschaft v Eurocontrol* [1994] ECR I-43, [1994] 5 CMLR 208; see similarly Case C-343/95 *Calì e Figli* [1997] ECR I-1547, [1997] 5 CMLR 484, dealing with the protection of the environment by preventing oil pollution at the port of Genoa.

Albany International

In the *Albany International* case[28] the ECJ was concerned with the application of the competition rules to a system of compulsory affiliation to pension schemes in the Netherlands. A request could be made for such a system by the representatives of employers and employees, and then made compulsory for all undertakings operating within a particular sector by Government decree. The case raised many complex issues, including whether Article 81 should apply at all to collective bargaining between employers' and employees' organizations (both the Advocate General and the ECJ were agreed that there should be some immunity for collective bargaining from the Treaty competition rules: the Advocate General's Opinion contains an interesting review of the position under the laws of many of the Member States and under US antitrust law). A further question was whether the Dutch pension funds were themselves undertakings for the purposes of the competition rules in the Treaty. The Opinion of Advocate General Jacobs contains considerable discussion of the meaning of the term 'undertaking'. From paragraphs 205 to 236 the position of employees, acting in their capacity as such, trade unions, when engaged in collective bargaining, and employers, when engaged in collective bargaining, is discussed. The Opinion also examines, from paragraphs 306 to 348, the position of the Dutch supplementary pension funds in that case, and concludes that they were acting as undertakings, a view endorsed by the ECJ. The Opinion is particularly helpful because of its explanation that, in approaching the term 'undertaking', it is necessary to adopt a 'functional' approach: the question to be asked is not whether a particular entity is an undertaking, but whether that entity, *when performing a particular activity*, is acting as an undertaking. This insight, which the Advocate General explains can be seen in the ECJ's jurisprudence, enables us to understand that the same entity can act as an undertaking when involved in one kind of activity but not when involved in another. It follows that, although individuals may be acting as an undertaking in some situations – for example when they are independent economic actors on the market – they are not when they are acting as an employee, in which capacity they do not accept direct commercial risk and are subject to the orders of their employers (see paragraphs 214 and 215 of the Opinion). Similarly a trade union when involved in collective bargaining would not be acting as an undertaking, but would be when running a bank or a travel agency (paragraph 226). Advocate General Jacobs referred again to this functional approach to the meaning of 'undertaking' in paragraph 26 of his

---

[28] Case C-67/96 *Albany International BV v Stichting Bedrijfspensioenfonds Textielindustrie* [1999] ECR I-5751, [2000] 4 CMLR 446.

Opinion in the *AOK Bundesverband* case,[29] where he was dealing with the question of whether German sickness funds were acting as undertakings when purchasing medicinal products:

> As to the status of the sickness funds, the Court's general approach to whether a given entity is an undertaking within the meaning of the Community competition rules can be described as functional, in that it focuses on the type of activity performed rather than on the characteristics of the actors which perform it, the social objectives associated with it, or the regulatory or funding arrangements to which it is subject in a particular Member State. Provided that the activity is of an economic character, those engaged in it will be subject to Community competition law.

Pavlov

In *Pavlov*[30] issues similar to those in *Albany* arose, except that in *Pavlov* the compulsory pension schemes were set up by members of a profession rather than pursuant to agreements between the representatives of employers and employees. The Advocate General considered that self-employed medical specialists could be classified as undertakings when they provide medical services for remuneration. However, he also noted that the question of *employed* medical specialists would be more problematic (on the facts of the case this point did not require to be answered): professional employees do not necessarily work under the express direction of their employers, and may bear economic risk in a way that 'ordinary' employees do not. They may be in a borderline category where it is difficult to determine whether they are acting as undertakings or not, a category that he had envisaged in paragraph 217 of his Opinion in *Albany*. The ECJ agreed with the Advocate General that the medical specialists were acting as undertakings. A further issue was whether they were acting as undertakings *when setting up the scheme for supplementary pensions*: an argument to the contrary was that, when doing so, they were spending their income and acting as consumers, not as undertakings, just as they would be when purchasing a holiday home or a valuable painting. The Advocate General rejected this argument, as the pension arrangements were related to their professional activities and so constituted economic activity: again the ECJ agreed. The Advocate General and the ECJ also concluded that the pension fund itself was acting as an undertaking when managing the supplementary pension scheme.

---

29 Joined Cases C-264/01, C-306/01, C-354/01 and C-355/01 *AOK Bundesverband and Others v Ichthyol-Gesellschaft Cordes, Hermani & Co., Mundipharma GmbH, Gödecke GmbH, Intersan, Institut für pharmazeutische und klinische Forschung GmbH* [2004] ECR I-2493, [2004] 4 CMLR 1261.

30 Cases C-180–184/98 [2000] ECR I-6451, [2001] 4 CMLR 30.

Ambulanz Glöckner

In *Ambulanz Glöckner v Landkreis Südwestpfalz*[31] the ECJ was asked to consider whether German legislation prohibiting the provision of private ambulance services was compatible with Article 86(1), read in conjunction with Article 82, where the grant of such authorization would be likely to have adverse effects on the operation and profitability of the public ambulance services. The public ambulance services were provided by medical aid organizations by virtue of an assignment made by designated public authorities. In the Opinion of the Advocate General, with which the ECJ agreed, there was no doubt that the medical aid organizations were undertakings: there was nothing to suggest that public ambulance services could only be carried out by public entities. However, the Advocate General was of the view that the designated public authorities, when granting or refusing authorizations for the provision of independent ambulance services, were not acting as undertakings, a point not dealt with in the ECJ's judgment. For both the Advocate General and the ECJ the crucial question in this case, assuming that the legislation in question could lead to an abuse of a dominant position (for example the exclusion of private operators from the market reserved to the medical aid organizations), was whether the legislation could be justified on the basis of Article 86(2) of the Treaty: that is to say, would exposure of the medical aid organizations to competition run the risk that they would be unable to perform the task entrusted to them? This, of course, is a complex issue, to be decided in a case such as this on the basis of the evidence before the referring court. The Opinion of the Advocate General, from paragraphs 174 to 189, sets out the issues that would have to be taken into account in making that assessment. This case is an example of the much deeper analysis that must be carried out in deciding whether a breach of competition law has taken place once it is determined that a particular entity is acting as an undertaking. Without such a determination there would be no need to conduct a justification review.

INAIL

In *Cisal di Battistello Venanzio & C Sas v INAIL*[32] the ECJ was asked by an Italian court whether a national regime of compulsory insurance against accidents at work and occupational diseases was acting as an undertaking so as to make it subject to the competition rules. On this occasion the Advocate General, with whom the ECJ agreed, concluded that INAIL was not acting as

---

31 Case C-475/99 [2001] ECR I-8089, [2002] 4 CMLR 726.

32 Case C-218/00 [2002] ECR I-691, [2002] 4 CMLR 833.

an undertaking. The link between contributions and benefits via the victim's earnings was too indirect to be regarded as analogous to private insurance, and the levels of both benefits and contributions were ultimately determined by the state. The Advocate General considered that, if INAIL were acting as an undertaking, there would have to be an examination of its behaviour under Article 86(2). The ECJ, having decided that INAIL was not an undertaking, did not address this issue. The contrast with *Ambulanz Glöckner* is obvious, where analysis of possible justification was precisely what had to be carried out following the determination that the public medical organizations were acting as undertakings.

AOK Bundesverband

One of the most interesting cases on social provision in which Advocate General Jacobs was involved was *AOK Bundesverband*. Associations of sickness funds in Germany, established under German law, collectively determined the maximum amounts that they would pay for certain medicinal products. In a number of cases referred under Article 234 by courts in Germany, the question for the ECJ was whether this collective action amounted to a cartel contrary to Article 81 and, if so, whether it could be justified under Article 86(2). Advocate General Jacobs considered whether the appellants in the German courts were acting as associations of undertakings from paragraphs 24 to 62 of his Opinion. This required an examination of three issues: first whether the sickness funds represented by the appellants in the German proceedings were themselves acting as undertakings; secondly, whether the setting of fixed amounts to be paid fell within the sphere of those funds' economic activities; and thirdly whether the appellants, when setting the maximum amounts, were acting as an association of undertakings. In the Advocate General's view the sickness funds were acting as undertakings and the competition rules were engaged. Although certain aspects of the arrangements resembled the facts, for example, of *Poucet and Pistre*[33] and *INAIL*,[34] where the ECJ had concluded that the element of solidarity in the schemes rendered them 'non-economic', in *AOK* the funds engaged in a certain degree of price competition between themselves, and employees had a choice as to which fund to join; there was potential for the funds to compete in relation to services as well; and the funds, and private health insurers, could compete for the business of workers not covered by the compulsory arrangements. The Advocate General suggested, at paragraph 27 of this Opinion, that the emphasis should be placed,

---

33 Cases C-159/91 and 160/91 [1993] ECR I-637.
34 See n. 32 above.

when interpreting whether an activity is economic, on whether it could, in principle, be carried on by a private undertaking in order to make profits. It followed that Article 81 was capable of applying, in principle, to the arrangements, but that either (a) a state action defence or (b) Article 86(2) might result in a finding that there had been no infringement. Each of these defences would, however, require further examination, as in *Ambulanz Glöckner*.

As is well known, however, the ECJ did not follow this Opinion. The ECJ concluded that the funds were involved in a social security scheme, like the bodies in *Poucet and Pistre*, fulfilling an exclusively social function on the principle of national solidarity and being entirely non-profit-making. It therefore followed that they were not acting as undertakings, with the result that the competition rules did not apply and there was no need for the more penetrating analysis of any possible distortion of competition envisaged by the Advocate General. The case vividly exposes the different outcomes that follow according to whether an entity is characterized as an undertaking or not. It is interesting to note that in the subsequent case of *FENIN v Commission*[35] the ECJ reached a similar conclusion in relation to 26 public bodies responsible for running the Spanish health system which were accused by suppliers of medical goods and equipment of excessive delays in settling bills, apparently abusive behaviour contrary to Article 82(a). The Court upheld the judgment of the CFI, albeit in very peremptory terms in three short paragraphs, that the public bodies were not acting as undertakings. Since they were purchasing goods and equipment in order to carry out a non-economic activity – the provision of healthcare to citizens on the basis of solidarity – the activity of purchasing could not be dissociated from the subsequent use to which the goods would be put; it followed that the purchasing activity was not, itself, economic and that FENIN's appeal failed. This was a judgment of 11 judges in the Grand Chamber of the ECJ, and one has to assume that the Court was mindful of the political sensitivity of applying the competition rules to the procurement activities of the health services of the Member States. However, it is interesting to speculate as to how, if the public bodies in question had been found to be acting as undertakings, they would have gone about justifying their behaviour of delaying the payment of bills to their suppliers by periods of nine months or longer, in circumstances where those same suppliers had to settle their own bills with their suppliers much more quickly. Again, the significance of classification as an undertaking is vividly exposed.[36]

---

35 Case C-205/03 P *Federación Española de Empresas de Tecnología Sanitaria (FENIN) v Commission* [2006] ECR I-000, judgment of 11 July 2006.

36 It is interesting to compare both *AOK* and *FENIN* with the judgment of the UK Competition Appeal Tribunal (CAT) in Case No. 1006/2/1/01 *BetterCare Group v Director General of Fair Trading* [2002] CAT 7, [2002] CompAR 299, where the CAT

Risparmio

In *Risparmio*[37] the ECJ was asked to consider whether certain banking foundations in Italy were undertakings for the purposes of Article 87 EC. In his Opinion Advocate General Jacobs repeated the idea in *AOK*, that one should ask whether the activity in question could be carried on by a private undertaking in order to make profits. He continued:

> 79. That interpretation is justified by the need to ensure the full effectiveness of the competition rules of the Treaty, in particular when read in the light of their ultimate rationale, namely to avoid any distortions of competition in the market caused by the conduct of any entity, whether public or private.

In the following paragraph the Advocate General suggested that it was necessary to avoid a narrow interpretation of the term 'undertaking' if that would mean 'that anti-competitive behaviour would escape the EC competition rules. Clearly, such a reading should be avoided.'

The ECJ has yet to adopt an approach as wide as this, which would mean that any anti-competitive behaviour would have to be scrutinized for its compatibility with the Treaty. It is certainly questionable whether the judgments of the ECJ in *AOK* and *FENIN* succeeded in avoiding distortions of competition by the entities involved in those cases.

CONCLUSION

The contribution of Advocate General Jacobs, to Community law generally and to competition law in particular, has been immense: a remarkable 18 years. As this short essay has attempted to demonstrate he was involved in many of the most important cases of the ECJ, and some of the most difficult ones, on matters of competition law. His Opinions on cases with a social dimension are of particular interest, and he leaves behind the largest contribution of learning on the difficult concept of undertakings in Community competition law made by anyone.

---

concluded that a Health Trust in Northern Ireland was acting as an undertaking when purchasing certain healthcare services; the CAT's judgment was given after Advocate General Jacobs's Opinion in *AOK*, but before the judgment of either the CFI or ECJ in *FENIN* or the judgment of the ECJ in *AOK*. It is also interesting to observe that the UK Government intervened in *FENIN* in order to support the argument that the Spanish health service was *not* an undertaking. One can only speculate therefore as to whether the UK Government supports the finding of the CAT in the *BetterCare* case.

[37] Case C-222/04 *Cassa di Risparmio di Firenze* [2006] ECR I-289, judgment of 10 January 2006.

6. Free movement of goods and services

Catherine Barnard[1]

INTRODUCTION

I feel honoured to be asked to participate in this collection. Francis Jacobs's Opinions have deepened my understanding of the debates surrounding the meaning and implications of the internal market. He has helped me frame my thinking and writing on the subject, and I am deeply grateful. Given the huge influence he has had on my thoughts, it is difficult to be critical of his contribution and so my aim in this chapter is to outline the areas in which Francis has made the most significant contribution to the jurisprudence on the internal market, and to focus on two particular areas where problems remain. I will begin by considering his approach to establishing breach of the treaty looking first at the free movement of goods.

FREE MOVEMENT OF GOODS

From *Keck* to *Leclerc-Siplec*

The *Keck*[2] case law was greeted with relief and criticism in equal measure. As is now well known, in *Keck* the Court drew a distinction between 'product requirements' and 'certain selling arrangements'. In respect of 'product requirements', the Court confirmed that the principles in *Cassis* continued to apply[3] and so any such national measures breached Article 28 unless they could be justified by mandatory requirements and the steps taken were proportionate. In respect of 'certain selling arrangements', the Court said in paragraph 16 that:

---

1 Fellow in Law, Trinity College, University of Cambridge.

2 Joined Cases C-267 & 268/91 *Keck and Mithouard* [1993] ECR I-6097.

3 The language of 'product requirements' is taken from AG Van Gerven's Opinion in Joined Cases C-401 & 402/92 *Boermans* [1994] ECR I-2199, para. 16.

> contrary to what has previously been decided, the application to products from other Member States of national provisions restricting or prohibiting certain selling arrangements is not such as to hinder directly or indirectly, actually or potentially, trade between Member States within the meaning of the *Dassonville* judgment . . . provided those provisions apply to all affected traders operating within the national territory and provided that they affect in the same manner, in law and in fact, the marketing of domestic products and those from other Member States.

The Court continued in paragraph 17 that:

> Where those conditions are fulfilled, the application of such rules to the sale of products from other Member States meeting the requirements laid down by that State is not by nature such as to *prevent* their [foreign goods'] access to the market or to *impede* access any more than it impedes the access of domestic products.[4]

Therefore overturning previous, unspecified case law, the Court said that 'certain selling arrangements' did not fall within the *Dassonville* formula and so, unlike quantitative restrictions and distinctly and indistinctly applicable measures having equivalent effect, these selling arrangements did not breach Article 28 where the two conditions set out in paragraph 16 were satisfied (the so-called 'paragraph 16 proviso'), namely: (1) the provisions applied to all affected traders operating in the territory, and (2) the provisions were non-discriminatory (same burden in law and in fact). National rules satisfying these two conditions did not breach Article 28 because, according to the Court, such rules did not prevent access to the market (first limb of paragraph 17) nor did they impede access for foreign goods more than they impeded access for domestic products (second limb of paragraph 17).

Whilst many congratulated the Court on finally recognizing that there were outer limits to the scope of Article 28 and that, in the day and age of subsidiarity, certain matters should be left to the Member States to regulate, others were critical of the crude way that this result was achieved. For example, many regretted that in its 'clarification' of the earlier case law,[5] the Court gave no indication of which cases it was overturning. More importantly, they bemoaned the new, formulistic classification, 'certain selling arrangements' and the fact that, in the cases immediately following *Keck*,[6] the Court unthinkingly equated a finding that a national measure constituted a certain selling

---

4 Emphasis added.

5 S. Weatherill, 'After *Keck*: Some thoughts on how to clarify the clarification' (1996) 33 CMLRev 885.

6 Case C-292/92 *Hünermund* [1993] ECR I-6787; Case C-412/93 *Leclerc-Siplec v TF1 Publicité SA* [1995] ECR I-179; Case C-391/92 *Commission v Greece* [1995] ECR I-1621.

arrangement with no breach of Article 28. *Leclerc-Siplec*[7] was one such case. French law prohibited the fuel distribution sector from advertising on television. The Court said that the French rule was a certain selling arrangement which did not breach Article 28, despite the fact that in a number of pre-*Keck* cases,[8] the Court said that a national rule prohibiting the advertising of alcohol in public places breached Article 28 but could be justified on the grounds of public health.

In reaching its conclusion in that case, the Court ignored, at least initially, the Opinion of its Advocate General (Francis Jacobs) who had argued that the (re)introduction of a discrimination test in *Keck* was inappropriate since the central concern of the Treaty provisions on the free movement of goods was to prevent unjustified obstacles to trade between Member States. He said that 'If an obstacle to trade exists it cannot cease to exist simply because an identical obstacle affects domestic trade.'[9] He therefore advocated a rather different approach which started from the premise that all undertakings which engage in a legitimate economic activity in a Member State should have unfettered access to the whole of the Community market, unless there is a valid reason why not. He then suggested his own test for determining whether non-discriminatory measures breach Article 28: is the measure liable 'substantially to restrict access to the market'?[10]

He said that where a measure prohibits the sale of goods lawfully placed on the market in another Member State (as in *Cassis*), it is presumed to have a substantial impact on access to the market, since the goods are either denied access altogether or can gain access only after being modified in some way; the need to modify goods is itself a substantial barrier to market access.[11] On the other hand, he said, where a measure restricts certain selling arrangements,

---

[7] See n. 6 above. The ruling in *Leclerc-Siplec* was confirmed in Case C-6/98 *ARD v PRO Sieben Media* [1999] ECR I-7599, para. 46, where the Court said that since the restriction on advertising in this case (limitation on transmission time) is of a 'similar, but less extensive, kind, it also concerns certain selling arrangements' and two conditions in paragraph 16 of *Keck* are 'clearly satisfied' (para. 48).

[8] Joined Cases C-1 & 176/90 *Aragonesa de Publicidad and Publivía* [1991] ECR I-4151, esp. para. 10.

[9] Para. 40.

[10] Paras 41 and 49. For academic support, see S. Weatherill, above n. 5, 900; C. Barnard, 'Fitting the remaining pieces into the goods and services jigsaw' (2001) 26 ELRev 35. See also: K. Mortelmans, 'Article 30 of the EEC Treaty and legislation relating to market circumstances: time to consider a new definition?' (1991) CMLRev 115 at 128 and the discussion there of AG Van Gerven's implicit introduction of a *de minimis* rule in *Torfaen*. See also J. Steiner, 'Drawing the line: uses and abuses of Article 30' (1992) 29 CMLRev 749. Cf. L. Gormley, 'Two years after *Keck*' (1996) *Fordham International Law Journal* 866, 882–3.

[11] Para. 44.

its impact will depend on whether it applies to some or all goods, the extent to which other selling arrangements remain available, and on whether the effect of the measure is 'direct or indirect, immediate or remote, or purely speculative and uncertain'. He continued that because the magnitude of the barrier to market access may vary enormously – from the insignificant to a quasi-prohibition – 'a *de minimis* test could perform a useful function'.[12]

Criticisms of the 'Substantial Hindrance' Test

Advocate General Jacobs's proposed test based on 'substantial' hindrance of market access has been subject to three criticisms: first, that it is a statistical test which the courts are ill-equipped to apply;[13] secondly, that it effectively reverses the well-established rule that the *de minimis* principle does not apply to Article 28;[14] and thirdly, that it is not clear whether the threshold to trigger Article 28 is set at a low level (i.e. more than *de minimis*) or at a higher level ('substantial'). For this reason some prefer a more legal test based on causation and remoteness. As Advocate General La Pergola said in *BASF*,[15] the aim of Article 28 is to verify whether a causal link exists between the national measure and the pattern of imports. The language used in the pre-*Keck* case *Krantz*,[16] and the post-*Keck* case *Graf*,[17] examining whether the effect on trade is 'too indirect and uncertain', supports the remoteness test. This might be another way in which the Court decides that certain national measures fall outside the scope of the Treaty.

However, others are dismissive of the difference between the two approaches. For example, Weatherill has argued that the remoteness test could equally be recast as an application of the notion that internal market law does not affect measures that cause no direct or substantial hindrance of access to the market of a Member State.[18] In practice, the Court seems to adopt a rather impressionistic approach. As we shall see, in cases such as *Graf*, if the Court

---

12 Para. 45. See also AG Jacobs's Opinion in Case C-112/00 *Schmidberger* [2003] ECR I-5659. Cf. Weatherill, who objects to the term '*de minimis*' because it requires numerical quantification ((1996) above n. 5, 900).

13 V. Hatzopoulos, 'Recent developments in the case law of the ECJ in the field of services' (2000) 37 CMLRev 43–82 at 82

14 Joined Cases 177 & 178/82 *van de Haar* [1984] ECR I-1797.

15 Case C-44/98 *BASF* [1999] ECR I-6269, para.18.

16 Case C-69/88 *Krantz* [1990] ECR I-583.

17 Case C-190/98 *Graf v Filzmozer Maschinenbau GmbH* [2000] ECR I-493.

18 Above n. 5, 900. See also Robert Walker, LJ in *R. (on the application of Professional Contractors Group Ltd) v Inland Revenue Commissioners* [2001] EWCA Civ 1945; [2002] 1 CMLR 46, para. 69, who talked of 'indirect or debateable' (para. 69) and 'direct and demonstrable' (para. 74).

considers that the rule challenged has such little effect on inter-state trade then it finds no breach of the Treaty provision.

Discriminatory Certain Selling Arrangements: *De Agostini*

Despite these criticisms of Francis Jacobs's approach, in fact the general thrust of his arguments has, almost imperceptibly, seeped into the pores of the Court's jurisprudence. Its first direct impact can be seen in *De Agostini*[19] where the Court had an opportunity to revisit its decision in *Leclerc-Siplec*, this time in respect of a prohibition on advertising which *prevented* access to the foreign market (as opposed to merely impeding access as in *Leclerc-Siplec*). The case concerned a Swedish ban on television advertising directed at children under 12 and a ban on misleading commercials for skin care products and detergents.

Advocate General Jacobs urged the Court to apply its own *Keck* proviso:

> The first condition is clearly satisfied in all these cases. In my view however the position is not so clear with regard to the second condition: I share the Commission's concern that the effect of the prohibition of all television advertising directed at children might in fact be greater on products from other Member States. As I argued in my Opinion in *Leclerc*, it would be inconsistent with the objectives of the Treaty to interpret *Keck* so as to exclude from the scope of Article [28] a total ban on the advertising of a product which may lawfully be sold in the Member State where the ban is applied and in other Member States: the effect of such a ban would be that manufacturers in other Member States would find it virtually impossible to penetrate the market in which the ban was imposed, so that the measure would be tantamount to a quantitative restriction on trade between Member States.

He concluded that 'However the discrimination test laid down by *Keck* is interpreted, it is difficult to resist the conclusion that in practice such a ban will almost certainly have a perceptible effect on imports.'[20]

This time the Court followed suit. Following *Leclerc-Siplec* the Court recognized that these restrictions constituted certain selling arrangements. However, unlike *Leclerc-Siplec*, the Court specifically addressed the proviso in paragraph 16 of *Keck*. It said that while the first condition of the paragraph 16 proviso (the measure applied to all traders operating within the national territory) was clearly fulfilled, the second condition (the measure affected all traders in the same manner in law and in fact) might not be. It said that an outright ban on a type of promotion for a product which is lawfully sold there

---

[19] Joined Cases C-34–6/95 *Konsumentombudsmannen (KO) v De Agostini (Svenska) Förlag AB and TV-Shop i Sverige AB* [1997] ECR I-3843, noted J. Stuyck (1997) 34 CMLRev. 1445, 1465.

[20] Para. 99.

might have 'a greater impact on products from other Member States'.[21] It continued that while the efficacy of various types of promotion was a question of fact to be determined by the national court, 'in its observations De Agostini stated that television advertising was *the only effective form* of sales promotion enabling it to penetrate the Swedish market since it had no other advertising methods for reaching children and their parents'.[22]

These paragraphs contain a strong hint that the Court thought that the Swedish measure had the same burden in law but a different burden in fact, a point reinforced by its reference to the fact that television advertising was the only effective form of sales promotion available to De Agostini. The Court concluded that if an unequal burden in law or fact was found, then the national restriction would be caught by Article 28 and the burden would shift to the Member State to justify it under one of the mandatory requirements in *Cassis*[23] or Article 30.[24]

This is the outcome the Advocate General had anticipated and it sits more comfortably with the pre-*Keck* case law. However, where *De Agostini* differs from the pre-*Keck* case law is that the Court took *Keck* as a starting point and decided that the measure constituted a certain selling arrangement. The measure therefore did not breach Article 28 *unless*, as the Court indicated in *De Agostini*, it was shown that the ban did not affect in the same manner, in fact and in law, the marketing of national products and products from other Member States.[25] In this situation the principles in *Cassis* would apply.

Thus, *De Agostini* helped to square the circle by creating a presumption of legality in respect of national measures classified as certain selling arrangements,

---

21 Para. 42.

22 Para. 43, emphasis added. Cf. Case C-412/93 *Leclerc-Siplec*, para. 19, where the Court noted that the French law which prohibited televised advertising in the distribution sector did not prevent distributors from using other forms of advertising.

23 Para. 45, although compare the bizarre and apparently contradictory wording in para. 47. See also Case C-376/98 *Germany v Parliament and Council (Tobacco Advertising)* [2001] ECR I-8419, para. 113, 'By imposing a wide-ranging prohibition on the advertising of tobacco products, the Directive would in the future generalize that restriction of forms of competition by limiting, in all the Member States, the means available for economic operators to enter or remain in the market'.

24 Para. 45.

25 *A fortiori*, if the measure has a different burden in law as well as in fact then there would also be a breach of Article 28: Case C-320/93 *Ortscheit v Eurim-Pharm Arzneimittel* [1994] ECR I-5243, which concerned a distinctly applicable measure. The Court said since the prohibition of advertising applied solely to foreign medicinal products it did not have the same effect on the marketing of medicinal products from other Member States as on the marketing of national medicinal products; it therefore fell within the scope of Article 28 (citing *Keck*, para. 16). See also the pre-*Keck* case, Case 152/78 *Commission v France* [1980] ECR 2299.

thereby providing some space for national legislative autonomy, while at the same time giving traders the opportunity to rebut that presumption when they could actually demonstrate that the measure had a disproportionate impact on them. In *GIP*[26] both Advocate General Jacobs and the Court emphasized that the trader needed to show *actual* disparate impact to rebut the presumption. This time the case concerned a Swedish ban on advertising alcohol not only on television but also on the radio and in magazines. Following *De Agostini*, Advocate General Jacobs and the Court assumed that this measure was a certain selling arrangement. They then considered the statistical evidence. The Swedish government had argued that there had been a constant increase in sales of wines (overwhelmingly imported, principally from other Member States) and a constant decrease in spirit sales (with an increase in the proportion of imported whiskies as opposed to Swedish-produced vodkas), the changing balance reflecting one of the aims of the legislation to wean consumers away from stronger beverages.[27] Therefore, the government argued, the ban on advertising did not have a disparate impact on importers: on the contrary, sales of imported drinks had increased.

However, Advocate General Jacobs was more persuaded by GIP's statistics, indicating Swedish domination of the domestic market in strong beer, and its arguments that ingrained consumer habits would always tend to favour national beverages, so that, without advertising, products from other Member States were at a disadvantage; that daily press information on other (e.g. economic) topics would keep the names of national producers to the forefront of consumers' minds; and that the lack of any restriction on the advertising of light beer enabled Swedish brewers of such beer to promote their brand names (which were the same as for their strong beers) and thus gain an advantage over brewers of imported beer, who generally did not produce a light beer.[28]

The Court broadly followed its Advocate General[29] and found the national law to breach Article 28. It then looked to see whether such a breach could be justified.[30] In subsequent cases the Court has gone further and demanded not only that there be an actual disparate impact but that the disparate impact be substantial: in *Burmanjer*[31] the Court talked of the national rules prohibiting itinerant sales without a licence as being 'too insignificant and uncertain to be

---

26 Case C-405/98 *Konsumentombudsmannen v Gourmet International Products (GIP)* [2001] ECR I-1795.
27 Para. 32.
28 Para. 33.
29 Paras 21–4.
30 Paras 25–6.
31 Case C-20/03 [2005] ECR I-4133.

regarded as being such as to hinder or otherwise interfere with trade between Member States'.[32]

Although these cases appear to turn on questions of discrimination, the heavy reliance on paragraph 17, rather than paragraph 16, of *Keck* tends to suggest that the effective denial of market access is a strong driving factor, as Advocate General Jacobs had argued in *Leclerc-Siplec*. This can be seen in *DocMorris*.[33] DocMorris had a pharmacy in the Netherlands and also offered medicines for sale over the internet. Both activities were licensed in the Netherlands. In Germany medicinal products could be sold but only in pharmacists' shops; sales by mail order were prohibited. The German pharmacists' association therefore tried to prevent DocMorris selling medicines to German consumers over the internet. The Court found in paragraph 74 that the prohibition of internet sales was 'more of an obstacle to the pharmacies outside Germany than to those within it'. While German pharmacies also could not sell their products over the internet, for them this was an 'extra or alternative method' of gaining access to the German market: they could still sell their products in their dispensaries. However, for pharmacies not established in Germany, the Court noted, 'the internet provides a more significant way to gain direct access to the German market'.[34] It concluded that '[a] prohibition which has a greater impact on pharmacies established outside German territory could impede access to the market for products from other Member States more than it impedes access for domestic products'. The German rule breached Article 28 because the prohibition did not affect the sale of domestic medicines in the same way as it affected the sale of those coming from other Member States.[35] While the breach could not be justified on public health grounds in respect of non-prescription medicines,[36] it could be justified in respect of prescription medicines.

DocMorris is a particularly important ruling for opening up the single market. New market entrants, however small, can now gain a foothold on markets in other states, via the internet, without having to incur the significant costs of setting up their own distribution and retail networks in those states. The striking feature of the case is that, whilst couched in the language of non-discrimination, in fact the need to secure market access pervades the

---

32 Para. 31.

33 Case C-322/01 *Deutscher Apothekerverband eV v 0800 DocMorris NV, Jacques Waterval* [2003] ECR I-14887, para. 74.

34 Ibid.

35 Ibid.

36 See also Case C-497/03 *Commission v Austria*, judgment of 28 October 2004, not reported: ban on mail order sale of food supplements breached Article 28, with the Court citing *DocMorris* to support this finding.

judgment,[37] as paragraph 74 makes clear.[38] The Court is therefore more likely to find discrimination and thus a breach of Article 28 where the measure prevents or significantly impedes market access (*De Agostini, DocMorris*[39]) than where the impediment to market access is slight (*Hünermund, Leclerc-Siplec*[40]). An approach based on market access would also pave the way for the Court to decide cases where there is a non-discriminatory measure that prevents market access. This would tend to support Advocate General Van Gerven's view in *Torfaen*[41] that Article 28 should catch only those measures that 'screened off the national market'.[42]

THE PERSONS AND SERVICES CASE LAW

Introduction

The *Keck* case law marked a sea change in approach. Prior to *Keck*, the emphasis was on removing national measures which, according to the famous *Dassonville* formula,[43] were capable of hindering, directly or indirectly, actually or potentially, intra-Community trade.[44] This 'market' access approach was apparently curtailed by *Keck* and a non-discrimination model (re)introduced in its place. By contrast, in the context of persons, and especially services, the case law appeared to be moving in the opposite direction. Initially, the focus of the case law was on the question of removing direct and indirect (overt and covert) discrimination. Measures that were not discriminatory were therefore lawful.[45]

---

37 G. Straetmans, (2002) 39 CMLRev 1407, 1418.

38 See also Case C-405/98 *Gourmet* [2001] ECR I-1795, paras 21 and 24.

39 This is particularly so given that these cases, viewed from a services perspective, would involve a breach of Article 49 due to the fact that the prohibition creates a hindrance to the provision of cross-border services (see e.g. Case C-405/98 *Gourmet* [2001] ECR I-1795).

40 See discussion in paras 71–2 of *DocMorris*.

41 Case C-145/88 *Torfaen* [1989] ECR I-3851.

42 See also Advocate General Tizzano's view in Case C-442/02 *Caixa-Bank v Ministère de l'Économie des Finances and de l'industrie* [2004] ECR I-8961, para. 58.

43 Case 8/74 *Procureur du Roi v Dassonville* [1974] ECR 837.

44 Para. 5.

45 See e.g. Case 221/85 *Commission v Belgium (Clinical Biology Laboratories)* [1987] ECR 719.

The *Säger* Ruling

Säger[46] (decided two years prior to *Keck*) marked a departure from this approach. The Court said that Article 49 required

> *not only* the elimination of all discrimination against a person providing services on the ground of his nationality *but also* the abolition of any restriction, even if it applies without distinction to national providers of services and to those of other Member States, when *it is liable to prohibit or otherwise impede* the activities of a provider of services established in another Member State where he lawfully provides similar services.[47]

It continued that any such restriction could be justified by imperative reasons relating to the public interest.[48] This judgment demonstrates a greater willingness by the Court to scrutinize national rules that, even potentially, interfere with the individual's right to free movement. From this perspective the Court is making a more significant incursion into national regulatory autonomy: unless Member States can justify their conduct, the national rule will breach Community law, even if it does not discriminate against nationals.

The hand of Francis Jacobs, the Advocate General in the case, was again much in evidence. He recognized that the Court's case law was at a cross-roads;[49] that most cases concerned discriminatory restrictions and that it was not clear that the Treaty provisions also caught non-discriminatory restrictions. However, he argued that services should be treated by analogy with goods, and that 'non-discriminatory restrictions on the provision of services should be approached in the same way as non-discriminatory restrictions on the free movement of goods under the *Cassis de Dijon* line of case law'.[50] He continued:

> But I do not think that it can be right to state as a general rule that a measure lies wholly outside the scope of Article [49] simply because it does not in any way discriminate between domestic undertakings and those established in other Member States. Nor is such a view supported by the terms of Article [49]: its expressed scope is much broader. If such a view were accepted, it would mean that restrictions on the freedom to provide services would have to be tolerated, even if they lacked any objective justification, on condition that they did not lead to discrimination against foreign undertakings. There might be a variety of restrictions in different Member

46 Case C-76/90 [1991] ECR I-4221, para. 12, emphasis added.

47 See the equivalent statement in respect of Article 39 in Case C-464/02 *Commission v Denmark (Company Vehicles)* [2005] ECR I-7929, para. 45.

48 Para. 15.

49 Para. 20.

50 Para. 24.

> States, none of them intrinsically justified, which collectively might wholly frustrate the aims of Article [49] and render impossible the attainment of a single market in services.

He therefore outlined the general principle that if an undertaking complies with the legislation of the Member State in which it is established it may provide services to clients in another Member State, even though the provision of such services would not normally be lawful under the laws of the second Member State. He continued that 'restrictions imposed by those laws can only be applied against the foreign undertaking if they are justified by some requirement that is compatible with the aims of the Community'. He added that the case for taking that approach is particularly strong when the service is provided by means of post or telecommunications without the provider of the service moving physically between Member States.

Two years later, the Court decided *Keck*,[51] where it made clear that certain non-discriminatory selling arrangements did not breach Article 28. This prompted various Member States to argue in the workers case, *Bosman*,[52] and in the services cases, *Schindler*[53] and *Alpine Investments*[54] that the *Keck* principle should also apply to persons and services. *Alpine Investments* concerned a Dutch law prohibiting cold-calling to sell financial services both within and outside the Netherlands. The Court said that the Dutch law was 'general and non-discriminatory and neither its object nor effect [was] to put the national market at an advantage over providers of services from other Member States'.[55]

The British and Dutch governments argued that since this case was analogous to a non-discriminatory measure governing selling arrangements the principles of *Keck* should apply, with the result that the rule should not breach Article 49. The Court disagreed, arguing that the rule deprived operators of a 'rapid and direct technique for marketing and for contacting potential clients in other Member States'.[56] For this reason the law was not analogous to the selling arrangements in *Keck*[57] because *Keck* concerned a situation where there was *no* hindrance of trade between Member States. By contrast, in *Alpine* the prohibition on cold-calling '*directly affect[ed] access to the*

---

[51] See n. 2 above.

[52] Case C-415/93 *Union Royale Belge de Société de Football Association v Bosman* [1995] ECR I-4921. See generally S. Weatherill (1996) 33 CMLRev 991.

[53] Case C-275/92 *Customs and Excise v Schindler* [1994] ECR I-1039.

[54] Case C-384/93 *Alpine Investments BV v Minister van Financiën* [1995] ECR I-1141.

[55] Para. 35.

[56] Para. 28.

[57] Para. 36.

markets in services in the other Member States and [was] thus capable of hindering intra-Community trade in services'.[58] Having established a breach, the Court then went on to consider the question of justification. It accepted that the prohibition on cold-calling could be justified by the need to safeguard the reputation of the Dutch financial markets[59] and that the measures taken were proportionate.

Alpine does not mean then that the *Keck* ruling does not apply to persons and services.[60] If *Keck* is removed from its specific goods context (certain selling arrangements, a non-legal category developed to curb the excesses of *Dassonville*) and considered instead in terms of its purpose (the removal of matters which do not substantially affect inter-state trade from the purview of Article 28), then it is possible to see how *Keck*-like principles will apply equally to the free movement of persons. *Graf*[61] provided a pointer in that direction. Graf, a German national, worked for his Austrian employer for four years when he terminated his contract in order to take up employment in Germany. Under Austrian law, a worker who has worked for the same employer for more than three years was entitled to a severance payment provided that he was dismissed (and did not just resign). Graf argued that this rule contravened Article 39 because the effect of the Austrian rule was that he lost the chance of being dismissed and so was unable to claim compensation.

The Court disagreed: the Austrian law was genuinely non-discriminatory and did not preclude or deter a worker from ending his contract of employment in order to take a job with another employer. The Court explained that the entitlement to unfair dismissal compensation was not dependent on the worker's choosing whether or not to stay with his current employer but on a future and hypothetical event (being dismissed). In paragraph 25 the Court concluded that 'Such an event is *too uncertain and indirect* a possibility for legislation to be capable of being regarded as liable to hinder free movement for workers.' Thus paragraph 25 of *Graf* says that the event was too remote to be considered liable to affect free movement.[62] Putting it another way, measures which do not substantially hinder access to the market fall outside Article 39 in much the

---

58 Para. 38, emphasis added. See also the 'Golden Shares' cases: See, e.g. Case C-463/00 *Commission v Spain* [2003] ECR I-4581 and Case C-98/01 *Commission v UK* [2003] ECR I-4641 on the free movement of capital.

59 Para. 43.

60 See D. O'Keeffe and A. Barasso, 'Four freedoms, one market and national competence. In search of a dividing line', in D. O'Keeffe (ed.), *Judicial Review in European Union Law: Liber Amicorum in Honour of Lord Slynn of Hadley* (The Hague: Kluwer, 2000).

61 See n. 17 above.

62 Cf. Case C-159/90 *SPUC v Grogan* [1991] ECR I-4685, para. 24; Case C-168/91 *Konstantinidis* [1993] ECR I-1191, para.15.

same way as certain selling arrangements cases (*Punto Casa* (ban on Sunday trading[63]), *Boermans* (restrictions on opening hours of shops)[64]) which do not substantially hinder access to the market fall outside Article 28.

Graf, *Punto Casa* and *Boermans* all concern non-discriminatory rules which did not substantially hinder access to the market and so did not breach the Treaty provision.[65] These rules stand at one stage removed from the individual good or person performing the economic activity. In the interests of subsidiarity, they are the very type of measures that should fall outside the purview of EC law. However, if the non-discriminatory measures had substantially hindered access to the market, then they would have breached the Treaty provision and would have had to be justified. This was the outcome in *Alpine* and *Bosman*, an outcome that may well apply to Article 28 if an equivalent case (e.g. a ban on the sale of a particular good) arose in the field of free movement of goods. This is essentially what Advocate General Jacobs advocated in *Leclerc-Siplec* and repeated in *Alpine*:[66]

> Whether a rule of the Member State of origin constitutes a restriction on the freedom to provide services should be determined by reference to a functional criterion, that is to say, whether it substantially impedes the ability of persons established in its territory to provide intra-Community services. It seems to me that that criterion is consonant with the notion of an internal market and more appropriate than the criterion of discrimination.

He continued that 'From the point of view of the realization of the internal market, what matters is not whether the rules of a Member State are discriminatory but whether they have an adverse effect on its establishment or functioning.'

Hindrance or Obstacle Approach

The formula used in *Säger* of measures 'liable to prohibit or otherwise impede' the activities of the service provider breaching Article 49 is sometimes simplified to 'obstacles' or 'restrictions' to the service provider breaching Article 49. For example, in *Alpine*, Advocate General Jacobs noted that

---

[63] Case C-69 & 258/93 *Punto Casa SpA v Sindaco de Commune di Capena and Others* [1994] ECR I-2355.

[64] Joined Cases C-401 & 402/92 *Criminal proceedings against Tankstation 't Heukske vof and Boermans* [1994] ECR I-2199.

[65] See also the views of Robert Walker LJ in the Court of Appeal of England and Wales in *Professional Contractors' Group v Commissioners of Inland Revenue* [2002] 1 CMLR 46, para. 69.

[66] Para. 47.

'[t]he Court has held that the concept of the common market involves the elimination of all *obstacles* to intra-Community trade "in order to merge the national markets into a single market bringing about conditions as close as possible to those of a genuine internal market"'. The language of 'obstacles' goes back to the simpler wording based on Article 3 EC, examining whether the national measure constitutes an obstacle to free movement.[67] For example, in *Bosman*[68] the Court concluded that the transfer rules constituted an 'obstacle to freedom of movement of workers prohibited in principle by Article [39]' and in *Carpenter*[69] the Court said that Mr Carpenter's freedom to provide services could not be 'fully effective' if he was 'deterred from exercising it by obstacles raised in his country of origin to the entry and residence of his spouse'.[70] Even in the context of goods, the Court still resorts to the language of 'obstacles' and 'hindrance'.[71]

There is little to choose between the *Säger* formula and that based on obstacles, and in cases such as *Kraus* and *Schindler* the Court used both,[72] although both have disadvantages. First, the meanings of the individual terms 'hindrance', 'restrictions' and 'obstacles' are far from clear. Take *Carpenter* as an example: what was the obstacle which 'deterred' Mr Carpenter from exercising his freedom to provide cross-border services – the separation of husband and wife which would be 'detrimental to their family life',[73] the potential loss of child care,[74] or the emotional distress involved? Secondly, the shift away from a model focused on removing *discriminatory* obstacles to free movement to one based on removing any (substantial) obstacles to free movement aligns

---

67 See e.g. Case 36/74 *Walrave and Koch* [1974] ECR 1405, para. 18, and Case 118/75 *Watson and Belmann* [1976] ECR 1185, para. 16.

68 Para. 104 (see n. 52 above). See also Case C-18/95 *Terhoeve* [1999] ECR I-345, para. 39; Case C-275/92 *Schindler* [1994] ECR 1039, para. 45. See also Case C-221/89 *ex parte Factortame Ltd and Others* [1991] ECR I-3905, para. 32; Case C-114/97 *Commission v Spain* [1998] ECR I-6717, para. 44.

69 Case C-60/00 *Mary Carpenter v Secretary of State for the Home Department* [2002] ECR I-6279.

70 Para. 39. See also para. 38.

71 E.g. Case C-36/02 *Omega Spielhallen* [2004] ECR I-9609, para. 25. Moreover, in so far as use of the form of the game developed by Pulsar involves the use of specific equipment, which is also lawfully marketed in the United Kingdom, the prohibition imposed on Omega is likely to deter it from acquiring the equipment in question, thereby infringing the free movement of goods ensured by Article 28.

72 Cf. paras 28 and 32 in Case C-19/92 *Kraus* [1993] ECR I-1663 and paras 43 and 45 in Case C-275/92 *Schindler* [1994] ECR I-1039. See also Case C-118/96 *Safir* [1998] ECR I-1897, paras 23 and 25; Case C-79/01 *Payroll Data Services* [2002] ECR I-8923, paras 26–7.

73 Para. 39.

74 Para. 44.

the persons jurisprudence more closely with that following the decision in *Dassonville*.[75]

Reversion to the Discrimination Model?

Just when it looked like the case law was reaching some sort of settled state, a number of cases were decided over a relatively short period suggesting that the Court was backtracking somewhat from a pure *Säger* market access approach. No explanation for this change of heart has been clearly articulated but it seems likely that the judges have become increasingly concerned that *Dassonville* might be repeating itself in the field of persons. Advocate General Tizzano came closest to identifying these concerns in his influential Opinion in *Caixa-Bank*.[76] He expressed profound misgivings about the 'rather broad concept of restriction' in the case law covering all 'national measures *liable* to hinder *or make less attractive the exercise of fundamental freedoms* guaranteed by the Treaty'.[77] He said that such a broad approach to the concept of restrictions allows economic operators, both national and foreign, to abuse the Treaty to oppose any national measure that, solely because it regulated the conditions for pursuing an economic activity, could in the final analysis narrow profit margins and hence reduce the attractiveness of pursuing that particular economic activity.[78] He continued: [79]

> However, that would be tantamount to bending the Treaty to a purpose for which it was not intended: that is to say, not in order to create an internal market in which conditions are similar to those of a single market and where operators can move freely, but in order to establish a market without rules. Or rather, a market in which rules are prohibited as a matter of principle, except for those necessary and proportionate to meeting imperative requirements in the public interest.

He therefore advocated a return to a non-discrimination combined with a market access approach:[80] where the principle of non-discrimination is

---

75 See n. 43 above.

76 See n. 42 above.

77 Para. 39, emphasis in the original, criticizing, in particular, Case C-255/97 *Pfeiffer Grosshandel* [1999] ECR I-2835.

78 Para. 62. The Court itself acknowledged this in Case C-290/04 *FKP Skorpio* [2006] ECR I-000, para. 46: 'the application of the host Member State's national rules to providers of services is liable to prohibit, impede or render less attractive the provision of services to the extent that it involves expense and additional administrative and economic burdens'.

79 Para. 63, echoing the sentiments expressed by AG Tesauro in his influential Opinion in *Hünermund*, para. 1 (see n. 6 above) which led to the ruling in *Keck*.

80 Para. 66.

respected a national measure cannot be described as a restriction on the freedom of movement of persons unless the measure 'directly affects market access'. This is resonant of the approach in *Keck*, where the presumption is that such national measures are lawful unless there are good reasons why they are not. Advocate General Tizzano added that this approach made it possible to reconcile the objective of merging the different national markets into a single common market with the continuation of Member States' general powers to regulate economic activities.[81]

Four cases illustrate this change of direction. The first, *Mobistar*,[82] concerned a request for the annulment of the taxes adopted by a community in Belgium on transmission pylons, masts and antennae for mobile phones on the grounds, *inter alia*, that it contravened Article 49 on the free movement of services. The Court, having cited the *Säger* market access test, said:

> By contrast, measures, the only effect of which is to create additional costs in respect of the service in question and which affect in the same way the provision of services between Member States and that within one Member State, do not fall within the scope of Article [49] of the Treaty.

One way of reading *Mobistar* is that the Court is reverting to a pure non-discrimination model.

The second case, *Weigel*,[83] concerned a German husband and wife who transferred their residence to Austria where Mr Weigel got a job. They both brought their cars with them but, due to their change of residence, they had to re-register their cars for which a fairly hefty tax was charged. The Court rejected their arguments that this breached Article 39(2), noting that the Austrian rule applied 'without regard to the nationality of the worker concerned to all those who registered a car in Austria and, accordingly, it is applicable without distinction'.[84] The Court then added that 'It is true that it is likely to have a negative bearing on the decision of migrant workers to exercise their right to freedom of movement'.[85] Under the *Säger* formula, this observation would have been enough for a finding of a breach of Article 39 which the Member State would then have had to justify. However, in *Weigel* the Court resorted to the pure non-discrimination approach and said that, provided that nationals and migrants were treated in the same way, the fact that

---

81 Para. 68.

82 Joined Cases C-544/03 and C-545/03 *Mobistar SA v Commune de Fleron* [2005] ECR I-7723.

83 Case C-387/01 *Weigel v Finanzlandesdirektion für Vorarlberg* [2004] ECR I-4981.

84 Para. 52.

85 Para. 54.

the tax regimes of the different Member States were different was neither here nor there.[86]

The third case, *Viacom II*,[87] also concerned taxation. At issue was a dispute between Giotto, a French estate agent, and Viacom, an Italian bill-posting company employed to put up posters in Genoa in Italy advertising Giotto's services. Giotto refused to reimburse Viacom for the sum of €226.92 (*c*. £150) paid to the Genoa authorities by way of an advertising tax on the grounds that the tax contravened Article 49 EC. The Court began by citing the *Säger* formula[88] but then noted the non-discriminatory nature of the tax: the rules on the levying of this tax did not 'draw any distinction based on the place of establishment or the provider or recipient of the bill-posting services or on the place of origin of the goods or services that form the subject-matter of the advertising messages disseminated'.[89] The Court then added that because the tax was applied only to outdoor advertising activities involving the use of public space administered by the municipal authorities and its amount was fixed at a level which might be considered 'modest in relation to the value of the services provided which are subject to it',[90] the levying of the tax was not liable to prohibit or impede the provision of services. It therefore did not breach Article 49. In other words, the tax regime was non-discriminatory and also did not create a substantial impediment to the free movement of services. This again reflects the approach in *Graf* and emphasizes the long-established rule that mere differences between national laws are not enough to trigger the application of the Treaty: there needs to be something more akin to protectionism for the Treaty to apply.[91]

Given that the Court has often relied on the non-discrimination model in respect of taxation, perhaps *Mobistar*, *Weigel* and *Viacom II* are not so remarkable. They also bear the hallmarks of the cases decided under Article 90 EC,[92] where the Court has long respected the principle of national fiscal autonomy, allowing Member States to tax (goods in the context of Article 90, the activity

86 Para. 55. The Court reached the same conclusion under Article 18 in Case C-365/02 *Lindfors* [2004] ECR I-7183.

87 Case C-134/03 *Viacom Outdoor Srl v Giotto Immobilier SARL (Viacom II)* [2005] ECR I-1167. The reference in Case C-190/02 *Viacom I* [2002] ECR I-8287 had been declared inadmissible due to the lack of sufficient information.

88 Para. 35.

89 Para. 37.

90 Para. 38.

91 See by analogy: Case C-391/92 *Commission v Greece (Baby Milk)* [1995]. ECR I-1621, paras 16–18 and the discussion in D. Chalmers *et al.*, *European Union Law* (Cambridge: CUP, 2006), 672–3.

92 Article 90 was also considered in *Weigel* and AG Kokott in *Viacom II* referred to the Article 90 case law.

in the services cases) as they choose, provided the tax does not discriminate on the grounds of origin and the effects of the tax are not protective. On the other hand they seem symptomatic of a more general change of approach, which can also be seen in the fourth case, *Innoventif*,[93] which does not concern tax as such but another type of charge. The question was raised in that case of whether Articles 43 and 48 EC precluded Germany from making registration, in the register of companies, of a branch of a limited company established in another Member State subject to the payment of an advance on the anticipated cost of the publication of the objects of the company as set out in its instruments of constitution. The Court said no, arguing that the payment of an advance was 'not liable to place companies from other Member States in a less favourable factual or legal situation than companies from the Member States of establishment',[94] and so a payment of an advance did not constitute an obstacle to the pursuit of the company's activities. This seems to be an application of the pure non-discrimination model.

Conclusions

The case law in this area is in flux. In more complicated cases, especially those involving legal persons, where there has been some impediment to market access, the Court has used and will continue to use the *Säger* approach.[95] However, there is a growing penumbra of cases where the Court thinks, at times, that Treaty intervention may well be going too far when, as in *Keck*, it feels that migrants are challenging any national rule which imposes costs on them, albeit that the rules are not specifically aimed at migrants from other Member States. In these cases there appears to be a shift away from a market access-inspired approach.

DEROGATIONS, JUSTIFICATIONS AND THE BALANCING ACT

The Basic Rules

So far we have concentrated on establishing breach. We turn now to the question

---

93 Case C-453/04 *Innoventif* [2006] ECR I-4929.

94 Para. 39.

95 See e.g. Case C-470/04 *N v Inspecteur van de Belastingdienst Oost/kantoor Almelo* [2006] ECR I-7409, para. 39 and Case C-196/04 *Cadbury's Schweppes v Commissioners of the Inland Revenue* [2006] ECR I-7995, para. 42 concerning Article 43 and both decided after *Innoventif*.

of derogations and justifications once a breach has been established. According to the orthodoxy, directly discriminatory measures breach the Treaty provision but defences can be found in one of the express derogations.[96] By contrast, indistinctly applicable, indirectly discriminatory and non-discriminatory measures which hinder free movement also breach Articles 28, 39, 43 and 49 unless the national measures can be objectively justified *or* saved by one of the express derogations. In *O'Flynn*[97] the language of objective justification was used in the context of free movement of workers. In respect of establishment and services, the Court tends to talk about justifications in the 'public' or 'general interest' or 'imperative requirements'.[98] It is likely that the term 'objective justification' is the functional equivalent to the 'public interest' requirements[99] that in turn are the law on persons' equivalent to mandatory requirements in goods. In all cases the Court recognizes that there existed certain national interests that are worthy of protection[100] and should take precedence over the free movement provisions.

In the services case, *Gouda*,[101] the Court listed the public interest grounds that it had already recognized:

- professional rules intended to protect the recipients of a service;[102]
- protection of intellectual property;[103]

---

[96] Case C-288/89 *Stichting Collectieve Antennvoorziening Gouda v Comissariaat voor de Media* [1991] ECR I-4007.

[97] Case C-237/94 *O'Flynn v Adjudication Officer* [1996] ECR I-2617.

[98] Case C-76/90 *Säger v Dennemeyer & Co. Ltd* [1991] ECR I-4221, para. 15; Case C-55/94 *Gebhard* [1996] ECR I-4165, para. 37.

[99] This view is supported by the workers case, Case C-195/98 *Österreicher Gewerkschaftsbund v Republik Österreich* [2000] ECR I-10497, para. 45, where the Court reported that the Austrian government contends that the restrictions on free movement are 'justified by overriding reasons of public interest and are consistent with the principle of proportionality', and the services case, Case C-118/96 *Safir v Skattemyndigheten i Dalarnas Län* [1998] ECR I-1897, para. 22: 'Article [49] of the Treaty precludes the application of any national legislation which, without objective justification, impedes a provider of services from actually exercising the freedom to provide them'.

[100] See AG Tesauro in Case C-118/96 *Safir* [1998] ECR I-1897, para. 29.

[101] Case C-288/89 [1991] ECR I-4007.

[102] Joined Cases 110 & 111/78 *Ministère public v Willy van Wesemael and Others* [1979] ECR 35, para. 28. In Case C-3/95 *Reisebüro Broede v Sandker* [1996] ECR I-6511, para. 38, the Court spelled out this justification more fully: 'the application of professional rules to lawyers, in particular those relating to organization, qualifications, professional ethics, supervision and liability, ensures that the ultimate consumers of legal services and the sound administration of justice are provided with the necessary guarantees in relation to integrity and experience'.

[103] Case 62/79 *Coditel* [1980] ECR 881.

- protection of workers;[104]
- consumer protection;[105]
- conservation of the national historic and artistic heritage;[106]
- turning to account the archaeological, historical and artistic heritage of a country and the widest possible dissemination of knowledge of the artistic and cultural heritage of a country;[107] and
- cultural policy.[108]

As with *Cassis*, the list in *Gouda* is not exhaustive. Other justifications have been recognized. For example, in *Alpine Investments*,[109] the Court said that a national law prohibiting cold-calling for sales of financial services could be justified by the need to safeguard the reputation of the Dutch financial markets and to protect the investing public.[110] In *Schindler*,[111] as justification for a national ban on lotteries, the Court recognized various grounds connected with the social ills of gambling (e.g. preventing gambling and avoiding the lottery from becoming the source of private profit; avoiding the risk of crime or fraud; avoiding the risk of incitement to spend, with damaging individual and social consequences). Most recently, the Court has recognized the prevention of social dumping[112] or unfair competition[113] as a public interest requirement.

---

104 Case 279/80 *Webb* [1981] ECR 3305, para. 19; Joined Cases 62–3/81 *Seco v EVI* [1982] ECR 223, para. 14; Case C-113/89 *Rush Portuguesa* [1990] ECR I-1417, para. 18. Subsequently in Case C-272/94 *Guiot* [1996] ECR I-1905, para. 16, the Court stressed the importance of the social protection of workers in the construction industry; Case C-79/01 *Payroll Data Services (Italy)* [2002] ECR I-8923, para. 31.

105 Case 220/83 *Commission v France* [1986] ECR 3663, para. 20; Case 252/83 *Commission v Denmark* [1986] ECR 3713, para. 20; Case 205/84 *Commission v Germany* [1986] ECR 3755, para. 30; Case 206/84 *Commission v Ireland* [1986] ECR 3817, para. 20; Case C-180/89 *Commission v Italy (Tourist Guides)* [1991] ECR I-709, para. 20.

106 Case C-180/89 *Commission v Italy* [1991] ECR I-709, para. 20.

107 Case C-154/89 *Commission v France* [1991] ECR I-659, para. 17; Case C-198/89 *Commission v Greece* [1991] ECR I-727, para. 21.

108 Case C-288/89 *Gouda* [1991] ECR I-4007, paras 22–3; Case C-353/89 *Commission v Netherlands* [1991] ECR I-4069 and Case C-23/93 *TV10* [1994] ECR I-4795.

109 Case C-384/93 [1995] ECR I-1141, para. 44.

110 See also Case C-222/95 *Parodi v Banque H. Albert de Bary* [1997] ECR I-3899, para. 22, where the Court noted that the banking sector is a particularly sensitive area from the perspective of consumer protection.

111 Case C-275/92 [1994] ECR I-1039, para. 60. See also Case C-124/97 *Läärä v Kihlakunnansyyttäjä* [1999] ECR I-6067.

112 Case C-244/04 *Commission v Germany* [2006] ECR I-885, para. 61.

113 Case C-60/03 *Wolff & Müller v Pereira Félix* [2004] ECR I-9553, para. 41.

Fundamental Rights

A Member State can invoke reasons of public interest to justify a national measure only if that measure is proportionate and compatible with fundamental rights.[114] This can be seen in *Carpenter*[115] where the UK proposed to deport Mrs Carpenter, a Filipino national, who, having overstayed her entry permit to the UK, married a British national. Faced with the threat of deportation, Mrs Carpenter argued that this would restrict her husband's ability to carry on business as a service provider in other Member States since she looked after his children while he was away.[116] The Court said that a Member State could 'invoke reasons of public interest to justify a national measure which is likely to obstruct the exercise of the freedom to provide services only if that measure is compatible with the fundamental rights whose observance the Court ensures'.[117] On the question of fundamental rights, the Court said that the decision to deport Mrs Carpenter constituted:

> an interference with the exercise by Mr Carpenter of his right to respect for his family life within the meaning of Article 8 of the [European Convention on Human Rights] . . . which is among the fundamental rights which, according to the Court's settled case-law, restated by the Preamble to the Single European Act and by Article 6(2) EU, are protected in Community law.[118]

Drawing on the case law of the European Court of Human Rights, the Court then said that even though no right of an alien to enter or to reside in a particular country was guaranteed by the Convention, 'the removal of a person from a country where close members of his family are living may amount to an infringement of the right to respect for family life as guaranteed by Article 8(1) of the Convention'. It continued that such an interference would infringe the Convention if it did not meet the requirements of Article 8(2), namely that the deportation had to be in accordance with the law, motivated by one or more of

---

114 Case C-260/89 *ERT* [1991] ECR I-2925, para. 43; Case C-368/95 *Vereinigte Familiapress Zeitungsverlags- und vertriebs GmbH v Heinrich Bauer Verlag* [1997] ECR I-3689, para. 24; Case C-413/99 *Baumbast and R v Secretary of State for the Home Department* [2002] ECR I-7091, para. 72.

115 N. 69 above, paras 40–41.

116 Para. 17.

117 Para. 40, citing Case C-260/89 *ERT* [1991] ECR I-2925, para. 43, and Case C-368/95 *Familiapress* [1997] ECR I-3689, para. 24.

118 Para. 41. See also Case C-63/99 *R v Secretary of State for the Home Department, ex parte Gloszczuk* [2001] ECR I-6369, para. 85; Case C-235/99 *R v Secretary of State for the Home Department, ex parte Kondova* [2001] ECR I-6427, para. 90; Case C-413/99 *Baumbast* [2002] ECR I-7091, para. 72; Case C-109/01 *Secretary of State for the Home Department v Akrich* [2003] ECR I-9607, paras 58–9.

the legitimate aims under Article 8(2) and 'necessary in a democratic society' (justified by a pressing social need and proportionate).[119] The Court concluded that a decision to deport Mrs Carpenter did not 'strike a fair balance' between the competing interests of the right of Mr Carpenter to respect for his family life on the one hand and the maintenance of public order and public safety, on the other.[120] Even though Mrs Carpenter had infringed UK immigration laws by overstaying she did not constitute a danger to public order and safety. Therefore, the decision to deport her was not proportionate.

As we have already seen in this volume,[121] one of Francis Jacobs's greatest contributions to the evolution of the European Union jurisprudence has been the prioritizing of fundamental human rights. One of his early opinions, in *Konstantinidis*,[122] demonstrated this clearly. Konstantinidis, a Greek national, worked in Germany as a self-employed masseur and assistant hydrotherapist. Although his name was entered into the marriage register as Konst*ad*inidis, he argued that the correct transcription of his name should have been Konst*ant*inidis. The Court said that the German rules breached Article 43 only in so far as their application caused a Greek national 'such a degree of inconvenience as in fact to interfere with his freedom to exercise the right of establishment'.[123] It continued that the interference would be sufficiently substantial if, as a result of the transliteration, the spelling of Konstantinidis' name led to a modification of the pronunciation with the risk that other clients might confuse him with others.[124]

Whilst Advocate General Jacobs reached much the same conclusion, his approach was inspired by fundamental human rights[125] and not market access. He said that a Community national who goes to another Member State as a worker or a self-employed person was entitled not just to pursue his trade or profession and to enjoy the same living and working conditions as nationals of the host state but also to assume that:

---

119 Para. 42, citing *Boultif v Switzerland*, No. 54273/00, paras 39, 41 and 46, ECHR 2001-IX.

120 Para. 43.

121 See Chapter 2.

122 Case C-168/91 *Christos Konstantinidis v Stadt Altensteig* [1993] ECR I-1191.

123 Para. 15. Cf. Case 379/87 *Groener v Minister of Education* [1990] ECR I-3967.

124 Para. 16.

125 See e.g. para. 40: 'A person's right to his name is fundamental in every sense of the word. After all, where are we without our name? It is our name that distinguishes each of us from the rest of humanity. It is our name that gives us a sense of identity, dignity and self-esteem. To strip a person of his rightful name is the ultimate degradation, as is evidenced by the common practice of repressive penal regimes which consists in substituting a number for a prisoner's name.'

> wherever he goes to earn a living in the European Community, he will be treated in accordance with a common code of fundamental values, in particular those laid down in accordance with the European Convention on Human Rights. In other words, he is entitled to say 'civis europeus sum' [I am a European citizen] and to invoke the status in order to oppose any violation of his fundamental rights.[126]

This Opinion, delivered just as the Treaty on European Union was being concluded, contained an important recognition of the changing attitude towards migrants: they were not only factors of production but were also citizens with fundamental (civil and political) rights. This approach eventually inspired decisions such as in *Martínez Sala*[127] and *Baumbast*[128] on the free movement of citizens.

In both *Carpenter* and *Konstantinidis* fundamental rights were used to limit the state's justifications. In more recent cases, such as *Schmidberger*[129] and *Omega*,[130] fundamental rights have constituted the justification. In other words, fundamental rights can be invoked defensively as a mandatory requirement to justify a restriction on trade. *Schmidberger* concerned an environmental association that organized a demonstration, blocking a stretch of the Brenner Motorway (the A13, the major transit route for trade between Northern Europe and Italy) for 30 hours, to draw attention to the threat to the environment and public health posed by the constant increase in the movement of heavy goods vehicles on the motorway.[131] Schmidberger, a German transport company, sought damages for the losses it suffered from its lorries not being able to use this route. The Court said that the fact that the competent authorities of a Member State did not ban this demonstration was capable of restricting intra-Community trade in goods and so breached Articles 28 and 29 EC on free movement of goods, read together with Article 10 on the duty of co-operation.[132]

However, the Austrian authorities justified their (in)action on the grounds of the fundamental rights of the demonstrators to freedom of expression and freedom of assembly guaranteed by the European Convention on Human

---

126 Para. 46.

127 Case C-85/96 *Martínez Sala v Freistaat Bayern* [1998] ECR I-2691.

128 Case C-413/99 *Baumbast and R v Secretary of State for the Home Department* [2002] ECR I-7091.

129 Case C-112/00 [2003] ECR I-5659.

130 Case C-36/02 *Omega Spielhallen- und Automatenaufstellungs-GmbH v Oberbürgermeisterin der Bundesstadt Bonn* [2004] ECR I-9609.

131 This is a matter of serious concern for the Tyrolean authorities who tried to ban from the A12 Inntal motorway all heavy goods vehicles over 7.5 tonnes carrying certain goods (e.g. logs, cork, stone, vehicles) (IP/03/984) but were stopped by the Court: Case C-320/03 R *Commission v Austria* [2003] ECR I-7029.

132 Para. 64.

Rights (ECHR) and the national constitution, principles which, the Court said, it recognized formed an integral part of the general principles of EC law.[133] It continued that 'since both the Community and its Member States are required to respect fundamental rights, the protection of those rights is a legitimate interest which, in principle, justifies a restriction of the obligations imposed by Community law, even under a fundamental freedom guaranteed by the Treaty such as the free movement of goods'.[134] Thus, the Court saw the fundamental rights as a freestanding justification or public interest requirement.[135]

However, since the two human rights at stake, described by the Court as 'fundamental pillars of a democratic society',[136] were not absolute, the Court recognized that their exercise could be restricted, provided that 'the restrictions in fact correspond to objectives of general interest and do not, taking account of the aim of the restrictions, constitute disproportionate and unacceptable interference, impairing the very substance of the rights guaranteed'.[137] The Court then tried to determine whether a fair balance had been struck between the competing interests.[138] It noted that the demonstration took place following a request for authorization, as required by national law, and after the Austrian authorities had decided to allow it to go ahead;[139] the obstacle to free movement was limited (a single event, on a single route, lasting for 30 hours); the demonstrators were motivated by a desire to express their opinion on a matter of public importance and not by a desire to restrict trade in goods of a particular type or from a particular source;[140] and various administrative and supporting measures had been taken by the Austrian authorities to limit the disruption to road traffic, including an extensive publicity campaign launched well in advance by the media and the motoring organizations, both in Austria and in neighbouring countries,[141] as well as the designation of alternative routes. The Court therefore concluded that the fact that the authorities of a Member State did not ban the demonstration in these circumstances was compatible with Community law.[142]

While the outcome of *Schmidberger* was broadly welcomed and not surprising, it paved the way for potentially more difficult balancing to be

---

133 Paras 71–3.
134 Para. 74.
135 See further C. Barnard, *The Substantive Law of the EU: The Four Freedoms* (Oxford: OUP, 2007) Ch. 6.
136 Para. 79.
137 Para. 80.
138 Para. 81.
139 Para. 84.
140 Para. 86.
141 Para. 87.
142 Para. 94.

carried out by the Court, problems created by the broad market access approach. *Viking*[143] demonstrates some of these difficulties.

A Difficult Balancing Act: The *Viking* Case

Viking Line, a Finnish company and one of the largest passenger ferry operators in the world, wanted to reflag its vessel, the *Rosella*, which traded the loss-making route between Helsinki and Tallinn in Estonia, under the Estonian flag so that it could man the ship with an Estonian crew to be paid considerably less than the existing Finnish crew.[144] The International Transport Workers' Federation (ITF), which had been running a flag of convenience (FOC) campaign trying to stop ship owners from taking such action, told its affiliates in the jurisdictions which the *Rosella* visited to boycott the *Rosella* and to take other solidarity industrial action against both the *Rosella* and other Viking vessels. The Finnish Seaman's Union (FSU) threatened strike action. Viking therefore sought an injunction in the English High Court (ITF had its base in London and so jurisdiction was established pursuant to the Brussels Regulation 44/2001[145]), restraining the ITF and the FSU from breaching, *inter alia*, Articles 43 and 49 EC.

In the High Court, Gloster J ruled that reflagging of a vessel in a Member State involved the exercise of establishment;[146] and that the ITF/FSU's proposed actions amounted to a restriction on the freedom of establishment under Article 43.[147] Applying *Gebhard*[148] and *Guiot*,[149] the judge ruled that 'Any measure which places an additional financial burden on a person so as to make the exercise of a free movement right more difficult constitutes a restriction on that free movement right.' She also thought that Article 43 applied to organizations like ITF/FSU which intended to create 'obstacles resulting from the exercise of their legal autonomy by associations or organisation not governed by public law'.[150] Indeed, she went so far as to say that the ruling in *Angonese*,[151] that Article 39

143 *Viking Line ABP v The International Transport Workers' Federation, the Finnish Seaman's Union* [2005] EWHC 1222 (QBD) and [2005] EWCA Civ. 1299 (Court of Appeal).

144 For a full description of the facts, see Waller LJ in the Court of Appeal [2005] EWCA Civ. 1299.

145 OJ [2001] L12/1.

146 Para. 106.

147 Para. 99.

148 Case C-55/94 [1995] ECR I-4165.

149 Case C-272/94 *Criminal Proceedings against Guiot* [1996] ECR I-1905.

150 Case C-415/93 *Bosman* [1995] ECR I-4921, paras 82–4.

151 Case C-281/98 [2000] ECR I-4139.

had full horizontal direct effect, was not confined to workers' cases, and applied equally to Article 43.[152]

The judge then ruled that the FOC policy was directly discriminatory: it prevented the owner of a Finnish vessel from reflagging so as to employ a crew of another Member State, and compelled the owner to retain its Finnish crew. Even if the policy was not directly discriminatory, it was, she said, indirectly discriminatory. She then considered whether the directly discriminatory conduct could be saved by reference to one of the express derogations, namely public policy. She said:[153]

> It is clear that the exercise of fundamental rights may fall within the scope of the public policy justification; . . . The right to take industrial action can, for present purposes, be characterized as part of the fundamental right of freedom of expression and of freedom of association and to take collective action.

However, since, as we have seen in *Carpenter*, the express derogations must also be appraised by reference to fundamental rights, Gloster J went on to find that the exercise of these fundamental rights could not, without more, authorize or justify discrimination on the grounds of nationality or sex.[154] Thus, she said it was not compatible with Article 14 ECHR (prohibition against discrimination) that workers have a fundamental right to strike to prevent women from being employed on ferryboats. In the same way, the exercise or enjoyment of the right to take industrial action to prevent the reflagging of a vessel could also be characterized as a fundamental right.[155] She therefore concluded that fundamental rights could not be invoked to justify discrimination on the grounds of nationality.

Gloster J then considered whether the FOC rule, if considered to be *indirectly* discriminatory, could be objectively justified. While acknowledging that the protection of workers was an acceptable public interest justification, she required more of the social purpose of the justification. The judge rejected the

---

152 Para. 115.

153 Para. 123.

154 Para. 124. See also AG Jacobs's opinion in Case C-67/96 *Albany International BV v Stichting Bedrijfspensioenfonds Textielindustrie* [1999] ECR I-5751, where he said that while management and labour are in principle free to enter into such agreements as they see fit, they must, like any other economic actor, respect the limitations imposed by Community law, such as sex equality and free movement of workers. He continues that this could be seen as an application of the general rule that the exercise of a fundamental right may be restricted provided that the restriction in fact corresponds to objectives of general interest pursued by the Community and does not constitute in relation to the aim pursued a disproportionate and intolerable interference, impairing the very substance of the rights guaranteed.

155 Para. 126.

first purpose offered, safeguarding the job opportunities of the FSU's members, on the grounds that Viking had given an undertaking that if it reflagged the *Rosella* none of its crew would be made redundant but would be transferred elsewhere in the group.[156]

She also rejected the second purpose put forward by the unions, safeguarding the level of terms and condition of employment and the living standards of all seafarers working on vessels trading in the Baltic and Nordic area, regardless of their nationality, on the grounds, first, that the primary purpose of the proposed action was to protect *Finnish* jobs; secondly, that it would be disproportionate to insist that Finnish terms and conditions be applied to all workers on board the *Rosella* even though the vessel was reflagged in Estonia; and lastly, if the vessel was reflagged in Estonia, the crew would be protected by an ITF-affiliated Estonian trade union and Estonian collective bargaining. If due regard was given to the principle of mutual recognition, the judge said that it did not seem proportionate that the FSU and ITF should be entitled to insist that the interests of workers on board the *Rosella* be protected by the FSU, as opposed to an ITF-affiliated trade union established in another Member State.[157] Thus the judge concluded that the unions' anticipated actions would not be objectively justified or were not appropriate or proportionate to secure the unions' purposes. As a result, she ordered interim relief in favour of Viking to restrain the unions from taking industrial action to deter Viking from (1) reflagging the *Rosella* and (2) if it did reflag, requiring Viking to continue paying its crew at Finnish rates negotiated with the FSU.

Gloster J's decision on interim relief was reversed by the Court of Appeal, which referred the case to the Court of Justice to rule on the issues considered by the judge at first instance. Before making the reference, Waller LJ, giving judgment on behalf of the court, expressed grave concerns about the view that Articles 43 and 49 applied to trade union acts.[158] While recognizing that there should not be a blanket exclusion of trade union activities from the free movement provisions, he thought the control mechanism should be the social policy Title of the Treaty; that is, 'if an activity plainly does not pursue a social object with Title XI, the free movement Articles will apply, whereas if it does they should not'.[159] He also suggested that if there was direct discrimination, the unions would be unlikely to justify any restriction but he thought it more likely that some indirect discrimination or other restriction would be found which, he recognized, might be justified by reference to fundamental rights. For these reasons, the Court of Appeal set aside Gloster J's decision and refused interim

---

156 Paras 133–4.
157 Para. 138.
158 Para. 62.
159 Para. 44.

measures because, as Waller LJ said, granting the injunction to Viking would be close to giving Viking the remedy which should only be available to it after a full trial of the action.[160]

AG Poiares Maduro, Opinion in *Viking* demonstrated an acute awareness of the need to balance the competing interests. He agreed that Community law did apply to the case, arguing that the inclusion of both single market and social policy objectives in the Treaty meant that the aim of the Community was to bring these policies together, not to give supremacy to one over the other. He also thought that the Treaty provisions should extend to private action – that is to say to action that does not ultimately emanate from the state and to which the competition rules do not apply[161] – where the individual's action was 'capable of effectively restricting others from exercising their right to freedom of movement'.[162] This was the situation in *Viking* where 'Taken together, the actions of the FSU and the ITF are capable of effectively restricting the exercise of the right to freedom of establishment of an undertaking such as *Viking*.'[163] Therefore Article 43 applied.

He then considered how to balance Viking's right of freedom of establishment under Article 43 with ITF and FSU's right to take industrial action to protect their members' interests. Having recognized the benefits of freedom of establishment, both to the undertaking and to the state where the (re)establishment occurred, he also acknowledged the 'painful consequences' workers could suffer as a result of the relocation. He said that the Treaty did not 'turn a blind eye' to such workers because the Treaty embodies a 'social contract'. Underpinning this social contract is the idea that 'workers throughout Europe must accept the recurring negative consequences that are inherent to the common market's creation of increasing prosperity, in exchange for which society must commit itself to the general improvement of their living and working conditions, and to the provision of economic support to those workers who, as a consequence of market forces, come into difficulties'.[164] In a strong endorsement of fundamental social rights he added 'The right to associate and the right to collective action are essential instruments for workers to express their voice and to make governments and employers live up to their part of the social contract.'[165]

The question, then, was whether the industrial action undertaken by ITF went too far. Advocate General Poiares Maduro distinguished between two types of industrial action:

---

160 Para. 64.
161 Para. 37.
162 Para. 43.
163 Para. 55.
164 Para. 59.
165 Para. 60.

1. Collective action in the interests of the jobs and working conditions of the *current crew*.
2. Collective action to improve the terms of employment of seafarers throughout the *Community*.

In respect of the first type of industrial action, which has the effect of restricting the right of establishment of an undertaking that intends to relocate to another Member State in order to protect the workers of that undertaking, the Advocate General said this was compatible with EC law provided that cases of intra-Community relocation (Finland–Estonia) were not treated less favourably than relocations within the national borders (one part of Finland to another).[166] However, he added a caveat: this presumption of legality did not apply to collective action that merely sought to prevent an undertaking that has moved elsewhere from lawfully providing its services in the Member State in which it had previously been established.[167] In other words, while the FSU could take collective action to stop Viking relocating from Finland, once Viking had relocated in Estonia it could not take such action because 'Blocking or threatening to block, through collective action, an undertaking established in one Member State from lawfully providing its services in another Member State . . . entirely negates the rationale of the common market.'[168]

In respect of the second type of collective action, the Advocate General sent out an important message that coordinating the national unions so as to promote a certain level of rights for seafarers was consistent with the unions' right to collective action because it constituted a reasonable method of counter-balancing the actions of undertakings who sought to lower their labour costs by exercising their rights to freedom of movement. He continued:

> One must not ignore, in that regard, the fact that workers have a lower degree of mobility than capital or undertakings. When they cannot vote with their feet, workers must act through coalition. The recognition of their right to act collectively on a European level thus simply transposes the logic of national collective action to the European stage.[169]

However, AG Poaires Maduro then distinguished between the situation where, on the one hand, all national unions were *obliged* to support collective

166 Para. 65.
167 Para. 67.
168 Para. 68.
169 Para. 70.

action by any of their fellow unions and, on the other, where they had a choice to offer such support. The former situation might constitute an abuse (and thus, presumably, could contravene Article 43), he said, because it would enable any national union to summon the assistance of other unions in order to make relocation to another Member State conditional on the application of its own preferred standards of worker protection, even after relocation had taken place.

He continued 'In effect, therefore, such a policy would be liable to protect the collective bargaining power of some national unions at the expense of the interests of others, and to partition the labour market in breach of the rules on freedom of movement.'[170] In other words, if ITF was able to summon all its affiliate unions to help the FSU, this would make Viking's relocation conditional on the continued application of Finnish labour standards, thus protecting the FSU's position to the detriment of the Estonian equivalent. By contrast, where other unions were, in effect, free to choose whether or not to participate in collective action, then the danger of discriminatory abuse of a coordinated policy would be prevented. Whether this was the situation in the circumstances of the present case was best left to the referring court.

Lessons from *Albany*

Francis Jacobs himself had already been involved in a case requiring a similarly difficult balancing act, *Albany*,[171] where the issue was whether collective agreements on wages and conditions, as well as those implementing Community directives, could be shielded from Community competition law (Article 81(1) and (2)). If collective bargaining had been a fundamental right then collective agreements might have been protected from Article 81,[172] although Advocate General Jacobs doubted this.[173] However, since collective bargaining was not, according to Advocate General Jacobs, a fundamental right then in principle collective agreements risked being exposed to the full rigours of Article 81 because, according to the Commission's submissions, collective agreements are, by their very nature, restrictive of competition since generally employees cannot offer to work for a wage below the agreed minimum, and

170 Para. 71.

171 Case C-67/96 *Albany* [1999] ECR I-5751, paras 66 and 67.

172 See the arguments of the Funds, the Dutch and French governments and the Commission.

173 Para. 163: 'The mere recognition of a fundamental right to bargain collectively would therefore not suffice to shelter collective bargaining from the applicability of the competition rules.'

they affect trade between Member States.[174] Such agreements would thus be prohibited and void unless exempted by the Commission under Article 81(3).[175] The granting of such an exemption would be unlikely since that provision does not allow social objectives to be taken into account.[176] This result would occur despite the fact that 'there is international consensus on the legitimate and socially desirable character of collective bargaining'[177] which is to prevent employees from engaging in a 'race to the bottom' with regard to wages and working conditions.[178]

Collective agreements therefore present a conflict between the social and competition provisions of the Treaty. As Advocate General Jacobs pointed out,[179] the authors of the Treaty either were not aware of the problem or could not agree on a solution[180] and so the Treaty does not give clear guidance as to which policy should take priority. He said that since both sets of rules were Treaty provisions of the same rank, one set of rules should not take absolute

---

174 Para. 175. Advocate General Jacobs in *Albany* doubted this (para. 182). He said that collective agreements on wages, working time or other working conditions, although they may restrict competition between employees, probably do not have an appreciable restrictive effect on competition between employers. As regards competition on the demand side of the labour market, normally each employer remains free to offer more advantageous conditions to his employees. As regards competition on the product or services markets on which the employers operate, first, agreements on wages or working conditions harmonize merely one of many production cost factors. Therefore only one aspect of competition is affected. Secondly, proximity to the market of the factor in issue is an important criterion for assessing appreciability. In the case of collective agreements on wages and working conditions, the final price of the products or services in question is influenced by many other factors before they reach the market. Thirdly, and perhaps most importantly, production factor costs are only apparently harmonized because in economic terms labour, in contrast to raw materials, is not a homogeneous commodity. The fact that employees earn nominally the same wage does not mean that the real costs for their respective employers are identical. Real costs can be determined only when the employees' productivity is taken into account. Productivity is determined by many factors, e.g. professional skills, motivation, technological environment and work organization. All those factors can be and are influenced by employers. That is precisely the task of efficient management of human resources. Thus, competition on labour as a cost factor is in fact strong.

175 This is increasingly unlikely: see Commission Notice, *Guidelines on the Application of Article 81(3) of the Treaty* OJ [2004] C101/97, where no reference is made to social (or environmental) considerations. Only economic considerations can be taken into account when deciding whether an agreement fulfils the conditions of Article 81(3).

176 Para. 175. Cf. para. 193.

177 Para. 164.

178 Para. 178.

179 Para. 179.

180 Ibid.

precedence over the other and neither set of rules should be emptied of its entire content. He therefore suggested the following reconciliation: since the Treaty rules encouraging collective bargaining presuppose that collective agreements are in principle lawful, Article 81(1) could not have been intended to apply to collective agreements between management and labour on core subjects such as wages and other working conditions. Accordingly, such collective agreements should enjoy automatic immunity from antitrust scrutiny.

He then proposed three conditions for *ipso facto* immunity: first, the agreement must be made within the formal framework of collective bargaining between both sides of industry. Unilateral co-ordination between employers unconnected with the collective bargaining process should not be automatically sheltered, whatever the subject of the co-ordination may be.[181] Secondly, the agreement should be concluded in good faith. In that context account must be taken of agreements which apparently deal with core subjects of collective bargaining such as working time but which merely function as cover for a serious restriction of competition between employers on their product markets. In those exceptional cases, too, competition authorities should be able to examine the agreement in question.[182] Thirdly, the immunity extends only to those agreements for which it is truly justified; that is, that the collective agreement deals with the core subjects of collective bargaining, such as wages and working conditions, and does not directly affect third parties or markets.

He suggested that the test should be 'whether the agreement merely modifies or establishes rights and obligations within the labour relationship between employers and employees or whether it goes beyond that and directly affects relations between employers and third parties, such as clients, suppliers, competing employers, or consumers'. The latter types of agreement have potentially harmful effects on the competitive process and therefore they should be subject to antitrust scrutiny by the Commission or other competent authorities, which would examine whether there was in fact an appreciable restriction of competition. If so, the Commission should be able to balance the different interests involved and, where appropriate, grant an exemption according to Article 81(3). He pointed out that both the Court and the Commission have, on occasions, recognized the possibility of taking account of social grounds in particular by interpreting the conditions of Article 81(3) broadly so as to include concerns for employment.[183]

---

181 Para. 191.

182 Para. 192.

183 Citing Case 26/76 *Metro v Commission* [1977] ECR 1875, para. 43, Case 42/84 *Remia v Commission* [1985] ECR 2545, para. 42; *Synthetic Fibres* (OJ [1984] L207/17), para. 37; and *Ford v Volkswagen* (OJ [1993] L20/14), para. 23. However, cf.

Thus, in Advocate General Jacobs's view, collective agreements concluded (1) in good faith and (2) on core subjects (such as wages and working conditions) which (3) do not directly affect third markets and third parties, are not caught by Article 81(1).[184] Agreements that do not satisfy one of these conditions are caught by Article 81(1) and will be subject to scrutiny by the Commission under Article 81(3) if notified. This is very much the perspective of a competition lawyer. The Court took a rather different, labour relations approach that offered greater respect to the autonomy of the Social Partners. It began by observing that the Community's activities include not only 'a system ensuring that competition in the internal market is not distorted'[185] but also 'a policy in the social sphere',[186] and that one of the Community's tasks is to promote a 'harmonious and balanced development of economic activities' and a 'high level of employment and social protection'.[187] It then pointed to the Commission's duties under Article 118 (new Article 140) and Article 118b (now amended Article 139) concerning collective bargaining and the role of the social dialogue under Article 1 SPA (now Article 136) and Article 4(1) and (2) SPA (now Article 139(1) and (2)).[188] It then said:

> 59. It is beyond question that certain restrictions of competition are inherent in collective agreements between organisations representing employers and workers. However, the social policy objectives pursued by such agreements would be seriously undermined if management and labour were subject to Article [81(1)] of the Treaty when seeking jointly to adopt measures to improve conditions of work and employment.
>
> 60. It therefore follows from an interpretation of the provisions of the Treaty as a whole which is both effective and consistent that agreements concluded in the context of collective negotiations between management and labour in pursuit of such objectives must, by virtue of their nature and purpose, be regarded as falling outside the scope of Article [81(1)] of the Treaty.

Thus, while the Advocate General thought that competition law applied to collective agreements but they were immune subject to three strict conditions being satisfied, the Court took the view that competition law did not apply at all provided that the collective agreement was aimed at improving working conditions.[189]

Commission Notice, *Guidelines on the Application of Article 81(3) of the Treaty* OJ [2004] C101/97 considered above, which refers only to economic considerations which can be taken into account when deciding whether an agreement satisfies Article 81(3).

184 Para. 194.

185 Article 3(g).

186 Article 3(j).

187 Para. 54.

188 Paras 55–8.

189 AG Fennelly in Case C-222/98 *Van der Woude v Stichting Beatrixoord* [2000]

The Validity of the Derogation/Justification Distinction

If community law is engaged and breached, then the other issue raised by the British courts in *Viking* is the validity of the distinction between derogations and justifications and, in particular, the fact that justifications cannot be invoked by the state in respect of directly discriminatory measures. As is well known, the Court itself has ignored the distinction between express derogations and mandatory requirements when it suits it.[190] Perhaps the most blatant example of this is *Walloon Waste*[191] which concerned a Decree of the Walloon Regional Council prohibiting the storage or dumping in Wallonia of waste originating in another Member State or in a region of Belgium other than Wallonia. Most commentators consider this rule to be directly discriminatory[192] and so should have been justified only by one of the express derogations. Instead, the Court applied the 'imperative requirements of environmental protection',[193] prompting some to call for the abolition of the distinction between the express derogations and mandatory requirements. For example, Advocate General Jacobs in *PreussenElektra*[194] pointed to a number of decisions where the Court has 'relied on imperative requirements in cases in which it was at least doubtful whether the measure could be considered as applying without distinction'.[195] He called on the Court to clarify the situation, especially because 'it is desirable that even directly discriminatory measures can sometimes be justified on grounds of environmental protection'.[196] To date the Court has ignored these calls but, in difficult cases, it has glossed over the issues of classification, thereby enabling Member States to rely on the broader list of mandatory requirements.

ECR I-7111, para. 26 said that '[A]s an exception to the general field of application of Article [81] of the EC Treaty, the scope of the *Albany* exception should be narrowly construed'.

190 See e.g. Case C-114/97 *Commission v Spain* [1998] ECR I-6717. The Court made no distinction between overriding interests and the derogations in the case of directly discriminatory measures (para. 43).

191 Case C-2/90 *Commission v Belgium* [1992] ECR I-4431.

192 The Commission argued this before the Court. See also e.g. N. Notaro, 'The new generation case law on trade and environment' (2000) 25 ELRev 467, 478–9 and 482. However, this is a difficult area because Article 174(2)EC recognizes that 'damage should as a priority be rectified at source'. This provision is difficult to reconcile with the broader principles of free trade.

193 Para. 32.

194 Case C-379/98 *PreussenElektra AG v Schleswag AG* [2001] ECR I-2099, para. 226. See also his comments in Case C-203/96 *Chemische Afvalstoffen Dusseldorp v Mininster van Milieubeheer* [1998] ECR I-4078 and in Case C-136/00 Rolf Dieter Danner [2002] ECR I-8147.

195 Citing Case C-389/96 *Aher-Waggon v Germany* [1998] ECR I-4473.

196 Para. 226.

CONCLUSIONS

Francis Jacobs's influence on the area of free movement of goods and persons has been immense. At times, this influence has been subtle and indirect but he has been responsible for framing the terms of the debate and commentators have responded to his proposals and interventions. He has highlighted the fundamental problem facing the free movement law at present: what are the outer limits of the Treaty provisions? In other words, where is it legitimate for the Treaty to intervene and what areas of law should be left to the Member States to regulate without risk of Community intervention? The Court has now equipped itself with a number of tools to limit its involvement in areas where it feels this is inappropriate – the rules about certain selling arrangements in *Keck*, the observation that the effect on inter-state trade is too indirect or uncertain, the rule that non-discriminatory measures do not breach the Treaty. The remaining problem is that it is not clear when the Court will resort to these techniques. It continues to need guidance from thoughtful academics.

7. Citizenship of the Union

Eleanor Sharpston[1]

It was, of course, Advocate General Jacobs in Case C-168/91 *Konstantinidis* [1993] ECR I-1191 who first coined the phrase, '*civis Europeus*', when he declared:

> A Community national who goes to another Member State . . . is entitled not just to pursue his trade or profession and to enjoy the same living and working conditions as nationals of the host state: he is in addition entitled to assume that . . . he will be treated in accordance with a common code of fundamental values, in particular those laid down in the European Convention on Human Rights. In other words, he is entitled to say, '*civis Europeus sum*' and to invoke that status in order to oppose any violation of his fundamental rights.[2]

Advocate General Jacobs, a civilized and well-read man, possibly had somewhere in mind the passage from Acts 22:25–30 where St Paul, about to have something nasty (like a flogging) happen to him in Jerusalem, pointed out that he was a Roman citizen; and was immediately set free. I add, in parentheses, that that particular episode did not, in the end, turn out to St Paul's advantage;[3] and that it shows that the exercise of citizenship rights is not always necessarily crowned with success.

Curiously, for so prolific and wide-ranging an Advocate General, Francis has given relatively few opinions in this area of EC law. Others – most notably Advocate General Geelhoed[4] – have drawn upon themselves the obloquy and

---

1 Advocate General of the Court of Justice of the European Communities (and successor to Francis Jacobs, as he then was).

2 At point 46 of his opinion.

3 Questioned further, Paul exercised his citizenship rights and appealed over the head of the Governor, Festus, to Caesar (Acts 25:9–12). Because he had appealed to the Emperor, he was subsequently shipped off to Rome where, in due course, he was martyred. King Agrippa, who had had extended discussions with Paul in the interim and became interested in the case, said expressly that 'This man might have been set at liberty, if he had not appealed unto Caesar' (Acts 26:32).

4 Advocate General Geelhoed delivered opinions in, *inter alia*, Case C-224/98 *D'Hoop v Office National de l'Emploi* [2002] ECR I-6191; Case C-413/99 *Baumbast and R. v Secretary of State for the Home Department* [2002] ECR I-7091; Case C-

opprobrium of irritated Member States by suggesting that citizenship of the Union is rather more than a convenient TEU sound-bite. Francis has – if I may put it this way – specialized in the quality end of the market.

This contribution concentrates on three specific issues that have arisen in the context of claims presented by virtue of, or analysed by reference to, 'citizenship of the Union' in which Francis has made a characteristically individual contribution: language rights enjoyed by defendants in criminal courts (*Bickel and Franz*[5]), calculation of a debtor's income before an attachment order is made (*Pusa*[6]) and the delicate issue of the name that someone is known by (*Garcia Avello*,[7] *Niebüll*[8]).

LANGUAGE OF CRIMINAL PROCEEDINGS

One of the by-products of the exercise of free movement rights is that, occasionally, people get prosecuted under the criminal justice system of a Member State other than their own. Mr Bickel, an Austrian national, was driving his lorry at Castelbello in the Trentino-Alto Adige region of Italy.[9] He was stopped by a carabinieri patrol and subsequently charged with driving while under the influence of alcohol. Mr Franz, a German national, was visiting Alto Adige as a tourist. In the course of a customs inspection, he was found to be in possession of a prohibited type of knife.

Mr Bickel and Mr Franz each made an official declaration that he had no knowledge of Italian and, relying on rules for the protection of the German-speaking community of the Province of Bolzano, requested that the proceedings against him be conducted in German. The national rules at issue concerned only residents of Bolzano. Other Italian citizens did not have the right to opt for the use of German in court proceedings. The national court was uncertain whether Community law required the benefit of the Bolzano rules to be extended upon request to nationals of other Member States, and therefore asked the European Court of Justice for a ruling on the question,

---

456/02 *Trojani*, judgment of 7 September 2004; and Case C-209/03 *Bidar*, judgment of 15 March 2005. However, other Advocates General have played their part, too – see, for example, Case C-184/99 *Grzelczyk* [2001] ECR I-6193 (AG Alber) and Case C-200/00 *Zhu and Chen*, judgment of 19 October 2004 (AG Tizzano).

5 Case C-274/96 [1998] ECR I-7637.

6 Case C-224/03, opinion of 20 November 2003, judgment 29 April 2004.

7 Case C-148/02 [2003] ECR I-11613.

8 Case C-96/04, opinion of 30 June 2005, judgment 27 April 2006.

9 The area was, historically, part of Austria and is invariably known north of the border as 'Südtirol'. Unsurprisingly, it therefore has a significant German-speaking population.

> Do the principle of non-discrimination as laid down in the first paragraph of Article 6, the right of movement and residence for citizens of the Union as laid down in Article 8a and the freedom to provide services as laid down in Article 59 of the Treaty require that a citizen of the Union who is a national of one Member State but is in another Member State be granted the right to have criminal proceedings against him conducted in another language where nationals of the host State enjoy that right in the same circumstances?

Francis defined the case as raising two issues: first, whether the choice of language in the criminal proceedings before the referring court comes within the scope of the Treaty; and secondly, whether the Italian rules, if construed so as to deny Mr Bickel and Mr Franz the right to use German, would entail discrimination on grounds of nationality.

On the first question, he recalled that the Court had already, in *Mutsch*,[10] considered whether a Luxembourg national had the right to use German in criminal proceedings in a German-speaking municipality of Belgium where Belgian law granted that right to Belgian nationals residing in that municipality. Mr Mutsch was a migrant worker residing in the Member State concerned; and the question had been answered affirmatively, on the basis of Articles 7 (now repealed) and 48 (now 9) EC and Article 7(2) of Regulation 1612/68. Mr Franz might (perhaps) have been able to show a link with Community law via Directive 91/447/EEC on control of the acquisition and possession of weapons;[11] Mr Bickel's prosecution for driving under the influence of alcohol disclosed no obvious link with Community law. His case therefore raised the general issue of whether criminal proceedings against a Community citizen based on alleged facts which occurred while that citizen exercised his right to free movement come within the scope of application of the Treaty and are therefore subject to the prohibition of discrimination on grounds of nationality.

Francis, applying *Cowan*,[12] considered that the equal treatment rule must apply to a tourist who was the accused in criminal proceedings just as it did to the tourist victim of criminal behaviour – the rights being claimed were, in both cases, the corollary of the right to free movement. He continued,

> The conclusion to be drawn from the *Cowan* case seems all the more compelling in the light of the subsequent amendments to the EC Treaty introduced by the Treaty on European Union. Part Two of the EC Treaty is now entitled 'Citizenship of the Union', and that citizenship is established by Article 8(1) . . .

---

10 Case 137/84 [1985] ECR 2681.

11 OJ 1991 L 256, p. 51.

12 Case 186/87 [1989] ECR 195.

> It may be concluded from that provision that, where a citizen exercises his right to move and reside within the territory of the Member States, his situation falls within the scope of the Treaty for the purposes of the prohibition of discrimination on grounds of nationality. It therefore re-affirms the conclusion that that prohibition applies to criminal proceedings arising in the course of the exercise of a citizen's freedom of movement.[13]

Francis left open the broader question of whether all criminal proceedings against a citizen of the Union fall within the scope of application of the Treaty for the purposes of Article 6, even where that citizen has not exercised his right to free movement. He suggested, however, that,

> It may be . . . that the time has come for even that question to be answered affirmatively. The notion of citizenship of the Union implies a commonality of rights and obligations uniting Union citizens by a common bond transcending Member State nationality. The introduction of that notion was largely inspired by the concern to bring the Union closer to its citizens and to give expression to its character as more than a purely economic union. That concern is reflected in the removal of the word 'economic' from the Community's name (also effected by the Treaty on European Union) and by the progressive introduction into the EC Treaty of a wide range of activities and policies transcending the field of the economy.
>
> Against that background it would be difficult to explain to a citizen of the Union how, despite the language of Articles 6, 8 and 8a [now Articles 12, 17 and 18 EC], a Member State other than his own could be permitted to discriminate against him on grounds of his nationality in any criminal proceedings brought against him within its territory. Freedom from discrimination on grounds of nationality is the most fundamental right conferred by the Treaty and must be seen as a basic ingredient of Union citizenship.[14]

Francis was careful to point out that the conclusion he proposed 'does not of course entail a transfer of Member States' competence in criminal matters to the Community. It merely recognises the fact that, as the Court noted in *Cowan*, Member States must exercise their powers in this area in conformity with the fundamental principle of equal treatment.'[15]

On the second issue (discrimination), Francis considered that the rule limiting the use of German to Bolzano residents, whilst not directly discriminatory on grounds of nationality, 'plainly' worked to the particular disadvantage of nationals of other Member States, that is, German-speaking visitors to Bolzano from Germany and Austria (who would be predominantly German and Austrian nationals). That was because the latter were all, without excep-

---

13 Points 20–21.
14 Points 23–4.
15 Point 25.

tion, prevented from choosing German for the conduct of criminal proceedings whereas most Italian residents being prosecuted in Bolzano who wished to use German would be able to do so.[16] With characteristic clarity of analysis, Francis dismissed the argument advanced by the Commission and the Italian Government that Italian nationals not resident in Bolzano could not choose German either as beside the point. Being Italian-speakers, the overwhelming majority of Italian residents would have no practical interest in choosing German. In other words, German and Austrian visitors were without exception denied an advantage granted to most Italian residents who actually wanted the advantage.[17]

The rest of the analysis flows smoothly forward. Was the restriction objectively justified? There was no administrative justification for it – local courts were, indeed, set up to operate primarily in German. Denying visitors from Germany or Austria the benefit of opting for proceedings in German was neither appropriate nor necessary as a means of achieving the (legitimate) aim of protecting the German linguistic minority in Alto Adige. Therefore, concluded Francis, the rule was disproportionate and hence impermissible.

The Court in its judgment followed Francis in every particular.

Here, in 1998, are most of the essential ingredients of the discussion that has subsequently developed over the scope and extent of the citizenship provisions. Is being a citizen of the Union just about economic rights, or does citizenship of the Union mean something more? Is discrimination on grounds of nationality compatible with the concept of citizenship of the Union? Can a Member State discriminate indirectly on grounds of nationality against citizens of the Union? If so, how is its defence of objective justification to be assessed?

ATTACHMENT OF EARNINGS

Just as people who move about the European Union sometimes get prosecuted for criminal offences, so too they find that different tax authorities make inroads into their disposable income. This can give rise to difficulty if they fall into debt and face having an attachment of earnings order made against them. Mr Pusa was a Finnish national, in receipt of a Finnish invalidity pension, who lived and paid income tax in Spain. As a result of a debt owed by him in Finland, there was an attachment order on his pension. Under the applicable

---

16 Point 36.

17 Point 37: see Case C-15/96 *Kalliope Schöning-Kougebetopoulou v Freie und Hansestadt Hamburg* [1998] ECR I-47.

Finnish legislation, the amount attached was calculated so as to leave him a minimum income, but in that calculation no account was taken of his Spanish income tax. Finnish income tax, had it been due and deducted at source, would have been taken into account. In consequence, Mr Pusa was left each month with less disposable income than the amount that would otherwise have been guaranteed to him under the applicable Finnish legislation. The Finnish Supreme Court asked whether the difference in the way that Finnish and Spanish income tax were treated in the calculation of disposable income was precluded by Community law, in particular in the light of the Treaty provisions on citizenship of the Union.

While accepting that 'it is quite true, as the Finnish Government points out, that national rules on the attachment of income for the recovery of debts do not as such fall within the sphere of Community law but are the responsibility of the Member States', Francis was clear that 'in exercising their powers in such matters, Member States must respect Community law, particularly when the exercise impinges on Treaty freedoms'.[18] Mr Pusa's circumstances clearly fell within the ambit of Community law. How was he to be treated? Francis pointed out that the issue in the case could be approached (conventionally and safely) in terms of discrimination on the basis of residence, since discrimination on the basis of residence had been a recurrent theme in the Court's case law as a form of indirect discrimination on grounds of nationality.

He then struck out more boldly. Discrimination on grounds of nationality, whether direct or indirect, was not necessary in order for Article 18 to apply. In particular, it was not necessary to establish that, for example, a measure adversely affects nationals of other Member States more than those of the Member State imposing the measure.[19] Francis pointed out that Article 39 EC (free movement of workers), although explicitly framed in terms of 'the abolition of any discrimination based on nationality' had nevertheless been interpreted as precluding also certain non-discriminatory measures.[20] The wording of Article 18, for its part, was clearly *not* limited to a prohibition of discrimination. He continued,

> freedom of movement entails more than simply the abolition of restrictions on a person's right to enter, reside in or leave a Member State. Such freedom cannot be assured unless all measures of any kind which impose an unjustified burden on those exercising it are also abolished. Whatever the context in which it may arise –

---

18 Points 12 and 13.

19 Point 18.

20 Point 20: Francis then referred to Case C-415/93 *Bosman* [1995] ECR I-4921, at paragraphs 103 and 104 of the judgment, and Case C-190/98 *Graf* [2000] ECR I-493, paragraph 18 and the case law analysed by Advocate General Fennelly in his opinion in that case.

including leaving or returning to the home Member State, or residing or moving elsewhere within the Union – no such burden may be imposed.

The conclusion – which is consistent with and complementary to the Court's judgments in *D'Hoop* and *Baumbast*[21] – must thus be that, subject to the limits set out in Article 18 itself, no unjustified burden may be imposed on any citizen of the European Union seeking to exercise the right to freedom of movement or residence. Provided that such a burden can be shown, it is immaterial whether the burden affects nationals of other Member States more significantly than those of the State imposing it.[22]

Against that background, Francis defined the issues in the case as being whether the Finnish legislation did in fact impose a burden on those exercising the right to freedom of movement and residence and whether, if so, it might none the less be justified on the ground that it was based on objective considerations and was proportionate to a legitimate aim.

The burden was not difficult to recognize: Francis felt that it was 'clear' that 'if a person receives a pension subject to an attachment order in one Member State, and the rules of that Member State mean that less will be withheld from his pension if he resides there than if he resides in another Member State . . . such treatment may deter him from moving to take up such residence'.[23]

A number of justifications were put forward by Finland at the hearing. It explained first that (although this was far from clear from the law itself) tax paid abroad might in fact be taken into account, upon proof of payment, by the official administering the attachment.[24] Thus, the system allowed income tax to be taken into account in all cases. Finland stressed the overall aim of ensuring that debts were paid as promptly as possible without placing the debtor in an intolerable financial position – in other words of safeguarding in so far as possible the interests of both the creditor and the debtor. The official body which administered attachments had to deal with a vast number of cases each year – 2.7 million in 2002. That required simplicity of operation and reliability of information. Tax not deducted at source could only be taken into account on production of proof that it had been paid. The debtor could provide

---

21 Case C-224/98 *D'Hoop* (*supra*, footnote 4); Case C-413/99 *Baumbast* (*supra*, footnote 4).

22 Points 21 and 22.

23 Point 24.

24 The national law allowed recalculation where the debtor's ability to pay was substantially reduced because of illness, unemployment or other special reason. The terms of that provision did not refer specifically to tax paid abroad (because such situations were not common at the time of its enactment), but in practice it was used for that purpose and a clarifying amendment was promised for the future.

such proof at any time in order to seek a recalculation of the part of his income which was excluded from attachment.[25]

Francis regarded the most important element in that catalogue as being that all tax may be taken into account upon proof of its payment. He considered that a requirement that the debtor must provide such proof where it is not automatically available seemed justified, provided that the requirement did not operate in such a way as to make it impossible in practice, or excessively difficult, for debtors resident in another Member State to obtain adjustment of the attachable portion on that basis, to the same extent as if tax had been deducted at source. However, an entitlement to equivalent treatment had to be clear from the legislation. A mere discretion on the part of the Finnish authorities was not sufficient.[26] He was also (let it be said) a little bit suspicious that the way in which the Finnish legislation actually operated might go beyond what was actually justified.[27]

In its judgment, the Court was a little opaque on whether it was applying a discrimination-based analysis or an approach based on obstacles to free movement.[28] Its subsequent analysis of the issues, and the conclusion it reached, followed the opinion, albeit at greater length.

Whether one takes a classic indirect discrimination approach or an 'obstacles to free movement' approach, it was – as Francis rightly said – clear that exercising free movement rights had placed Mr Pusa in a worse position, when his pension was attached, than if he had stayed put in Finland. From Finland's presentation of the case, it looks as though inertia (failing to adjust legislation to reflect greater mobility within the Union) rather than active unhelpful intent was probably the explanation for the system being applied. Although there was indeed *an* economic effect (on the unfortunate debtor) in the way the rules operated, it was not one that affected the Member State's own interests in any way. Rather, the central issue was one of equitable treatment. Disposable income that is to be attached to pay off a debt should be assessed realistically. That means that tax paid must be taken into account. Whichever Member State's tax authorities the money has been paid to, it is no longer in the debtor's bank account. The taxpayer-debtor is in the best position to provide proof that the tax has been paid but, once he does so, he must be treated in the same way whether he lives in Tampere or Talavera.

---

25 See points 26–30.
26 Points 30–32.
27 See points 33–4.
28 See paragraphs 16–21 of the judgment.

WHAT'S IN A NAME?

The name we are known by matters. God gave Adam the right to name all the creatures of the earth.[29] Adam's first response to Eve's creation was to name her.[30] Moses, faced with being sent off to introduce himself to the people of Israel and to confront Pharoah, asks (a little plaintively) for God's name.[31] He is given the unanswerable reply, 'I AM THAT I AM . . . Thus shalt thou say unto the children of Israel, I AM hath sent me unto you.'[32]

Francis had already, in *Konstantinidis*, explored the symbolic importance of names. In a passage of considerable eloquence and force, he had argued,

> A person's right to his name is fundamental in every sense of the word. After all, what are we without our name? It is our name that distinguishes each of us from the rest of humanity. It is our name that gives us a sense of identity, dignity and self-esteem. To strip a person of his rightful name is the ultimate degradation, as is evidenced by the common practice of repressive penal regimes which consists in substituting a number for the prisoner's name. In the case of Mr Konstantinidis the violation of his moral rights, if he is compelled to bear the name 'Hrestos' instead of 'Christos', is particularly great; not only is his ethnic origin disguised, since 'Hrestos' does not look or sound like a Greek name and has a vaguely Slavonic flavour, but in addition his religious sentiments are offended, since the Christian character of his name is destroyed. At the hearing Mr Konstantinidis pointed out that he owes his name to his date of birth (25 December), Christos being the Greek name for the founder of the Christian – not 'Hrestian' – religion.[33]

---

29 Gen. 2:18–19.

30 Gen. 2:23: in deriving the new name, 'woman' (*ishah*), from 'man' (*ish*), Adam symbolically stresses that Eve was 'bone from my bone and flesh from my flesh'.

31 Gen 3:13: 'When I come unto the children of Israel, and shall say to them, The God of your fathers hath sent me unto you; and they shall say to me, What is his name? What shall I say unto them?'

32 Gen. 3:14. The next verse sees the first appearance of the tetragram (יהוה) as God's name forever, splendidly but erroneously promoted thereafter in English translations of the Bible as 'Jehovah' by adding in (and then Anglicizing) the vowel combination from 'Adonai' ('Lord'), the word invariably used to substitute, in reading, for the not-to-be-pronounced name of God. If the magnificent hymn originally penned by William Williams (Halleluiah, Bristol, 1745) as 'Arglwydd, arwain trwy'r anialwch' and translated from Welsh to English by Peter Williams (Hymns on Various Subjects, Carmarthen, Wales, 1771) as 'Guide me, o thou great Jehovah' were rewritten so as to replace Jehovah with modern Biblical scholars' guess of 'Yahweh', something more than the scansion would be lost. (Nowadays when it is sung – to John Hughes's equally magnificent tune 'Cwm Rhondda' – the first line is usually rendered 'Guide me, o thou great Redeemer'.)

33 Point 40.

The Court in that case had stuck to the more prosaic and the economic, limiting itself to ruling that 'Article 52 of the Treaty must be interpreted as meaning that it is contrary to that provision for a Greek national to be obliged, under the applicable national legislation, to use, in the pursuit of his occupation, a spelling of his name whereby its pronunciation is modified and the resulting distortion exposes him to the risk that potential clients may confuse him with other persons.'

Garcia Avello concerned the surname borne by children born in Belgium to a married couple resident there. The father was a Spanish national, the mother Belgian. The children had dual nationality. On registration of their births in Belgium, the children were given the double surname borne by their father, 'Garcia Avello'. That name was composed, in accordance with Spanish law and custom, of the first element of his own father's surname and the first element of his mother's surname. In 1995, the parents subsequently applied to the Belgian authorities to have the children's surname changed to 'Garcia Weber' so that, in turn, it reflected the Spanish pattern and comprised the first element of their father's surname, followed by their mother's (maiden) surname. They pointed out that the Spanish system of surnames was deeply rooted in Spanish law, tradition and custom, to which the children felt more intimately related. For the children to bear the surname of 'Garcia Avello' suggested, under that system, that they were siblings rather than children of their father and deprived them of any link by name to their mother. The requested change would mean that the children could bear the same surname in Belgium as in Spain; it was in no way likely to cause harm to anyone else or to give rise to confusion, and the stable presence of the element 'Garcia' was sufficient to meet any need for continuity of name in the paternal line.

In 1997, the Belgian Ministry of Justice suggested that the children's surname be simplified to 'Garcia'. The parents did not accept that suggestion, explaining (reasonably enough) that such a change would not reflect either the Spanish or the Belgian system and that Garcia was an extremely common surname. The Ministry then informed Mr Garcia Avello that the Government considered there was no adequate reason to propose acceptance of their original request because 'any request for the mother's surname to be added to the father's, for a child, is usually refused on the ground that, in Belgium, children bear their father's surname'.[34]

Mr Garcia Avello challenged the refusal to change his children's name, claiming in particular that it infringed both the Belgian Constitution and Article 18 EC because it treated two different situations (that of children with purely Belgian nationality and that of those with dual nationality) in the same

34 See points 38 and 39 of the opinion.

way without any objective justification. In its reference to the Court of Justice, the Belgian Conseil d'Etat (Council of State) asked whether such a refusal might be precluded by principles of Community law such as those relating to citizenship of the European Union and freedom of movement for citizens.

In his opinion, Francis dealt with the question of names and their importance with characteristic scholarship and thoroughness. After a delightful survey of the range and variety of the rules and practices of a number of Member States in relation to determining the name to be given to a child and subsequent change of surname, he placed the analysis of the EC Treaty provisions against the background of Article 8 of the European Convention on Human Rights (ECHR) and international instruments such as the International Commission on Civil Status (ICCS) Convention on the law applicable to surnames and forenames,[35] the Hague Convention on certain questions relating to the conflict of nationality laws,[36] the ICCS Convention on the issue of a certificate of differing surnames[37] and the United Nations Convention on the Rights of the Child.[38]

He had first to deal with the argument (advanced by Belgium and two intervening Member States, Denmark and the Netherlands) that the situation fell outwith the scope of Community law, because only the children, who had dual nationality and had never exercised free movement rights, were affected by the refusal. Francis, however, agreed with the Commission that Mr Garcia Avello as well as the children was affected:

> the issue is not the choice of a surname for the children viewed independently but the way in which the surname borne by one generation is to be determined by the name or names borne by the previous generation; indeed, the Belgian Government lays great stress on this aspect of the case. Clearly such an issue concerns both generations and it is just as much in the father's interest to ensure that his surname is passed on in accordance with the principles on which it was formed as it is in the children's interest to inherit a surname in the appropriate manner and form.[39]

Since Mr Garcia Avello was a national of one Member State who had exercised his right to move to and work in another Member State, and a citizen of the Union who had exercised his right to move and reside freely within the

---

35 ICCS Convention No. 19, signed at Munich on 5 September 1980 ('the Munich Convention').

36 Of 12 April 1930, League of Nations Treaty Series, vol. 179, p. 89 ('the 1930 Hague Convention').

37 ICCS Convention No. 21, signed at The Hague on 8 September 1982 ('the 1982 Hague Convention').

38 Adopted and opened for signature, ratification and accession by General Assembly Resolution 44/25 of 20 November 1989.

39 Point 50.

territory of the Member States, his situation fell well within the sphere of Community law.[40]

Francis was prepared to go further:

> I cannot in any event agree that the situation of the children themselves is wholly internal to Belgium. Even if they have Belgian nationality, were born in Belgium and have never resided outside that country, they none the less also possess the nationality of another Member State. That fact is inseparable from the exercise by their father, whose dependants they are, of his right to freedom of movement . . . If their mother had not had Belgian but Spanish nationality, their situation as dependent children of nationals of a Member State having exercised freedom of movement within the Community would clearly have fallen within the sphere of Community law. From the point of view of that law, the fact that they possess the nationalities of two Member States is relevant and it cannot be acceptable that one nationality should eclipse the other depending on where they happen to be.[41]

Francis then identified two adverse effects produced by the refusal to allow a name change. First,

> both Mr Garcia Avello and his children may object to the fact that he cannot pass his surname on to them – and they cannot inherit it from him – in accordance with the principles on which it was formed. That is no mere abstract objection since, as has been pointed out, application of the Belgian system to a Spanish surname is liable to present a distorted image of family relationships to those familiar with the Spanish system: Mr Garcia Avello's children appear to be his siblings.[42]

Secondly,

> obvious practical difficulties may ensue for the children from the fact that their surname as recorded by the Belgian authorities differs from that recorded by the Spanish authorities. One example, pointed out by counsel for Mr Garcia Avello at the hearing, might be the possession of an educational qualification issued in Belgium in a name not recognised as that of the holder.[43]

Belgium had argued that the administrative practice on which the refusal was based applied to a single category of persons who could be objectively

---

40 Point 51, citing Case C-224/98 *D'Hoop* [2002] ECR I-6191, paragraphs 27 to 29 of the judgment.

41 Point 52.

42 Point 55. Francis went on to give a further delicious (if perhaps slightly mischievous) illustration in a footnote: 'An even more striking example, outside the scope of Community law, would be the daughter, born in Belgium, of an Icelandic father and a Belgian mother. If the Belgian rule were applied, she would appear to an Icelander to be her grandfather's son rather than her father's daughter.'

43 Point 56.

distinguished from others – children of dual Belgian and Spanish nationality, born in Belgium – and that it was therefore not discriminatory. With painstaking care, Francis unpicked that argument:

> What is at issue is a refusal to change a surname so that it (i) reflects the paternal surname in accordance with the way that surname itself was formed and (ii) avoids any discrepancy between the forms of surname registered by the authorities of two Member States both of whose nationalities are held by the bearer of the surname. It appears that the Belgian authorities will not consider themselves competent to make any change to the name of a person who is not a Belgian national, whether that person possesses any other nationality or not. The first aim described above would appear to be relevant above all, and the second aim only, when another nationality is also present. Since a change of surname may be accorded under Belgian law when serious grounds are given for the application, a systematic refusal to grant a change when the grounds given are linked to or inseparable from the possession of another nationality must be regarded as discriminating on grounds of nationality. Such a practice in fact accords the same treatment both to those who, as a result of possessing a nationality other than Belgian, bear a surname or have a parent who bears a surname not formed in accordance with Belgian rules and to those who possess only Belgian nationality and bear a surname formed according to those rules, despite the fact that their situations are objectively different.[44]

That similar treatment of situations that were *not* similar discriminated against both Mr Garcia Avello and the children.

Francis then turned to the question of objective justification. He accepted that the aim of preventing confusion over identity by placing limitations on the right to change surnames was legitimate, although he felt that the dangers of such confusion should not be exaggerated.[45] Moving to the broader social context, he examined and expressly rejected the argument that non-discrimination as applied to free movement seeks essentially to ensure the integration of migrant citizens into their host Member State.[46] 'The intention is rather to allow free, and possibly repeated or even continuous, movement within a single "area of freedom, security and justice", in which both cultural diversity and freedom from discrimination are ensured.'[47]

After that strong statement, Francis was (characteristically) careful to conclude by stressing that none of what he had said

> should be construed as a criticism of the Belgian or any other rules governing the attribution of surnames. The point is rather that such rules should not be applied in such a way as to infringe the Community-law principle of non-discrimination.

---

44 Point 63.
45 Points 69 to 70.
46 Point 72.
47 *Ibid.*

> Belgium has a procedure whereby surnames can be changed if sufficiently serious grounds are present. The only point on which Belgian practice appears to conflict with Community law lies in the systematic refusal to consider a situation such as that of Mr Garcia Avello and his children as constituting such grounds.

The Court decided (after a rather lengthy analysis) to approach the question of the link with Community law from the sole perspective of the children (Francis's alternative position). It shared his analysis that there was discrimination arising from treating different situations in the same way; and concluded (perhaps less elegantly) that none of the grounds of justification advanced by Belgium stood up to scrutiny.

Niebüll provided Francis with a final opportunity, shortly before stepping down as Advocate General,[48] to analyse names. This time, the question was whether a national choice of law rule may assign the determination of a name solely to the law of the child's (and/or parents') nationality – in this case, German – without regard to the law of the state of his or her place of birth – in this case, Denmark – with the result that the name is different under the two legal systems.

The child in question ('Leonhard Matthias') was born in Denmark in 1998. The surname 'Grunkin-Paul' was entered on his Danish birth certificate by virtue of an administrative certificate attesting to that name, issued in accordance with Danish law.[49] The parents (Stefan Grunkin and Dorothee Paul, both of German nationality) initially lived together in Denmark. They then separated – it appears, fairly amicably – and by 2002 the four-year-old Leonhard Matthias was living principally with his mother in Tønder (Denmark), where she had set up residence and established her medical practice, but regularly stayed with his father in Niebüll (Germany) some 20 km away.

The parents, who had themselves never used a joint surname, wished to register him with the German authorities in Niebüll, again under the surname 'Grunkin-Paul' given to him in Denmark. Pursuant to German legislation, the Niebüll authorities refused to recognize that name, insisting that the surname chosen must be either 'Grunkin' or 'Paul'.

It was clear that Leonhard Matthias, as a national of one Member State lawfully resident in the territory of another Member State, was within the

48 The opinion was delivered on 30 June 2005. Francis left the Court on 10 January 2006.

49 'It may be presumed that the certificate was issued on the basis that the child was domiciled in Denmark for purposes of Danish private international law, so that Danish substantive law applied to the determination of his surname': point 22 of the opinion.

ambit of Community law.[50] Francis accepted that there was no discrimination on grounds of nationality (indeed, all the parties agreed on that point, even Mr Grunkin). On a restrictive interpretation of what citizenship and non-discrimination means, that might have been the end of the story.[51]

Building succinctly but powerfully on the foundations already laid in *Garcia Avello*, Francis pointed out that from a practical point of view, Leonhard Matthias was in a position closely comparable to that of the Garcia Avello children. In the Member State of his nationality, he had apparently to be registered under a different surname from that which he bore in the Member State of his birth. Francis continued,

> While the practical difficulties which he is likely to encounter may not stem from discrimination on grounds of nationality, they constitute a clear obstacle to his right as a citizen to move and reside freely within the territory of the Member States. Although such difficulties may be of a similar kind to those encountered by Mr Konstantinidis, the combined effects of Articles 17 and 18(1) EC mean that it is now unnecessary to establish any economic link in order to demonstrate an infringement of the right to freedom of movement.
>
> In addition to practical matters, which may range from the merely annoying to – in the climate of suspicion which has followed the events of 11 September 2001 – the extremely serious, a person's name is a fundamental part of his or her identity and private life, the protection of which is widely recognised in national constitutions and international instruments.[52]

He concluded, roundly,

> It thus seems to me totally incompatible with the status and rights of a citizen of the European Union – which, in the Court's phrase, is 'destined to be the fundamental status of nationals of the Member States' – to be required to bear different names under the laws of different Member States.[53]

---

50 *Garcia Avello* at paragraph 27; see also Case C-200/02 *Zhu and Chen* (*supra*, footnote 4), paragraph 19.

51 But certainly not with Francis as the Advocate General. He had already stated unequivocally in his opinion in *Pusa* (see earlier discussion) that discrimination on grounds of nationality is *not* necessary for Article 18 EC to apply.

52 Points 54 and 55, referring back to his opinions in *Konstantinidis*, at points 35 to 40, and in *Garcia Avello*, in particular at points 5, 27 and 36, together with the sources cited there.

53 Point 56. Francis cited Case C-209/03 *Bidar* [2005] ECR I-2119, paragraph 31, as the (then) most recent use of this formula by the Court. It finds its origin in Case C-184/99 *Grzelczyk* (*supra*, footnote 4) at paragraph 31: 'Union citizenship is destined to be the fundamental status of nationals of the Member States, enabling those who find themselves in the same situation to enjoy the same treatment in law irrespective of their nationality, subject to such exceptions as are expressly provided for.' (Advocate

Sadly, we cannot tell whether the Court would have followed him in this further step in the evolution of *civis europeus*, as it declared the reference inadmissible[54] and thus never ruled on the substance.[55]

What do these three areas have in common? Unlike the cases concerning access to social security benefits, where the host Member State has an obvious interest in resisting a claim, these are *not* areas where it is easy to see what a Member State has to lose by extending appropriate equal treatment based on citizenship of the Union to nationals of another Member State who are in its territory (*Bickel and Franz*, *Garcia Avello*), or recognizing the impact on its own nationals of exercising rights to move and reside as a citizen (*Pusa*). There was no obvious extra cost to Italy in allowing the proceedings against Mr Bickel and Mr Franz to take place in German rather than Italian. Calculating a debtor's disposable income in the same way, regardless of which Member State's authorities have claimed tax, before making an attachment of earnings order merely seems fair. And would it really be so subversive of good order to allow a mixed Spanish–Belgian nationality couple living in Belgium to reflect Spanish tradition by naming their children in the way that makes clear to other Spaniards whose children they are? Francis reminds us that we

---

General Alber, in a detailed opinion, had reached the same conclusion in more prosaic language.) In its prophetic luminosity – highly unusual in recent Court drafting – the Court's vision of citizenship of the Union in *Grzelczyk* is reminiscent of its famous statement in Case 26/62 *Van Gend* [1963] ECR 1 at p. 4 that, 'the Community constitutes a new legal order of international law for the benefit of which the states have limited their sovereign rights, albeit within limited fields, and the subjects of which comprise not only Member States but also their nationals . . . Community law therefore not only imposes obligations on individuals but is also intended to confer upon them rights which become part of their legal heritage.'

54 Francis had also had serious doubts as to admissibility (see points 30–44 of his opinion), but had considered it 'preferable' to answer the question raised. The Court held that the functions being exercised by the Amtsgericht were administrative rather than judicial. It was not, accordingly, a 'court or tribunal' entitled to make a reference under Article 234 EC.

55 The reader may wonder a little what the parents were meant to do next. They had already challenged the refusal to accord recognition to the surname given to Leonhard Matthias in Denmark, leading to a final dismissal of their challenge by the Kammergericht (Court of Appeal) in Berlin, and had sought to challenge the latter decision before the Bundesverfassungsgericht. Francis hints (point 33) that a reference could (and probably should) have been made in one or other of those earlier proceedings, all of which were clearly judicial. However, the parents were nothing if not persistent. They made a further application to the registrar of births, mariages and deaths at the Standesamt Niebüll to have their son registered under the surname Grunkin-Paul. The registrar refused. They promptly applied to the Amtsgericht Plensburg for an order requiring the registrar to register their son under that surname. The Amtsgericht duly made a new reference which is pending before the Grand Chamber of the Court as Case C-353/06 *Grunkin and Paul.*

should be prepared to question the premise for Member States' reflex reaction to a non-economic claim based upon citizenship of the Union ('well of course you're not entitled to that – we just don't do it that way here'). In a European Union in which nationals of Member States are indeed citizens of the Union with corresponding free movement rights, what (apart from natural administrative inertia) is the real problem about recognizing that administrative rules should not automatically be applied in a rigidly national way; but that cultural diversity allied to the consequences of free movement may sometimes require greater flexibility of thought and spirit?

Viewed quantitatively, Francis's contribution in this area of EC law may not have been that large. In qualitative terms, however, it has been both thoughtful and significant. Above all, it has helped to remind us all that there is rather more to citizenship of the Union than whether an enterprising claimant who has exercised free movement rights of some kind can get his hands on a particular social security benefit.[56]

---

56 For a thoughtful recent academic contribution extending beyond the conventional case-based analysis of the impact of citizenship of the Union on the substantive content of free movement rights for non-economically active persons, see M. Dougan, 'The constitutional dimension to the case law on Union citizenship' (2006) 31 ELRev 613.

8. External relations

Richard Plender*

Sir Francis Jacobs began his professional career as a public international lawyer. One of his earliest publications, if not his first, was a contribution to the *International and Comparative Law Quarterly* entitled 'Varieties of Treaty Interpretation'.[1] It should be no cause for surprise, therefore, that several of his more influential Opinions are concerned with the European Community's external relations. In this chapter we shall be able to review only four of them: not all being among the best-known of the Court's cases on the subject: *VOF Schieving-Nijstad*,[2] *Bosphorus Airways v Minister of Transport*,[3] *Regione Autonoma Friuli-Venezia*[4] and *Wählergruppe Gemeinsam Zajedno*.[5] This quartet of Opinions also provides us with an opportunity to review four current controversies: the European Court's jurisdiction to interpret treaties between the Community and third States; the application to the European Community of Security Council resolutions; the interpretation of the European Convention on Human Rights (ECHR); and the association between the European Community and Turkey.

JURISDICTION TO INTERPRET AGREEMENTS WITH THIRD STATES

In *Commission v Council, 'Convention on Nuclear Safety'*, Mr Advocate General Jacobs reaffirmed the consistent line of judgments of the European Court holding that a provision of an international agreement concluded by one of the Communities forms, as from its entry into force, an integral part of

* QC, LLD; successor to Professor Francis Jacobs (as he then was) as Director of the Centre of European Law, King's College, London.

1 18 ICLQ (1969) 318–46.
2 Case C-89/99, 25 February 2001; [2001] ECR I-5851.
3 Case C-84/95 [1996] ECR I-3953.
4 Case C-347/03, 18 December 2004; [2005] ECR I-3785.
5 Case C-171/01, 12 December 2002; [2003] ECR I-4301.

Community law which the Court of Justice has jurisdiction to construe.[6] The cases to which he was referring include *Haegeman*,[7] *Hauptzollamt Mainz v Kupferberg and Co*,[8] *Sevince v Staatssecretaris van Justitie*[9] and many others.[10] Originally those cases were concerned only with treaties concluded by the Community to the exclusion of the Member States. But in *Demirel v Stadt Schwäbish Gmünd* the Court applied similar reasoning to 'mixed agreements' concluded between third States and the Community together with some or all Member States.

In Case C-13/00, *Commission v Ireland* the Court of Justice concluded that it had jurisdiction to construe the Berne Convention because its provisions fall 'in large measure' within Community competence. The expression is imprecise and for that reason unsatisfactory.

Mixed agreements contain as parties both the Community and the Member States because they contain some provisions beyond the scope of Community competence.[11] It is generally accepted that the jurisdiction of the Court of Justice extends not only to the interpretation of provisions in mixed agreements which are matters of Community competence but also to the identification of

---

6 Case C-29/99 [2002] ECR I-11221, paragraph 79, reiterating a well-established rule.

7 Case 181/73, *Haegeman v Belgium* [1974] ECR 449, paragraph 5.

8 Case 104/81, *Hauptzollamt Mainz v Kupferberg and Co.* [1982] ECR 3641, paragraph 13.

9 Case C-192/89, *SZ Sevince v Staatssecretaris van Justitie* [1990] ECR 3461, paragraph 8 of the Opinion, paragraph 10 of the judgment.

10 See also Joined Cases 267/81, 268/81 and 269/81, *Amministrazione delle Finanze dello Stato v Società Petrolifera Italiana SpA (SPI) and SpA Michelin Italiana* [1983] ECR 801, paragraph 15; Case 30/88, *Greece v Commission* [1989] ECR 3711, paragraphs 12 to 14; Opinion of Mr Advocate General Darmon and judgment of Court in Opinion 1/91, '*EEA Agreement*' [1991] ECR I-6079, paragraph 37; Case T-115/94, *Opel Austria GmbH v Council* [1997] ECR-II 39, paragraph 101; Case C-321/97, *Ulla-Brith Andersson and Susannne Wåkerås-Andersson v Svenska Staten* [1991] ECR-I 3551, paragraph 25; Case T-174/00, *Biret International SA v Council* [2002] ECR II-17, paragraph 60.

11 Case C-13/00, *Commission v Ireland* [2002] ECR I-2943, paragraph 14 referring to Case 12/86, *Demirel v Stadt Schwäbish Gmünd* [1987] ECR 3719, paragraph 9. The principle to be applied for the purpose of ascertaining the extent of the transfer of competence to the Community was established in Case 22/70, *Commission v Council ('ERTA' or 'AETR')* [1971] ECR 263, paragraphs 15–17. '[E]ach time the Community, with a view to implementing a common policy envisaged by the Treaty, adopts provisions laying down common rules, whatever form these may take, the Member States no longer have the right, acting individually or even collectively, to undertake obligations with third countries which may affect those rules.' That principle was reiterated, in particular, in Opinion 1/94, *WTO Agreement* [1994] ECR I-5267, paragraph 77 which confirms that where the Community's external competence is not conferred expressly it is defined by the exercise of internal competence.

the provisions in mixed agreements that are matters of Community competence.[12] Greater controversy applies to the question of the jurisdiction of the Court of Justice to interpret provisions of a mixed agreement that are not matters of Community competence.

In accordance with the judgment of the Court of Justice in *Opinion 1/94 on the WTO Agreement*:

> the Member States, whether acting individually or collectively, only lose their right to assume obligations with non-member countries as and when common rules which could be affected by those obligations come into being. Only in so far as common rules have been established at internal level does the external competence of the Community become exclusive.

In other words (those of Dashwood and Heliskoski):

> Treaty-making power becomes the sole prerogative of the Community once measures have been adopted by the institutions pursuant to an objective authorised by the Treaty, in so far as acceptance of international commitments by the Member States might interfere with the operation of those measures.

In *VOF Schieving-Nijstad*,[13] the Hoge Raad referred to the Court of Justice for preliminary ruling a series of questions concerning Article 50(6) of the Agreement on Trade-Related Aspects of Intellectual Property Rights ('TRIPS'). That paragraph of Article 50 provides for the lapsing of any provisional measures that national judicial authorities may prescribe, to prevent the infringement of an intellectual property right, if proceedings leading to a decision on the merits are not taken within a reasonable period.

Messrs Schieving and Nijstad operated a discothèque in Meppel, incorporating a café called Route 66. Mr Groenvelt was the registered proprietor of a pictorial trade mark of the interstate highway sign for Route 66. He obtained an order from the Rechtsbank, Assen, restraining Messrs Schieving and Nijstad from using the 'Route 66' sign. On appeal Messrs Schieving and Nijstad argued that the order of the Rechtsbank must be taken to have lapsed, by reason of the operation of Article 50(6) of TRIPS. The premise of the case appears to have been that Article 50(6) was, or at least might be, a matter of Community competence. Since, however, the Court was invited to construe it

---

[12] Opinion 1/94, *WTO Agreement* [1994] ECR I-5267, paragraph 77; Opinion 2/94, *European Convention on Human Rights* [1996] ECR I-1759 paragraphs 24–6; A. Dashwood and J. Heliskoski, 'The classic authorities revisited', in A. Dashwood and C. Hillion, *The General Law of EC External Relations* (London: Sweet & Maxwell, 2000) 3.

[13] Case C-89/99, 25 February 2001.

in the context of a dispute between private parties, the question of its direct effectiveness was raised.

Mr Advocate General Jacobs concluded, as he was bound to do, that Article 50(6) of TRIPS does not produce direct effects. The Court of Justice had already decided in *Parfums Christian Dior* that Article 50 does not create rights upon which individuals can rely by virtue of Community law. However, in that case the Court of Justice had added that:

> In a field to which TRIPS applies and in respect of which the Community has already legislated, as is the case with the field of trade marks, it follows from the judgment in *Hermès*,[14] in particular paragraph 28 thereof, that the judicial authorities of the Member States are required by virtue of Community law, when called upon to apply national rules with a view to ordering provisional measures for the protection of rights falling within such a field, to do so as far as possible in the light of the wording and purpose of Article 50 of TRIPS.[15]

In the light of that statement, it was not decisive that Article 50(6) failed to produce direct effects. It remained necessary to ascertain the true meaning of Article 50(6) of TRIPS so that national rules could be interpreted consistently with it. After referring to the French and Spanish versions, as well as the English version, of Article 50(6), Mr Advocate General Jacobs concluded that it is only when the defendant so requests that provisional measures lapse, or are revoked, in consequence of the failure to institute the substantive proceedings within the prescribed period. In that conclusion there is, perhaps, an unconscious reiteration of the view expressed by Francis Jacobs some thirty years earlier when he pleaded for the imposition of limits to teleological interpretation, stating 'the main limiting factor adopted by the [Vienna] Convention [on the Law of Treaties] is text'.[16]

Mr Advocate General Jacobs went on to conclude, in his Opinion in *VOF Schieving-Nijstad,* that it is for the national law of each Member State to determine when a time limit commences: this might be the date of the decision ordering the provisional measures or the date of service of that decision. He thought it was also for national law to determine whether the court ordering a provisional measure must of its own motion fix a time limit within which proceedings on the merits must be instituted and whether an appellate court may of its own motion fix a time limit within which proceedings on the merits must be instituted.

---

14 C-53/96, *Hermès International v FHT Marketing* [1998] ECR 1-3603.

15 C-300/98 and C-392/98, *Parfums Christian Dior SA v Tuk Consultancy BV* and *Assco Gerüste GmbH v Wilhelm Layher GmbH & Co. KG* [2000] ECR I-11307, paragraph 47.

16 18 ICLQ (1969) 318–46 at 338.

His conclusions were upheld by the Court.[17]

The case presents at least one feature that demands explanation. This is that the rights and obligations applying between two litigants in a Dutch court, charged with the application of a Benelux Uniform Law, are determined by reference to a ruling of the Court of Justice on the meaning of provisions in a mixed agreement that do not produce direct effects.

It should be a source of no surprise that the Court assumes jurisdiction to interpret the provisions of a mixed agreement that are matters of Community competence. That follows from the judgment in *Parfums Christian Dior*[18] if not from *Demirel v Stadt Schwäbish Gmünd.*[19] Nor should it be a source of surprise that an applicable rule of Community law affects the application of a Benelux Uniform Law as it affects the application of Dutch law. The obligation of a national court to apply a rule of Community law cannot be diminished by reason of the fact that it is charged by national law to apply the law of a regional organization wholly subsumed within the Community. The feature that demands some explanation is the rule requiring the national court to interpret the applicable law by reference to provisions of a mixed agreement that do not produce direct effects. Mr Advocate General Jacobs suggested that the phenomenon might be explained by a practical consideration: it would be too cumbersome to have two distinct legal regimes, one governing the Community trade mark and the other governing national trade marks.[20] But there may be a wider and more theoretical explanation. In accordance with the principle in *Marleasing*,[21] national courts must construe national law, as far as possible, in the light of the wording and purpose of a directive in order to comply with the obligation imposed by Article 249 (formerly 189) of the EC Treaty. That being the case, should not those courts also apply national law (including the

---

17 13 September 2001, [2001] ECR I-5851.

18 *Supra* note 11.

19 *Supra* note 7.

20 Opinion in *VOF Schieving-Nijstad* paragraph 40.

21 Case C-106/89 *Marleasing v La Comercial Internacional de Alimentación* [1990] ECR I-4135, paragraph 8. See further Joined Cases C-297/88, 197/89, *Dzodzi v Belgium* [1990] ECR I-3763; Case C-231/89, *Gmurzynska v Oberfinanzdirektion Köln* [1990] ECR I-4003; Case C-106/89, *Marleasing SA v La Comercial Internacional de Alimentación SA* [1992] 1 CMLR 305. See also *Litster v Forth Dry Dock and Engineering Co. Ltd* [1990] 1 AC 546, [1989] 1 All ER 1134. Where the national legal provision is incapable of being construed in conformity with Community legislation, and that legislation produces legal effects, the national legal provision must be declared inapplicable: Case 157/86, *Murphy v Bord Telecom Eireann Ltd* [1988] ECR 673; *Customs and Excise Commissioners v Apple and Pear Development Council* [1987] 2 CMLR 634; *Duke v GEC Reliance Ltd (formerly Reliance Systems Ltd)* [1988] AC 618; [1988] 1 CMLR 719.

Benelux Uniform Law) consistently with the terms of a mixed agreement? There is reason to think that they should do so since those terms become, from their entry into force, 'an integral part of European Union law' and so impose obligations on Member States.[22]

Since the judgment in *VOF Schieving-Nijstad* the Court of Justice has added significantly to its case law on mixed agreements. In *Opinion 1/03 'Brussels Convention'*, it held that '*in all the areas corresponding to the objectives of the EC Treaty*, Article 10 of the EC Treaty requires Member States to facilitate the achievement of the Community's tasks and to abstain from any measure which could jeopardise the attainment of the objectives of the Treaty'.[23] Building upon that judgment, and upon *Parfums Christian Dior*, the Court concluded in *Commission v Ireland ('the Mox Plant case')* that the Community's competence and the duty of loyal cooperation extend to the case of a dispute which relates *essentially* to undertakings resulting from a mixed agreement which relates to an area, namely the protection and preservation of the marine environment, in which the respective areas of competence of the Community and the Member States are liable to be closely interrelated.[24]

A different problem arises in the case of mixed agreements containing provisions alleged to conflict with rules of Community law. In *Tod's SpA and Tod's France SARL v Heyraud SA* (30 June 2005) an Italian shoe manufacturer and its French distributor brought an action for copyright protection against a French retailer whose shoes were said to be based on Tod's design. The Defendant relied on Article 2(7) of the Berne Convention for the Protection of Literary and Artistic Works, which, in the Defendant's view, provided that the protection granted in respect of designs and models should extend only to those who enjoy the right to bring proceedings for such protection in the country of origin of the work. The Defendant argued that since Tod's design did not qualify for copyright protection in Italy, it could not bring proceedings in France, where the rules governing copyright protection were less restrictive. The Berne Convention required reciprocity.

The Court insisted that it was not construing the Berne Convention – a point which tends to reinforce the view that it does not have jurisdiction to

---

22 Case 26/62, *Van Gend en Loos v Nederlandse Administratie der Belastingen* [1963] ECR 1. On the duty to construe national law in conformity with European Community law, see Joined Cases C-297/88, 197/89, *Dzodzi v Belgium* [1990] ECR I-3763; Case C-231/89, *Gmurzynska v Oberfinanzdirektion Köln* [1990] ECR I-4003; Case C-106/89, *Marleasing SA v La Comercial Internacional de Alimentación SA* [1990] ECR I-4135, [1992] 1 CMLR 305 applied in numerous subsequent cases, most recently in Case C-371/02, *Björnekulla Fruktindustrier AB v Procordia Food AB*, 29 April 2004, paragraph 13.

23 7 February 2006, paragraph 119 (emphasis added).

24 Case C-459/03, 30 May 2006, paragraph 176 (emphasis added).

construe provisions of a mixed agreement falling outside Community competence. It stated:

> it is not for the Court of Justice to rule on the applicability of provisions of national or, in this case, international law which are relevant to the outcome of the main proceedings. The Court must take account, under the division of jurisdiction between the Community Courts and the national courts, of the legislative context, as described in the order for reference, in which the question put to it is set.

Nevertheless, it concluded that the Berne Convention did not avail the Defendant. The Berne Convention required reciprocity; but did not determine the applicable law. Application of the principle of reciprocity would be inconsistent with Community law. As the Court put it: 'the application of rules such as those at issue in the main proceedings is liable to operate mainly to the detriment of nationals of other Member States and thus give rise to indirect discrimination on grounds of nationality.'

APPLICATION OF SECURITY COUNCIL RESOLUTIONS

The young Francis Jacobs's insistence on the importance of text, as the main limiting factor in the interpretation of treaties, is echoed in the Opinion of the mature Francis Jacobs, as Advocate General, in *Bosphorus Airways v Minister of Transport*.[25]

Bosphorus Airways was a Turkish company operating as an air charterer. In April 1992 it took dry leases for four years of two aircraft owned by the Yugoslav national airline JAT. The leases were concluded in good faith and were not intended to circumvent the sanctions later imposed against the Federal Republic of Yugoslavia. Indeed once sanctions were imposed, Bosphorus Airways' payments pursuant to the lease were made into a blocked account.

By Resolution 820 of 17 April 1993 the Security Council of the United Nations decided

> that all States shall impound all vessels, freight vehicles, rolling stock and aircraft in their territories in which a majority or controlling interest is held by a person or undertaking in or operating from the Federal Republic of Yugoslavia (Serbia and Montenegro) and that those freight vehicles, rolling stock and aircraft may be forfeit to the seizing State upon a determination that they have been in violation of resolutions 713 (1991), 757 (1992), 787 (1992), or the present resolution.[26]

---

[25] Case C-84/95 [1996] ECR I-3953; Opinion of 30 April 1996.

[26] S/RES/820 (1993) paragraph 24.

That paragraph was implemented in the European Community by Article 8 of EC Council Regulation 990/93 of 26 April 1993.[27] This provided that:

> All vessels, freight vehicles, rolling stock and aircraft in which a majority or controlling interest is held by a person or undertaking in or operating from the Federal Republic of Yugoslavia (Serbia and Montenegro) shall be impounded by the competent authorities of the Member States.

On 16 April 1993 one of the aircraft was flown to Dublin airport for maintenance. On 8 June 1993 it was impounded on the direction of the Minister of Transport, acting on the basis of Regulation 990/93. Not unnaturally, Bosphorus Airways challenged the Minister's decision. It pleaded that the aim of Regulation 990/93 was to penalize the Federal Republic of Yugoslavia; but not to extend sanctions unnecessarily against wholly innocent parties in a neighbouring State with which the Community enjoys friendly relations.

Upon a reference from the Irish Supreme Court, the first question arising was whether Article 8 of EC Council Regulation 990/93 applies to an aircraft leased for a period of four years to an undertaking the majority of controlling interest in which is not held by a person or undertaking in or operating from the Federal Republic of Yugoslavia.

Mr Advocate General Jacobs found it unnecessary to consider the 'very interesting' question of whether Security Council resolutions, as such, are binding on the Community. Nor did he find it necessary to consider the effect of the decision taken by the Committee established by Resolution 724 (1991) which took the view that the aircraft had to be impounded. For him the question was one of determining whether Security Council Resolution 820 warranted departure from the clear wording of Article 8 of EC Council Regulation 990/93. He concluded that no departure from that wording was warranted. The Court of Justice agreed. It stated at paragraph 8 of the judgment: 'Nothing in the wording of the first paragraph of Article 8 of Regulation No 990/93 suggests that it is based on a distinction between ownership of an aircraft, on the one hand, and day-to-day operation and control, on the other.'

That aspect of the case may appear straightforward, even pedantic. But it is not without significance. In asserting the primacy of the text, the Advocate General and the Court eschewed the technique applied in certain other cases, in which the Court's identification of the legislator's intention was preeminent, even in the face of contrary indications in the wording.[28] Alexander Hamilton would have approved. In the seventy-eighth of the *Federalist Papers* he wrote: 'The courts must declare the sense of the law; and if they should be

---

27 OJ 1993 L102/4.

28 See the author's article 'The interpretation of Community acts by reference to the intentions of the authors' (1982) 2 Yearbook of European Law 57.

disposed to exercise will instead of judgment, the consequence would equally be the substitution of their pleasure to that of the legislative body.'

In reaching their conclusions both the Advocate General and the Court referred to Security Council Resolution 820, which they considered consistent with the view they took of the Regulation. This entailed, of course, taking a view as to the apparent meaning of the Resolution. On that point Advocate General Jacobs expressed the view that the primary object of the Security Council Resolution appeared to be to deprive Yugoslav undertakings, in a case such as the present, of even the indirect benefit that a means of transport will continue to operate and to be maintained. The Court, on the other hand, was careful not to speak of the Security Council's object but only to quote and comment on the language that it had employed. It stated that the use of the word 'interest' in paragraph 24 of the Resolution cannot, on any view, exclude ownership as the defining criterion.

Mr Advocate General Jacobs and the Court had to revert to the issue of interpretation only a few months later in the *Ebony Maritime* case.[29] One of the issues arising in that case was whether Article 10 of Regulation 990/93 authorizes the seizure of cargoes of vessels. On that point the Italian version of the Regulation alone mentioned means of transport but failed to mention their cargoes; the other official versions specified both cargoes and vessels. The Advocate General and the Court were not, of course, bound by the obvious error on the part of the Italian translator. In view of the need for uniform interpretation, they held that the Regulation was to be given the meaning expressed in all languages other than the Italian.

The two decisions reflect Articles 31(1) and 33(3) of the Vienna Convention on the Law of Treaties, which was the subject of Francis Jacobs's early article. Article 31(1) requires that a 'treaty shall be interpreted in good faith in accordance with the ordinary meaning to be given to the terms of the treaty'. Article 33(3) provides that 'The terms of the treaty are presumed to have the same meaning in each authentic text.'

The question of whether Security Council resolutions are binding on the Community was not mentioned at all by the Court in *Bosphorus Airways*. It was not necessary to address the question in that case; and indeed the question is one of some difficulty.

Some authors maintain that Security Council resolutions are not binding on the European Community, even when adopted under Chapter VII of the United Nations Charter.[30] Writing in the *European Journal of International Law*,

---

29 Case C-177/95 [1997] ECR I-1111.

30 A. Vedder in (1991) Schweizer Zeitschrift für Internationales und Europäisches Recht 561 and in *Kommentar zum EWG-Vertrag* (1989) 46 *Kommentar zum EWG-Vertrag* para. 65.

Sebastian Bohr concludes that 'the EC is not bound by public international law to implement sanctions adopted by the Security Council'.[31]

That conclusion cannot be dismissed out of hand. In accordance with Article 4(1) of the UN Charter, only States are eligible for membership. It is by joining the Organization that a member agrees to be bound by any resolutions that may be adopted under Chapter VII. Even if there is a basis for the contention that Security Council resolutions adopted under Chapter VII of the Charter may also bind States other than members,[32] the position of international organizations remains ambiguous. Certain resolutions adopted under Chapter VII call upon all States and international organizations to act in accordance with their terms; but the explicit language of those resolutions could be cited as evidence of the absence of a general principle whereby international organizations are bound.

The position of the European Community is, however, different from that of international organizations in general. On the establishment of the European Community five of the six original Member States were already members of the United Nations. They were therefore bound by Article 103 of the Charter to ensure that in the event of a conflict between their obligations under the Charter and their obligations under any other international agreement, the former should prevail. In accordance with the principle of good faith[33] they could not escape that obligation by concluding, after 1945, a treaty pursuant to which the competence to take measures to comply with a Security Council decision, adopted under Chapter VII, might be transferred to an entity having no obligation to comply with such a decision. It is therefore to be inferred that upon any transfer of competence to the Community pursuant to the EC Treaty, the Community will act consistently with a decision of the Security Council binding under Chapter VII. In other words, as the Member States were not free to act inconsistently with binding Security Council resolutions adopted under Chapter VII of the Charter, they could not transfer to the Community the

31 'Sanctions by United Nations Security Council and the European Community', (1993) 4 EJIL 256.

32 By Article 2(6) the Organization is to ensure that States not being members act in accordance with the principles set out in the Charter 'so far as may be necessary for the maintenance of international peace and security'. Some resolutions request 'all States, including States non-members of the United Nations' to act in accordance with their provisions, see K. Widdows, 'Security Council resolutions and non-members of the United Nations' (1978) 27 ICLQ 459.

33 The principle is expressed in Article 2(2) of the United Nations Charter: 'All members, in order to ensure to all of them the rights and benefits resulting from membership, shall fulfil in good faith the obligations assumed by them in accordance with the present Charter.' See Bin Cheng, *General Principles of Law as Applied by International Courts and Tribunals*, London: Stevens and Sons, 1953, 207–16.

competence to act inconsistently with such resolutions: *nemo dat quod non habet*. When the Federal Republic of Germany and the DDR joined the United Nations in 1973, they too subscribed to Article 103, thereby confirming the prevalence of the Charter over any obligations under the EC Treaty, including an obligation to transfer competence to the Community.[34]

This is consistent with the reasoning of the European Court of Justice in the *International Fruit Company* case where the Court, referring to the antecedent obligations of the Member States under GATT, said: 'By concluding a treaty between them they [the Member States] could not withdraw from their obligations towards third countries.'[35]

In that case the Court of Justice declared that, with regard to the rights and duties arising from the GATT, the EC has replaced the Member States as the relevant actor. In the words of the Court: 'By conferring those powers on the Community, the Member States showed their wish to bind it by the obligations entered into under the General Agreement.'

Likewise, by conferring on the Community powers in respect of the common commercial policy, the Member States showed their wish to bind it by the obligations entered into under the United Nations Charter, in so far as the latter may entail the imposition of economic sanctions.

PRIMACY OF THE EUROPEAN CONVENTION ON HUMAN RIGHTS

Security Council resolutions, adopted on the basis of Chapter VII of the United Nations Charter, present a rare if not rarefied instance of the primacy of an international obligation over the EC Treaty. A more recurrent problem of primacy arises in the case of the ECHR. The relations between that Convention and the EC Treaty are a matter on which Sir Francis Jacobs has special expertise, as a former legal officer in the Council of Europe and as author of a treatise on the subject.[36]

Among his more recent Opinions on the subject is that of 16 December

---

[34] Ernst Schenck, 'Das Problem der Beteiligung der Bundesrepublik Deutschland an Sanktionen der Vereinten Nationen, besonders im Falle Rhodesiens', (1969) 29 Zeitschrift für Ausländisches Öffentliches Recht und Völkerrecht 257.

[35] Joined Cases 21 to 24/72, *International Fruit Company and Others v Produktschap voor Groetnen en Fruit* [1972] ECR 1219 paragraph 11. Article XXI(c) of the General Agreement on Tariffs and Trade confers the contracting parties with the right to invoke obligations under the UN Charter against GATT provisions.

[36] F. Jacobs, *The European Convention on Human Rights* (Oxford: OUP, 1974).

2004 in *Regione autonoma Friuli-Venezia Giulia and Agenzia regionale per lo sviluppo rurale v Ministero delle Politiche Agricole e Forestali.*[37]

Notwithstanding its rather technical facts, the case merits greater attention than it has yet received. The issues of public international law raised in that case were several. The Court of Justice had to interpret a treaty concluded between the European Community and Hungary together with a simultaneous exchange of letters and a Declaration between those parties. In doing so it was called upon to consider general principles of international law, Articles 48 and 59 of the Vienna Convention on the Law of Treaties, the TRIPS Agreement and the European Convention on Human Rights.

The Claimants were *Regione autonoma Friuli-Venezia Giulia and Agenzia regionale per lo sviluppo rurale*. The Defendant was the Italian Ministry for Agriculture and Forestry. The Claimants applied for the annulment of a ministerial Decree prohibiting the use of the word '*Tocai friulani*' for the description and presentation of certain Italian wines at the end of a transitional period expiring on 31 March 2007. The Claimants considered it unfair that of the 106 wines with homonymous names, only Italian and French *Tocai* were required, at the end of a transitional period, to alter the name under which they were presented. They argued that there was no risk of confusion with Hungarian *Tokaj* (differently spelled) because the two products were entirely different, Hungarian *Tokaj* being a sweet wine and Italian *Tocai* being dry. Moreover, Italian *Tocai* had been marketed under that name since time immemorial.

Since the ministerial decree was based on Council Decision 93/724 of 23 November 1993 on the conclusion of an Agreement between the European Community and Hungary on wine names, the Tribunale amministrativo de Lazio referred to the European Court for preliminary ruling certain questions as to the validity of that Decision.

The Claimants argued that an exchange of letters on *Tocai*, annexed to the EC–Hungary Agreement, was inconsistent with the Agreement itself. From this they invited the Court to deduce that the Council Decision was invalid to the extent that it was based on that exchange. According to the Claimants the exchange of letters gave priority to Hungarian *Tokaj* whereas Article 4(5) of the Agreement guarantees the coexistence of homonymous geographical indications of origin, provided that they are not likely to cause confusion. On this point, the Advocate General concluded that there is 'no inconsistency between the prohibition arising from the exchange of letters and the rules governing geographical homonyms in Article 4(5) of the Agreement on wine names'[38] The Court of Justice agreed: the word *Tocai*, as it appears in the expression

---

37 Case C-347/03; judgment given 12 May 2005.

38 Paragraph 67 of the Opinion.

Tocai friulani, is not a geographical indication of origin but the name of a variety of vine.

The Claimants then referred to a Declaration made simultaneously with the EC–Hungary Agreement, by which the parties stated that at the time of negotiations they were not aware of any homonymic designations liable to cause confusion of Community and Hungarian wines. They argued that the Declaration was a misrepresentation of reality, which vitiated the EC–Hungary Agreement. In that context they invoked Article 48 of the Vienna Convention on the Law of Treaties which provides that a State may invoke an error in a treaty as invalidating its consent to be bound if that error relates to a fact or situation which was assumed by that State to exist at a time when the treaty was concluded and formed an essential basis of its consent to be bound. There were obvious difficulties for this argument: the Community had not invoked error as invalidating its consent; and it is doubtful that any error as the consumer's propensity to distinguish between Italian *Tocai* and Hungarian *Tokaj* formed an essential basis of the Community's consent to be bound. But the Advocate General and the Court detected no error and no inconsistency between the treaty and the Declaration. That followed from their view that the Joint Declaration was concerned only with homonymous geographical indications of origin.

Next the Claimants invoked Articles 22 to 24 of the TRIPS Agreement, which govern the prevention of the use of geographical indications of origin in relation to wines other than those originating in the place so indicated. Article 24 reads as follows:

> 1. Members agree to enter into negotiations aimed at increasing the protection of individual geographical indications under Article 23. …
> …
> 4. Nothing in this Section shall require a Member to prevent continued and similar use of a particular geographical indication of another Member identifying wines or spirits in connection with goods or services by any of its nationals or domiciliaries who have used that geographical indication in a continuous manner with regard to the same or related goods or services in the territory of that Member either (a) for at least 10 years preceding 15 April 1994 or (b) in good faith preceding that date.
> …
> 6. Nothing in this Section shall require a Member to apply its provisions in respect of a geographical indication of any other Member with respect to products of the vine for which the relevant indication is identical with the customary name of a grape variety existing in the territory of that Member as of the date of entry into force of the WTO Agreement.

The Claimants' submission as to the meaning of these words was unsustainable. Article 24 established a right, not an obligation, for the Community to grant protection to a particular grape or vine variety if that variety is the homonym of a geographical designation of origin of a wine originating in a third country. On this the Advocate General and the Court were agreed, as was to be expected.

Finally, the Claimants relied on their right to property in accordance with Article 1 of the First Protocol to the European Convention on Human Rights. This presented the most interesting and difficult of the issues in the case. It prompted the referring court to ask the following question:

> Does the right of ownership set out in Article 1 of Protocol No 1 to the European Convention on Human Rights and Fundamental Freedoms . . . also cover intellectual property in the names of the places of origin of wines and the exploitation thereof, and, consequently, does the protection of that right preclude application of the agreement set out in the exchange of letters annexed to the Agreement between the European Community and the Republic of Hungary on reciprocal protection and control of wine names . . ., but not included in the body of that agreement, under which wine producers of the Friuli region will not be permitted to use the name 'Tocai friulano', particularly in view of the total lack of any compensation to the wine producers of the Friuli region thus dispossessed, the lack of any general public interest justifying their dispossession and the disregard for the principle of proportionality?

The difficult part of the question is in the opening three lines: 'Does the right of ownership set out in Article 1 of Protocol No 1 . . . cover intellectual property in the names of the places of origin of wines?'

The Court of Justice did not answer that part of the question directly. Instead it concentrated on the referring court's closing words, which refer to 'the total lack of any compensation to the wine producers of the Friuli region thus dispossessed, the lack of any general public interest justifying their dispossession and the disregard for the principle of proportionality'. The question addressed by the Court of Justice is whether the prohibition of the use of *Tocai* for the description and presentation of certain Italian wines constitutes a disproportionate and intolerable interference, impairing the very substance of the fundamental right to property of the economic operators concerned. The Court's answer was 'No'.

In avoiding a response to the opening three lines of the question, the Court of Justice spared itself the task of determining the meaning of 'property' or 'possessions' as those expressions are found in Article 1 of the First Protocol. To answer that question directly would present a hostage to fortune and might risk inconsistent judgments in Luxembourg and Strasbourg. But Mr Advocate General Jacobs did not flinch from responding directly to the whole of the question, including the opening three lines.

His point of departure could only be that the word 'possessions' in the Protocol is an autonomous notion extending to incorporeal goods of economic value. The European Court of Human Rights had said so more than once. It has in several instances made the point that:

> The concept of 'possessions' in the first part of Article 1 of Protocol No. 1 has an autonomous meaning which is not limited to the ownership of material goods and is independent from the formal classification in domestic law. In the same way as material goods, certain other rights and interests constituting assets can also be regarded as 'property rights', and thus as 'possessions' for the purposes of this provision.[39]

In *Tre Traktörer Aktiebolag v Sweden*[40] the Court of Human Rights accepted, in the context of the withdrawal of a licence to serve alcoholic beverages at a restaurant, that the economic interests connected with the running of the restaurant were 'possessions' for the purposes of Article 1 of the Protocol. Since the maintenance of the licence was one of the principal conditions for the carrying on of the business, and its withdrawal had adverse effects on the goodwill and value of the restaurant, the Court of Human Rights held that the withdrawal constituted an interference with the restaurant manager's right to the 'peaceful enjoyment of [his] possessions'.

Mr Advocate General Jacobs considered however that the decision in *Tre Traktörer Aktiebolag v Sweden* was not analogous to the *Friuli-Venezia Giulia* case. There is indeed this difference between the two cases: use of the words '*Tocai friulano*' was not essential for the sale of wines from the Friuli Venezia Giulia region in the same way that possession of a licence is a prerequisite for the conduct of the business of a restaurant in *Tre Traktörer Aktiebolag*.[41] But that difference is more in degree than in kind. In both cases the applicant was deprived of an incorporeal right, of monetary value, to conduct a business as it wished. Commercial conduct which previously had been lawful, and valuable, became unlawful in consequence of the State's action.

It might perhaps be contended (although there is no such contention in the Opinion of Advocate General Jacobs) that the right conferred by a licence (as in *Traktörer Aktiebolag v Sweden*) is proprietary whereas a right granted by operation of law to all inhabitants of a region is not of a proprietary nature. But the answer to that point is to be found in the judgment of the European Court of Human Rights in its judgment in *Broniowski v Poland*:[42] a case decided

---

39 Paragraph 129 of the judgment. See *Iatridis v Greece* Application No. 31107/96, paragraph 54, ECHR 1999-II, and *Beyeler v Italy* Application No. 33202/96, paragraph 100, ECHR 2000-I. See more recently *Kanayev v Russia*, 27 July 2006, Application No. 43726/02.

40 10873/84 [1989] ECHR 15 (7 July 1989).

41 In the French version the word *biens* ('possessions') appears to have the same meaning as *propriété* ('property').

42 Application No. 31443/96.

only six months before the Advocate General's Opinion in the *Friuli-Venezia* case.

In *Broniowski v Poland* the right at issue was a right to compensation granted by Polish law to persons who were 'repatriated' from the 'territories beyond the Bug River'. The right was not granted individually and attested by a document. It was granted by operation of law to those originating in a certain region. This suggests that a right to market wines by reference to a particular regional designation, when granted by law to all inhabitants of a defined region, is to be considered as a form of possession within the meaning of Article 1 of the First Protocol to the European Convention.

This conclusion is consistent with a passage in the judgment of the European Court of Justice in Case C-306/93 *SMW Winzersekt v Land Rheinland-Pfalz.*[43] The point at issue there was whether the prohibition of use of the term *méthode champenoise* for the marketing of wines amounted to breach of the property rights of a German producer. The Court of Justice stated that:

> the designation *méthode champenoise* is a term which, prior to the adoption of the regulation, all producers of sparkling wines were entitled to use. The prohibition of the use of that designation cannot be regarded as an infringement of an alleged property right vested in Winzersekt.

The reasoning in that case was that no property right was vested in Winzersekt since use of the term had formerly been open to all producers of sparkling wines irrespective of their region. Conversely in the *Friuli-Venezia Giulia* case, use of the term *Tocai friulano* had been limited to wine producers of the Friuli Venezia Giulia region. It was a right vested in them.

This objection is inadequately addressed by the submission, made by the Council and the Commission in the *Friuli-Venezia Giulia* case, that the right involved was not a property right even in the sense of intellectual property. While it is true that neither the Paris Convention[44] nor the TRIPS Agreement[45] mentions grape variety names as a category of intellectual property, that submission pays insufficient regard to the insistence of the European Court of Human Rights that the concept of 'possessions' in the first part of Article 1 of Protocol No. 1 has an autonomous meaning.

Moreover, it would be consistent with the facts of the case to recognize a

---

43 [1994] ECR I-5555, paragraph 25.

44 Convention for the Protection of Industrial Property, Paris, 20 March 1883, 74 BFSP 44.

45 Annex IC to the Agreement establishing the World Trade Organization, Marrakesh, 15 April 1994.

proprietary right to use the name of the region in which the wine is produced. The grievance expressed by the Claimants in the national court was that those engaged in the production and marketing of wines from the Venice region were to be deprived of an entitlement, long recognized by national law, which the relevant producers considered to be valuable. It is of little comfort to the producers that (in the Advocate General's words, quoting those of the Commission) there are acceptable synonyms such as *sauvignonasse* and *trebbianello*. If the Claimants had thought those synonyms equally valuable, they would presumably have refrained from instituting the proceedings.

The Advocate General in the *Friuli-Venezia* case doubted whether the applicants could properly plead an infringement of the right to property under the Convention, given that they are not wine producers and have not shown how they would be affected. It is submitted, however, that on a reference for preliminary ruling, it must be for the national court rather than for the Court of Justice to determine whether a claimant has a sufficient interest or other entitlement to invoke the European Convention on Human Rights for the purpose of determining the applicability of a Community regulation. It is by no means inconceivable that Italian law might permit a public authority to do so.

Having concluded that the right to use the name of a grape variety in marketing a given wine is not a property right covered by Article 1 of the First Protocol, 'at least in the circumstances of the present case', Mr Advocate General Jacobs went on to consider whether the prohibition of the use of that name is precluded by that Article. Here he was on secure ground.

Even if the prohibition on use of *Tocai friulano* amounted to deprivation of a 'possession' it would be consistent with Article 1 of the First Protocol if done 'in the public interest and subject to the conditions provided for by law and by the general principles of international law'. There is a clear public interest in the Community's entering into reciprocal arrangements for the protection of wine names. There is a clear basis in Community law for the legislative regulation of the description of wines. There was nothing to suggest that the prohibition is contrary to any principle of international law. The effect of the long transitional period, the limited effect of the prohibition and the availability of alternative vine names were such as to exclude any entitlement to compensation.

A fortiori the prohibition would be consistent with the Protocol if it were to be seen as an interference with peaceful enjoyment of property, not amounting to deprivation. In *SMW Winzersekt v Land Rheinland-Pfalz*[46] the Court of Justice held that the Council took account of the interests of those affected by

[46] [1994] ECR I-5555.

the prohibition of the use of the designation *méthode champenoise* and so acted proportionately by adopting transitional arrangements for and by allowing traders who had formerly used that expression to use alternative expressions. Similar considerations applied in the *Friuli-Venezia* case.

THE ASSOCIATION AGREEMENT WITH TURKEY

The European Convention on Human Rights has played a large part in the negotiations, and public debate, on the question of Turkish accession to the European Community. In Case C-275/02, *Engin Ayaz v Land Baden-Württemberg*[47] a question arose as to the interpretation of the term 'member of the family' in Article 7 of Decision No. 1/80.[48] In that context both Mr Advocate General Geelhoed and the Court had to take account of the European Convention on Human Rights. Mr Advocate General Jacobs and the Court had to address the question of rights of Turkish workers more recently in *Wählergruppe Gemeinsam Zajedno*.[49] Before considering the issues raised in that case, we must establish the legislative context.

The 'Ankara Agreement' of 12 September 1963 established an Association between Turkey and what was then the European Economic Community.[50] It provided for the establishment of a Customs Union in three stages: the preliminary, transitional and final stages. It also contains 'other economic provisions'. Among these are:

1. Article 14, whereby the parties agree to be guided by Articles 55 and 56 and 58 to 65 of the Treaty establishing the European Economic Community [now Articles 45 and 46 and 49 to 55 of the EC Treaty] for the purpose of abolishing restrictions on the freedom to provide services between them; and
2. Article 15 which contemplates the extension to Turkey, with appropriate modifications, of the provisions of the EC Treaty relating to transport.

Article 22 provides for the establishment of an Association Council, comprising representatives of both sides, having the power to take by unanim-

---

47 25 May 2004.

48 Decision No. 1/80 of 19 September 1980 on the development of the Association, adopted by the Council of Association created under the Agreement establishing an Association between the European Economic Community and Turkey.

49 Case C-171/01 [2003] ECR I-4301.

50 OJ 1964, 3687; OJ 1973 C113/1. Annexed to the Ankara Agreement were Protocol No. 1 (Provisional Protocol) and Protocol No. 2 (Financial Protocol).

ity decisions binding on both sides. Article 28 states that when the operation of the Agreement has advanced sufficiently far, the Contracting Parties will examine the possibility of Turkish accession to the Community.

The preliminary stage for the completion of the Customs Union, lasting five years, was instituted by the Ankara Agreement itself. The transitional phase, lasting twenty-two years, began on 1 January 1973 with the entry into force of the Additional Protocol and Financial Protocol of 23 November 1970, annexed to the Ankara Agreement.[51] The final phase was instituted by Decision 1/95 of the Association Council of 22 December 1995 which entered into force on 31 December 1995 and remains in force.

It was in the course of the transitional phase that the Association Council formed under Article 22 of the Ankara Agreement made Decision 1/80 of 19 September 1980 on the application of the social security schemes of the Member States to Turkish workers. That Decision applies to workers who are or have been subject to the legislation of one or more Member States and who are Turkish nationals, and to the members of the families and survivors of these workers, resident in the territory of one of the Member States. It provides, subject to express exceptions, that persons resident in the territory of one of the Member States to whom this Decision applies shall be subject to the same obligations and enjoy the same benefits under the legislation of any Member State as the nationals of that State. Article 10(1) provides: 'The Member States of the Community shall as regards remuneration and other conditions of work grant Turkish workers duly registered as belonging to their labour forces treatment involving no discrimination on the basis of nationality between them and Community workers.'

In *Wählergruppe Gemeinsam Zajedno* a question arose as to the application of Article 10(1) of Decision 1/80 in the face of a provision of Austrian law[52] which made possession of Austrian nationality a condition for election to the general assembly of a chamber of workers. Wählergruppe Gemeinsam put forward a list of twenty-six candidates for the elections to the general assembly of the chamber of workers for the *Land* of Vorarlberg which took place in April 1999. Of those candidates five were Turkish nationals. They fulfilled the criteria for eligibility, save for that relating to nationality. On 8 February 1999, the principal election committee decided to delete the five Turkish nationals from the list of candidates submitted by Wählergruppe Gemeinsam on the ground that they did not have Austrian nationality and were therefore ineligible. Voting was by proportional representation. The result of the election was

---

[51] OJ 1972 L293/4.

[52] Paragraph 21 of the Arbeiterkammergesetz (Law on Chambers of Workers, BGBl. 1991/626, read with Article 26(4) of the Bundesverfassungsgesetz (Federal Constitutional Law)).

such as to give Wählergruppe Gemeinsam two delegates. Wählergruppe Gemeinsam then contested the validity of the election. The competent Federal Minister rejected their complaint, reasoning that the deletion of the names of the Turkish nationals from the list of Wählergruppe Gemeinsam was not such as to influence the result, in view of the non-personalized list voting system prescribed for elections to the general assembly.

Wählergruppe Gemeinsam appealed to the Verfassungsgerichtshof, which referred the following questions to the Court for a preliminary ruling:

> 1. Is Article 10(1) of Decision No 1/80 . . . to be interpreted as precluding a provision of a Member State which excludes Turkish workers from eligibility for the general assembly of a chamber of workers?
> 2. If so, is Article 10(1) of Decision No 1/80 . . . directly applicable Community law?

The principal concern of the Verfassungsgerichtshof, when asking the first question, appears to have been to ascertain whether eligibility for election to the general assembly of a chamber of workers fell within the expression 'other conditions of work' for the purposes of Article 10(1) of the Decision. Some support might be found for a negative answer to that question in Article 8(1) of Regulation 1612/68,[53] which provides expressly that a worker who is a national of a Member State employed in the territory of another Member State shall enjoy, among other rights, 'the right of eligibility for workers' representative bodies'.

Since, however, the aim of the Ankara Agreement is 'to promote the continuous and balanced strengthening of trade and economic relations between the Contracting Parties, including in the labour sector, by progressively securing freedom of movement for workers', there was good reason to construe that Agreement and Decisions of the Association Council established thereby in the light of European Community law. In *Ahmet Bozkurt v Staatssecretaris van Justitie*[54] the Court of Justice had gone so far as to say that it is 'essential to transpose so far as possible' the principles contained in Articles 48 to 50 of the EC Treaty to Turkish workers who enjoy rights pursuant to Decision 1/80.

Consistently with that injunction, it was incumbent on the Court of Justice to construe the provisions in Decision 1/80 governing the treatment of Turkish workers consistently with the provisions in the EC Treaty governing the treatment of workers having the nationality of Member States. It is very clear that Community nationals are entitled to be treated equally with nationals of

---

53 OJ Sp Ed 1968, 475.
54 Case C-343/93 [1995] ECR I-1475 paragraph 19.

Member States for the purpose of election to membership of occupational guilds to which they are compulsorily affiliated.[55]

The Advocate General therefore concluded that on the proper construction of Article 10(1) of Decision No. 1/80 eligibility for election to the general assembly of a chamber of workers fell within the expression 'other conditions of work'. By parity of reasoning he concluded that eligibility for such election did not fall within the exception for offices involving the exercise of powers conferred by public law. The Court of Justice agreed. It stated at paragraph 93 of the judgment:

> with respect to foreign workers enjoying equal treatment as regards remuneration and other conditions of work, the denial of the right to stand as a candidate for election to a body representing and defending the interests of workers, such as the chambers of workers in Austria, can be justified neither by the legal nature of the body in question under national law nor by the fact that certain of its functions could involve participation in the exercise of powers conferred by public law.

The technique of construing an association agreement by reference to the principles of the EC Treaty is not new. It can be traced at least as far back as 1980.[56] But the specific reiteration of that principle in the context of the Ankara Agreement is of special interest at present in view of a much-publicized difference between Turkey and certain Member States over access to ports. Decision 1/95 uses language similar to that found in Articles 28 and 29 (formerly 30 and 34) of the EC Treaty when prohibiting quantitative restrictions and equivalent measures. It may be appropriate to read the language of Decision 1/95 in the light of the judgment in *Corsica Ferries,*[57] where the Court of Justice stated legislation providing for certain mooring charges is not to be regarded as being capable of hindering trade between Member States when it makes no distinction according to the origin of the goods transported, its purpose is not to regulate trade in goods with other Member States and the restrictive effects which it might have on the free movement of goods are too uncertain and indirect for the obligation which it imposes.

A decision on the correct meaning of Article 10(1) of Decision 1/80 was not enough to dispose of the issues raised in *Wählergruppe Gemeinsam*

---

55 Case C-213/90, *Association de soutien aux travailleurs immigrés v Chambre des employés privés* [1991] ECR I-3507.

56 Case 270/80, *Polydor and Others v Harlequin and Others* [1982] ECR 329, paragraphs 14 to 20; Case 104/81, *Hauptzollamt Mainz v Kupferberg & Cie* [1982] ECR 3641, paragraphs 28 to 30; and Case C-312/91, *Metalsa* [1992] ECR I-3751, paragraphs 10 to 12.

57 Case 266/96 [1989] ECR 4441.

Zajedno. It remained necessary to respond to the Verfassungsgerichtshof's second question, which enquired as to the direct applicability of that provision.

On that issue the point of departure is that a provision in the Ankara Agreement must be regarded as being directly applicable when, regard being had to its wording and to the purpose and nature of the Agreement, it contains a clear and precise obligation which is not subject, in its implementation or effects, to the adoption of any subsequent measure;[58] and the same conditions apply in determining whether the provisions of a decision of the EEC–Turkey Association Council may have direct effect.[59]

Both Mr Advocate General Jacobs and the Court concluded that Article 10(1) of Decision No. 1/80 contains a clear and precise obligation which is not conditional on the adoption of any subsequent measure. In reaching that conclusion both referred to the judgment in *Sürül*:[60] a case in which the Court held that Article 3(1) of Decision 3/80 produced direct effects, while adding that those direct effects may not be relied on in support of claims relating to benefits in respect of periods prior to the date of this judgment except as regards those persons who, before that date, initiated proceedings or made an equivalent claim.

In fact, the issue in *Wählergruppe Gemeinsam Zajedno* appears considerably simpler than that in *Sürül*. In the latter case the prohibition of discrimination was entirely general. Article 3(1) of Decision No. 3/80, which is entitled 'Equality of treatment' and adopts the wording of Article 3(1) of Regulation No. 1408/71, provides:

> Subject to the special provisions of this Decision, persons resident in the territory of one of the Member States to whom this Decision applies shall be subject to the same obligations and enjoy the same benefits under the legislation of any Member State as the nationals of that State.

There was a respectable argument to be advanced in that case that Article 3(1) is of general scope; and programmatic in the sense that it is intended to be supplemented and implemented in the Community by a subsequent act of the Council. In the case of Article 10(1) of Decision 1/80, on the other hand, its scope is limited to 'remuneration and other conditions of work'; and there is no reason to expect further supplementation by subsequent Council acts.

---

[58] Case 12/86, *Demirel v Stadt Schwäbisch Gmünd* [1987] ECR 3719 paragraph 14.

[59] Case C-192/89, *Sevince Staatssecretaris van Justitie* [1990] ECR I-3461 paragraphs 14 and 15.

[60] Case C-262/96, *Sema Sürül v Bundesanstalt für Arbeit* [1999] ECR I-2685, paragraph 60.

CONCLUSION

In his seventeen years at the European Court of Justice Sir Francis Jacobs brought, among other attributes, an experience in public international law such as to set him apart from most of his colleagues. The experience was of value both to him and to the Court. It is reflected in his Opinions.

There was a time, however, when this expertise would have been considered by some to be foreign to the Court of Justice, which sought to set itself apart from courts of international law. It is noteworthy that in recent years the Court has been prepared to acknowledge its debt to international law: for instance by referring expressly to the Vienna Convention on the Law of Treaties: not only in cases such as *Regione Autonoma Friuli-Venezia*, when it has to construe treaties concluded with third States; but also when interpreting instruments governed by Community law, as in Case C-37/00, *Herbert Weber v Universal Ogden Services Ltd.*[61]

It is not that the European Court now sees itself more as an international court than it used to do. The opposite is probably the case. More confident, now, that its distinctive status is recognized and understood, the Court no longer expresses sensitivity that once it showed towards acknowledging the paternity of its law. On matters as diverse as State immunity,[62] State responsibility,[63] flags of convenience,[64] the elimination of statelessness,[65] and the constitutional relations between the United Kingdom and Jersey[66] or Gibraltar[67] there are recent judgments of the European Court of Justice. In a case brought by the Kurdistan Workers' Party the Court of First Instance even had something brief to say about the right of self-defence in international law.[68] For those whose desks already groan under the weight of accumulated information from a multitude of judicial bodies, committees, commissions and States the lesson may be unwelcome: the judgments of the European Courts constitute an indispensable source of international law.

---

61 [2002] ECR I-2013.

62 Case T-306/01, *Ahmed Ali Yusuf, Al Barakaat International Foundation v Council and Commission*, 21 September 2005, not yet reported in ECR.

63 Case C-224/01, *Köbler* [2003] ECR I-10239.

64 Case C-405/01, *Colegio de Oficiales de la Marina Mercante Española v Administracion del Estado*, 30 September 2003, not yet reported in ECR.

65 Case C-95/99, *Khalil, Chaaban and Osseili v Bundesanstalt für Arbeit* [2001] ECR I-7413.

66 Case C-293/02 *Jersey Produce Marketing Organisation* [2005] ECR I-9543.

67 Case C-168/93 *Government of Gibraltar & Gibraltar Development Council* [1993] ECR I-4009.

68 Case T-229/02 *PKK and KNK v Council* [2005] ECR II-539; on appeal: Case C-229/05 P, judgment, 18 January 2007.

9. Intellectual property

Christopher Morcom*

INTRODUCTION

At the UKAEL Conference in Honour of Sir Francis Jacobs held on 30 June 2006, a number of distinguished speakers paid tribute to his outstanding contribution over his 18 years as Advocate General to the European Court of Justice (ECJ), in different areas of the law. Although there was mention of his Opinions in some Intellectual Property cases, this area of his work did not receive the attention which it deserves. However, no account of his role as Advocate General could ever be complete without reference to his contribution to the law of Intellectual Property.

INTELLECTUAL PROPERTY LAW IN THE EU

For reasons which are perfectly understandable, there have been very few patent and design cases before the Court. There is still no Community Patent system and there is no harmonised patent law in the EU; such developments in the area of designs[1] have been quite recent, only becoming effective during 2002–3. Although there has been some harmonisation in the field of copyright law, this is far from being comprehensive, being confined to a few directives dealing with specific topics, and there have been comparatively few cases before the Court involving copyright issues; Sir Francis has been involved with some of them. Another area in which he has had some involvement is that of protected designations of origin and protected geographical indications, which are now covered by EU legislation[2] and can be said to have some overlap with trade mark law. In the Intellectual Property field it is trade mark law which has been much the most affected by legislation in the EU. There has

* QC, Hogarth Chambers, Lincoln's Inn.

1 See in particular Council Regulation (EC) No. 6/2002 of 12 December 2001 on Community Designs and Directive 98/71/EC of the European Parliament and of the Council of October 1998 on the legal protection of Designs.

2 See Council Regulation (EC) 2081/92 of 14 July 1992, as later amended.

been a Community Trade Mark ('CTM') Regulation[3] in force for over 10 years, providing for a single registration having unitary effect throughout all 25 Member States, and national trade mark laws of Member States have been required to conform to a harmonisation Directive[4] for more than 12 years. These measures have given rise to a considerable number of trade mark cases before the ECJ. Even before then, during Sir Francis's first six years as Advocate General, he was responsible for guiding the ECJ in a number of highly significant trade mark cases. In this appreciation of his work it is proposed primarily to consider his contribution in the area of trade marks. It would be an almost Herculean task to review all such cases in which he has provided Opinions, and this chapter will concentrate on the most important examples. These include in particular: cases concerned in some way with the principle of free movement of goods; a line of cases which lay down the criteria for registration of trade marks; and some others relating to refusal of registration and infringement.

FREE MOVEMENT OF GOODS

The principle of the free movement of goods in the EU has long been established as a fundamental principle of Community law. However, there was a stage in the development of the law in the ECJ, when there was very grave concern that the principle was being applied in a way that was in danger of causing serious damage to some Intellectual Property rights, and to trade marks in particular. There were views being expressed within certain directorates of the European Commission to the effect that trade mark rights should not be capable of being enforced so as to prevent the import of goods from one Member State into another. Unfortunately such views appeared to find favour in the ECJ. For instance, in the case of *Sirena Srl v Eda Srl*,[5] the Advocate General said that 'the interests which patent legislation is intended to protect are economically and humanely more respectable than those protected by the law of trade marks'. The Court appeared to accept this without question. So perhaps one should not have been surprised by the ruling of the Court in *Van Zuylen Freres SA v HAG AG*[6] (now known as '*HAG I*') that the owner of rights to a trade mark in the Benelux countries could not prevent the import

[3] Council Regulation 40/94/EC of 23 December 1993 on the Community Trade Mark, as amended on a number of occasions.

[4] First Council Directive 89/104/EC to approximate the laws of the Member States relating to trade marks.

[5] Case 40/70 [1971] ECR 69.

[6] Case 192/73 [1974] ECR 731.

from Germany of goods bearing the same mark but manufactured by an unrelated company which owned the rights to the mark in Germany, for the sole reason that the German company had many years previously been the owner of the rights to the mark in the Benelux countries which the claimant sought to enforce, losing these as a result of a compulsory assignment. The case was referred to and distinguished by Advocate General Jean-Pierre Warner in his lucid Opinion in *EMI Records Ltd v CBS United Kingdom Ltd*,[7] in which the defendant sought to rely upon the 'common origin' doctrine of *HAG I* where the goods in question came from outside the Community. It is worth noting that the Court did not even refer to *HAG I* in its judgment.

There never was any proper justification for the common origin doctrine, but the decision was left alone, and indeed approved,[8] until Advocate General Jacobs came to the rescue in the sequel, now known as '*HAG II*' *Cnl-Sucal NV SA v Hag GF AG*.[9] In his masterly Opinion the fallacy, indeed the heresy, of the *HAG I* common origin doctrine was exposed, with references to more recent decisions of the Court and a recommendation that the Court should overrule its decision in *HAG I*. This was a truly historic moment in the history of trade mark law in the Community. The Court accepted the Advocate General's Opinion, and thus *HAG I* was duly buried. The *HAG II* ruling was applied and extended soon afterwards, to a case in which the rights in a trade mark in Germany and France had become vested in unconnected companies as a result of voluntary assignments.

Subsequent Cases Concerning Free Movement of Goods

Also falling under the general heading of free movement of goods are the cases concerned with 'exhaustion of rights'. Once a trade mark owner has placed his goods on the market, or consented to them being placed on the market, under the trade mark, he is said to have exhausted his rights in the mark, with the result that he cannot then generally object to the further marketing of the goods. There are two kinds of 'exhaustion'. One is 'Community exhaustion', where the goods are first marketed in the EU (the same rules apply to goods first marketed in the European Economic Area (EEA)); the goods are considered then to be in free circulation, and national trade mark rights can only be exercised to prevent further circulation in the EU (or EEA) if there are proper reasons. The second kind of exhaustion is called 'international exhaustion', where (it is said) a trade mark owner should not, without a

[7] Case C-51/75 [1976] ECR 811.

[8] See the ruling of the Court in Case 119/75, *Terrapin v Terranova* [1976] ECR 1039, which was not a 'common origin' case.

[9] Case C-10/89 [1990] ECR 3711.

proper reason, be allowed to object to further marketing of his trade marked goods in the EU even if they were first marketed outside the EU. International exhaustion had been recognised in several cases before English courts before the adoption of the trade marks Directive. However, as will be seen, the position has now changed.

Community exhaustion

Many cases before the Court, in which trade mark owners have sought to prevent goods marketed by them in one Member State from being sold into other Member States, have been concerned with pharmaceutical products. Often there are significant price differences between one Member State and another, but because of local regulations the products have to be re-labelled or repackaged before they can be sold in other Member States. Francis Jacobs has made a significant contribution in this area, and also in cases involving other products, such as perfumes and alcoholic drinks.

In a leading case involving repackaging of pharmaceutical products, *Bristol-Myers Squibb v Paranova A/S*,[10] Advocate General Jacobs laid down the basic rules, which the Court largely followed, as to the circumstances in which a trade mark owner was entitled to object to the marketing of repackaged goods imported from another Member State. The Court held that the trade mark owner was only barred from enforcing his rights if (a) use of the trade mark right to prevent imports would contribute to the artificial partitioning of markets between Member States, (b) the repackaging did not adversely affect the original condition of the product, and (c) the parallel importer complied with certain obligations as to labelling and provision of samples. These basic rules continue to be applied, although further clarification has necessarily been required from the Court as different situations have arisen in the cases subsequently referred to it. The first of the conditions mentioned above involves, in particular, consideration of the question whether it is 'necessary' for the parallel importer to repackage or re-label the goods in order to secure access to the market in the importing Member State. In the case of *Frits Loendersloot v George Ballantine & Son Ltd*[11] the Advocate General had to consider this question in a case involving parallel imports of Scotch whisky, which had been re-labelled. A different question arose in a case[12] involving parallel imports of perfumes; the goods had not been repackaged but were being sold in a chain of chemists' shops which were outside the trade mark

10 Cases C-427, 429, 436/93 [1996] ECR I-3457. In a comprehensive Opinion the Advocate General also dealt with four other cases, which were the subject of separate references to the Court, in which separate judgments were given.

11 Case C-349/95 [1997] ECR I-6227.

12 Case C-337/95, *Parfums Christian Dior SA v Evora BV* [1997] ECR I-6013.

owner's selective distribution network for such goods. The Court, again following the Advocate General's clear Opinion, held that a trade mark owner was not entitled to exercise his rights so as to prevent importation from another Member State unless it was shown that the use of the mark in question seriously damaged the reputation of the mark. The same approach was adopted in relation to enforcement of copyright in images of the bottles and packaging.

In yet another case,[13] the Advocate General had to deal with a situation in which a trade mark owner used (and registered) slightly different trade marks for the two Member States concerned, and the parallel importer, as well as repackaging the goods to meet local requirements, replaced the trade mark with the one that was used and protected in the Member State of importation. The Court again accepted his view, that the importation could be prevented unless changing the mark was necessary in order to market the product in the Member State of import. He adopted a similar approach in *Boehringer Ingelheim KG v Swingward Ltd*,[14] where the Court had to determine the circumstances in which a parallel importer should not be prevented from repackaging the goods, as opposed to re-labelling. Again the Advocate General's view, in another most thorough and clear Opinion, that this depended upon whether repackaging was objectively 'necessary' for effective access to the market concerned, was accepted by the Court.

These few cases alone demonstrate the very significant contribution of Advocate General Jacobs to the development of the law in this area, so as to achieve a proper balance between the rights of Intellectual Property right owners and the need to maintain the free movement of goods between Member States. This is still a developing area, and the Court's position may yet change, but there is no doubt that the basic foundations have been well laid.

International exhaustion

Here again Advocate General Jacobs was involved in two of the earliest cases heard by the Court in which the question of international exhaustion was raised. In the first of these, *Silhouette International Schmied GmbH & Co KG v Hartlauer Handelsgesellschaft mbH*,[15] his very clear and firm Opinion, that the trade mark owner's rights were not exhausted where the goods were put on the market by him outside the EEA and that the relevant provision of the

---

13 Case C-379/97, *Pharmacia & Upjohn SA v Paranova A/S* [2000] ECR I-6927.

14 Case C-143/00 [2002] ECR I-3759, considered together with Case C-443/99, *Merck, Sharp & Dohme GmbH v Paranova*, in which similar issues arose. See also a later Opinion in another repackaging case, *Aventis Pharma Deutschland GmbH v Kohlpharma GmbH* (Case C-433/00) [2002] ECR I-7761.

15 Case C-355/96 [1998] ECR I-4799.

Directive precluded Member States from adopting the principle of international exhaustion, was accepted. The decision in *Silhouette* was followed in the second case, *Sebago Inc v GB-Unic SA*.[16] These two decisions, and the Advocate General's Opinion in each of them, have paved the way for similar rulings in a number of cases.[17]

It is also worth mentioning one of his last cases concerned with parallel importation, *Class International BV v Colgate Palmolive Company & Others*.[18] This involved a different situation, the goods in question – toothpaste – being the genuine goods of the trade mark owner, having been placed in a warehouse in the Netherlands and subject to the 'external transit procedure'. Such goods come from non-EEA countries and are not in free circulation in the EU. This case called for a full analysis of the relevant Customs legislation and procedures, as well as the applicable trade mark law. In his detailed Opinion, which again the Court accepted, the Advocate General concluded that the applicant was not using the trade mark 'in the course of trade' in the Netherlands and was therefore not infringing the trade mark, because the goods were still, while in the warehouse, 'non-Community goods'.

REGISTRABILITY OF TRADE MARKS

The work of the Court in the area of trade mark registration has significantly increased since the coming into effect of the CTM Regulation on 1 April 1996. Appeals from the Boards of Appeal in the Office (OHIM, or Office for Harmonisation in the Internal Market) in Alicante are to the Court of First Instance, but from there, there may be a further appeal to the ECJ. These cases are of course in addition to references from the national courts. Advocate General Jacobs was particularly involved in some of the cases on registrability of trade marks under the CTM Regulation. It is only possible to mention a few of these. Because the requirements for registering a trade mark as a CTM are the same as those established under the Directive for national registrations, the principles of the Court's decisions in these cases apply generally to the registration of trade marks throughout the EU.

---

16 Case C-173/98 [1999] ECR I-4103.

17 See, for example, Cases C-414 –16/99, *Zino Davidoff SA v A & G Imports Ltd* and *Levi Strauss & Co. & Levi Strauss (UK) Ltd v Tesco Stores Ltd & Tesco plc* and *Levi Strauss & Co. & Levi Strauss (UK) Ltd v Costco Wholesale UK Ltd* [2001] ECR I-8691.

18 Case C-405/03 [2005] ECR I-8735.

The first of these cases concerned an application to register the mark 'BABY DRY'[19] for disposable babies' nappies, the Office having raised objections on the ground of the mark's descriptiveness. In his Opinion, which is a very clear exposition of the principles involved, Advocate General Jacobs considered that the Board of Appeal and OHIM had erred in law in failing to give due consideration to the mark's 'unusual and opaque grammatical structure', and the Court accepted this and allowed the appeal. The decision has, as the Advocate General would be the first to agree, been considered controversial.[20] In this connection it is worth mentioning that when he delivered his Opinion, the Court of First Instance had upheld an appeal against the refusal to register the mark DOUBLEMINT for chewing gum; although that decision was subsequently reversed by the ECJ, it is possible that the decision of the Court of First Instance had some influence on the BABY DRY case. Advocate General Jacobs himself was involved in the DOUBLEMINT case before the Court.[21] His Opinion merits careful reading, and it is interesting to see the way in which he explained and clarified the BABY DRY decision. The Court accepted his Opinion and overturned the decision of the CFI.

The subsequent case of *OHIM v Zapf Creations AG*[22] arose from an application to register 'NEW BORN BABY' for dolls and accessories for dolls, which had been refused registration by OHIM on the ground of its descriptiveness, but the Court of First Instance had reversed the decision of the Board of Appeal. This provided the Advocate General with the opportunity to summarise the position, regarding a suggested conflict between BABY DRY and an earlier case, and he expressed the view that any such conflict had been settled by the DOUBLEMINT decision, concluding with the advice that the appeal should be allowed. There was no decision in the case because the applicant withdrew the application and the Court merely ordered the applicant to pay the costs. There can be no doubt, it is considered, that the Advocate General's Opinion would have been accepted.

The above are the main cases on registrability in which the Court has had the benefit of the Advocate General's Opinions; there are several others, but it

---

19 Case C-383/99 P, *Procter & Gamble Company v OHIM* [2001] ECR I-6251.

20 In Case C-363/99, *Koninklijke Nederland NV v Benelux Merken Bureau* [2004] I-1619, a case arising from the refusal of the Benelux Office to accept POSTKANTOOR (the Dutch word for Post Office) for postal services and related goods, the Advocate General (who has been known to disagree with Advocate General Jacobs on at least one other occasion) was critical of the BABY DRY decision and thus by implication, of the Advocate General's Opinion in the case. It is to be noted that the Court's decision in that case was delivered more than two years after the delivery of the Advocate General's Opinion.

21 Case C-191/01, *OHIM v Wm Wrigley JR Company* [2004] ECR I-12447.

22 Case C-498/01 P [2004] ECR I-11349.

is not possible here to mention all of them.[23] One final case can be mentioned, being of interest because it concerned a national registration of a mark which was descriptive of the goods in question but only in a language of a different Member State. In *Matratzen Concord AG v Hulka Germany SA*[24] a Spanish registration had been obtained for the word 'Matratzen' for a variety of goods, which included mattresses, the mark being the German word for such goods. A German company sought to cancel the registration. Such cases have often caused problems, and the Advocate General in his Opinion reviewed the positions taken by the trade mark offices of other Member States. He concluded that under the relevant provision of the Directive, a sign consisting solely of a word or words which are descriptive of the product in question in the language of one Member State 'may not be registered as a trade mark in another Member State where a significant proportion of traders in and consumers of that product can reasonably be expected to understand the meaning of the word or words'. The Court however preferred a different form of wording, holding that the relevant provision of the Directive

> does not preclude the registration in a Member State, as a national trade mark, of a term borrowed from the language of another Member State in which it is devoid of distinctive character or descriptive of the goods or services in respect of which registration is sought, unless the relevant parties in the Member State in which registration is sought are capable of identifying the meaning of the term.

With all due respect, it is suggested that the Advocate General's wording provides a rather more practical guide to offices and practitioners than does the Court's ruling.

INFRINGEMENT OF REGISTERED TRADE MARKS AND OPPOSITION TO REGISTRATION

There have been a considerable number of references to the Court of questions concerning conflicts between the trade marks of different parties. These questions arise both in infringement cases and in cases in which one party is opposing or seeking to cancel a registration of another party, the tests being the same for all these purposes. Additional cases, mainly in opposition proceedings at OHIM, reach the Court on appeal from the Court of First Instance. In this area again Advocate General Jacobs has played a prominent part in the develop-

---

[23] One recent case is Case C-329/02 P, *Sat.1 Satellitenfernsehen GMBH v OHIM* [2004] I-8317 – another appeal from the Court of First Instance.

[24] Case C-421/04 [2006] ECR I-2303.

ment of the law of trade marks. One of the earliest cases was *Sabel BV v Puma AG*,[25] in which the Court had to consider the nature of the 'confusion' between two trade marks which must be likely to occur among members of the public, for the purpose of the provisions of the Directive which require a likelihood of confusion. The contention was between confusion as to trade origin of the goods or services (the traditional view) or mere 'association' (a concept recognised in Benelux Law). The Court, accepting the Opinion of the Advocate General, came down in favour of the traditional view. The decision continues to be cited in the courts and the trade mark registry, together with other decisions in which the Advocate General was again involved[26] and which further clarified the law. In other cases, the Advocate General has been involved in defining the rights of third parties in the honest use of registered trade marks.[27]

Special mention should be made of some of the cases concerning enhanced protection, under the Directive and the CTM Regulation, to trade marks having a 'reputation'. According to the literal text of the provisions concerned, such protection could only be given where the allegedly infringing mark is used for goods or services which are not similar to goods or services covered by the registration claimed to have been infringed. In *Davidoff & Cie SA v Gofkid Ltd*[28] the question arose as to whether the Directive permitted the Member States to confer this enhanced protection in cases where the goods or services concerned were identical or similar to those covered by the allegedly conflicting trade mark. According to the usual principles of construction applied in the English courts the answer would be in the negative, and Advocate General Jacobs so concluded. However the Court, in an unusually short judgment, reached the opposite conclusion. The

---

25 Case C-251/95 [1997] ECR I-6191.

26 See, in particular, Case C-39/97, *Canon Kabishiki Kaisha v Metro-Goldwyn-Mayer Inc.* [1999] ECR I-5507; Case C-342/97, *Lloyd Schufabrik Meyer & Co. v Klijsen Handel BV* [1999] ECR I-3819, and, more recently, Case C-425/98, *Marca Mode CV v Adidas AG* [2000] ECR 4861, in which the Court, again on the basis of the Advocate General's Opinions, laid down the rules to be applied in assessing the likelihood of confusion. See also Case C-291/00, *LTJ Diffusion v Sadas Vertbaudet SA* [2003] ECR I-2799 on the question: when are two marks 'identical'?

27 See, for example, Case C-63/97, *Bayerische Motorenwerke AG v Deenik* [1999] ECR I-905 (use of the BMW mark by a garage proprietor specialising in BMW cars) and Case C-2/00, *Hölterhoff v Friesleben* [2002] ECR I-4187 (use of descriptions of the cut of gemstones).

28 Case C-292/00 [2003] ECR I-389. Note that in between the delivery of the Advocate General's Opinion and the judgment, another Advocate General had delivered an Opinion in Case C-206/01, *Arsenal Football Club PLC v Reed* [2002] ECR I-10273, in which, in a footnote to paragraph 33 (footnote 20) he criticised the Opinion of Advocate General Jacobs in *Davidoff*. The remarks had no obvious relevance to the *Arsenal* case, but may well have influenced the Court in *Davidoff*.

decision has been questioned,[29] but it was followed in a decision in which the same issue arose in a case referred to the ECJ by a Dutch court.[30] It fell to Advocate General Jacobs to deliver an Opinion in this case. The *Davidoff* ruling had been delivered after the reference from the Dutch court. As was expected, the Advocate General followed the *Davidoff* ruling. In fact he went a little further, concluding that Member States were not merely permitted to confer the enhanced protection where there was identity or similarity of goods or services; they were, he said, obliged to do so if it conferred the protection where the goods or services were not similar. The Court agreed.

TRADE MARKS: A SIDELINE

Before leaving the subject of trade marks, the Advocate General's involvement extended, rather surprisingly, beyond matters of protection of such rights, to a language issue.[31] When the CTM was established, it was realised that to allow the use of all of the languages spoken in the Community would involve such expense as would make the system prohibitively expensive to use. Accordingly, whilst applications can be filed in any one of the official languages of the Community, of which there are now 23, for the purpose of proceedings at OHIM there are just five languages of the Office (English, French, German, Italian and Spanish). The applicant, a Dutch trade mark lawyer, had filed an application to register her name in Dutch (which was permitted) but identified Dutch as the 'second language'. Her application was refused because Dutch was not one of the languages of the Office. She appealed to the Board of Appeal and then to the Court of First Instance, both times unsuccessfully; her appeal to the ECJ was not heard until after her death, and was dismissed. Essentially, her challenge was on the ground of discrimination. In the result, the Court accepted the Opinion of Advocate General Jacobs and thus, no doubt, saved the CTM system from an inevitable demise.

---

[29] See, for example, C. Morcom, 'Extending protection for marks having a reputation. What is the effect of the decision of the European Court of Justice in Davidoff v Gofkid?' (2003) European Intellectual Property Review, 279.

[30] Case C-408/01, *Adidas-Salomon AG v Fitnessworld Trading Ltd* [2004] ECR I-12537.

[31] Case C-361/01 P, *Kik v OHIM* [2003] ECR I-8283.

OTHER INTELLECTUAL PROPERTY AND SIMILAR RIGHTS

Mention has already been made of the Advocate General's contribution in other areas of Intellectual Property. The cases are quite few in number, compared to his prodigious output in the field of trade marks, and space does not permit any discussion of them here. But it can be said that he brought to the areas of patents, copyright and protected designations of origin the same degrees of learning and clarity as are displayed in the trade mark cases.

CONCLUSIONS

Little more needs to be said. It can be asserted with some considerable confidence that the due protection of Intellectual Property rights in the EU has been greatly enhanced as a result of the work of Sir Francis Jacobs and that his contribution in particular to the development of trade mark law in the Community has been truly outstanding.

10. Temporal limitation in EU law

David Vaughan[1]

INTRODUCTION

The basic principle in EU law (as in many other legal systems) is that, in the absence of express legislative powers and subject to rulings as to temporal limitation, judgments of the European Court of Justice (ECJ) (and of the Court of First Instance) establish the law as it ought to have been understood and applied from the date of its entry into force. That is to say, a ruling is to apply *ex tunc* and not *ex nunc*. It is in this field of temporal limitation that Sir Francis Jacobs has very recently delivered an Opinion of the very greatest importance inviting the Court to adopt an innovative step.

In the case of a regulation, Article 231 EC makes express provision to permit the Courts, as an exception to annulling the measure, to state which of the effects of that measure should be considered as being definitive, if the Court considers this to be necessary. This Article has been applied by the Court to measures other than regulations, such as directives and decisions. In so doing the Court takes into account in particular the aims of the measure in question and the need to ensure legal certainty. Thus these powers have been used in certain cases to preserve the past effects of an annulled act (e.g. a budget) or to declare that the measure is to remain in force until the competent authority has taken the appropriate remedial actions under Article 233 EC to give effect to the judgment of the Court.

In cases of preliminary rulings made under Article 234 EC, whether they are rulings of validity or interpretation, EU law has been applied so as exceptionally to allow for the possibility of the application of a temporal limitation on the effect of such a ruling, even though the EC Treaty does not make any express provision for such an application.

Before considering the conditions for such an exceptional application and its effect, it is relevant to look at some different jurisdictions to see how they deal with equivalent situations.

[1] CBE QC, Brick Court Chambers.

THE APPROACH TO TEMPORAL LIMITATION IN ENGLAND AND WALES

The idea that English law should apply some doctrine of temporal limitation (usually referred to as prospective overruling) was previously regarded with abhorrence, being said to be inconsistent with the common law and having no place in the English legal system (see, for example, Lord Reid in *West Midland Baptist Association*[2] and Lord Goff in *Kleinwort Benson v Lincoln City Council*[3]), although some high judicial authorities and several academic commentators had expressed the view that the technique was worthy of consideration. Lord Devlin considered that application of such a rule crossed the divide between judicial and legislative powers. However, notwithstanding such objections, there have been certain public law cases where courts have restricted the effects of their rulings to the future, for example in the field of mergers and rating (see, for example, *Datafin*[4] and *ex parte Peachey*[5]) to avoid what would otherwise be 'chaos' or unacceptable consequences. In the context of Scotland and Wales, the devolution legislation makes provision in appropriate cases for some temporal limitation for particular classes of decision.

Very recently the House of Lords (sitting with seven judges) decided that prospective ruling was not in principle incompatible with English law, although in that particular case it did not give effect to such an application: *Spectrum Plus*.[6] *Spectrum* concerned an issue involving charges over book debts and issues of priority. In that case charges had been consistently and in good faith drafted and agreed upon on the basis of a decision which had been adopted some 25 years earlier and which had remained unchallenged in the intervening period. However, it was clear that the earlier case had been decided on the basis of a mistaken view of the law. In *Spectrum* the House of Lords considered some of the practical and principled objections to prospective overruling. Of particular relevance to this chapter, the House considered the Opinion of Advocate General (AG) Sir Francis Jacobs in Case C-475/03 *Banco Populare di Cremona*, to which I shall return later.

In *Spectrum* the House of Lords ruled that the established practice of judicial precedence derived from the common law and consequently judges had power to modify that practice. Their Lordships held that there could be cases, in which a particular decision on the law was unavoidable, where the flexibility inherent in the system allowed in exceptional circumstances for the ruling

---

2 [1970] AC 874, 898–9.
3 [1999] 2 AC 349, 379.
4 [1989] QB 815, 842.
5 [1966] 1 QB 360, 402.
6 [2005] UKHL 41; [2005] 3 WLR 58.

of the House of Lords to be prospective only in order to avoid gravely unfair and disruptive consequences for prior transactions and happenings; and they further held (by a majority) that this could occur even in the case of the interpretation or application of statutes. The effect of the judgment was 'never say never' in order to provide for exceptional cases when justice required this to be done.

Accordingly, in the light of *Spectrum* it can be seen that much still remains uncertain:

- Applying this rationale it would seem probable that the House of Lords can limit the normal retrospective application of the law. This would limit the availability of this exceptional remedy to those cases which were given permission to enable the case to reach the House of Lords because of their importance or because of the financial strength of the entities involved.
- What could possibly be considered as exceptional and what would be the pre-conditions for its application have yet to be defined.
- What particular form a prospective ruling should take remains to be decided. (Would it protect the litigant in question and cases in the pipeline?)
- What are the classes of case to which it could apply? (Could it ever apply to criminal cases?)
- Could it apply to cases of statutory interpretation or statutory application (usurpation)?

Although the House of Lords made brief reference to the powers of the ECJ to make prospective rulings, the application of the rule and when and how it is to be applied in English law could well merit a more detailed examination of EU law.

THE APPROACH TO TEMPORAL LIMITATION IN OTHER JURISDICTIONS

It is also relevant to consider how some other jurisdictions have dealt with the same issue of temporal limitation or prospective overruling (deriving much of my information from the speeches in *Spectrum*):

In Ireland, in *Murphy v Attorney General*[7] the Supreme Court held that certain tax provisions were unconstitutional and void; and that they were

---

7 [1982] IR 241.

invalid from the date of enactment. However, the Supreme Court restricted the effect of such a ruling by limiting the claim in issue only back to the first year in which the objections were raised and by limiting their effect only to other taxpayers who had already made claims. Recently the Irish Supreme Court has refused to apply retrospectively a previous ruling declaring a criminal offence to be unconstitutional: *A v Governor of Arbour Hill Prison*.[8]

In the USA, as was pointed out in *Spectrum*, the prospective overruling by the Supreme Court had waxed and waned in its application, reaching its apogee in the 1960s and 1970s (when it applied to both civil and criminal cases) but is much less common nowadays (and not in criminal cases).

In India the power derives from the constitution itself and applies consequently only in constitutional cases.

In Canada it has 'not found favour' for much the same reason as it was previously rejected by the English courts (but see the *Language Rights under the Manitoba Act 1870*[9] case where, wholly exceptionally, the Supreme Court allowed temporary validity to all laws enacted since 1870 which would otherwise have been unlawful because of a statutory defect so as to allow for rectification of that defect).

According to the House of Lords other common law countries do not accept the exceptional jurisdiction to overrule prospectively.

Interestingly enough, in France, according to my information, the issue of temporal limitation remains very much an open issue, with two very high-powered working parties having recently reviewed the situation. In France traditionalists have rejected the possibility of temporal limitation because 'Judges do not make the law'. However, it is my understanding that the courts (both Cour de Cassation and Conseil d'Etat) are likely to side with the possibility of imposing a temporal limitation as and when the situation requires it. For the position in Germany, at least in constitutional cases, see the reference in AG Jacobs's Opinion in *Cremona*, discussed below.

THE APPROACH TO TEMPORAL LIMITATION IN EU LAW

The origins of temporal limitation in EU law are to be found in the famous case *Defrenne No. 2*.[10] Interestingly enough, although the Court referred to the immense 'financial consequences – including the bankruptcy of firms' which

---

8 [2006] 1 ESC 45.

9 (1985) 90 DLR (4th) 1.

10 43/75 [1976] ECR 455, 480–81.

the Court considered would have followed from retrospective effect, this was not held to be sufficient in itself to justify a temporal limitation on the ruling. The limitation there was justified in particular by the inactivity of the Commission, having led Member States to believe that the relevant article of the Directive had no direct effects. It was thus likely to lead to the incorrect impression of the effects of the relevant article. The Court there held that considerations of legal certainty made it impossible in principle to re-open the question as regards the past. It is significant that in that case there was no consideration given to the principles involved in giving effect to the temporal limitation or its legal justification, and it is also significant that in that case the Advocate General in his Opinion rejected any argument based on financial expediency as having no relevance in law.

It is difficult to define from the decided cases (including the cases where such a contention has been rejected) the precise limits of the exceptional situation in which such a temporal limitation can or cannot in principle be applied. It would seem from decided cases that financial cost is unlikely by itself to amount to a justification for applying such a ruling. However, it could be a justification when linked to the Commission's or other Member States' conduct, the Court's earlier case law and existing measures of other Community institutions, allied to the large number of legal relationships entered into in good faith on the assumption that the law was valid or because the practices were adopted because of objective uncertainty as to the law (Case C-209/03 *Bidar*[11]). One thing that is reasonably clear is that the temporal limitation can only be imposed in the same ruling in which the interpretation is given.[12] In this context it should be appreciated that the national court on receiving a decision in which no temporal limitation has been imposed cannot of its own right impose a temporal limitation, although obviously, in exercise of its ordinary procedural rules, it can make appropriate rulings which could in a particular case have the same effect (e.g. limitation periods) provided that such an application of national procedure rules complies with the Community law requirements of equivalence and effectiveness, on which there could be a further preliminary reference.

Furthermore, even where temporal limitation of a ruling is introduced, it cannot, at least in the ordinary event (for exceptions have been recognized: see for example Case 145/79 *Roquette*[13]), be introduced to deprive the applicant

[11] C-209/03 *Bidar* [2005] ECR I-2119.

[12] Case 309/85 *Barra* [1988] ECR 355, paragraph 13; Case 24/86 *Blaizot* [1988] ECR 379, paragraph 28; Case C-163/90 *Legros and Others* [1992] ECR I-4625, paragraph 30; Case C-415/93 *Bosman and Others* [1995] ECR I-4921, paragraph 142; and Case C-437/97 *EKW and Wein & Co.* [2000] ECR I-1157, paragraph 57.

[13] [1980] ECR 2917.

of his rights or the rights of those who had already brought legal proceedings or made equivalent claims at the date of the judgment. This latter requirement has led to many claims being brought in national courts between the date of the Opinion of the Advocate General (the first time at which most interested parties will normally become formally aware that there is even a possibility of a temporal limitation being considered by the Court) and the judgment of the Court. In *References to the European Court* by Anderson and Demetriou it is pointed out that this led in the *Coloroll*[14] litigation to some 220,000 male employees lodging pre-emptive claims before the date of the judgment.[15] It in fact turned out in that case that the claims were unnecessary but shows that, as the temporal limitation can only be introduced by the Court, advisers should consider very carefully bringing relevant claims prior to the date of the judgment in the type of case in which temporal limitation might be a possibility. To exclude existing claims would be a draconian step and one which is most unlikely to occur (see Anderson and Demetriou *op cit* at 14-079-081 for discussion of this issue).

The same issue of temporal limitation also applies in the case where the preliminary ruling declares a Community measure to be invalid and probably also could be applied only exceptionally and where no other solution appears to be appropriate, although in some such cases the Court has applied Article 231 EC by analogy and adopts the test of 'overriding considerations' as being necessary to justify such a measure.

In the two most recent cases before the ECJ, the Advocates General have suggested novel ways to apply temporal limitation to the judgments. In both cases the Court responded by transferring the cases to the Grand Chamber and re-opening the oral procedure in order for the issue of temporal limitation to be fully argued and considered.

In Case C-475/03 *Cremona*, in which AG Francis Jacobs gave his Opinion on 17 March 2005, the issue was whether a regional tax on production levied in Italy was compatible with the Community prohibition on national turnover taxes other than VAT. The tax had been levied since 1997 in order to provide regional authorities with a source of revenue to fund the exercise of their devolved powers. AG Jacobs concluded that the tax possessed the same essential features as VAT and was therefore caught by the prohibition embodied in Article 33 of the Sixth Directive.

Advocate General Jacobs went on to consider that there should be a temporal limitation on any judgment reaching the conclusion of incompatibility of

---

14 Case C-200/91 *Coloroll Pension Trustees* [1994] ECR I-4389.

15 D.W.K. Anderson and M. Demetriou, *References to the European Court* (London: Sweet & Maxwell, 2nd edn, 2002) at 14-078.

the tax, because the requirements of good faith and risk of serious difficulties were established. As regards the Italian Government's good faith, Jacobs noted that the law had been notified to the Commission and that the competent Director General had written in unambiguous terms that 'after careful examination of the documentation provided, I can inform you that, in its present state, the proposal for this new tax does not appear incompatible with the legislation applicable in the field of value added tax'. The Advocate General was not persuaded by the Commission's reliance on the qualification added in the letter in which the Director General had continued, 'none the less, I reserve the right to re-examine it in the light of any amendments and/or of the implementing provisions to be adopted'.

As regards the risk of serious difficulties, Advocate General Jacobs concluded that in the absence of a limitation of temporal effect, the judgment might retroactively cast into confusion the system whereby Italian regions are financed.

The particularly innovative aspect of this Opinion is the approach Advocate General Jacobs took regarding the date that should be set as the limit for temporal effect. Given the very large number of claims that had already been made even prior to the date of the Opinion, Jacobs suggested that the Court should consider making the finding of incompatibility subject to a future date before which individuals would not be entitled to rely on the incompatibility in any claims against the State. The date in question should be chosen in order to allow sufficient time for new legislation to be enacted. In this proposal, the Advocate General drew inspiration from the German constitutional court, remarking that it was an approach frequently taken by that court, and it was this innovation which is particularly emphasized by the House of Lords in *Spectrum*.

Advocate General Jacobs pointed out that the whole field of temporal limitation had been subject to innovative steps from the date of its original inception (in 1976 with *Defrenne*[16]), and it would seem that he was of the view that this would be a further acceptable innovative step.

In Case C-292/04 *Meilicke*, the issue of the date from which the temporal limitation should take effect was once again the subject of innovative proposals. Advocate General Tizzano suggested that in a case where he considered temporal limitation to be appropriate, it should relate back to the date of a prior judgment in another case (6 June 2000), which had for the first time made clear the scope of provisions on the free movement of capital in relation to equivalent tax measures to the case in question. AG Tizzano did not consider that the approach suggested by AG Jacobs in the *Cremona* case, which he said

---

16 Case 43/75 [1976] ECR 455, at paragraphs 69 to 75.

was entirely reasonable in that case, would be appropriate in the *Meilicke* case. In addition he suggested that:

- the right to tax credit should relate to dividends received after 6 June 2000 or to cases where tax credits had been applied for before that date;
- the terminal date should not be the date of judgment in that particular case for that would amount to a generalized refund involving serious economic repercussions;
- account should be taken of the diligence of persons covered and that they should have taken action by the date when the reference in this particular case had been published in the Official Journal (11 September 2004), notwithstanding this would give an entirely new significance to such a publication.

In *Cremona*, the subsequent Opinion of Advocate General Stix-Hackl, on 14 March 2006 (to which reference should also be made in particular for a useful description of the varying approaches of Member States to this question), delivered following the oral argument before the Grand Chamber, very much followed the same line of argument as that of Advocate General Jacobs. She additionally raised the interesting question as to the spatial effect of a temporal limitation in one Member State when applied to other States. Advocate General Stix-Hackl also added that if the approach of Advocate General Tizzano in *Meilicke* were to be adopted, the relevant date for existing claims should be the date of Advocate General Jacobs's Opinion (17 March 2005).

In *Meilicke* the subsequent Opinion was again delivered by Advocate General Stix-Hackl (on 5 October 2006). In the light of the importance of the question of a possible limitation of the temporal effects of a judgment, the case had been reassigned to the Grand Chamber of the ECJ, principally to give the parties the opportunity to make submissions on the possible effects of an adverse judgment. At the re-opened oral hearing, no fewer than ten Member States, the Commission and Mr Meilicke made submissions. The majority of Governments submitted that a decision should only be made about a temporal limitation on the basis of the 'specific circumstances' in each relevant Member State, especially as regards national taxation systems which are often 'complex'. Accordingly they submitted that any bar to an application to limit the temporal effects had to be limited to 'exceptional cases'. However, the German Government also submitted that in the event that the judgment to be delivered would have effect *ex tunc*, there would be a risk of serious economic repercussions as a result of the probable shortfall in tax revenue and in this case there should be a temporal limitation. AG Stix-Hackl, recalling the earlier Opinion of Advocate General Tizzano, recognized that 'the situation of

Member States should not be made any more difficult than is absolutely necessary', but that for temporal limitation to apply there had to be (1) objective and significant legal uncertainty; and (2) the risk of serious economic repercussions. The Advocate General found that neither had been established by the German Government on the facts. In conclusion, she proposed that the Court should not limit the temporal effects of the judgment in the present case.

In the event, from the point of view of clarifying the law on temporal limitation, both judgments (and particularly *Cremona*) were disappointing. In *Cremona*[17] the ECJ held that the EU provision in question did not preclude the maintenance of a charge to tax with the characteristics of the national tax in issue in the Italian proceedings, so that the question of a temporal limitation did not have to be considered. Accordingly, we are left with the innovative Opinion of Francis Jacobs, but no ruling from the ECJ.

In *Meilicke*[18] the Court did find that the national tax was contrary to the relevant provisions of EU law; however, the Court went on to find that it was not appropriate to limit the temporal effects of its judgment. In so finding, the Court relied principally on the fact that it should have been clear to the Member State from an earlier case, *Verkooijen*,[19] that EU law precluded such tax provisions. The Court recalled that:

> It is only exceptionally that, in application of a general principle of legal certainty which is inherent in the Community legal order, the Court may decide to restrict the right to rely upon a provision, which it has interpreted, with a view to calling in question legal relations established in good faith (see, in particular, Case C-104/98 *Buchner and Others* [2000] ECR I-3625, paragraph 39, and *Linneweber and Akritidis*, [[2005] ECR I-1131], paragraph 42).[20]

The Court reasoned that since it had not limited the temporal effects of *Verkooijen* it would be inappropriate to limit the temporal effects in *Meilicke*.[21]

The judgment and the (second) Opinion of the Advocate General in *Meilicke* are useful illustrations of the approach the Court will take in cases of this particular type, and that temporal limitations will always be exceptional. However, *Meilicke* failed to provide an answer to the wider questions posed by AG Jacobs in *Cremona*.

---

17 Judgment, 3 October 2006.
18 Judgment, 6 March 2007.
19 Case C-35/98 *Verkooijen* [2000] ECR I-4071.
20 Para. 34.
21 Paras 39 and 41.

CONCLUSION

When this paper was first delivered, to the conference held in honour of Francis Jacobs in 2006, the relevant judgments of the ECJ were still pending. At the time it concluded thus: 'So it is very much a question of "watch this space" not only from the EU perspective but from the point of view of national jurisdictions such as England and Wales and France.' That conclusion still stands and it remains to be seen what will happen when the Court next has the opportunity to return to these issues.

Postscript

Anthony Arnull[1]

The preceding chapters reveal the richness of Francis Jacobs' contribution as Advocate General to the development of Community law. Hardly any area of the discipline was untouched by his Opinions. In this brief afterword, I would like to reflect on the qualities that enabled Francis to exploit the potential of his office to such great effect. I had the privilege of serving as a référendaire in his chambers at the Court from 1989 to 1992, so I shall also say a few words in passing about what he was like to work for.

Francis' influence is of course to some extent attributable to his longevity: he is the second longest-serving Advocate General after Advocate General Roemer, who held office from 1953 to 1973. A more important factor was Francis' professional background. Lord Mackenzie Stuart once remarked that an Advocate General was like the holder of a professorial chair in Community law.[2] That remark could hardly be repeated in today's world of 'Research Assessment Exercises' and increasing managerialism in universities, but I doubt whether it was entirely apt even when it was made. Francis was indeed the holder of a chair in Community law when he was appointed as Advocate General; he was also a successful QC. I believe that his capacity to combine an academic's sensitivity to the deep rhythms of Community law with a practitioner's ability to identify the really crucial issues played a big part in his success.

We can only really start to understand Francis' influence when we examine the intellectual rigour he brought to the job of Advocate General. This manifested itself in a number of ways: awareness of the importance of context,[3] a willingness to confront inconvenient problems and dilemmas, independence of mind, sensitivity to the limits of the judicial function, to mention just a few.

Francis' keen awareness of the importance of context produced some fasci-

---

1 Professor of European Law and Head of the School of Law, University of Birmingham.

2 See L.N. Brown and T. Kennedy, *Brown and Jacobs' The Court of Justice of the European Communities* (5th edn, London: Sweet & Maxwell, 2000), p. 67.

3 See also the chapter by Stephen Weatherill in this volume (Chapter 1).

nating passages. The Opinion in *Konstantinidis*,[4] for example, contains an erudite examination of the problem of converting names from one alphabet to another (as well as the wry observation that the Court's word processors could not reproduce some of the accents used in the system of transliteration laid down by the International Organization for Standardization).[5] The Opinion in *Garcia Avello*[6] contains an equally interesting discussion of the personal naming systems used in Europe. The case concerned a Belgian rule requiring children to take their father's surname. Francis' Opinion revealed the intriguing fact that, if that rule were applied to the daughter, born in Belgium, of an Icelandic father and a Belgian mother, to an Icelander the daughter would appear to be her grandfather's son.[7]

One of the best examples of Francis' willingness to confront the inconvenient is *HAG II*,[8] decided in 1990 at a time when the Court was searching for a way of dealing effectively in its judgments with the growing body of previous case law. In *HAG II*, the Court abandoned the much-criticized doctrine of common origin laid down in *HAG I*.[9] That doctrine limited the right of an owner of a trade mark in one Member State to restrain imports of products legally bearing the mark in another Member State. The result was in accordance with Francis' advice,[10] but there was an issue as to whether *HAG I* could be distinguished. Francis rejected that approach: it would, he said, 'be healthier to recognize that *HAG I* was wrongly decided, rather than to compound that error by inventing a spurious distinction between the two cases'.[11] Francis stated that, if he were to be followed, 'the Court should in my view make it clear, in the interests of legal certainty, that it is abandoning the doctrine of common origin laid down in *HAG I*'.[12] He went on: 'That the Court should in an appropriate case expressly overrule an earlier decision is I think an inescapable duty, even if the Court has never before expressly done

4 Case C-168/91 [1993] ECR I-1191.

5 Ibid, p. I-1201, n. 4.

6 Case C-148/02 [2004] 1 CMLR 1. Cf. the Opinion of AG Jacobs in Case C-96/04 *Standesamt Stadt Niebüll*, judgment of 27 April 2006. These cases are discussed in the chapter by Eleanor Sharpston in this volume (Chapter 7).

7 See [2004] 1 CMLR 1, 15, n. 25.

8 Case C-10/89 *CNL-Sucal v HAG GF* [1990] ECR I-3711.

9 Case 192/73 *Van Zuylen v HAG* [1974] ECR 731. See further D. Keeling, *Intellectual Property Rights in EU Law (Vol I)* (Oxford: OUP, 2003), pp. 161–74.

10 In a striking display of judicial open-mindedness, Francis thereby departed from the view he had expressed in an article published in 1975, where he had stoutly defended *HAG I*: see 'Industrial property and the EEC Treaty – a reply' (1975) 24 ICLQ 643. The article was a response to F.A. Mann, 'Industrial property and the EEC Treaty' (1975) 24 ICLQ 31.

11 [1990] ECR I-3711, 3749.

12 Ibid.

so.'[13] Francis' advice produced the desired result, for the Court said that it considered it 'necessary to reconsider the interpretation given in [*HAG I*]'.[14] The remainder of the judgment made it clear that the doctrine of common origin no longer formed any part of the Community rules on intellectual property. The case was the harbinger of a radical change in the way the Court dealt with its own case law.[15]

At the time, a correspondent rightly described Francis' Opinion in *HAG II* as a tour de force, but its tone was lightened by a joke that caused some soul-searching in chambers. One of the issues addressed was the effect on trade of differing national views on whether trade marks are confusingly similar. The Opinion refers to a decision of the German Bundespatentgericht holding that the mark 'LUCKY WHIP' was liable to be confused with the mark 'Schöller-Nucki'. Francis observed that the decision seemed 'to postulate a body of consumers afflicted with an acute form of dyslexia'.[16]

Jokes can be risky in a multi-national setting because they are hard to translate and do not always move freely across cultural borders. A quick-witted interpreter highlighted this in one hearing by saying: 'Counsel has just started to tell a joke. It is completely impossible to translate. However, it would be polite to laugh . . . now!' At which point the members of the Court dutifully obliged. Counsel was blissfully unaware that they were not laughing at him but at the interpreter.

The LUCKY WHIP joke was the product of collaboration between Francis and the référendaire who had primary responsibility for working on the *HAG II* Opinion. He had worked at the Court for many years and was a stalwart of the staff association. He had grown concerned at what he saw as the Court's growing tendency to parachute into jobs people who had not formally applied for them over the heads of people who had. When a vacancy arose for the post of Head of Personnel, he wrote a letter to the President of the Court applying for it. He explained in the letter that he had absolutely no interest in being Head of Personnel but thought that the only way he could be certain of not being awarded the job was to apply for it. Brits at the Court thought this was an audacious and effective way of making an important point about the Court's

13 Ibid, I-3750.

14 At para. 10.

15 For further discussion, see A. Arnull, *The European Union and its Court of Justice* (2nd edn, Oxford: OUP, 2006), ch. 17. The normative character of the case law was recognized in the Constitutional Treaty, according to which it 'shall remain, *mutatis mutandis*, the source of interpretation of Union law and in particular of the comparable provisions of the Constitution' (Art. IV-438(4)).

16 [1990] ECR I-3711, 3740.

recruitment practices, but the President, who was not British, was said not to have been in the least amused.

However, the LUCKY WHIP joke caused soul-searching for a quite different reason. The issue was whether it was offensive, not to the Bundespatentgericht but to dyslexics. The matter was resolved when the father of a dyslexic child said he found it very funny. I do not think it is criticized in any of the many publications in which the case is discussed.[17]

Another good example of Francis' willingness to confront inconvenient dilemmas is *Extramet Industrie v Council*.[18] That case concerned the standing of a business affected by an anti-dumping regulation to challenge its validity. I was the référendaire with principal responsibility for *Extramet* and I subsequently published a couple of articles about the standing rules that apply in annulment proceedings.[19] However, I am ashamed to say that I did not immediately spot the case's potential. Under the case law as it stood at that time, the application was clearly inadmissible and I produced a draft Opinion saying so. Francis considered the consequences unsatisfactory and asked me to produce a draft arguing for a relaxation in the case law.

A particular problem with the existing case law was how to distinguish the requirement for a decision from the requirement of individual concern. The problem arose because in a number of cases where challenges to measures called regulations had been held to be admissible, the Court had not considered whether in reality they constituted decisions. In a characteristic passage, Francis advised the Court to 'make clear what is already implicit in the prevailing trend of its case-law, namely that the requirement of a decision does not exist independently of the requirement of individual concern'.[20] The Court endorsed that view, acknowledging that a measure might, without losing its character as a regulation, be open to challenge by a private party who could show individual concern.[21] In a significant departure from the earlier case law, the application was therefore declared admissible. It led to a second Opinion,

---

17 For other examples of Francis' use of humour, see his Opinions in Case C-405/98 *Gourmet International Products* [2001] ECR I-1795 (where the careful reader is rewarded with two jokes) and Case C-329/03 *Trapeza tis Ellados AE v Banque Artesia*, judgment of 27 October 2005.

18 Case C-358/89 [1991] ECR I-2501. See the chapter by Takis Tridimas and Sara Poli in this volume (Chapter 3).

19 See 'Private applicants and the action for annulment under Article 173 of the EC Treaty' (1995) 32 CMLRev 7; 'Private applicants and the action for annulment since Codorniu' (2001) 38 CMLRev 7.

20 [1991] ECR I-2501, 2520.

21 The Court later appeared to retreat from that position: see Case C-50/00 P *Unión de Pequeños Agricultores v Council* [2002] ECR I-6677, para. 36.

less well known perhaps but equally interesting, on the relationship between anti-dumping measures and competition policy.[22]

It was the *Extramet* case which sparked my interest in the standing rules. My initial mistake was not to sound Francis out before putting pen to paper (as we used to do in those days). I tended not to do this with every case but only those where I had doubts about the line he would want to take. *Extramet* was not the only one I failed to call correctly. In fact I acquired the dubious reputation of being able to turn a draft suggesting one result very quickly into a draft suggesting precisely the opposite. Getting it right first time was very satisfying, but getting it wrong more educational, as one was then treated to a private tutorial in which the error of one's ways was gently but firmly pointed out.

Francis' independence of mind was evident in his willingness to question both conventional wisdom and new orthodoxies. It is easy to forget that several of his Opinions did not enjoy a favourable critical reception. An example is *TWD Textilwerke Deggendorf*.[23] There the Court held, following Francis' advice, that an applicant who clearly has standing to challenge a Community act under Article 230 EC but who fails to do so within the deadline laid down cannot later contest its validity before a national court. The judgment was delivered at a time when the Court seemed to be relaxing the standing rules applicable to private applicants under Article 230. It appeared to reflect a desire to channel validity disputes away from the national courts. That desire was based on the perceived defects of the preliminary rulings mechanism by comparison with the action for annulment as a mechanism for reviewing the legality of Community acts, which is emphasized by Francis in his Opinions in *Extramet*,[24] *TWD* itself and later in *UPA*.[25]

Notwithstanding the criticism it received, *TWD* did challenge the received wisdom that the action for annulment and the preliminary rulings mechanism were separate and independent ways of reviewing the validity of Community acts. Some commentators were unhappy with the apparent restriction of the rights of applicants involved in the *TWD* case. One commentator, for example, argued that whether the preliminary rulings mechanism was considered deficient as a means of reviewing the validity of Community acts depended on the perspective taken.[26] He pointed out that the ability to bring proceedings in the national courts long after the deadline for bringing annulment proceedings had

---

22 Case C-358/89 [1992] ECR I-3813, Opinion of 8 April 1992.

23 Case C-188/92 [1994] ECR I-833.

24 Above n. 18.

25 Above n. 21.

26 J.A. Usher, 'Direct and individual concern – an effective remedy or a conventional solution?' (2003) 28 ELRev 575, 586.

expired was, from the point of view of the applicant, 'highly beneficial and protective of his or her rights'.[27] Francis' point, I think, was that the annulment action was better adapted to balancing the private interests of the applicant against the public interest in effective legislative and administrative action.

In the law of equal treatment of men and women, Francis' respect for the limits of the judicial function led him to treat fashionable opinion with caution. An early example is *Integrity*.[28] In that case, the Court was asked about the effect of the Social Security Directive[29] on a national rule exempting married women, widows and students from the requirement to pay certain social security contributions. The Court held that such a rule was incompatible with the Directive because the exemption did not extend to married men and widowers. Francis explained that the Directive made

> no distinction between positive discrimination in favour of the members of a particular sex and negative discrimination. Within its field of application, it requires all discrimination on the grounds of sex to be abolished. Member States cannot therefore justify inequalities of treatment on the basis that the provisions at issue are favourable to women.[30]

That remark acquired a certain notoriety. One commentator objected:

> Such a view illustrates the central flaw of equality as neutrality. It assumes that equality is an end in itself, rather than a mechanism for correcting disadvantage, and in doing so, it makes it impossible for the anti-discrimination principle to make real inroads into the disadvantaged position of women.[31]

But Francis was expressing no view about the desirability in principle of a neutral application of the principle of equal treatment. He was merely summarizing the effect of the Directive, which it was the task of the Court to apply.

Francis took a similar approach in *Marschall v Land Nordrhein-Westfalen*.[32] That case was a sequel to *Kalanke v Bremen*,[33] where the Court took a restrictive view of the circumstances in which so-called positive action could be justified under the original version of the Equal Treatment

27 Ibid, 587.

28 Case C-373/89 [1990] ECR I-4243.

29 Dir. 79/7, OJ 1979 L 6/24.

30 [1990] ECR I-4243, 4254.

31 S. Fredman, 'European Community discrimination law: a critique' (1992) 21 ILJ 119, 129. See also S. Fredman, 'Reversing discrimination' (1997) 113 LQR 575, 585.

32 Case C-409/95 [1997] ECR I-6363.

33 Case C-450/93 *Kalanke v Bremen* [1995] ECR I-3051.

Directive.[34] The judgment caused widespread consternation, but in *Marschall* Francis took the opportunity to emphasize that

> the Court is not being asked – nor would it be appropriate for it to be asked – to rule on the desirability of positive discrimination or affirmative action generally: the national court's question concerns the conformity of the national rule at issue with two specific provisions of the Equal Treatment Directive. Similarly the Court in its recent decision in *Kalanke* relating to a similar national rule was focusing solely – notwithstanding the tenor of some of the academic reaction to the case – on the compatibility of that rule with those provisions.[35]

This was clearly right: whether or not positive action ought to be permitted is a matter for political judgment. At Amsterdam in October 1997, the Member States agreed to insert in the EC Treaty a new provision[36] apparently designed to make it easier to justify positive action (although in practice it does not seem to have made much difference).[37]

The Opinions I have mentioned represent only a small, idiosyncratic selection of the many delivered by Francis between 1988 and 2006. I hope I have done enough to illustrate various facets of the intellectual rigour with which he approached his work as an Advocate General. I have not mentioned the cases, from *Wachauf v Bundesamt für Ernährung und Forstwirtschaft*[38] to *Richards v Secretary of State for Work and Pensions*,[39] where Francis dealt, directly or indirectly, with the protection of fundamental rights in the Community. It was perhaps cases like these that underlined most clearly his profound belief in an open Europe based on liberal, humane values. History may have ended while he was in Luxembourg, but that vision remains as important as ever.[40]

---

[34] Dir. 76/207, OJ 1976 L 39/40. The Directive has now been amended: see Dir. 2002/73, OJ 2002 L 269/15.

[35] [1997] ECR I-6363, 6367-8. See also ibid, 6378-9.

[36] Art. 141(4).

[37] See further Arnull, above n. 15, pp. 590-600.

[38] Case 5/88 [1989] ECR 2609.

[39] Case C-423/04 [2006] 2 CMLR 49.

[40] See F. Fukuyama, *The End of History and the Last Man* (London: Hamish Hamilton, 1992). In an article published in the summer 1989 issue of the journal *The National Interest* on which that book was based, Fukuyama described the end of history as 'the end point of mankind's ideological evolution and the universalization of Western liberal democracy as the final form of human government'. Fukuyama attributed the origins of the notion of the end of history to Hegel and Marx.

ANNEX: FRANCIS JACOBS'S OPINIONS (IN OPINION DATE ORDER)

	Case No.	Date of Hearing	Date of Opinion	Date of Judgment	ECR	Keywords
1	182/87 *Trouw*	09/11/88	30/11/88	28/02/89	[1989] 469	Lait écrémé en poudre: modalités d'octroi des aides
2	307/87 *Klein*	01/12/88	07/12/88	31/01/89	[1989] 125	Fonc: allocation de foyer – dégagement volontaire
3	324/87 *Italy*	19/01/89	19/01/89	27/04/89	[1989] 1013	Police sanitaire – importations – pays tiers
4	100, 146 & 153/87 *Basch*	01/12/88	20/01/89	28/02/89	[1989] 447	Fonc: recrutement – non-admission concours interne
5	341/85 etc. *Van der Stijl*	30/11/88	24/01/89	28/02/89	[1989] 511	Fonc: nomination agent temporaire
6	358/87 *Drewes*	26/01/89	26/01/89	18/04/89	[1989] 891	Lait – prime de non-commercialisation – remboursement
7	141/87 *Italy*	22/11/88	31/01/89	25/04/89	[1989] 943	Vin – VQPRD – Lago di Caldaro
8	128/88 *Di Felice*	24/01/89	02/02/89	18/04/89	[1989] 923	LCP – sec. soc.: cumul de prestations
9	51/88 *Hamann*	14/02/89	21/02/89	15/03/89	[1989] 767	Fiscalité - TVA: yacht à voile de haute mer
10	368/87 *Troiani*	14/02/89	22/02/89	18/05/89	[1989] 1333	LCP – sec. soc.: assurance viellesse, cotisation volontaire
11	76/86 *Germany*	22/02/89	28/02/89	11/05/89	[1989] 1021	LCM – lait – mesures d'éffet équivalent
12	50/88 *Kühne*	25/01/89	02/03/89	27/06/89	[1989] 1925	Fiscalité – VAT utilisation privé – voiture de service
13	344/87 *Bettray*	18/01/89	08/03/89	31/05/89	[1989] 1621	LCP – travailleurs – activité exerçée – emploi social
14	113/88 *Leukhardt*	28/02/89	09/03/89	27/06/89	[1989] 1991	Lait – prélèvement suppl.
15	380/87 *Enichem*	02/03/89	16/03/89	13/07/89	[1989] 2491	Environnement – prévention et élimination de déchets
16	305/87 *Greece*	14/03/89	13/04/89	30/05/89	[1989] 1461	LCP – lég. nat. – biens immobiliers
17	198/87 *Kerzmann*	16/02/89	18/04/89	04/07/89	[1989] 2083	Fonc: recrutement – avis de vacance
18	43/88 *Netherlands*	11/04/89	19/04/89	31/05/89	[1989] 1649	LCM – mesure d'effet équiv.

Annex *continued*

Case No.		Date of Hearing	Date of Opinion	Date of Judgment	ECR	Keywords
19	77/88 *Stute*	28/02/89	20/04/89	15/06/89	[1989] 1755	Fruit/légume – organis. de producteurs – reconnaissance
20	88/88 *Rewe*	19/04/89	26/04/89	27/06/89	[1989] 1959	Oeuf/volaille – teneur en eau des volailles congelées
21	5/88 *Wachauf*	28/02/89	27/04/89	13/07/89	[1989] 2609	Lait – prime à l'abandon déf. de production
22	323/87 *Italy*	15/03/89	27/04/89	11/07/89	[1989] 2275	Fiscalité – taxation différencié – rhum/eaux de vie
23	173/88 *Henriksen*	18/04/89	17/05/89	13/07/89	[1989] 2763	Fiscalité – TVA – exonérations – garages
24	395/87 etc. *Sacem*	08/03/89	26/05/89	13/07/89	[1989] 2521	Concurrence: position dominante – discothèques
25	170/88 *Ford Espana*	25/05/89	26/05/89	11/07/89	[1989] 2305	LCM – taxe d'effet équiv. – dédouanement des marchandises
26	4/88 *Lambregts*	25/05/89	15/06/89	13/07/89	[1989] 2583	Transports – route – retrait d'autorisation
27	12/88 *Schäfer Shop*	17/05/89	22/06/89	21/09/89	[1989] 2937	LCM – interdiction d'importations
28	201/88 *Atala Palmerini*	14/06/89	22/06/89	10/10/89	[1989] 3109	Fonc: indemnité de dépaysement
29	81 & 95/88 *Mullers & Laval*	20/04/89	27/06/89	07/02/90	[1990] I-0249	Fonc: promotion – revalorisation d'un emploi
30	214/88 *Politi*	28/06/89	28/06/89	13/07/89	[1989] 2785	Agri. viande porcine – taxe de contrôle sanitaire
31	281/87 *Greece*	06/06/89	06/07/89	29/11/89	[1989] 4015	Agri. céréales: achat de blé dur dégradé
32	386/87 *Bessin*	29/06/89	26/09/89	09/11/89	[1989] 3551	LCM – remboursement des droits à l'importation
33	301/87 *France*	08/06/89	04/10/89	14/02/90	[1990] I-307	Aides d'Etat – aide à une entreprise du secteur textile
34	353/88 *Briantex*	27/09/89	11/10/89	09/11/89	[1989] 3623	Pol. comm. – résponsabilité non contractuelle
35	249/87 *Mulfinger*	04/07/89	17/10/89	06/12/89	[1989] 4127	Fonc: Professeur de langue – contrat d'emploi
36	228/88 & 12/89 *Bronzino/Gatto*	19/09/89	17/10/89	22/02/90	[1990] I-3387	LCP – sec. soc.: allocation familiale – jeune chomeur

37	329/88 *Greece*	19/10/89	19/10/89	06/12/89	[1989] 4159	Environnement – protection des consommateurs – publicité
38	360/88 *Belgium*	19/10/89	19/10/89	16/11/89	[1989] 3803	Environnement – protection des consommateurs – publicité
39	163/88 *Kontogeorgis*	26/09/89	07/11/89	12/12/89	[1989] 4189	Fonc: sec. soc.. – régime commun d'assurance maladie
40	346/88 *Lactina*	11/10/89	07/11/89	14/12/89	[1989] 4579	Lait écrémé en poudre: aliments composés – étiquetage
41	153-7/88 *Fauque*	10/10/89	21/11/89	07/03/90	[1990] I-649	Politique commerciale – importations pays tiers – textiles
42	345/88 *Butter-Absatz*	11/10/89	22/11/89	18/01/90	[1990] I-0159	Lait écrémé – aide spéciale – délai de déclaration
43	206/88 etc. *Vessoso & Zanetti*	21/11/89	13/12/89	28/03/90	[1990] I-1461	Environnement – déchets toxiques et dangereux
44	108-9/89 *Pian & Bianchin*	09/01/90	07/02/90	05/04/90	[1990] I-1599	LCP – sec. soc: pension d'invalidité ou de retraite
45	85/89 *Ravida*	09/01/90	07/02/90	21/03/90	[1990] I-1063	LCP – sec. soc: cumul de prestations – indexation
46	199/88 *Cabras*	12/12/89	08/02/90	21/03/90	[1990] I-1023	LCP – sec. soc: prestation d'invalaidité – remboursement
47	333/88 *Tither*	10/01/90	08/02/90	22/03/90	[1990] I-1133	Privilèges et immunities: Miras
48	201/89 *Le Pen*	11/01/90	08/02/90	22/03/90	[1990] I-1183	Droit institutionnel – délit de diffamation
49	62/89 *France*	01/02/90	20/02/90	20/03/90	[1990] I-0925	Pêche – régime des quotas pour la pêche
50	251/88 *Germany*	30/01/90	22/02/90	23/05/90	[1990] I-2107	Ressources propres – TVA – télécommunications
51	111/89 *Bakker*	11/01/90	06/03/90	02/05/90	[1990] I-1735	LCM – taxe d'effet équivalent – contrôles phytosanitaires
52	10/89 *HAG CNL-Sucal*	18/01/90	13/03/90	17/10/90	[1990] I-3711	LCM – propriété industrielle – droit de marque
53	354–6/88 *Roermond*	06/03/90	29/03/90	04/07/90	[1990] I-2753	Agric. – restitution à l'exportation – porc
54	119/88 *Aerpo*	07/03/90	29/03/90	06/06/90	[1990] I-2189	Fruits et légumes: coeff. d'adaptation aux prix d'achat
55	67/89 *Berkenheide*	07/03/90	29/03/90	27/06/90	[1990] I-2637	Lait – prélèvement supplementaire
56	305/88 *Lancray*	28/03/90	03/05/90	03/07/90	[1990] I-2725	Convention de Bruxelles

Case No.		Date of Hearing	Date of Opinion	Date of Judgment	ECR	Keywords
57	217/88 *Germany*	21/03/90	15/05/90	10/07/90	[1990] I-2879	Vin – mesures de distillation – contrainte nationale
58	48/89 *Italy*	17/05/90	17/05/90	14/06/90	[1990] I-2425	Environnement – déchets – informations
59	172/89 *Vandemoortele*	02/05/90	12/06/90	12/12/90	[1990] I-4677	Relations ext. – aide alimentaire
60	128/89 *Italy*	15/05/90	12/06/90	12/07/90	[1990] I-3239	LCM – pamplemousses
61	34/89 *Italy*	14/06/90	12/07/90	11/10/90	[1990] I-3603	FEOGA – apurement des comptes – ex./1986
62	189 & 217/89 *Spagl & Pastätter*	26/06/90	02/10/90	11/12/90	[1990] I-4539	Lait – quantités de référence
63	226/89 *Haniel Spedition*	27/06/90	23/10/90	21/03/91	[1991] I-1599	Relations ext. – aide alimentaire
64	215/89 *Eddelbüttel*	02/10/90	23/10/90	15/01/91	[1991] I-1	Lait – prime de reconversion de troupeaux bovins
65	343/89 *Witzemann*	02/10/90	25/10/90	06/12/90	[1990] I-4477	LCM – droit de douane – TVA – fausse monnaie
66	373/89 *Rouvroy*	04/10/90	25/10/90	21/11/90	[1990] I-4243	Pol. soc. – égalité de traitement – hommes
67	22/89 *Netherlands*	14/06/90	07/11/90	13/12/90	[1990] I-4799	FEOGA – apurement des comptes – beurre
68	28/89 *Germany*	09/10/90	20/11/90	21/02/91	[1991] I-581	FEOGA – apurement des comptes – ex. 1986
69	240/89 *Italy*	20/11/90	20/11/90	13/12/90	[1990] I-4853	Pol. soc. – protection des travailleurs – amiante
70	384/89 *Tomatis*	28/06/90	22/11/90	24/01/91	[1991] I-127	LCM – TDC – clasement tarifaire véhicules mixtes
71	32/89 *Greece*	08/11/90	06/12/90	19/03/91	[1989] I-985	FEOGA – apurement des comptes: ex./1986
72	244/89 *France*	20/11/90	10/01/91	31/01/91	[1991] I-163	Pêche – régime des quotas pour la pêche
73	2/90 *Belgium*	27/11/90	10/01/91	09/07/92	[1992] I-4431	Environ. – déchets provenant d'un autre EM (réouv.)
74	355/89 *Barr*	29/11/90	10/01/91	03/07/91	[1991] I-3479	LCP travailleurs – discrimination – Ile de Man
75	41/90 *Höfner*	13/11/90	15/01/91	23/04/91	[1991] I-1979	LCP – conseil en recrutement de cadre d'entreprise
76	93/90 *Cassamali*	12/12/90	16/01/91	20/03/91	[1991] I-1401	LCP – sec. soc.. – revalorisation des prestations

77	328/89 *Berner*	15/01/91	07/02/91	15/05/91	[1991] I-2431	LCM – transit comm – libération de la caution
78	109/90 *Giant*	15/01/91	07/02/91	19/03/91	[1991] I-1385	TVA – taxe spéciale sur spectacles et divertissements
79	310/89 *Netherlands*	20/02/91	20/02/91	19/03/91	[1991] I-1381	Rapproch. légis. – matériel électrique – médecine humaine
80	76/90 *Säger*	15/01/91	21/02/91	25/07/91	[1991] I-4221	LCP – prest. services – droits de propriété ind.
81	230/89 *Greece*	22/01/91	21/02/91	18/04/91	[1991] I-1909	TVA – taxation différenciée – boissons spiritueuses
82	152–3/89 *Lux./ Belgium*	10/01/91	28/02/91	26/06/91	[1991] I-3141	Fiscalité – impositions intérieures – accise sur la bière
83	354/89 *Schiocchet*	05/02/91	07/03/91	16/04/91	[1991] I-1775	Transport – services autocars – Luxembourg/France
84	358/89 *Extramet* (Interlocutory)	19/02/91	21/03/91	16/05/91	[1992] I-3813	Admissibility – dumping – calcium-métal de Chine et URSS
85	97/90 *Lennartz*	07/03/91	30/04/91	11/07/91	[1991] I-3795	TVA – déduction taxe payée pour bien d'investissement
86	367/89 *Richardt*	13/03/91	08/05/91	04/10/91	[1991] I-4621	LCM – transit communautaire – matériel stratégique
87	213/90 *ASTI*	14/03/91	08/05/91	04/07/91	[1991] I-3507	LCP – travailleurs – fonction de droit public
88	58/89 *Germany*	19/03/91	08/05/91	17/10/91	[1991] I-4983	Environnement – qualité des eaux
89	44/89 *Von Deetzen*	30/04/91	04/06/91	22/10/91	[1991] I-5119	Agriculture – quantité de référence spécifique
90	121/90 *Posthumus*	05/06/91	04/07/91	06/12/91	[1991] I-5833	Lait – quan. réf.- recession de l'exploitation agric.
91	24–26/90 *Faust*	06/06/91	11/07/91	16/10/91	[1991] I-4905	Agri. produits transformés – champignons – mes. sauvegarde
92	269/90 *Univ. München*	11/06/91	11/07/91	21/11/91	[1991] I-5469	LCM – TDC – appareils scientifiques
93	185/90-P Rev. *Gill*	N/H	19/09/91	04/10/91	[1992] I-993	Procédure – Révision d'un arrêt sur pourvoi
94	2/90 *Belgium*	04/07/91	19/09/91	09/07/92	[1992] I-4431	Env. – Gestion des déchets provenant d'un autre EM
95	354/90 *FN Prod. Al.*	11/07/91	03/10/91	21/11/91	[1991] I-5505	Aide – Projet – Mise à exéc. avant la décision finale

Case No.		Date of Hearing	Date of Opinion	Date of Judgment	ECR	Keywords
96	284/90 *Council/Parl.*	19/09/91	17/10/91	31/03/92	[1992] I-2277	Procédure budgétaire – Budget rectificatif
97	164/90 *Muwi Bouwgroep*	24/09/91	24/10/91	13/12/91	[1991] I-6049	Fiscalité – rass. capitaux – société filiale
98	301/90 *Comm/Council*	01/10/91	07/11/91	23/01/92	[1992] I-221	Fonc: Rémuneration – Coef. correct. Munich
99	260/90 *Leplat*	03/10/91	07/11/91	12/02/92	[1992] I-643	Rel. ext. – Pays et territoires d'outre-mer
100	163/90 *Legros*	03/10/91	21/11/91	16/07/92	[1992] I-4625	LCM – TEQ – Octroi de mer
101	328/90 *Greece*	21/11/91	21/11/91	30/01/92	[1992] I-425	Arrêt de la Cour – Etablissement et prestation de services
102	334/90 *Marichal-Margreve*	22/10/91	28/11/91	16/01/92	[1992] I-101	Agri. – MCM – Condition d'octroi
103	84/90 *Dent*	22/10/91	29/11/91	19/03/92	[1992] I-2009	Agri.- Lait – Quantité de référence spécifique
104	1/91 *Avis*	26/11/91	03/12/91	14/12/91	[1991] I-6079	Demande d'avis – Projet d'accord CEE/AELE
105	330-31/90 *Lopez Brea*	12/11/91	13/12/91	28/01/92	[1992] I-323	LCP – Etab. et prest. de services – Immobilières
106	358/90 *Ital. Alcool*	13/11/91	16/01/92	07/04/92	[1992] I-2457	Vin – Alcool d'orig. vinique
107	311/90 *Hierl*	29/11/91	16/01/92	19/03/92	[1992] I-2061	Agri. – Lait – Suspension – quantités de référence
108	2/90 *Belgium*	28/01/92	29/01/92	09/07/92	[1992] I-4431	Environ. – déchets provenant d'un autre EM (réouv.)
109	237/90 *Germany*	14/01/92	12/02/92	24/11/92	[1992] I-5973	Env. – Eaux destinées à la consommation humaine
110	60/91 *Batista Morais*	14/01/92	13/02/92	19/03/92	[1992] I-2085	Transports – Permis de conduire
111	104/91 *Agentes de la Prop.*	21/01/92	26/02/92	07/05/92	[1992] I-3003	LCP – Affaires immobilières
112	45/91 *Greece*	29/01/92	26/02/92	07/04/92	[1992] I-2509	Env. – Gestion des déchets
113	256/90 *Mignini*	24/01/92	27/02/92	08/04/92	[1992] I-2651	Agri. – Matières grasses – Graines de soja
114	20/91 *De Jong*	24/01/92	27/02/92	06/05/92	[1992] I-2847	Fisc – TVA

115	195/90 *Germany*	15/01/92	13/03/92	19/05/92	[1992] I-3141	Transports – Routes allemandes
116	62/90 *Germany*	28/01/92	13/03/92	08/04/92	[1992] I-2575	MEQ – Importation de médicaments – Usage privé
117	347/90 *Bozzi*	13/02/92	19/03/92	07/05/92	[1992] I-2947	TVA – Rémuneration des avocats
118	106/91 *Ramrath*	13/02/92	19/03/92	20/05/92	[1992] I-3351	LCP – Réviseur d'entreprises
119	351/90 *Luxembourg*	10/03/92	25/03/92	16/06/92	[1992] I-3945	LCP – Etablis. – Unicité du cabinet médical
120	26/91 *Handte*	25/02/92	08/04/92	17/06/92	[1992] I-3967	Compétence – Matière contractuelle – Chaîne de contrats
121	358/89 *Extramet*	27/02/92	08/04/92	11/06/92	[1992] I-3813	PCOM – Dumping – Calcium-métal
122	85/90 *Dowling*	27/02/92	08/04/92	22/10/92	[1992] I-5305	Agri. – Quantité de référence spécifique
123	86/90 *O'Brien*	27/02/92	08/04/92	03/12/92	[1992] I-6251	Agri. – Quantité de référence spécifique
124	90–91/91 *di Crescenzo*	19/03/92	08/04/92	11/06/92	[1992] I-3851	LCP – Séc. sociale – Retraite et invalidité
125	49/91 *Weber Haus*	02/04/92	14/05/92	13/10/92	[1992] I-5207	Fisc. – Droit d'apport – Transfert des résultats
126	50/91 *Commerz-Credit Bank*	02/04/92	14/05/92	13/10/92	[1992] I-5225	Fisc. – Rassemblement de capitaux
127	295/90 *Parl./Council*	25/03/92	20/05/92	07/07/92	[1992] I-4193	LCPE – Etudiants – Droit de séjour
128	271, 281 & 289/90 *Spain e.a.*	31/03/92	20/05/92	17/11/92	[1992] I-5833	Conc. Services de télécommunication
129	163/90 *Legros*	31/03/92	20/05/92	16/07/92	[1992] I-4625	LCM – TEQ – Octroi de mer (réouv.)
130	73/89 *Fournier*	12/03/92	21/05/92	12/11/92	[1992] I-5621	RAPP – Véhicule à moteur
131	240/90 *Germany*	01/04/92	03/06/92	27/10/92	[1992] I-5383	Agri. – Viandes ovine et caprine
132	147/91 *Laderer*	07/05/92	04/06/92	25/06/92	[1992] I-4097	LCPE – Etablissement – Affaires immobilières
133	67/91 *Asociacón Española*	12/05/92	10/06/92	16/07/92	[1992] I-4785	Conc. – Utilisation d'informations
134	156/91 *Hansa Fleisch*	14/05/92	25/06/92	10/11/92	[1992] I-5567	Agri. – Police sanitaire – Redevances
135	376/90 *Belgium*	13/05/92	30/06/92	25/11/92	[1992] I-6153	CEEA – Contrôles de sécurité
136	142/91 *Cebag*	N/H	01/07/92	11/02/93	[1993] I-553	Clause compromissoire – Aide alimentaire
137	81/91 *Twijnstra*	21/05/92	02/07/92	19/05/93	[1993] I-2455	Agri. – Lait – Prime de non-commerc.
138	123/91 *Minalmet*	11/06/92	08/07/92	12/11/92	[1992] I-5661	Reconnaissance des décisions
139	79/91 *Knufer*	N/H	09/07/92	17/12/92	[1992] I-6895	Agri. – Lait – Production laitière

Case No.		Date of Hearing	Date of Opinion	Date of Judgment	ECR	Keywords
140	275/91 *Iacobelli*	02/07/92	30/09/92	03/02/93	[1993] I-523	LCPE – Sécurité sociale – Invalidité et vieillesse
141	71 & 178/91 *Ponente Carni*	08/07/92	30/09/92	20/04/93	[1993] I-1915	Fisc. – Rassemblement de capitaux
142	2/91 Avis	30/06/92	23/10/92	19/03/93	[1993] I-1061	Demande d'avis – Convention de l'OIT (Court Avis only published)
143	193/91 *Mohsche*	08/10/92	10/11/92	25/05/93	[1993] I-2615	Fisc. – TVA – Voiture de service
144	308/90 *Adv. Nuclear Fuels*	15/10/92	19/11/92	21/01/93	[1993] I-309	CEEA – Contrôles de sécurité
145	263/91 *Kristoffersen*	22/10/92	26/11/92	25/05/93	[1993] I-2755	Priv. – Fonctionnaire – Logement
146	282/91 *de Wit*	29/10/92	26/11/92	30/03/93	[1993] I-1221	LCPE – Sec. soc. assurance vieillesse – NL
147	173/91 *Belgium*	20/10/92	02/12/92	17/02/93	[1993] I-673	PSOC – Egalité de rémunération
148	168/91 *Konstantinidis*	29/10/92	09/12/92	30/03/93	[1993] I-1191	LCPE – Travailleurs – Noms grecs
149	56/91 *Greece*	21/10/92	15/12/92	22/06/93	[1993] I-3433	Agri. – FEOGA – 1988
150	181 & 248/91 *Parl./Council*	28/10/92	16/12/92	30/06/93	[1993] I-3685	Compétences budgétaires du Parlement
151	197/91 *Asprofrut*	12/11/92	16/12/92	25/05/93	[1993] I-2639	Agri. – FEOGA – 1987
152	111/91 *Luxembourg*	17/11/92	16/12/92	10/03/93	[1993] I-817	LCPE – Travailleurs – Allocations de naissance
153	280/91 *Viessman*	12/11/92	17/12/92	18/03/93	[1993] I-971	Fisc. – Rassemblement de capitaux
154	308/91 *Süddeutsche Zucker*	26/11/92	14/01/93	25/05/93	[1993] I-2787	Agri. – Restitution à l'exportation – Sucre
155	304/91 *Van Doesselaar*	17/12/92	28/01/93	11/05/93	[1993] I-2303	Transport – Absence de disposition nationale
156	65/92 *ONP/Levatino*	17/12/92	28/01/93	22/04/93	[1993] I-2005	LCPE – Pension de vieillesse – Cumul de prestations
157	193/92 *Bogana*	17/12/92	28/01/93	18/02/93	[1993] I-755	LCP – Sécurité sociale – Prestation d'invalidité
158	290/91 *Peter*	03/12/92	17/02/93	27/05/93	[1993] I-2981	Agri – Lait – Prélèvement supplémentaire
159	364/90 *Italy*	15/12/92	17/02/93	28/04/93	[1993] I-2097	Aides – Mezzogiorno

160	281/91 *Muys*	21/01/93	03/03/93	27/10/93	[1993] I-5405	Fisc. TVA – Opérations immobilières
161	10/92 *Balocchi*	10/02/93	24/03/93	20/10/93	[1993] I-5105	Fisc. TVA – Fait générateur et l'exigibilité de la taxe
162	111/92 *Lange*	N/H	01/04/93	02/08/93	[1993] I-4677	Fisc. TVA – Exon. – Transactions illicites – Ordinateurs
163	121/92 *Zinnecker*	04/03/93	22/04/93	13/10/93	[1993] I-5023	LCPE – Travailleur non salarié – Législation applicable
164	312/91 *Metalsa*	11/03/93	22/04/93	01/07/93	[1993] I-3751	Rel. ext. Accord CEE/Autriche
165	28/92 *Leguaye-Neelsen*	11/03/93	22/04/93	16/12/93	[1993] I-6857	LCPE – Ass. vieillesse – Cotisation volontaire
166	272/92 *Spotti*	N/H	12/05/93	20/10/93	[1993] I-5185	LCP – Travailleurs – Lecteurs de langue étrangère
167	125/92 *Mulox*	N/H	26/05/93	13/07/93	[1993] I-4075	CCJE – Compétence – Contrat de travail
168	13–16/92 *Driessen*	22/04/93	27/05/93	05/10/93	[1993] I-4751	Tran. – Assainissement structurel – navigation intérieure
169	297/92 *Baglieri*	N/H	09/06/93	20/10/93	[1993] I-5211	LCP – Séc. soc. – Pension d'invalidité – Cotis. volontaire
170	212/91 *Angelopharm*	11/05/93	16/06/93	25/01/94	[1994] I-171	RAPP – Produits cosmétiques
171	21/92 *Kamp*	22/04/93	30/06/93	05/05/94	[1994] I-1619	Agri. Lait – Quantité de référence spécifique
172	92 & 326/92 *Collins*	19/05/93	30/06/93	20/10/93	[1993] I-5145	PCOM – Propriété industrielle – Droit d'auteur – Disque CD
173	188/92 *TWD*	29/06/93	15/09/93	09/03/94	[1994] I-833	Aides – Fils de polyamide et de polyester
174	377/92 *Koch*	30/06/93	16/09/93	05/10/93	[1993] I-4795	LCM – Nomenclature combinée
175	316/91 *Parliament*	14/09/93	10/11/93	02/03/94	[1994] I-625	Budget – Règlement financier – Convention ACP-CEE
176	53/92-P *Hilti*	29/09/93	10/11/93	02/03/94	[1994] I-667	Conc. – Pourvoi – Position dominante – Fabricant de clous
177	36/92-P *SEP*	N/H	15/12/93	19/05/94	[1994] I-1911	Conc. – Pourvoi – Demande de renseignements – Gaz naturel
178	419/92 *Scholz*	10/11/93	15/12/93	23/02/94	[1994] I-507	LCPE – Emploi dans l'administration publique
179	11/93 *Siemens Nixdorf*	N/H	27/01/94	19/05/94	[1994] I-1945	LCMA – Nomenclature combinée – Moniteur couleur

Case No.		Date of Hearing	Date of Opinion	Date of Judgment	ECR	Keywords
180	316/93 *Vaneetveld*	N/H	27/01/94	03/03/94	[1994] I-763	Droit institutionnel. – directive – effet direct – assurance respons.civile
181	403/92 *Baux*	02/12/93	10/02/94	29/06/94	[1994] I-2961	Agri. – Désignation des vins – Dénom. 'Château de Calce'
182	38/93 *Glawe*	20/01/94	03/03/94	05/05/94	[1994] I-1679	TVA – Base d'imposition – Appareils automat. de jeu
183	353 & 385/92 *Greece*	18/01/94	09/03/94	14/07/94	[1994] I-3411	Agri. – Cultures arables
184	118/92 *Luxembourg*	15/03/94	15/03/94	18/05/94	[1994] I-1891	LCPE – Travailleurs – Fonction de droit public
185	278–280/92 *Spain*	01/02/94	23/03/94	14/09/94	[1994] I-4103	Aides – en faveur des sociétés
186	42/93 *Spain*	01/02/94	23/03/94	14/09/94	[1994] I-4175	Aides – aide en faveur de la société MERCO
187	303/93 *Italy*	13/04/94	13/04/94	18/05/94	[1994] I-1901	Rapp. lég. ascenseurs mus électroniquement
188	301/93 *Bettaccini*	N/H	14/04/94	22/09/94	[1994] I-4361	LCP – Sécurité sociale – Allocation pour le noyau familial
189	438/92 *Rustica Semences*	03/03/94	14/04/94	14/07/94	[1994] I-3519	Agri. – MCM – Semences et plants
190	7/93 *Beune*	09/03/94	27/04/94	28/09/94	[1994] I-4471	Egalité de traitement – Cumul des pensions de retraite
191	312/93 *Peterbroeck*	16/03/94	04/05/94	–	[1995] I-4599	Droit institutionnel droit commun. – application par le juge national
192	187/93 *Parliament*	N/H	18/05/94	28/06/94	[1994] I-2857	Env – gestion des déchets – transfert des déchets – base juridique
193	133, 300 & 362/93 *Crispoltoni e.a.*	24/03/94	19/05/94	05/10/94	[1994] I-4863	Agr – tabac – quantités maximales garanties
194	359/92 *Germany*	03/05/94	08/06/94	09/08/94	[1994] I-3681	Env. – Produits dangereux
195	395/93 *Neckermann Versand*	N/H	09/06/94	09/08/94	[1994] I-4027	LCM – TDC – Nomenclature combinée – pyjamas

196	406/93 *Reichling*	N/H	09/06/94	09/08/94	[1994] I-4061	LCP – Séc. soc. – prestation d'invalidité – calcul de la prestation
197	76/93-P *Scaramuzza*	21/04/94	09/06/94	20/10/94	[1994] I-5173	Statut – Pourvoi Fonc. – Rémunération – lieu d'affection
198	55/93 *Van Schaik*	28/04/94	09/06/94	05/10/94	[1994] I-4837	LCM – véhicule à moteur – contrôle technique et révision périodique
199	297/93 *Grau-Hupka*	N/H	29/06/94	13/12/94	[1994] I-5535	Politique sociale – égalité de rémuneration – travailleur à temps partiel
200	401/93 *Goldstar Europe*	07/07/94	21/09/94	13/12/94	[1994] I-5587	LCM – TDC – Classement tarifaire – Mecadecks
201	1/94 *Avis*	11/10/94	19/10/94	–	[1994] I-5267	GATT (AG's Obs not published)
202	412/93 *Leclerc-Siplec*	07/07/94	24/11/94	09/02/95	[1995] I-179	Concurrence – publicité télévisée – Secteur de la distribution
203	345/93 *Nunes Tadeu*	17/11/94	13/12/94	09/03/95	[1995] I-479	Fiscalité – imposition intérieures – taxe automobile – véhicules d'occasion
204	349/93 *Italy*	N/H	19/01/95	23/02/95	[1995] I-343	Aides – accordée par le gouv. italien à Aluminia et Comsal
205	384/93 *Alpine Investments*	29/11/94	26/01/95	10/05/95	[1995] I-1141	LCP – prestation de services – pratique du 'cold calling'
206	348/93 *Italy*	06/12/94	02/02/95	04/04/95	[1995] I-673	Aides – accordée par le gouv. italien à Alfa Romeo
207	350/93 *Italy*	06/12/94	02/02/95	04/04/95	[1995] I-699	Aides – Remboursement des aides – Groupe ENI-Lanerossi
208	451/93 *Delavant*	N/H	09/02/95	08/06/95	[1995] I-1545	LCP – séc soc. – notion de 'membre de famille'
209	350/92 *Spain*	N/H	09/03/95	13/07/95	[1995] I-1985	RAPP – Spécialité pharmaceutique
210	147/94 *Spain*	N/H	09/03/95	06/04/95	[1995] I-1015	LCP – assurances – resp. civile – véhicule automoteur
211	62/93 *BP Soupergaz*	19/01/95	09/03/95	06/07/95	[1995] I-1883	Fiscalité – TVA – régime héllenique applicable aux produits petroliers
212	59/94 & 64/94 *Pardo & Fils*	N/H	16/03/95	17/10/95	[1995] I-3159	LCM – TDC – classement tarifaire – sangria
213	422/92 *Germany*	17/01/95	16/03/95	10/05/95	[1995] I-1097	Env. – Gestion des déchets – toxiques et dangereux

Annex *continued*

Case No.		Date of Hearing	Date of Opinion	Date of Judgment	ECR	Keywords
214	414/93 *Teirlinck*	26/01/95	16/03/95	01/06/95	[1995] I-1339	Transports – navigation intérieure – assainissement structurel
215	119/94-P *Coussios*	02/02/95	23/03/95	01/06/95	[1995] I-1439	Fonc. – recrutement – dommages-intérêts
216	2/92 *Avis*	11/10/94	24/03/95	–	[1995] I-521	Décision du Conseil de l'OCDE (AG's Obs not published)
217	120/94 *Greece*	01/02/95	06/04/95	Order 19/3/96	[1996] I-1513	Pol. com. – Commerce Grèce/ancienne Rép. yougoslave de Macédoine
218	291/92 *Armbrecht*	14/03/95	06/04/95	04/10/95	[1995] I-2775	Fiscalité – TVA – Opérations immobilières
219	474/93 *Hengst Import*	N/H	04/05/95	13/07/95	[1995] I-2113	Conv. Brux. – Acte introductif d'instance ou équiv.
220	170/94 *Greece*	N/H	04/05/95	29/06/95	[1995] I-1819	Env. – Biotechnologie – micro-organismes génétiquement modifiés
221	391/93 *Perrotta*	30/03/95	11/05/95	13/07/95	[1995] I-2079	LCP – séc. soc. – prestation de maladie – travailleur en chomage
222	51/94 *Germany*	30/03/95	11/05/95	26/10/95	[1995] I-3599	LCM – Mesure d'effet équivalent – sauce hollandaise
223	156/93 *Parliament*	07/03/95	18/05/95	13/07/95	[1995] I-2019	Env – protection consommateurs – Agriculture – production biologique
224	70/94 & 83/94 *Werner*	21/03/95	18/05/95	17/10/95	[1995] I-3189	Pol. com. – Exportation – interdiction (sécurité publique)
225	426/93 *Germany*	15/03/95	15/06/95	09/11/95	[1995] I-3723	Droit des entreprises – répertoires utilisés à des fins statistiques
226	312/93 *Peterbroeck*	04/04/95	15/06/95	14/12/95	[1995] I-4599	Droit institutionnel droit commun. – application par le juge national
227	430/93–431/93 *Van Schijndel*	04/04/95	15/06/95	14/12/95	[1995] I-4705	Concurrence – entreprise – fonds prof. de pension

228	457/93 *Lewark*	02/05/95	29/06/95	06/02/96	[1996] I-243	Pol soc – égal. rémun. – fonc. membre du comité d'entreprise
229	144/94 *Italittica*	08/06/95	13/07/95	26/10/95	[1995] I-3653	Fiscalité – TVA – Fait générateur et exigibilité de la taxe
230	151/94 *Luxembourg*	15/06/95	19/09/95	26/10/95	[1995] I-3685	LCP – travailleurs – impôt sur revenu – remb. trop-perçu
231	113/94 *Casarin*	22/06/95	12/10/95	30/11/95	[1995] I-4203	Fiscalité – taxation différenciée – véhicules à moteur
232	166/94 *Pezzullo*	N/H	26/10/95	08/02/96	[1996] I-331	LCM – droit douanier – perfectionnement actif – intérêts moratoires
233	25/94 *Commission v Council*	27/06/95	26/10/95	19/03/96	[1996] I-1469	Rel. ext – projet d'accord – compétence commun exclusive – pêche
234	274/93 *Luxembourg*	12/10/95	23/11/95	25/04/96	[1996] I-2019	Env – protection des animaux utilisés à des fins scientifiques
235	215/94 *Mohr*	12/10/95	23/11/95	29/02/96	[1996] I-959	Fiscalité – TVA – Indemnité à l'abandon de la production laitière
236	86/94 *van Iersel*	N/H	30/11/95	24/10/96	[1996] I-5261	Agri – Police sanitaire – inspections/contrôles sanitaires – redevances
237	427, 429 & 436/93, 71–73/94, 232/94 *Paranova*	04/10/95	14/12/95	11/07/96	[1996] I-3457	LCM – prop. ind et comm. – droit de marque – pharmaceutique
238	39/94 *SFEI*	24/10/95	14/12/95	11/07/96	[1996] I-3547	Aides d'Etat – sociétés de courrier express inter national
239	191/94 *AGF Belgium*	28/11/95	15/02/96	28/03/96	[1996] I-1859	Priv. & immunités – Suppléments prime d'assurance – Financ. fonds sociaux
240	2/94 *Denkavit*	30/01/96	07/03/96	11/06/96	[1996] I-2827	Fiscalité – rassemblement de capitaux – impôts indirects
241	295 & 296/94 *Hüpeden & Pietsch*	01/02/96	14/03/96	04/07/96	[1996] I-3375	Agri. – Produits transformés – mesures de sauvegarde – champignons
242	205/94 *Binder*	14/03/96	30/04/96	13/06/96	[1996] I-2871	Agri – Produits transformés – Mesure de sauvegarde – fruits rouges
243	84/95 *Bosphorus*	27/03/96	30/04/96	30/07/96	[1996] I-3953	Rel. ext – Echanges CE/Yougoslavie – Saisie d'un avion

Case No.		Date of Hearing	Date of Opinion	Date of Judgment	ECR	Keywords
244	245/94 & 312/94 *Hoever & Zachow*	14/03/96	02/05/96	10/10/96	[1996] I-4895	LCP – Séc. soc – Prestations familiales – Erziehungsgeld
245	283/94, 291–2/94 *Denkavit*	21/03/96	02/05/96	17/10/96	[1996] I-5063	Fisc. – Régime des soc. mères et filiales d'EM différents
246	241/94 *France*	26/03/96	07/05/96	26/09/96	[1996] I-4551	Aides d'Etat – Kimberley Clark
247	163/95 *Von Horn*	24/04/96	14/05/96	09/10/97	[1997] I-5451	Conv. comp. jud – Conv. Bruxelles – Litispendance
248	313/94 *Graffione*	23/04/96	06/06/96	26/11/96	[1996] I-6039	LCM – Prop. ind & comm. – Marques – Cotonelle
249	91/95-P *Tremblay*	N/H	20/06/96	24/10/96	[1996] I-5547	Conc. – Position dominante – SACEM
250	78/95 *Hendrikman*	23/05/96	04/07/96	10/10/96	[1996] I-4943	Conv. comp. jud. -Reconn/exécut. décisions – validité représentation
251	Défendeur					
252	320/94, 328–9, 337–9/94 *RTI*	23/05/96	11/07/96	12/12/96	[1996] I-6471	LCP – Libre prestation de services – radiodiffusion télévisuelle
253	28/95 & 130/95 *Leur-Bloem & Giloy*	04/06/96	17/09/96	17/07/97	[1997] I-4161	Fiscalité – Régime des soc. mères et filiales d'EM différents
254	34/95-36/95 *De Agostini*	11/06/96	17/09/96	17/07/97	[1997] I-3843	LCP – services – activités radiodiffusion télévisuelle
255	178/95 *Wiljo*	20/06/96	19/09/96	30/01/97	[1997] I-585	Transport – Navigation intérieure – Bateaux nouv. construits (spécialisés)
256	124/95 *Centro-Com*	25/06/96	24/09/96	14/01/97	[1997] I-81	Pol. com. – Serbie et Monténégro – Déblocage de fonds
257	298/95 *Germany*	N/H	17/10/96	12/12/96	[1996] I-6747	Env. – Pollution – qualité des eaux – vie des poissons
258	383/95 *Rutten*	N/H	24/10/96	09/01/97	[1997] I-57	Conv. Brux – contrat de travail – plusieurs Etats contractants

259	321/94–324/94 *Pistre*	13/06/96	24/10/96	07/05/97	[1997] I-2343	LCM – Mesures d'effet équiv. – Provenance – charcuterie
260	304/94, 330, 342/94 & 224/95 *Tombesi*	27/06/96	24/10/96	25/06/97	[1997] I-3561	Env. – Gestion des déchets – Notion de déchets
261	352/95 *Phytheron Int.*	12/09/96	24/10/96	20/03/97	[1997] I-1729	LCM – prop. ind. – droit de marque – produit phytosanitaire
262	24/95 *Alcan*	10/09/96	12/11/96	20/03/97	[1997] I-1591	Aides – aide illégale – récupération – application droit national
263	177/95 *Ebony Maritime*	22/10/96	19/11/96	27/02/97	[1997] I-1111	Rel. ext. Yougoslavie – Saisie d'un navire
264	220/95 *Van den Boogard*	24/10/96	12/12/96	27/02/97	[1997] I-1147	Conv. Brux. – Rég. matrim. – Obligation alimentaire entre époux
265	135/96 *Belgium*	N/H	16/01/97	20/02/97	[1997] I-1061	Rapp. lég. – amiante
266	147/95 *Evrenopoulos*	21/11/96	16/01/97	17/04/97	[1997] I-2057	Pol. soc. Egalité hommes/femmes – sec. soc. prestation de survivants
267	316/95 *Generics*	07/01/97	27/02/97	09/07/97	[1997] I-3929	LCM – ind. prop. – droit de brevet – pharmaceutiques
268	349/95 *Loendersloot*	07/01/97	27/02/97	11/11/97	[1997] I-6227	LCM – prop. ind. – droit de marque – boissons alcoolisées
269	90/94 etc. *Haahr Petroleum*	09/01/97	27/02/97	17/07/97	[1997] I-4085	LCM – taxe d'effet equiv. Utilisation des ports publics et privés
270	248–9/95 *SAM Schiffahrt*	16/01/97	27/02/97	10/07/97	[1997] I-4475	Transport – navigation intérieure – fonds de déchirage
271	313, 356 & 358/96 *Belgium*	N/H	13/03/97	29/05/97	[1997] I-2953	Rapp. leg. – substances dangereuses
272	45/96 *Dietzinger*	22/01/97	20/03/97	17/03/98	[1998] I-1199	Env. – Protection des consommateurs – Contrat de cautionnement
273	283/95 *Fischer*	30/01/97	20/03/97	11/06/98	[1998] I-3369	Fiscalité – TVA – Jeux de hasard illicites (roulette)
274	144/96 *Cirotti*	06/02/97	20/03/97	02/10/97	[1997] I-5349	LCP – sec. soc.. – assurance vieillesse/invalidité
275	329/96 *Greece*	N/H	24/04/97	26/06/97	[1997] I-3749	Env. – conservation habitats naturels
276	331/96 *Greece*	N/H	24/04/97	Withdrawn	—	Env. – pollution d'air par l'ozone

Annex *continued*

Case No.		Date of Hearing	Date of Opinion	Date of Judgment	ECR	Keywords
277	129/96 *Inter-Envir Wallonie*	05/02/97	24/04/97	18/12/97	[1997] I-7411	Env. – Déchets – production industrielle
278	251/95 *SABEL*	28/01/97	29/04/97	11/11/97	[1997] I-6191	Rapp. lég. – droit de marque – risque de confusion
279	337/95 *Christian Dior*	05/02/97	29/04/97	04/11/97	[1997] I-6013	LCM – prop. ind. – droit de marque/auteur – parfum
280	409/95 *Marschall*	11/03/97	15/05/97	11/11/97	[1997] I-6363	LCP – égalité – promotions favorisant femmes
281	314/96 *Djabali*	07/05/97	15/05/97	12/03/98	[1998] I-1149	Rel. ext. – CEE/Algérie – adultes handicapés
282	188/95 *Fantask*	29/04/97	26/06/97	02/12/97	[1997] I-6783	Fiscalité – Impôts ind. rassemb. de capitaux – Droits caractère rémunératoire
283	177/96 *Banque Indo-Suez*	N/H	03/07/97	16/10/97	[1997] I-5659	CECA – Dumping – Tôles de fer/acier (FYROM)
284	338/95 *Wiener*	17/04/97	10/07/97	20/11/97	[1997] I-6495	LCM – TDC – Classement tarifaire – chemise de nuit
285	15/96 *Schöning-Kougebetopoulou*	13/05/97	17/07/97	15/01/98	[1998] I-47	LCP – travailleurs – egalité – service public national et autre EM
286	284/96 *Tabouillot*	05/06/97	17/07/97	18/12/97	[1997] I-7471	Tax – véhicules à moteur – puissance fiscale
287	225/96 *Italy*	N/H	25/09/97	04/12/97	[1997] I-6887	Env. – pollution – qualité des eaux
288	236/96 *Germany*	N/H	25/09/97	13/11/97	[1997] I-6397	Rapp. leg. – sub. dang. – piles et accumulateurs
289	92/97 *Belgium*	N/H	25/09/97	Withdrawn	–	Transports combinés de marchandises entre EM
290	384/95 *Landboden-Agrardienste*	15/05/97	25/09/97	18/12/97	[1997] I-7387	Fisc. – TVA – prestation de service – pommes de terre
291	346/95 *Blasi*	05/06/97	25/09/97	12/02/98	[1998] I-481	Fisc. – TVA – Exonérations – location chambres meublées
292	132/96 *Stinco*	24/06/97	25/09/97	24/09/98	[1998] I-5225	LCP – sec. soc. – pension vieillesse

293	192/96 *Beside*	03/07/97	23/10/97	25/06/98	[1998] I-4029	Env. – Transfert des déchets
294	203/96 *Dusseldorp*	03/07/97	23/10/97	25/06/98	[1998] I-4075	Env. – Transfert des déchets
295	113/97 *Babahanini*	N/H	13/11/97	15/01/98	[1998] I-183	Accord CEE/Algérie – séc. soc. – allocation handicapé
296	213/96 *Outokumpu*	24/06/97	13/11/97	02/04/98	[1998] I-1777	LCM – production/importation éléctricité
297	43/96 *France*	25/09/97	13/11/97	18/06/98	[1998] I-3903	Fisc. – TVA – Activité de l'assujetti – Moyens de transport
298	162/96 *Racke*	15/07/97	04/12/97	18/06/98	[1998] I-3655	Rel. ext. – Accord CEE/Yougoslavie – comp. droit int.
299	56/97 *France*	N/H	16/12/97	Withdrawn	–	Agri – pol. san – abattage des animaux
300	275/96 *Kuusijärvi*	06/11/97	16/12/97	11/06/98	[1998] I-3419	LCP – sec. soc. maternité – conditions de résidence
301	24/97 *Germany*	N/H	22/01/98	30/04/98	[1998] I-2133	LCP – trav. – droit de séjour – documents d'identité
302	313/97 *Italy*	N/H	22/01/98	12/03/98	[1998] I-1191	Transport maritime – inspection des navires – organismes habilités
303	319/96 *Brinkmann*	13/11/97	22/01/98	24/09/98	[1998] I-5255	Fisc. – imports directs – tabacs
304	286/96 *Italy*	N/H	29/01/98	Withdrawn	–	Rapp. leg. – sub. dang.- pollution de l'air
305	355/96 *Silhouette*	14/10/97	29/01/98	16/07/98	[1998] I-4799	Droit de marque – pays tiers – opposition du titulaire
306	52–4/97 *Viscido*	29/01/98	12/02/98	07/05/98	[1998] I-2629	Aides d'Etat – contrats de travail à durée déterminée
307	213/97 *Portugal*	N/H	12/03/98	28/05/98	[1998] I-3289	Env. – pollution – substances dangereuses
308	415/96 *Spain*	N/H	19/03/98	12/11/98	[1998] I-6993	Aides d'Etat – textiles
309	274/96 *Bickel*	27/01/98	19/03/98	24/11/98	[1998] I-7637	Egalité de traitement – discrim. nat.
310	368/97 *Belgium*	N/H	26/03/98	14/05/98	[1998] I-2967	Transports maritimes – inspection navires – organismes habilités
311	63/97 *BMW*	13/01/98	02/04/98	23/02/99	[1999] I-905	Rapp. lég – droit de marque – mesures transitoires
312	39/97 *Canon*	20/01/98	02/04/98	29/09/98	[1998] I-5507	Droit de marque – risque confusion – notoriété
313	268/97 *Belgium*	N/H	14/05/98	15/10/98	[1998] I-6069	Env. – protection animaux

Case No.		Date of Hearing	Date of Opinion	Date of Judgment	ECR	Keywords
314	7/97 *Bronner*	10/02/98	28/05/98	26/11/98	[1998] I-7791	Conc.- pos. dom. – presse – distrib. à domicile de quotidiens
315	36/97 & 37/97 *Kellinghusen*	26/03/98	28/05/98	22/10/98	[1998] I-6337	Agri – pol. agr. com. – soutien producteurs cultures arables
316	247/97 *Schoonbroodt*	30/04/98	25/06/98	03/12/98	[1998] I-8095	LCM – droit douanier – franchises douanières – réservois de carburant
317	431/97 *Ireland*	N/H	14/07/98	15/09/98	[1998] I-5055	Transports maritimes – inspections navires – organismes habilités
318	211/97 *Gomez Rivero*	N/H	16/07/98	03/06/99	[1999] I-3219	LCP – sec. soc. – prestations familiales – conjoint – poste consulaire
319	256/97 *DM Transport*	25/06/98	24/09/98	29/06/99	[1999] I-3913	Aides d'Etat – contributions sociales – facilités de paiement
320	342/97 *Lloyd Schufabrik Meyer*	22/09/98	29/10/98	22/06/99	[1999] I-3819	Droit de marque – confusion – similarité deux marques limité à la sonorité
321	379/97 *Upjohn*	15/09/98	19/11/98	12/10/99	[1999] I-6927	LCM – droit de marque – pharmaceutiques – reconditionnement
322	375/97 *General Motors*	22/09/98	26/11/98	14/09/99	[1999] I-5421	Droit de marque – marque jouissant d'une renommée
323	87/97 *Consorzio Gorgonzola*	24/09/98	17/12/98	04/03/99	[1999] I-1301	LCM – appellation d'origine – Cambozola/Gorgonzola
324	164/97 & 165/97 *Parl v Council*	29/10/98	17/12/98	25/02/99	[1999] I-1139	Env. – pollution – protection des forêts contre incendies
325	192/97 *Germany*	N/H	21/01/99	Withdrawn	–	Pol. soc. – protection travailleurs – risques d'accidents
326	198/97 *Germany*	N/H	26/01/99	08/06/99	[1999] I-3257	Env. – pollution – qualité des eaux de baignade
327	67/96 *Albany*	17/11/98	28/01/99	21/09/99	[1999] I-5751	Conc. – Ent. pub. – Pensions

328	115/97–117/97 *Brentjen's*	17/11/98	28/01/99	21/09/99	[1999] I-6025	Rég. nat – affiliation obligatoire – régime de pension de retraite
329	219/97 *Maatschappij Drijvende Bokken*	17/11/98	28/01/99	21/09/99	[1999] I-6121	Conc. – rég. nat. – affiliation obligatoire à un fonds de pension propre
330	202/97 *Fitzwilliam Tech Services*	24/11/98	28/01/99	10/02/00	[2000] I-883	LCP – sec. soc. – travailleur détaché dans un autre Etat membre
331	421/97 *Tarantik*	25/11/98	28/01/99	15/06/99	[1999] I-3633	Fisc. – taxation differenciée – puissance fiscale – critères de détermination
332	66/98 *Italy*	N/H	04/02/99	Withdrawn	–	Rapp. leg. – substances dangereuses – emballage
333	14/98 *Battital*	21/01/99	11/03/99	01/07/99	[1999] I-4039	Agr. – police sanitaire – dangers phytosanitaires – végétaux du genre citrus
334	61/98 *De Haan Beheer*	14/01/99	11/03/99	07/09/99	[1999] I-5003	LCM – transit communautaire – infractions/irregularités
335	336/97 *Italy*	04/02/99	25/03/99	17/06/99	[1999] I-3771	Pol. soc. – risque accidents – activités industrielles
336	173/98 *Sebago*	28/01/99	25/03/99	01/07/99	[1999] I-4103	Rapp. leg. – marque – consentement du titulaire
337	48/98 *Söhl & Söhlke*	11/02/99	29/04/99	11/11/99	[1999] I-7877	LCM – dette douanière – dépôt temporaire
338	215/98 *Greece*	N/H	29/04/99	08/07/99	[1999] I-4913	Rapp. leg. – sub. dang. – piles et accumulateurs
339	186/98 *Nunes et de Matos*	N/H	20/05/99	08/07/99	[1999] I-4883	Pol. soc. – détournement de fonds communautaires – sanctions
340	6/98 *ARD/PRO-Sieben*	22/04/99	24/06/99	28/10/99	[1999] I-7599	LCP – libre prest. services – radiodiffusion télévisuelle – limitation publicité
341	309/98 *Holz Geenen*	10/06/99	08/07/99	28/03/00	[2000] I-1975	Customs classification
342	238/98 *Hocsman*	17/06/99	16/09/99	14/09/00	[2000] I-6623	Equivalent qualifications
343	355/98 *Belgium*	N/H	16/09/99	09/03/00	[2000] I-1221	Freedoms/companies
344	228/98 *Dounias*	22/06/99	23/09/99	03/02/00	[2000] I-577	Goods tax
345	315/98 *Italy*	N/H	23/09/99	11/11/99	[1999] I-8001	Maritime safety
346	138/99 *Luxembourg*	N/H	14/10/99	16/12/99	[1999] I-9021	Civil aviation accidents
347	339/98 *Peacock*	16/09/99	28/10/99	19/10/00	[2000] I-8947	Customs classification
348	78/99 *France*	N/H	28/10/99	Withdrawn	–	Financial services
349	386/98 *Italy*	N/H	16/11/99	09/03/00	[2000] I-1277	Working time

Case No.		Date of Hearing	Date of Opinion	Date of Judgment	ECR	Keywords
350	153/99-P *Commission/ Giannini*	N/H	25/11/99	13/04/00	[2000] I-2891	Staff case
351	236/98 *Svenaeus (Jämo)*	21/10/99	16/12/99	30/03/00	[2000] I-2189	Equal pay
352	359/98-P *Ca'Pasta*	N/H	20/01/00	25/05/00	[2000] I-3977	Fisheries/annulment
353	195/98 *Östereichisscher Gewerkschaftsbund*	N/H	27/01/00	30/11/00	[2000] I-10497	LCP – égalité de traitement – travailleurs – ancienneté/étranger
354	443/98 *Unilever Italia*	16/11/99	27/01/00	26/09/00	[2000] I-7535	Technical standards – olive oil labelling
355	425/98 *Marca Mode*	24/11/99	27/01/00	22/06/00	[2000] I-4861	Trade marks/confusion
356	13/99-P *TEAM*	24/11/99	17/02/00	15/06/00	[2000] I-4671	Tender offer/annulment Commission decision
357	16/98 *France*	16/11/99	24/02/00	05/10/00	[2000] I-8315	Droit des entreprises – marchés publics de fourniture – éléctrification
358	154/99-P *Politi/ETF*	N/H	24/02/00	29/06/00	[2000] I-5019	Staff case/admissibility
359	236/99 *Belgium*	26/01/00	16/03/00	06/07/00	[2000] I-5657	Urban waste water – force majeure
360	456/98 *Centrosteel*	N/H	16/03/00	13/07/00	[2000] I-6007	Article 52 – agency contract
361	180/98–184/98 *Pavlov*	11/01/00	23/03/00	12/09/00	[2000] I-6451	Conc. – entreprise – pensions médecins spécialistes
362	73/99 *Movrin*	13/01/00	23/03/00	06/07/00	[2000] I-5625	Social security – sickness insurance
363	337/98 *France*	02/02/00	23/03/00	05/10/00	[2000] I-8377	Public procurement
364	160/99 *France*	N/H	30/03/00	13/07/00	[2000] I-6137	Maritime transport
365	210/98-P *Salzgitter*	11/11/99	30/03/00	13/07/00	[2000] I-5843	State aid – annulment Commission decision
366	216/98 *Greece*	17/02/00	13/04/00	19/10/00	[2000] I-8921	Fiscalité – impôts indirects – tabacs – prix minimum de vente
367	408/98 *Abbey National*	23/02/00	13/04/00	22/02/01	[2001] I-1361	VAT – services
368	312/98 *Warsteiner*	22/03/00	25/05/00	07/11/00	[2000] I-9187	Designation of origin
369	478/98 *Belgium*	28/03/00	15/06/00	26/09/00	[2000] I-7587	Article 73B – bond issue
370	404/98 *Josef Plum*	N/H	15/06/00	09/11/00	[2000] I-9379	Social security – posted workers

371	384/99 *Belgium*	N/H	15/06/00	03./11/00	[2000] I-10633	Telecommunications – tariffs – cost of service
372	79/99 *Schnorbus*	N/H	06/07/00	07/12/00	[2000] I-10997	Equal treatment
373	99/98 *Austria*	28/03/00	13/07/00	15/02/01	[2001] I-1101	State aid – Siemens
374	150/99 *Stockholm Lindöpark*	29/06/00	26/09/00	18/01/01	[2001] I-493	VAT – state liability
375	347/99 *Ireland*	N/H	12/10/00	14/12/00	[2000] I-11647	Transport of dangerous goods by road
376	379/98 *PreussenElektra*	27/06/00	26/10/00	13/03/01	[2001] I-2099	State aid – free movement
377	201/99 *Deutsche Nichimen*	19/09/00	09/11/00	05/04/01	[2001] I-2701	Customs classification
378	239/99 *Nachi Europe*	26/09/00	16/11/00	15/02/01	[2001] I-1197	Anti-dumping – Japanese ball bearings
379	276/98 *Portugal*	03/10/00	23/11/00	08/03/01	[2001] I-1699	VAT
380	219/99 *France*	N/H	23/11/00	14/02/01	[2001] I-1093	Technical standards – lifts
381	95–98/99 & C-180/99 *Khalil e.a.*	10/10/00	30/11/00	11/10/01	[2001] I-7413	Social security – stateless persons/refugees
382	258/99 *BASF*	12/10/00	30/11/00	10/05/01	[2001] I-3643	Plant protection products
383	322 & 323/99 *Fischer & Brandenstein*	12/10/00	14/12/00	17/05/01	[2001] I-4049	VAT – private use
384	405/98 *Gourmet International*	19/10/00	14/12/00	08/03/01	[2001] I-1795	Article 30 – prohibition of advertising
385	108/00 *SPI*	09/11/00	14/12/00	15/03/01	[2001] I-2361	VAT – advertising services
386	191/99 *Kvaerner*	08/11/00	18/1/01	14/06/01	[2001] I-4447	Insurance – services
387	100/00 *Italy*	N/H	18/1/01	05/04/01	[2001] I-2785	Manquement – electricity
388	253/99 *Bacardi*	23/11/00	25/1/01	27/09/01	[2001] I-6493	Import duties
389	463/98 *Cabletron*	30/11/00	01/02/01	10/05/01	[2001] I-3495	Customs classification
390	283/99 *Italy*	14/12/00	15/02/01	31/05/01	[2001] I-4363	Security firms – nationality condition
391	89/99 *Schieving-Nijstad*	17/10/00	15/02/01	13/09/01	[2001] I-5851	TRIPS – direct effect
392	43/99 *Leclere et Deaconescu*	22/11/00	15/02/01	31/05/01	[2001] I-4265	Social security
393	326/99 *'Goed Woenen'*	07/12/00	22/02/01	04/10/01	[2001] I-6831	VAT – rights in real property
394	494/99 *Greece*	N/H	22/02/01	05/04/01	[2001] I-2761	Civil aviation
395	100/99 *Italy/ Commission & Council*	18/01/01	15/03/01	05/07/01	[2001] I-5217	Annulment Regulations – euro and agriculture

Case No.		Date of Hearing	Date of Opinion	Date of Judgment	ECR	Keywords
396	270/99-P *Z/Parliament*	01/0.2/01	22/03/01	27/11/01	[2001] I-9197	Staff case – demotion
397	393 & 394/99 *Hervein e.a.*	07/02/01	05/04/01	19/03/02	[2002] I-2829	Social security – applicable legislation
398	383/99 P *Procter & Gamble/OHMI*	30/01/01	05/04/01	20/09/01	[2001] I-6251	Trade marks – designation intended purpose
399	269/99 *Kühne*	31/01/01	05/04/01	06/12/01	[2001] I-9517	Designation of origin
400	368/00 *Sweden*	N/H	05/04/01	14/06/01	[2001] I-4605	Bathing water
401	19/00 *SIAC Construction*	08/03/01	10/05/01	18/10/01	[2001] I-7725	Public procurement
402	475/99 *Ambulanz Glöckner*	22/02/01	17/05/01	25/10/01	[2001] I-8089	Competition – ambulance services
403	377/98 *Netherlands/ EP & Council*	13/02/01	14/06/01	09/10/01	[2001] I-7079	Biotechnological inventions – annulment
404	79/00 *Telefónica de España*	22/03/01	21/06/01	13/12/01	[2001] I-10075	Telecommunications
405	370/00 *Ireland*	N/H	05/07/01	20/09/01	[2001] I-6329	Transport of dangerous goods by rail
406	130/99 *Spain/ Commission*	N/H	12/07/01	21/03/02	[2002] I-3005	FEOGA
407	443/99 *Merck, Sharp & Dohme*	03/04/01	12/07/01	23/04/02	[2002] I-3703	Trade marks – repackaging
408	143/00 *Boehringer*	03/04/01	12/07/01	23/04/02	[2002] I-3759	Trade marks – repackaging
409	218/00 *Cisal di Battistello Venanzio*	07/06/01	13/09/01	22/01/02	[2002] I-691	Competition – sickness insurance body
410	427/98 *Germany*	29/05/01	20/09/01	15/10/02	[2002] I-8315	VAT – discount vouchers
411	2/00 *Hölterhoff*	12/06/01	20/09/01	14/05/02	[2002] I-4187	Trade marks – descriptive use
412	162/00 *Pokrzeptowicz-Meyer*	19/06/01	20/09/01	29/01/02	[2002] I-1049	Association agreement – equal treatment

413	451/99 *Cura Anlagen*	21/06/01	25/09/01	21/03/02	[2002] I-3193	Freedom of services – cross-border carleasing
414	274/00-P *Simon*	27/06/01	25/09/01	27/06/02	[2002] I-5999	Staff case
415	28/00 *Kauer*	28/06/01	25/09/01	07/02/02	[2002] I-1343	Social security – pension insurance
416	37/00 *Weber*	N/H	18/10/01	27/02/02	[2002] I-2013	Brussels Convention – employment contract
417	107/01 *Luxembourg*	N/H	25/10/01	13/12/01	[2001] I-10357	Road haulage and passenger transport operators
418	127/01 *Greece*	N/H	25/10/01	Withdrawn	–	Road haulage and passenger transport operators
419	306/99 *BIAO*	03/07/01	15/11/01	07/01/03	[2003] I-1	Article 234 – EC law not directly applicable
420	6/00 *ASA Abfall*	12/07/01	15/11/01	27/02/02	[2002] I-1961	Waste – transfer
421	314/99 *Netherlands/ Commission*	11/09/01	15/11/01	18/06/02	[2002] I-5521	Dangerous substances directive – legal basis
422	386/00 *Axa Royale Belge*	20/09/01	15/11/01	05/03/02	[2002] I-2209	Life assurance
423	290/00 *Duchon*	N/H	22/11/01	18/04/02	[2002] I-3567	Social security
424	10/00 *Italy*	12/09/01	22/11/01	07/03/02	[2002] I-2357	Own resources
425	428/99 *van den Bor*	04/10/01	29/11/01	08/01/02	[2002] I-127	BSE – compensation for slaughter of calves from UK
426	507/99 *Denkavit Nederland*	04/10/01	29/11/01	08/01/02	[2002] I-169	Veterinary controls – slaughter of calves
427	396/00 *Italy*	N/H	11/12/01	25/04/02	[2002] I-3949	Urban waste water treatment
428	29/99 *Commission/ Council*	05/06/01	13/12/01	10.12/02	[2002] I-11221	EAEC – annulment Council decision
429	482/99 *France/ Commission*	10/07/01	13/12/01	16/05/02	[2002] I-4397	State aid – annulment Commission decision
430	96/00 *Gabriel*	11/10/01	13/12/01	11/07/02	[2002] I-6367	Brussels Convention – consumer contract
431	174/00 *Kennemer*	26/09/01	13/12/01	21/03/02	[2002] I-3293	VAT – non-profit-making organization
432	267/00 *'London Zoo'*	26/09/01	13/12/01	21/03/02	[2002] I-3353	VAT – non-profit-making organization
433	287/00 *Germany*	N/H	13/12/01	20/06/02	[2002] I-5811	VAT – scientific research
434	268/00 *Netherlands*	N/H	17/01/02	19/03/02	[2002] I-2995	Bathing water
435	159/00 *Sapod Audic*	23/10/01	17/01/02	06/06/02	[2002] I-5031	Article 30 – technical regulations
436	291/00 *LTJ Diffusion*	10/10/01	17/01/02	20/03/03	[2003] I-2799	Trade marks – confusion

Case No.		Date of Hearing	Date of Opinion	Date of Judgment	ECR	Keywords
437	9/00 *Palin Granit*	N/H	17/01/02	18/04/02	[2002] I-3533	Waste – leftover stone
438	113/00 *Spain/ Commission*	N/H	24/01/02	19/09/02	[2002] I-7601	State aid
439	114/00 *Spain/ Commission*	N/H	24/01/02	19/09/02	[2002] I-7657	State aid
440	150/01 *France*	17/01/02	28/02/02	Withdrawn	–	Mutual recognition – trade mark and patent rights
441	384/00 *Bredemeier*	N/H	28/02/02	16/05/02	[2002] I-4517	Milk quotas
442	333/00 *Maaheimo*	10/01/02	07/03/02	07/11/02	[2002] I-10087	Social security – 'family benefits'
443	433/00 *Aventis Pharma Deutschland*	29/11/01	07/03/02	19/09/02	[2002] I-7761	Trade marks – repackaging
444	372/01 *Luxembourg*	N/H	07/03/02	16/05/02	[2002] I-4553	Marketing of biocidal products
445	167/00 *Henkel*	11/12/01	14/03/02	01/10/02	[2002] I-8111	Brussels Convention – consumer contract
446	325/00 *Germany*	N/H	14/03/02	05/11/02	[2002] I-9977	Article 28 – origin and quality mark
447	221/01 *Belgium*	N/H	14/03/02	19/09/02	[2002] I-7793	Telecommunications
448	50/00-P *Unión de Pequeños Agric.*	06/11/01	21/03/02	25/07/02	[2002] I-6677	Annulment – olive oil regulation
449	136/00 *Danner*	06/12/01	21/03/02	3/10/02	[2002] I-8147	Capital/services – pension contributions
450	292/00 *Davidoff*	13/12/01	21/03/02	09/01/03	[2003] I-389	Trade marks – reputation
451	76/00-P *Petrotub e.a./ Council & Commission*	30/01/02	25/04/02	09/01/03	[2003] I-79	Anti-dumping
452	184/01-P *Hirschfeldt*	N/H	25/04/02	07/11/02	[2002] I-10173	Staff case
453	413/00 *Netherlands*	N/H	25/04/02	Withdrawn	–	Passenger boats
454	391/01 *Portugal*	N/H	25/04/02	Withdrawn	–	Marketing of biocidal products
455	126/01 *GEMO*	17/01/02	30/04/02	20/11/03	[2003] I-13769	State aid – charge on meat purchases
456	269/00 *Seeling*	07/02/02	16/05/02	08/05/03	[2003] I-4101	VAT – rented property

457	315/00 *Maierhofer*	07/02/02	06/06/02	16/01/03	[2003] I-563	VAT – rented property
458	110/01 *Tennah-Durez*	05/03/02	06/06/02	19/06/03	[2003] I-6239	Mutual recognition of medical diplomas
459	371/01 *Greece*	N/H	06/06/02	Withdrawn	–	Genetically modified organisms
460	47/01 *Spain*	N/H	06/06/02	03/10/02	[2002] I-8231	Disposal of PCBs/PCTs
461	112/00 *Schmidberger*	12/03/02	11/07/02	12/06/03	[2003] I-5659	State liability – demonstration on motorway
462	457/00 *Belgium/ Commission*	11/06/02	19/09/02	03/07/03	[2003] I-6931	State aid
463	437/00 *Pugliese*	13/06/02	19/09/02	10/04/03	[2003] I-3573	Brussels Convention – employment contract
464	228/00 *Germany*	25/04/02	26/09/02	13/02/03	[2003] I-1439	Transfer of waste
465	458/00 *Luxembourg*	25/04/02	26/09/02	13/02/03	[2003] I-1553	Transfer of waste
466	497/01 *Zita Modes*	N/H	26/09/02	27/11/03	[2003] I-14393	VAT – transfer of totality of assets
467	11/00 *European Central Bank*	03/07/02	03/10/02	10/07/03	[2003] I-7147	OLAF – annulment ECB Decision
468	15/00 *European Investment Bank*	03/7/02	03/10/02	10/07/03	[2003] I-7281	OLAF – annulment EIB Decision
469	116/01 *SITA EcoService (Verol)*	19/09/02	14/11/02	03/04/03	[2003] I-2969	Waste
470	478/01 *Luxembourg*	N/H	14/11/02	06/03/03	[2003] I-2351	Patent agent – residence requirement
471	485/01 *Caprini*	N/H	21/11/02	06/03/03	[2003] I-2371	Commercial agents
472	15/01 *Paranova*	10/10/02	12/12/02	08/05/03	[2003] I-4175	Free movement of goods – parallel imports
473	113/01 *Paranova*	10/10/02	12/12/02	08/05/03	[2003] I-4243	Free movement of goods – parallel imports
474	171/01 *Wählergruppe*	24/10/02	12/12/02	08/05/03	[2003] I-4301	EEC/Turkey Association Agreement – direct effect
475	438/01 *Design Concept*	14/11/02	12/12/02	05/06/03	[2003] I-5617	VAT – advertising – place of supply
476	85/02 *France*	N/H	12/12/02	13/02/03	[2003] I-1693	Driving licences
477	436/01 *Belgium*	N/H	14/01/03	13/03/03	[2003] I-2633	Genetically modified organisms
478	76/01-P *Eurocoton e.a.*	22/10/02	16/01/03	30/09/03	[2003] I-10091	Anti-dumping
479	223/01 *AstraZeneca*	10/10/02	23/01/03	16/10/03	[2003] I-11809	Medicinal product – marketing authorization
480	106/01 *Novartis Pharmaceuticals*	07/11/02	23/01/03	29/04/04	[2004] I-4403	Medicinal product – marketing authorization
481	152/01 *Kyocera Electronics Europe*	N/H	23/01/03	20/11/03	[2003] I-13821	Customs – value of goods

Case No.		Date of Hearing	Date of Opinion	Date of Judgment	ECR	Keywords
482	198/01 *Consorzio Industrie Fiammiferi*	24/09/02	30/01/03	09/09/03	[2003] I-8055	Competition – Article 81
483	345/01 *Austria*	N/H	30/01/03	Withdrawn	–	Genetically modified organisms
484	419/01 *Spain*	N/H	30/01/03	15/05/03	[2003] I-4947	Urban waste water treatment
485	383/01 *De Danske Bilimportorer*	06/11/02	27/02/03	17/06/03	[2003] I-6065	Articles 28 and 30 EC – tax on new cars
486	305/01 *MKG-Kraftfahrzeuge-Factoring*	09/01/03	06/03/03	26/06/03	[2003] I-6729	VAT – factoring
487	207/01 *Altair Chimica*	16/01/03	13/03/03	11/09/03	[2003] I-8875	Competition – electricity prices
488	361/01-P *Kik/OHMI*	26/11/02	20/03/03	09/09/03	[2003] I-8283	OHMI – language regime
489	147/01 *Weber's Wine World*	12/12/02	20/03/03	02/10/03	[2003] I-11365	Recovery of unlawful tax passed on
490	261/01 & 262/01 *Van Calster e.a.*	10/12/02	10/04/03	21/10/03	[2003] I-12249	State aid – animal health and production fund
491	191/01-P *OHMI/Wrigley*	21/01/03	10/04/03	23/10/03	[2003] I-12447	Trade marks – descriptive use
492	114/01 *AvestaPolarit Chrome*	23/01/03	10/04/03	11/09/03	[2003] I-8725	Waste – definition
493	290/01 *Derudder*	05/02/03	10/04/03	04/03/04	[2004] I-2041	Customs code – samples
494	153/02 *Neri*	13/02/03	10/04/03	13/11/03	[2003] I-13555	Mutual recognition – teaching
495	264, 306, 354 & 355/01 *AOK Bundesverband*	14/01/03	22/05/03	16/03/04	[2004] I-2493	Competition – social security rules – ceilings for reimbursement of medicines
496	245/01 *RTL Television*	29/01/03	22/05/03	23/10/03	[2003] I-12489	TV without frontiers – advertising
497	148/02 *Garcia Avello*	11/03/03	22/05/03	02/10/03	[2003] I-11613	European citizenship – change of name
498	263/02-P *Jégo-Quéré*	22/05/03	10/97/03	01/04/04	[2004] I-3425	'Direct and individual concern'
499	408/01 *Adidas & Adidas Benelux*	3/04/03	10/07/03	23/10/03	[2003] I-12537	Trade marks – protection of marks with reputation

500	91/01 *Italy/Commission*	05/06/03	18/09/03	29/04/04	[2004] I-4355	State aid – SMEs
501	18/02 *DFDS Torline*	20/05/03	18/09/03	05/02/04	[2004] I-1417	Brussels Convention – 'tort and delict'
502	236/02 *Slob*	26/06/03	18/09/03	12/02/04	[2004] I-1861	Milk levy – accounting records
503	285/02 *Elsner-Lakeberg*	N/H	16/10/03	27/05/04	[2004] I-5861	Equal pay – part-time workers
504	90/02 *Bockemühl*	11/09/03	23/10/03	01/04/04	[2004] I-3303	VAT – right to deduct
505	137/02 *Faxworld*	11/09/03	23/10/03	29/04/04	[2004] I-5547	VAT – transfer of assets
506	167/02-P *Rothley*	23/09/03	20/11/03	30/03/04	[2004] I-3149	OLAF – EP rules
507	224/02 *Pusa*	25/09/03	20//11/03	29/04/04	[2004] I-5763	Free movement (Article 18 EC) – tax
508	110/02 *Commission/ Council*	N/H	11/12/03	29/06/04	[2004] I-6333	State aid – Portuguese pig farmers
509	292/02 *Meiland Azewijn*	20/11/03	15/01/04	09/09/04	[2004] I-7905	Excise duties – freedom to provide services
510	332/01 *Greece/ Commission*	13/11/03	22/01/04	09/09/04	[2004] I-7699	FEOGA
511	173/02 *Spain/ Commission*	N/H	22/01/04	14/10/04	[2004] I-9735	State aid – milk reference quantities
512	498/01-P *OHMI/ Zapf Creations*	08/01/04	19/02/04	01/12/04 (Order)		Trade mark – 'New born baby'
513	166/03 *France*	N/H	19/02/04	08/07/04	[2004] I-6535	Article 28 – gold
514	329/02-P *SAT 1/OHMI*	08/01/04	11/03/04	16/09/04	[2004] I-8317	Trade mark – descriptive sign
515	297/02 *Italy/ Commission*	N/H	18/03/04	23/09/04 (Order)		FEOGA
516	372/02 *Adanez-Vega*	N/H	25/03/04	11/11/04	[2004] I-10671	Social security – unemployment benefit
517	422/02-P *Europe Chemi-Con*	N/H	29/04/04	27/01/05	[2005] I-791	Anti-dumping
518	31/03 *Pharmacia Italia*	17/03/04	29/04/04	19/10/04	[2004] I-10001	Supplementary protection certificate
519	113/02 *Netherlands*	N/H	06/05/04	14/10/04	[2004] I-9707	Waste – recovery or disposal
520	123/03-P *Greencore*	01/04/04	06/05/04	09/12/04	[2004] I-11647	Article 230 – 'Decision'
521	312/02 *Sweden/ Commission*	N/H	17/06/04	07/10/04	[2004] I-9247	FEOGA
522	36/03 *Approved Prescription Services*	25/05/04	08/07/04	09/12/04	[2004] I-11583	

Case No.		Date of Hearing	Date of Opinion	Date of Judgment	ECR	Keywords
523	27/02 *Engler*	26/05/04	08/07/04	20/01/05	[2005] I-481	Brussels Convention – misleading prize allocation
524	203/03 *Austria*	N/H	08/07/04	01/02/05	[2005] I-935	Equal treatment of men and women
525	464/01 *Gruber*	24/06/04	16/09/04	20/01/05	[2005] I-439	Brussels Convention – consumer contract
526	74/03 *SmithKline Beecham*	25/05/04	16/09/04	20/01/05	[2005] I-595	Abridged procedure – 'essentially similar'
527	198/03-P *CEVA Santé animale*	06/07/04	23/09/04	12/07/05	[2005] I-6357	Veterinary medicine – residues in food
528	53/03 *Syfait e.a.*	18/05/04	28/10/04	31/05/05	[2005] I-4609	Abuse of dominant position
529	32/03 *I/S Fini H*	15/09/04	28/10/04	03/03/05	[2005] I-1599	VAT – 'economic activity'
530	378/02 *Waterschap Z. V.*	23/09/04	18/11/04	02/06/05	[2005] I-4685	VAT – public authority
531	342/03 *Spain/ Commission*	N/H	02/12/04	10/03/05	[2005] I-1975	Customs – tariff quota (tuna)
532	39/04 *Laboratoires Fournier*	28/10/04	09/12/04	10/03/05	[2005] I-2057	Freedom to provide services – tax credit
533	267/03 *Lindberg*	07/10/04	16/12/04	21/04/05	[2005] I-3247	Technical regulations
534	347/03 *Friuli-Venezia Giulia*	14/10/04	16/12/04	12/05/05	[2005] I-3785	Association Agreement – protection of 'Tokay'
535	434/03 *Charles et Charles-Tijmens*	16/11/04	20/01/05	14/07/05	[2005] I-7037	VAT – private use
536	464/02 *Denmark*	24/11/04	20/01/05	15/09/05	[2005] I-7929	Danish car registration
537	147/03 *Austria*	25/11/04	20/01/05	07/07/05	[2005] I-5969	Mutual recognition (teachers)
538	287/02 *Spain/ Commission*	N/H	20/01/05	09/06/05	[2005] I-5093	FEOGA
539	208/03-P *Le Pen*	N/H	27/01/05	07/07/05	[2005] I-6051	Article 230 – 'act' of European Parliament
540	77/04 *GIE Réunion européenne e.a.*	08/12/04	24/02/05	26/05/05	[2005] I-4509	Brussels Convention – insurance and guarantees

541	394/02 *Greece*	08/12/04	24/02/05	02/06/05	[2005] I-4713	Public procurement
542	227/03 *van Pommeren-Bourgondiën*	09/12/04	24/02/05	07/07/05	[2005] I-6101	Social security – residence requirement
543	465/03 *Kretztechnik*	15/12/04	24/02/05	26/05/05	[2005] I-4357	VAT – sale of shares
544	78/03-P *Commission/ ARE*	N/H	24/02/05	13/12/05	[2005] I-10737	State aid
545	281 & 282/03 *Cindu Chemicals e.a.*	27/01/05	17/03/05	15/09/05	[2005] I-8069	Hazardous substances
546	329/03 *Trapeza tis Ellados*	03/02/05	14/04/05	27/10/05	[2005] I-9341	Free movement of capital – bonds
547	276/03-P *Scott/ Commission*	03/02/05	14/04/05	06/10/05	[2005] I-8437	State aid – recovery
548	174/03 *Impresa Portuale di Cagliari*	17/02/05	21/04/05	Withdrawn	–	Public procurement
549	30/04 *Koschitzki*	17/03/05	04/05/05	21/07/05	[2005] I-7389	Social security – aggregation
550	405/03 *Class International*	15/03/05	26/05/05	18/10/05	[2005] I-8735	Trade marks – exhaustion of rights
551	151/04-P & 152/04 *Nadin*	24/02/05	26/05/05	15/12/05	[2005] I-11203	Freedoms – car registration requirements
552	71/04 *Xunta de Galicia*	N/H	26/05/05	21/07/05	[2005] I-7419	State aid – shipbuilding
553	525/03 *Italy*	06/04/05	02/06/05	27/10/05	[2005] I-9405	Public suppliers – adjudication
554	33/04 *Luxembourg*	03/03/05	02/06/05	08/12/05	[2005] I-10629	Telecommunications
555	120/04 *Medion AG*	14/04/05	09/06/05	06/10/05	[2005] I-8551	Trade marks – confusion
556	96/04 *Standesamt Stadt Niebüll*	28/04/05	30/06/05	2704/06	[2006] I-3561	Citizenship – surnames
557	201/04 *Molenbergnatie*	N/H	30/06/05	23/02/06	[2006] I-2049	Customs code – debt
558	26/04 *Spain*	N/H	07/07/05	15/12/05	[2005] I-11059	Bathing water
559	197/04 *Germany*	12/05/05	14/07/05	10/11/05	[2005] I-9739	Tax on tobacco
560	316/04 *Zuid-Hollandse Milieufederatie*	02/06/05	14/07/05	10/11/05	[2005] I-9759	
561	301/03 *Italy/Commission*	16/06/05	15/09/05	01/12/05	[2005] I-10217	Structural funds

Case No.		Date of Hearing	Date of Opinion	Date of Judgment	ECR	Keywords
562	415/04 *Kinderopvang Enschede*	N/H	15/09/05	09/02/06	[2006] I-1385	VAT – childcare services
563	341/04 *Eurofood*	12/07/05	27/09/05	02/05/06	[2006] I-3813	Insolvency – jurisdiction
564	213/04 *Burtscher*	05/07/05	29/09/05	01/12/05	[2006] I-10309	Free movement of capital
565	227/04-P *Lindorfer*	N/H	27/10/05	[not yet decided]		Transfer of pension rights
566	222/04 *Cassa di Risparmio di Firenze*	07/07/05	27/10/05	10/01/06	[2006] I-289	State aid, privatization of banking
567	493/04 *Piatkowski*	N/H	17/11/05	09/03/06	[2006] I-2369	Social security
568	371/03 *Aulinger*	12/10/05	17/11/05	09/03/06	[2006] I-2207	Sanctions against Serbia & Montenegro
569	421/04 *Matratzen Concord*	N/H	24/11/05	09/03/06	[2006] I-2303	Trade marks – Article 30 EC
570	368/04 *Transalpine Ölleitung*	14/09/05	29/11/05	05/10/06	[2006] I-9957	State aid
571	5/05 *Joustra*	N/H	01/12/05	23/11/06	[2006] I-11075	Excise duty – wine
572	167/04-P *JCB*	19/10/05	15/12/05	21//09/06	[2006] I-8935	Article 81 EC – Cartels
573	423/04 *Richards*	20/10/05	15/12/05	27/04/06	[2006] I-3585	Equal treatment – transsexual's pensionable age
574	416/04-P *Sunrider/OHMI*	17/11/05	15/12/05	11/05/06	[2006] I-4237	Trade marks – use of earlier marks

Index